The Digital Weaver

Architecting connected digital systems for the AI era

Syam Madanapalli

www.bpbonline.com

First Edition 2026

ISBN: 978-93-78546-549

Distributors:

BPB PUBLICATIONS
20, Ansari Road, Darya Ganj
New Delhi-110002
Ph: 23254990/23254991

DECCAN AGENCIES
4-3-329, Bank Street,
Hyderabad-500195
Ph: 24756967/24756400

MICRO MEDIA
Shop No. 5, Mahendra Chambers,
150 DN Rd. Next to Capital Cinema,
V.T. (C.S.T.) Station, MUMBAI-400 001
Ph: 22078296/22078297

Published by Manish Jain for BPB Publications, 20 Ansari Road, Darya Ganj, New Delhi-110002 and Printed by him at Repro India Ltd., Rewari.

www.bpbonline.com

Dedicated to

My parents,
Smt. Lakshmi Kanthamma and Sri Ramaiah Madanapalli,
whose hard work and sacrifices gave me the chance to pursue
an education and begin a journey from a small village to
take part in shaping the connected world.

Every system begins with a single thread.
What matters is how that thread is woven.

About the Author

Syam Madanapalli is a technology leader and systems architect with more than twenty-five years of experience designing connected digital systems. His work spans Internet infrastructure, IoT platforms, data systems, artificial intelligence, and cybersecurity governance.

Over the course of his career, he has led large engineering teams, contributed to Internet standards, and holds multiple patents in networking and connected systems. Working across industries including manufacturing, healthcare, infrastructure, and life sciences, he has focused on translating emerging technologies into scalable and reliable digital platforms.

The digital weaver reflects his effort to provide a practical framework for understanding and designing the complex digital systems that increasingly shape modern society.

Acknowledgement

Writing a book is never a solitary effort. It is sustained by the patience, encouragement, and generosity of many people.

I am deeply grateful to my wife, Kavitha, and to my children, Ramasri and Sriram, whose constant support made this book possible. They generously gave their evenings, weekends, and holidays so that I could devote time to writing. Their patience carried this work through many late nights and revisions.

My thanks also go to the editors from BPB Publications for their support and thoughtful feedback throughout the development of the manuscript.

I also remember with gratitude my elder brothers, Madhu and Raghu. As the youngest, they took on my share of the field work and encouraged my studies.

I am equally grateful to my teachers and professors at the National Institute of Technology, Warangal, whose discipline and example shaped my approach to learning and work. They taught us to pursue ideas with persistence and curiosity, to keep moving forward with the restless energy of an electron, and to approach engineering with both rigor and humility.

Over the years, I have also benefited from conversations with many friends, colleagues, engineers, and practitioners whose ideas helped shape the perspectives presented in this book. Many of these exchanges took place through technology forums, standards communities, and professional networks that foster open collaboration. Engagements through forums such as the ATM Forum and WiMAX Forum, standards organizations including the IPv6 Forum, the **Institute of Electrical and Electronics Engineers** (IEEE), and the **Institution of Engineering and Technology** (IET), as well as interactions within online technical communities, the startup ecosystem, TiE networks, NASSCOM, the **India Electronics and Semiconductor Association** (**IESA**), and discussions with officials from MeitY, provided opportunities to exchange ideas and learn from scholars and practitioners.

I am particularly grateful to Brian Calder, Basavaraj Patil, and Ajay Jasti for their encouragement and for the many thoughtful conversations we shared over the years. Many of the seeds that eventually grew into the perspectives presented in this book were planted through these exchanges.

This work reflects a journey that began far from the digital systems described in these pages. I remain grateful to everyone who, in ways both small and large, helped make that journey possible.

Preface

A clinician in a rural hospital requests a unit of blood during an emergency.

Within minutes, an autonomous drone begins its flight. Sensors monitor weather conditions, navigation systems adjust the route, and a dispatch platform coordinates delivery before the patient's condition worsens.

At a different moment, a commuter taps a phone to pay for transportation. The transaction travels through identity systems, banking networks, data platforms, and fraud detection algorithms in a fraction of a second.

Elsewhere, a city adjusts traffic signals based on real-time sensor data, while an artificial intelligence system helps doctors interpret medical images.

These situations appear unrelated. They belong to different industries and technologies. Yet each of them depends on the same underlying structure, which consists of networks that connect devices, sensors that capture signals, data systems that organize information, intelligent algorithms that interpret patterns, and security mechanisms that maintain trust.

Together, these elements form the digital systems that increasingly shape modern life.

Most discussions of technology focus on individual tools such as networks, devices, data platforms, or artificial intelligence. In practice, however, modern digital systems rarely operate as isolated technologies. They function as interconnected structures where connectivity, sensing, data, intelligence, and trust interact continuously.

Understanding how these components interact is becoming one of the most important skills for anyone working with modern technology.

This book presents digital weaving, a framework for understanding how modern digital systems are structured and how they can be designed to remain reliable and accountable as they scale.

Digital weaving treats connectivity, sensing, data, intelligence, and trust as structural threads that combine to form digital systems. When these threads are woven deliberately, systems become coherent, resilient, and adaptable. When they are assembled without attention to structure, systems become fragmented and difficult to govern.

The goal of this book is to help readers understand these structures and design digital systems that remain reliable in real-world conditions.

The book is written for students, engineers, architects, and technology leaders who want to understand how modern digital systems are designed and integrated. It is particularly useful for undergraduate students studying computing and engineering, practitioners building connected infrastructures, and decision makers responsible for governing digital platforms.

Readers can approach the book sequentially to build a layered understanding of modern digital systems. It can also serve as a reference for specific topics such as networking, IoT systems, data platforms, artificial intelligence, and cybersecurity. Each chapter introduces concepts that connect to later chapters, gradually revealing how individual technologies combine to form larger digital systems.

By the end of the book, readers will understand how the major components of modern digital systems interact, how these systems behave under scale and automation, and how to design connected digital infrastructures that remain reliable, secure, and trustworthy.

Chapter 0: The First Stitch - This opening chapter introduces the posture that frames the book. It invites readers to see digital systems not as distant technologies but as structures that shape everyday decisions and outcomes. Through the idea of the loom, it offers a way to notice patterns, relationships, and responsibilities within the systems that increasingly organize modern life.

Chapter 1: The Internet – This chapter represents the loom beneath our lives, and introduces the Internet as the foundational infrastructure of modern digital systems. It explains how networking protocols, routing systems, and distributed architectures allow devices and services to communicate globally and form the base layer of the digital ecosystem.

Chapter 2: The Internet of Things– This chapter represents the sensory threads and explores IoT as the layer that enables digital systems to observe and interact with the physical world. It examines sensors, embedded devices, and edge computing systems that convert physical signals into digital information.

Chapter 3: Data – This chapter represents the design blueprint and explains how data functions as the structural blueprint of digital systems. It introduces data architectures, pipelines, and governance practices that enable information to move across platforms and organizations.

Chapter 4: Artificial Intelligence – This chapter represents the master weaver and examines artificial intelligence as the capability that interprets data and supports automated decision-making. It introduces machine learning systems and explores the opportunities and challenges of algorithmic decision processes.

Chapter 5: Security – This chapter explores the trust framework and introduces cybersecurity as the mechanism that protects digital systems and establishes trust. It discusses identity systems, encryption, system resilience, and governance practices required to secure interconnected infrastructures.

Chapter 6: The Digital Weaving – This chapter focuses on designing coherent systems and presents the digital weaving framework in detail. It explains how connectivity, sensing, data, intelligence, and trust operate as structural threads and introduces principles for designing integrated digital systems.

Chapter 7: The Real-world Applications – This chapter explores the systems under strain and examines digital systems operating in healthcare, identity platforms, infrastructure, and civic systems. These cases illustrate how systems behave under real-world pressure and how design decisions affect reliability and legitimacy.

Chapter 8: The Future Weaving – This is the final chapter focusing on designing for a changing world and looks ahead to the future of digital systems as artificial intelligence, automation, and global connectivity continue to evolve. It explores how engineers and policymakers can design systems that remain adaptable, responsible, and resilient.

Digital systems are not static technologies. They are evolving structures shaped by human decisions. Understanding these structures allows us not only to build technology but to guide how it shapes the world we live in.

Every digital system begins with a thread.

What we choose to weave determines how the system holds.

Coloured Images

Please follow the link to download the
Coloured Images of the book:

https://rebrand.ly/6318b6

We have code bundles from our rich catalogue of books and videos available at https://github.com/bpbpublications. Check them out!

Errata

We take immense pride in our work at BPB Publications and follow best practices to ensure the accuracy of our content to provide an indulging reading experience to our subscribers. Our readers are our mirrors, and we use their inputs to reflect and improve upon human errors, if any, that may have occurred during the publishing processes involved. To let us maintain the quality and help us reach out to any readers who might be having difficulties due to any unforeseen errors, please write to us at:

errata@bpbonline.com

Your support, suggestions and feedback are highly appreciated by the BPB Publications' Family.

Piracy

If you come across any illegal copies of our works in any form on the Internet, we would be grateful if you would provide us with the location address or website name. Please contact us at **business@bpbonline.com** with a link to the material.

If you are interested in becoming an author

If there is a topic that you have expertise in, and you are interested in either writing or contributing to a book, please visit **www.bpbonline.com**. We have worked with thousands of developers and tech professionals, just like you, to help them share their insights with the global tech community. You can make a general application, apply for a specific hot topic that we are recruiting an author for, or submit your own idea.

Reviews

Please leave a review. Once you have read and used this book, why not leave a review on the site that you purchased it from? Potential readers can then see and use your unbiased opinion to make purchase decisions. We at BPB can understand what you think about our products, and our authors can see your feedback on their book. Thank you!

For more information about BPB, please visit **www.bpbonline.com**.

Join our Discord space

Join our Discord workspace for latest updates, offers, tech happenings around the world, new releases, and sessions with the authors:

https://discord.bpbonline.com

Table of Contents

CHAPTER 0

The First Stitch

Where systems begin

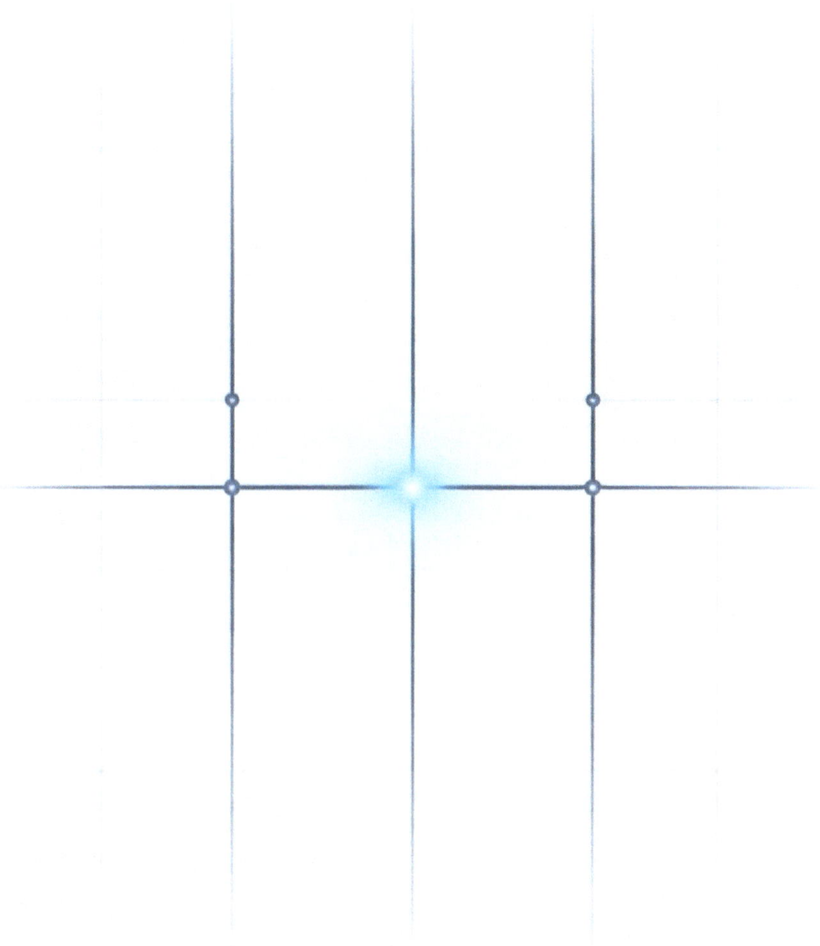

Every system begins when the first connection is made.

CHAPTER 0
The First Stitch

Introduction

This book begins with a way of seeing.

Digital systems surround us so completely that they often disappear from view. We interact with screens, follow prompts, accept defaults, and adapt our behavior without seeing the structures that shape those interactions. The systems feel finished, distant, and inevitable.

They are not.
They were built. They continue to act, and they can be read.

The first stitch does not introduce technologies or techniques. It introduces a posture. It asks how to step into complex systems without assuming mastery, how to notice patterns before naming them, and how to recognize responsibility before prescribing solutions.

This chapter offers a pause.

To enter the digital world beyond the role of consuming tools, and to recognize participation in systems that carry history, strain, and intention. Before we examine networks, data, intelligence, or security, we begin by learning how to see the structure that holds them together.

We begin here.

Entering the loom

Every weave begins with what we inherit.

I was born in a remote village, long before the Internet, cloud servers, and satellite constellations became part of daily life. It was a time when an app could not summon groceries to your door or a doctor to your screen.

Connections arrived slowly, if they arrived at all. A letter could take weeks to reach its destination, carried along roads, then by bicycle, and finally on foot. A phone call, if you were lucky, would come through the village post office and be passed from hand to hand like a sacred object.

And yet, systems were already at work around us.

We marked the changing seasons by watching the sky and sensing shifts in the wind. We repaired our tools with care and patience. Knowledge moved through gestures at shared meals, beneath trees, and in moments of silence. I did not recognize it then, but I was already living inside a system: a network of people, memory, and meaning.

Figure 1: *Village to loom*

Thread by thread, through books, mentors, and machines, my world expanded beyond that village. I learned to write my first lines of code. I studied engineering. I later found myself contributing to the standards that shape how the Internet works today.

I did not inherit a fully woven world.

I inherited the loom.
And I learned how to use it.

This book is about that loom. Not mine alone, but ours.

It is about the structures, visible and invisible, that shape the systems we live inside. The platforms that decide what we see. The protocols that allow one device to communicate with another. The algorithms that act before we can blink.

We now walk streets where data adjusts traffic lights. We live in homes that respond to spoken commands. We consult maps that shift with every tap. We carry devices that quietly listen, learn, and anticipate.

None of this appeared by accident.

These systems were built and shaped through choices. Some were deliberate. Others accumulated quietly through use and habit.

Every digital system is more than code. It reflects decisions about access, power, ethics, and intent.

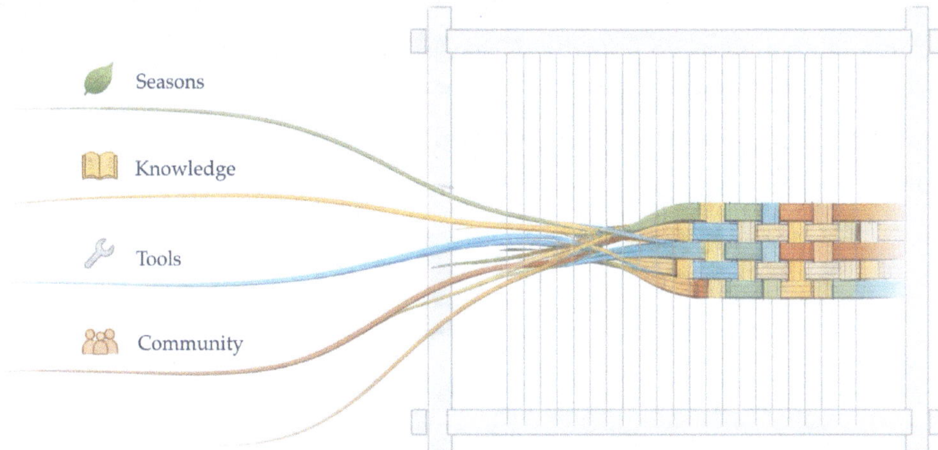

Every system begins with inherited threads. Knowledge, tools, communities, and environments carry patterns forward from the past. When these threads enter a structural frame, they interlock and form the patterns from which new systems emerge.

***Figure 2**: From lived systems to technical structure*

This book invites you to step inside those systems. Not only as a user of technology, but as someone who participates in shaping it.

You do not need to be an engineer to begin.
You only need to be curious.

We do not inherit a world that is fully woven.
We inherit the loom and the responsibility of deciding what to weave next.

Patterns that repeat

The world is not just made. It is woven, choice by choice.

Digital systems often feel complex because we encounter them in fragments. An interface here. An alert there. A decision made elsewhere. Yet beneath this variety, familiar structures recur. When we slow down and look closely, we begin to notice that many systems, despite their differences, are organized in similar ways.

This section introduces a way of seeing that makes those repetitions visible.

Seeing with the loom

To begin, we must notice the loom around us.

Whether you realize it or not, you already hold a thread. Not because you have written code or studied systems, but because you live inside them. You navigate platforms. You respond to alerts. You notice when something works smoothly and when it fails without explanation.

Each time a digital tool helps you quietly or leaves you confused, an unseen structure is at work, and whether you recognize it or not, you are already part of its design.

This book does not simply describe the digital world.
It looks at how it is held together.

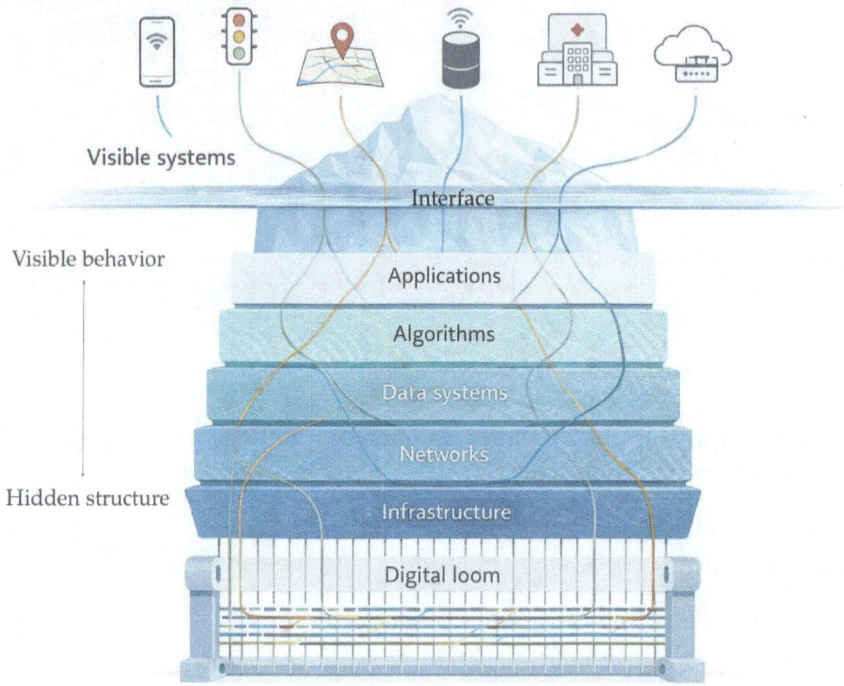

Figure 3: *Structure beneath the interface*

To understand systems, diagrams, and dashboards is not enough. We need a way of seeing that reveals what usually remains hidden: the structure beneath the interface, the assumptions behind defaults, and the values embedded in everyday technical choices.

This requires more than observation.
It requires attention.

We must learn to notice how systems are framed. What they make visible. What they leave out. Where signals travel without context, and where responsibility fades as systems scale. This kind of seeing does not come from expertise alone. It comes from learning to look differently.

To support that shift, this book turns to one of humanity's oldest technologies—*weaving*.

Weaving is not introduced here as a metaphor alone. It is used as a working lens for seeing systems. A loom holds threads under tension so patterns can emerge. In the same way, digital systems hold signals, data, rules, and decisions within a structured frame.

The loom helps us see systems as constructed, not inevitable. It draws attention to the connection rather than the components. It makes strain, fray, and repair visible rather than abstract.

When we look closely, the pace of creating systems gives way to their structure. Novelty gives way to recombination. What appears new is often a rearrangement of familiar threads.

Fractal patterns across scales

Patterns do not belong to a single scale.

The same patterns appear in small systems and large ones, in a sensor and in a city, in a data pipeline and in a policy framework. The details differ, but the underlying structure often feels familiar.

Digital systems grow by layering systems within systems. A component becomes part of a service. Services combine into platforms. Platforms extend into infrastructures that shape institutions and everyday life.

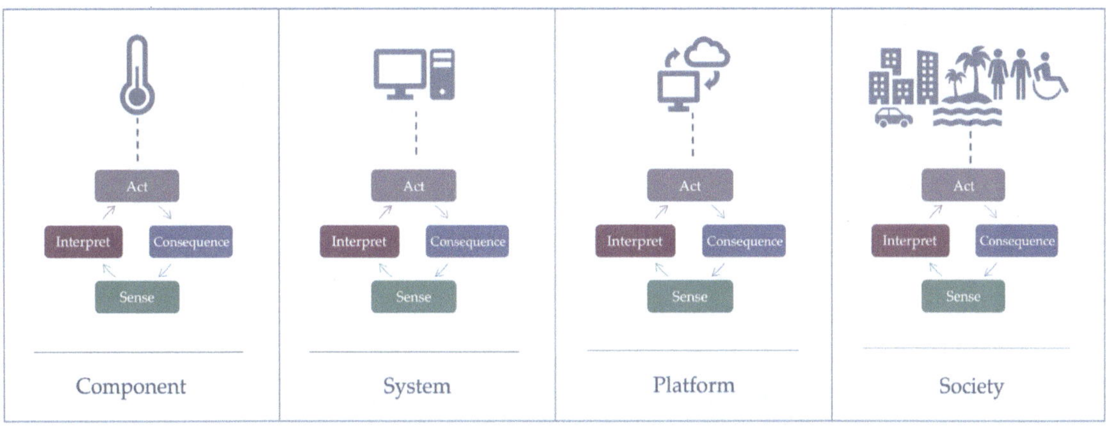

The same structure appears at different scales.

***Figure 4:** Recurring structure across scale*

As scale increases, complexity grows, but the relationships between sensing, interpretation, action, and consequence recur. You will see this same sequence appear again and again as the book moves from small systems to large ones, offering a consistent way to read systems at any scale.

The loom allows us to trace these recurring patterns without collapsing their differences.

Pattern as the first code

Long before digital systems, humans encoded meaning through patterns.

Across cultures, people learned to bend material into structure, and in doing so, they learned how to store and transmit meaning. Weaving was never only about cloth.

It was *communication.*
It was *memory.*
It was *identity.*

Patterns carried memory across generations. Repeated motifs signaled belonging, season, or obligation. Instructions were held not in words, but in structure. The pattern itself was the record.

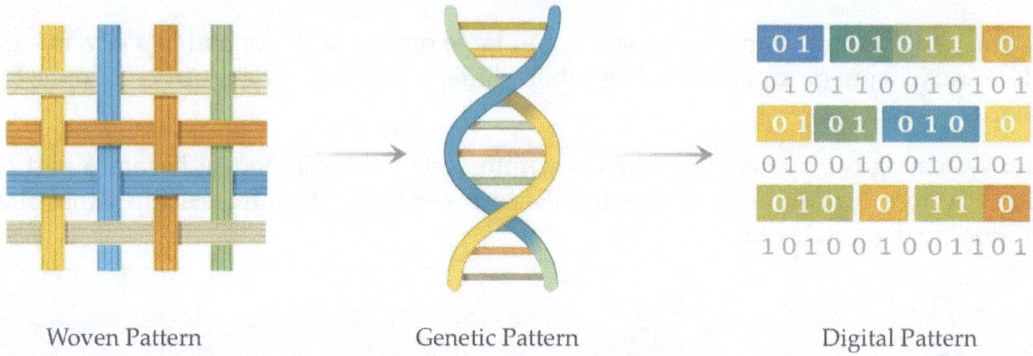

Across craft, nature, and computation, patterns store instruction. Woven structures carry cultural memory, DNA encodes biological development, and digital code organizes computation.

***Figure 5:** Instruction encoded in structure*

This matters because digital systems do the same thing.

Before software, humans already understood how to embed instruction in form. A repeated knot, a colored thread, or a woven symbol could carry knowledge across time and distance. The pattern functioned as code.

In this sense, pattern was the first code.

Nature follows the same logic. DNA stores instructions in sequences. Neural pathways strengthen through repetition. Tree rings record time through accumulation.

Digital systems extend this lineage.

A program is a pattern of instructions.
A database is a pattern of memory.
An interface is a pattern of expectation.

Once encoded, patterns tend to persist. They repeat quickly. They travel far. They shape behavior long after their original context has faded.

Learning to see patterns does not require prediction.
It requires noticing structure.

As this book progresses, these patterns will appear in more concrete forms. For now, it is enough to recognize that digital systems echo themselves as they grow.

When you can see that echo, understanding begins to shift. The chapters that follow ground these ideas in concrete systems, beginning with the Internet.

The loom we inherited

Every system carries the past forward.

Digital systems do not begin when we encounter them. They arrive already shaped by earlier decisions, assumptions, and limits. Before anyone can choose how to act within a system, they must contend with what has already been woven.

We are not the first to build such structures.

Long before screens, signals, or silicon, people created systems that carried knowledge across time and space. They wove calendars from stars, warnings from smoke, and memories from ritual. These early looms were not machines. They were social structures made of symbols, practices, and shared understanding.

Most of their makers are unnamed. Indigenous technologists, oral knowledge keepers, and community builders shaped systems that endured for generations. Their work reminds us that technology has always been social before it was digital, and collective before it was computational.

Over time, weaving began to change.

Patterns were no longer held only in human hands or memory. They could be stored, repeated, and executed without the presence of the maker. This shift did not happen all at once, but one moment makes it visible.

In the early nineteenth century, *Joseph Jacquard* designed a loom controlled by punched cards. Each card encoded a choice. Together, they formed a pattern that could be reproduced precisely, again and again. For the first time, design and execution were separated. A system could remember.

This idea did not remain confined to textiles.

A century later, *Alan Turing* described a universal machine, not as a device, but as a principle. Any process that could be described formally could be represented, simulated, and executed. Logic itself could be woven into a structure.

Claude Shannon then showed that information could be treated as a signal independent of meaning. Voice, text, and image could all be encoded, transmitted, and reconstructed using the same underlying rules. Patterns became portable. Systems could act across distance and time without carrying context with them.

The loom stretched outward, across wires and waves, towers and satellites, until it wrapped the planet.

With each extension, the capability increased. So did constraint.
Even the strongest patterns face tension.

In the nineteenth century, *Rudolf Clausius* articulated a principle that applies far beyond physics. Without care, systems tend toward disorder. Structure erodes. Signals drift. What once held begins to loosen.

Digital systems are no exception. Sensors fall out of calibration. Models inherit outdated assumptions. Infrastructure expands faster than oversight. Security thins quietly. Patterns persist long after their context has changed.

Human societies have long encoded knowledge in patterns. Mechanical looms stored patterns in structure, computation encoded logic as instruction, communication systems carried signals across distance, and modern digital networks extend these patterns across the planet.

***Figure 6:** Inherited structure and accumulated constraint*

These thinkers did more than introduce mechanisms. They left us ways of understanding systems.

Jacquard showed that patterns could be stored and repeated.
Turing showed that logic itself could be woven.
Shannon showed that information could move independent of its form.
Clausius reminded us that no system holds without attention.

Their ideas shape the systems we rely on today. They appear in networks that coordinate billions of devices, in algorithms that learn from data, and in platforms that carry decisions across distance and time.

These lineages matter not because the names must be memorized, but because they reveal continuity. Each generation inherits a loom shaped by those before it. Each adds new threads and new constraints.

The loom we work with now is programmable, global, and deeply entangled with human life. It is also unfinished.

Strain reveals structure

The weave shows itself under pressure.

Most systems appear stable until they are pressed. Their structure recedes into the background as long as conditions remain familiar. It is only when demands shift or intensify that assumptions surface and limits become visible.

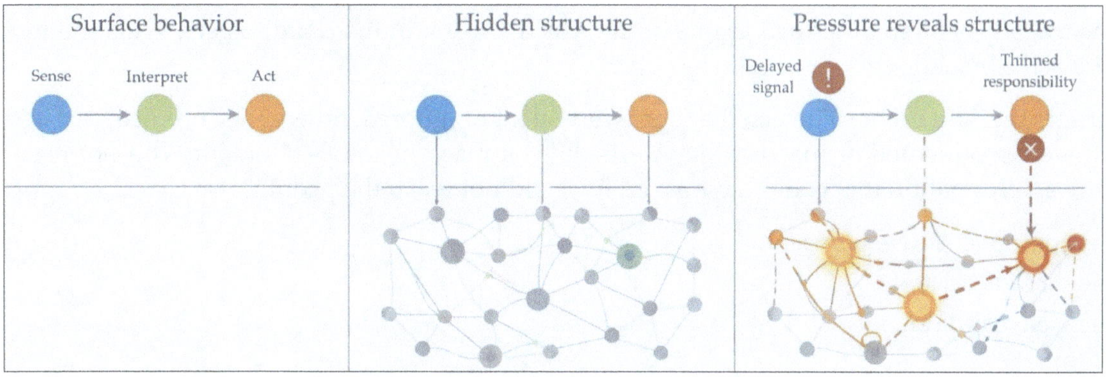

Figure 7: *System behavior under pressure*

Strain does not create structure.
It reveals it.

The weave under shock

When the COVID-19 pandemic spread across the world, digital systems were asked to do more than they were designed to. Networks carried unprecedented volumes of traffic. Platforms mediated work, education, and care. Models informed policy under conditions of deep uncertainty.

Many systems continued to function. Some adapted quickly. Others exposed gaps that had gone unnoticed.

Contact tracing struggled with fragmented data and uneven adoption. Dashboards aggregated numbers faster than they could explain them. Automated decisions scaled rapidly, while accountability lagged behind. The strain did not come from a single failure, but from the accumulation of small mismatches between design assumptions and lived reality.

The pandemic did not invent these weaknesses.
It made them visible.

Threads at failure

Decades earlier, in Bhopal, a different form of strain unfolded. Industrial controls, maintenance practices, organizational decisions, and regulatory oversight combined into a system that appeared stable until it was not.

In the early hours of December 3, 1984, a cloud of methyl isocyanate gas drifted across the city. Nearly invisible. Heavier than air. Lethal when inhaled.

By morning, thousands were dead. Hundreds of thousands were exposed. The effects did not end that day. They continue in bodies, soil, and memory decades later.

The tragedy is often described as one of the world's worst industrial disasters. What matters here is the breakdown.

Sensors that should have detected danger were silent or ignored. Emergency protocols existed but were fragmented or inaccessible. Alerts did not reach hospitals. Guidance did not reach homes. Information that could have saved lives did not reach the people.

The components were present.
The threads existed.
The weave did not.

Doctors treated patients without knowing what they faced. Hospitals descended into chaos. Families fled without understanding where safety lay because the gas hugged the ground, and many ran directly into danger. Survival often depended on chance rather than knowledge.

The failure was not a lack of expertise.
It was a failure of connection.

The system did not fail because it was complex. It failed because responsibility was distributed without coordination, and signals were separated from action.

The loom was incomplete.

Threads that should have connected sensing to response, expertise to guidance, and knowledge to care were left loose. When the strain arrived, there was nothing to hold.

Bhopal reminds us that systems do not fail all at once.
They fail where threads were never stitched.

Here, the strain revealed structure.

Persistent fraying

Not all strain arrives as shock. Some appear suddenly, while other forms accumulate slowly through continuous use, erosion, and neglect.

Many digital systems operate under continuous tension. Infrastructure expands faster than oversight. Sensors drift out of calibration. Models inherit assumptions that no longer hold. Security thins gradually as systems scale and interconnect.

These forms of fraying rarely trigger alarms. They accumulate quietly. Systems continue to function even as trust erodes and corrective pathways narrow. Over time, what once felt reliable becomes brittle.

In these cases, failure is not sudden.
It is delayed.

Across these cases, the lesson is not that systems are inherently fragile. It is that structure that matters most when conditions change.

Under strain, certain questions become unavoidable. *Who can intervene?* When correction is possible. How signals travel. Where responsibility remains reachable.

Strain does not point to a single fix.
It points to a pattern.

Systems that endure are not those that avoid pressure, but those whose structure allows learning, adjustment, and correction before harm hardens into consequence.

Intention in the weave

The loom does not evaluate intention. It holds choices in structure.

Technology is never just technical.
It shapes how decisions travel, how consequences unfold, and who bears their weight.
What strain makes visible, intention must address.

Systems do not act on their own. They act through choices made earlier, often quietly, and then repeat them at scale. When consequences appear, they are not accidents. They reflect intention, whether explicit or implied.

Responsibility is not confined to moments of failure.
It begins with design.

Designing with intention

Design was never neutral.

Every digital system encodes assumptions about how the world works and how people should behave within it. These assumptions appear in defaults, thresholds, and automated decisions. They shape which actions are easy to take, which require effort or permission, and which never surface at all, often long before their effects are visible.

Design is often described as problem-solving. In practice, it is also a problem-framing exercise. *What is measured? What is optimized? What is excluded?* Each choice expands some possibilities while narrowing others.

At small scales, these decisions can feel reversible. At larger scales, they harden quickly.

A model trained on partial data shapes future data collection.
An interface guides behavior until it becomes a habit.
A workflow optimized for speed reshapes judgment.

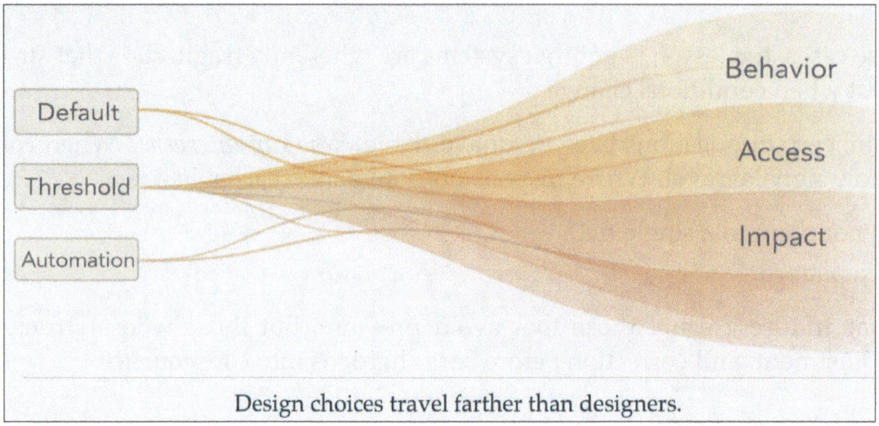

Figure 8: *Design choices and downstream consequences*

Intention does not disappear as systems grow.
It compounds.

We do not just build tools anymore.
We build tools that shape the world.

Learning to weave with care

Assuming responsibility means recognizing that systems continue to act long after their designers step away. Correction, if it comes, often arrives downstream, carried by people who did not make the original choices but must live with their effects.

To weave with care is to design with the expectation that systems will be used in ways their creators cannot fully anticipate. It is to leave room for pause, explanation, and adjustment. It is to recognize that learning must remain possible even as systems scale.

Care also means resisting the temptation to confuse delegating decisions with giving up responsibility for their consequences. Automation can extend human capability, but it cannot absorb responsibility. When decisions are embedded in systems, responsibility remains with those who shape and deploy them.

This posture does not guarantee correct outcomes.
It preserves the ability to correct.

Responsibility in digital systems is not a single act. It is an ongoing commitment to remain present as systems evolve, to attend to their effects, and to intervene when structure no longer serves the people who depend on it.

This posture has a name.

Digital weaving is the practice of shaping systems with awareness of structure, strain, and consequence over time. It is also a method of digital innovation for solving problems across industry, society, and the environment without severing responsibility from action.

It treats design not as a one-time act, but as an ongoing commitment to coherence, accountability, and care as systems evolve. The chapters ahead return to this practice repeatedly, deepening it from intuition into method.

Reading as a weaver

Understanding deepens through return and attention.

Digital systems rarely reveal themselves all at once. They are encountered in fragments—a feature here, an outcome there, a decision made elsewhere. Learning to work with such systems requires a different posture than learning a single tool or technique.

This book asks for that shift.

Reading this book like a weaver

There is more than one way to move through this book.
One approach, however, is deliberate.

Reading in sequence allows the threads to build carefully, chapter by chapter. Ideas introduced early provide the structure needed to understand what follows. Concepts return with greater specificity. Patterns become visible only after they have been encountered more than once.

At the same time, this book is not meant to be read only once.

You may return to chapters as reference points when designing systems, questioning assumptions, or navigating unfamiliar challenges. Sections are written to stand on their own, even as they contribute to a larger pattern.

Reading like a weaver means staying alert to connection.

As you move through the chapters, notice how themes recur. How questions raised in one domain reappear in another. How choices made at one layer shape behavior elsewhere. The same tensions surface across infrastructure, sensing, data, intelligence, and security, even when the technologies differ.

You are not expected to understand everything at once.

Some sections are meant to be revisited. Some ideas settle only after you have seen them applied. Others remain open, inviting reflection rather than resolution. This is part of learning. It is part of working with systems that resist simplification.

Reading the stories in this book

Throughout this book, you will encounter people navigating real systems under real constraints. Some are composites drawn from lived experience. Others reflect common roles across engineering, policy, care, and civic life.

These stories are not included for illustration or relief. They are part of the method.

Each character appears at moments where structure meets consequence. They surface assumptions that diagrams alone cannot reveal. They show how decisions travel through systems, how strain is felt unevenly, and how responsibility shifts across roles.

You are not asked to track their biographies. You are invited to notice what they encounter, what options are available, and what remains out of reach.

As the chapters progress, some characters return. Not to advance a plot, but to reveal how the same system appears from another position, or how earlier decisions reshape what follows.

Read these narratives as diagnostic lenses. They help make the structure legible by showing where it presses against lived reality.

The threads ahead

The chapters that follow trace several foundational dimensions that shape how digital systems operate and endure.

They begin with connectivity and infrastructure, examining how networks create both reach and constraint. They move through sensing and data, where visibility expands even as context thins. They turn to intelligence, where systems learn from patterns and act with increasing autonomy.

They then examine trust, where security, governance, and legitimacy intersect. Security appears here not as an end in itself, but as one of several mechanisms through which trust is earned, maintained, or lost as systems operate at scale.

The book then returns to digital weaving, where innovation is understood as remixing what already exists while holding responsibility under change. It concludes with applications and futures, where these dimensions converge in lived systems, and where emerging possibilities are tested against responsibility, constraint, and care.

These dimensions are not independent. They cross, reinforce, and sometimes pull against one another. Decisions made in one domain shape what is possible in another. Understanding emerges not from mastering each in isolation, but from learning how they interact.

This book does not aim to close conversation.

It aims to equip you to participate in one.

Weavers toolkit

Every weaver carries more than thread.

This section emphasizes the tools that support the weave. Understanding systems requires more than insight. It requires support, ways to hold ideas steady, to practice seeing structure, and to return to questions as they deepen over time. This book is designed with that need in mind.

Throughout the chapters, you will encounter a small set of tools intended to support learning rather than mastery. They do not provide answers in advance or close inquiry. They help you recognize what kind of system you are examining, where it is under strain, and which questions deserve sustained attention.

Together, these tools form the weaver's toolkit.

Weaver's lexicon

This book relies on a shared language.

Across chapters, certain terms recur, words such as loom, thread, pattern, fray, repair, and intention, alongside technical concepts drawn from networking, data, intelligence, and security. These terms are not decorative. They function as analytic tools for describing structure, strain, and responsibility in complex systems.

Their core meanings are defined canonically and remain stable across the book. As you move through the chapters, you will also encounter short, chapter-level lexicons. These do not redefine terms. They clarify how shared concepts are being used, stressed, or examined in a particular context.

As the language shapes how systems are understood, the book is careful about how agency is described. When it refers to systems as acting, deciding, or learning, it describes the structured delegation of human choice through design, not independent moral or intentional agency.

Meaning in this book deepens through use, comparison, and return. The lexicons exist to help you keep terms aligned as ideas resurface and sharpen over time.

Weaver's workshop

Seeing structure requires practice.

Each chapter includes exercises and prompts designed to help you work with the ideas rather than simply read them. These activities invite you to examine real or imagined systems, surface hidden assumptions, and notice where constraints tighten or choices harden.

Some prompts trace how decisions move through a system. Others ask how a design behaves under pressure. None require specialized tools or advanced technical skills.

The workshop is not about finding the correct solution.
It is about learning how to frame better questions.

Weaver's library

Learning does not end with a single book.

Each chapter concludes with a small, curated set of readings drawn from multiple disciplines, including technical foundations, design practice, social analysis, and reflections on governance and trust.

The library is not exhaustive. It is an invitation to explore further, guided by the threads that matter most to you.

Working with the toolkit

The weaver's toolkit is not a checklist.

It will not tell you exactly what to build or how to fix every system you encounter. Instead, it helps you recognize what kind of problem you are facing, how it fits within a larger structure, and which questions require care.

These tools support learning that is iterative, reflective, and grounded in systems that continue to act long after design decisions are made.

Beginning the weave

Every system begins with a first stitch.

A small decision. A framing choice. An assumption that shapes what follows. These early stitches do not determine the final pattern, but they influence how the weave responds when pulled.

This book does not claim to predict the future.
It offers a way to participate in shaping it.

As you move forward, remember that systems are never finished. They are held, adjusted, and repaired by the people who live within them. The loom you inherit is not neutral, and it is not fixed.

It is responsive.

What comes next is not about control, but about attention. Not about certainty, but about responsibility. The next stitch is already yours to make.

From posture to structure

Posture shapes what structure can hold.

The First Stitch has focused on posture—how to enter systems, how to see their patterns, how to recognize inheritance, strain, and responsibility, and how to read what unfolds across scale and time.

What follows turns from posture to structure.

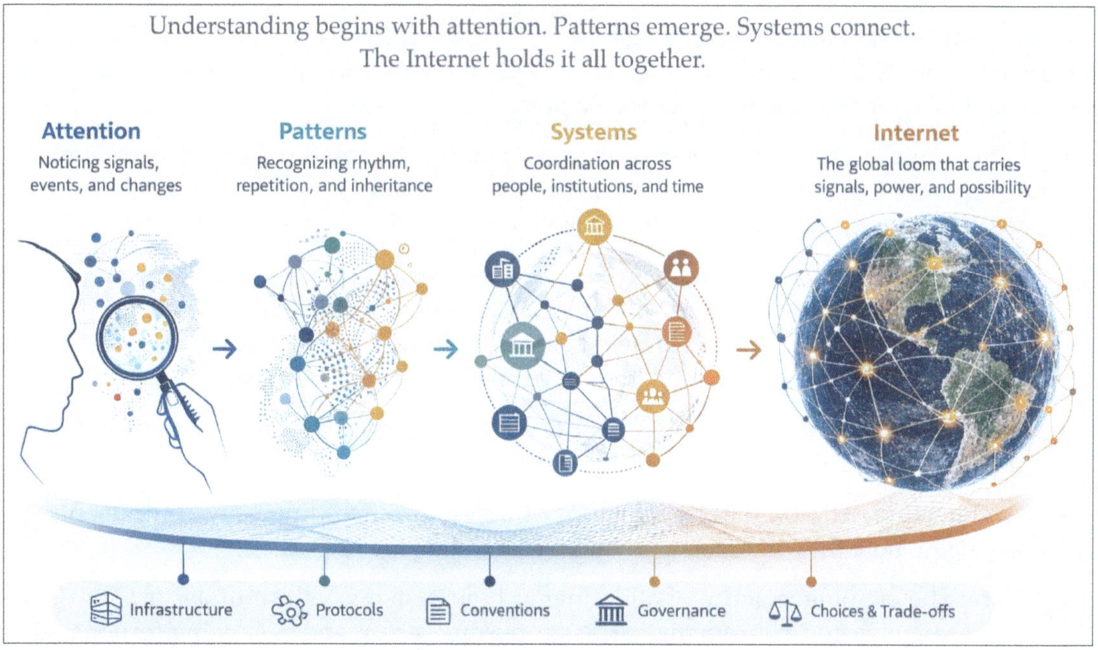

Figure 9: *From attention to architecture*

The loom we inherit is not abstract. It is built from layers of infrastructure, protocols, and conventions that shape how signals move, how reach expands, and how constraints accumulate. Among these, one system stands apart in both scope and consequence.

The Internet is *the foundational loom upon which all modern digital systems are built.*

It is the largest loom humanity has ever built. It connects devices, institutions, and people across distance and time. It carries information, coordination, and power at the planetary scale. Its structure shapes what can be seen, what can be reached, and how quickly action becomes consequence.

The Internet is often described as neutral infrastructure or invisible plumbing. In practice, it is neither. It is a designed system, built through specific technical choices, economic pressures, and governance decisions. Those choices continue to act, even when they are no longer visible.

To understand digital systems, we must begin here.

Chapter 1, The Internet, examines the Internet not as a collection of technologies, but as a loom—a structure that holds signals under tension, enables patterns to form, and constrains what can be woven next.

Metaphorical and conceptual terms

How to read the language of the loom.

This lexicon introduces a shared language used throughout The First Stitch. The terms listed here are not meant to be memorized. They are reference points you can return to as ideas recur, sharpen, and take on new meaning across chapters.

Many of these words appear in everyday conversation. In this book, they carry precise, consistent meanings grounded in how systems are designed, stressed, and sustained over time. Definitions deepen through use, not in isolation:

- **Accountability**: The condition in which responsibility for a system's behavior and consequences remains identifiable, reachable, and enforceable over time, even as the system operates at scale or under delegation. In this book, accountability includes answerability during execution, not only traceability after outcomes.
- **Algorithm**: A structured set of instructions that governs how a system processes inputs, makes decisions, or produces outputs.
- **Architecture**: The organized structure of a system, including how components are arranged, how they interact, and where constraints are imposed.
- **Care**: The ongoing practice of attending to how systems behave under use, pressure, and change, including noticing harm, supporting repair, and sustaining responsibility over time.
- **Code**: A patterned set of instructions that directs system behavior. In digital systems, code encodes intention into structure, enabling actions to be repeated consistently.
- **Connection**: The linkage between components, people, or processes that allows signals, information, or responsibility to move through a system.

- **Consequence**: The effects that follow from system decisions or actions often unfold over time, across distance, or across populations beyond the original point of choice.
- **Constraint**: A boundary or limitation that shapes how a system can act, what it can see, or which outcomes are possible.
- **Data**: Information that is captured, structured, and stored so it can be interpreted, reused, or acted upon by systems.
- **Default**: An embedded choice that governs system behavior when no explicit decision is made, often persisting silently over time.
- **Design**: The intentional arrangement of technical, social, and organizational elements to shape system behavior and outcomes.
- **Digital weaving**: The practice and method of shaping digital systems with awareness of structure, strain, and consequence over time, holding responsibility as systems evolve across industry, society, and the environment.
- **Digital system**: An interconnected set of technical and human components that processes information, makes decisions, and produces effects in the world.
- **Endurance**: The capacity of a system to continue functioning meaningfully under changing conditions, stress, or uncertainty.
- **Entropy**: The tendency of systems to drift toward disorder, misalignment, or degradation unless actively maintained or repaired.
- **Fray**: A weakening of system coherence where connections loosen, signals misalign, or responsibility thins, often appearing before outright failure.
- **Governance**: The structures and processes through which authority, oversight, and decision rights are exercised within a system.
- **Infrastructure**: The foundational systems and arrangements that enable connection, coordination, and operation across other systems.
- **Intention**: The purposes, values, or assumptions embedded in a system through design choices, whether explicit or implicit.
- **Interface**: The point where people interact with a system, shaping what is visible, usable, and understandable.
- **Layer**: A distinct level within a system that performs a specific function and interacts with other levels through defined relationships.
- **Loom**: The structured frame that holds system elements under tension, allowing patterns to form. In digital systems, the loom refers to the combined infrastructure, architecture, and governance that shape what can be woven.

- **Maintenance**: The ongoing activities required to keep a system functioning, including updates, calibration, repair, and adaptation over time.
- **Pattern**: A recurring structure or arrangement that encodes meaning, guides behavior, and persists through repetition.
- **Repair**: An intervention that restores or improves system function by reconnecting threads, correcting assumptions, or adjusting structure.
- **Responsibility**: The obligation to answer for system behavior and its consequences, including the duty to correct harm when it appears.
- **Scale**: The extent to which a system operates across size, population, time, or complexity often amplifies both benefit and harm.
- **Sensor**: A device or component that detects signals from the environment and converts them into data for system interpretation.
- **Signal**: An input captured by a system that carries information requiring interpretation.
- **Strain**: The pressure placed on a system when demands exceed its structural capacity, often revealing hidden assumptions or weak connections.
- **Structure**: The arrangement of components and relationships that shapes how a system behaves over time.
- **System**: An organized set of interacting elements, human, technical, or both, that produces patterned behavior and outcomes.
- **System of systems**: A collection of independent systems that interact to produce effects no single system controls alone.
- **Tension**: The productive or destabilizing force created when system elements pull in different directions under constraint.
- **Thread**: A single element within a system, such as data, code, a rule, or a relationship, that gains meaning through connection and can traverse multiple layers of a system.
- **Trust**: Confidence that a system will behave reliably, transparently, and in good faith, especially under conditions of stress.
- **Uncertainty**: The condition in which outcomes cannot be fully predicted, requiring systems to remain correctable rather than merely optimized.
- **Weave**: The combined result of connecting threads into a coherent system through design, use, and time.
- **Weaver**: A person or group who shapes, maintains, questions, or repairs systems through intentional action.
- **Weaving**: The ongoing process of constructing, adjusting, and sustaining systems by connecting elements under changing conditions.

CHAPTER 1

The Internet

The loom beneath our lives

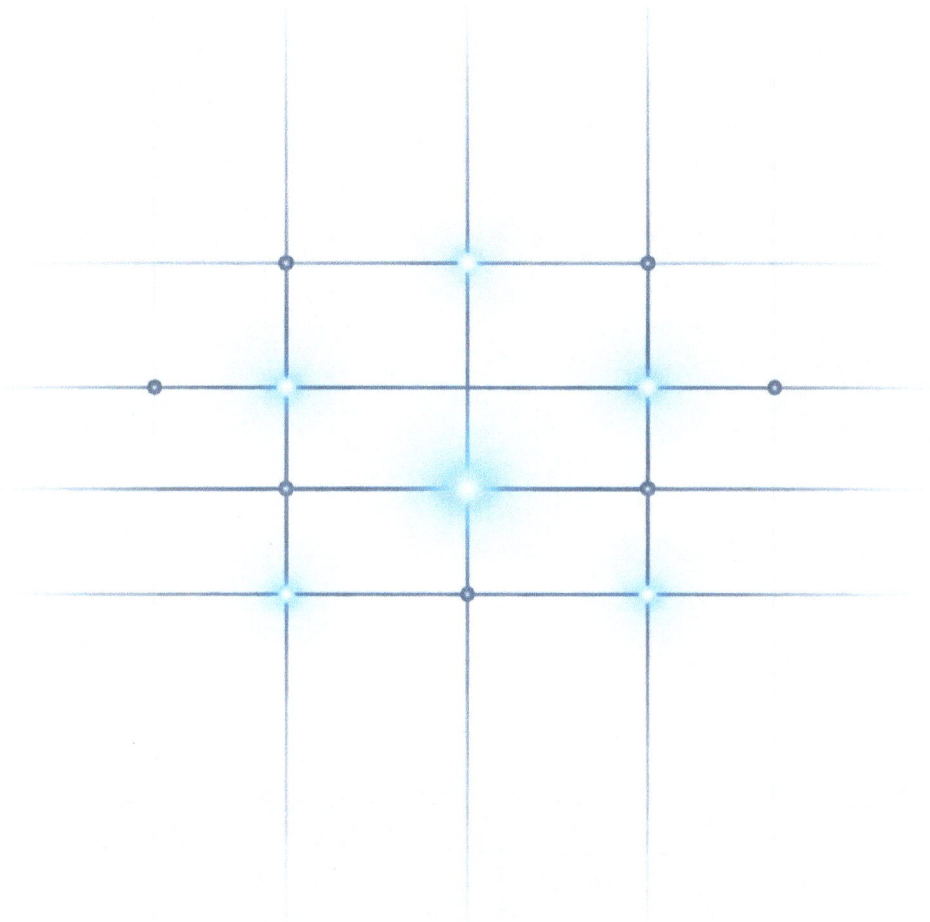

A system can grow only where connections are able to endure.

CHAPTER 1
The Internet

Introduction

The Internet forms the underlying loom of contemporary life. It enables the exchange of information, the coordination of activity, and the sustaining heartbeat of the digital age, operating quietly, invisibly, and everywhere. What began as a research network designed for resilience has evolved into the global infrastructure that supports communication, commerce, education, healthcare, and governance.

Its enduring strength arises not from speed or scale but from architectural principles that foster openness, decentralization, and adaptability. The Internet's design distributes intelligence to the edges, ensures interoperability through shared standards, and maintains reliability through redundancy and routing diversity. Information travels through multiple possible paths across interconnected networks, automatically adapting when congestion or failure occurs. These qualities have allowed it to expand, recover from disruption, and integrate new technologies without requiring fundamental redesign.

This chapter examines the origins, structure, and societal role of the Internet as the foundation of connected systems. It outlines the principles that shaped its evolution and provides a framework for understanding how this digital fabric continues to influence daily life and transform modern institutions.

Structure

This chapter covers the following topics:

- The loom unseen
- The loom beneath our lives
- A message's journey across the Internet
- Tapestry of industry and society transformation
- Fraying edges of the loom
- Reinforcing the frame with new threads

Objectives

To study the Internet is to uncover the loom beneath every click and the weave that binds global connection. By the end of this chapter, the readers will recognize the Internet as digital infrastructure and as the foundational loom for building enduring and sustainable systems. They will understand how packet switching, layered architecture, and open standards provide resilience and adaptability at scale. Core principles of decentralization, interoperability, end-to-end design, and statelessness will be examined in relation to both technical reliability and social trust. They will explore major applications of the Internet, from communication and commerce to education, health, and governance, and understand their societal impact. The reader will also evaluate vulnerabilities such as privacy erosion, security risks, and the digital divide, and see how these challenges shape system design. Finally, they will study how technologies such as IPv6, edge computing, and artificial intelligence are extending the Internet's reach and strengthening its resilience. This grounding prepares the reader to design and assess digital systems that remain durable under strain, sustainable in growth, and trustworthy in practice.

The loom unseen

At 2:14 a.m., Samir's room glowed with the pale light of his screen.
His phone vibrated once and then again.
Hashtags. Livestreams. Voice notes from a city on edge.
Outside, chants from Tahrir Square ricocheted off stone walls.

But Samir was not there.
He did not carry a sign.
He did not march in the square.
And yet, he was part of it.

From the quiet of his bedroom, he translated tweets, uploaded protest footage, tunneled **virtual private networks (VPNs)** for journalists, and relayed encrypted messages through servers in Reykjavik and San Francisco. His fingers flew across keys while buried fiber carried intent beneath oceans and borders.

I have not left my house, he typed to a friend in Berlin, *but I think I am helping shape history.*

This was not just the Internet at work.
This was the Internet at its most human, connecting voices, bypassing censors, stitching a collective will across continents.

Local actions enter shared Internet infrastructure and propagate across borders through packets, protocols, and routing agreements, linking individual intent to global participation while remaining largely invisible to those who rely on it.

***Figure 1.1**: The loom unseen, but felt everywhere*

It did not speak, but it carried every voice.
It did not lead, but it made direction possible.
It was not seen, yet it was felt everywhere.

The Internet is the most intricate system humanity has built, second only to language itself. Like language, it did not just change how we communicate; it reshaped who we are.

Just as the earliest looms enabled weavers to create fabric at scale, the Internet allows humanity to weave knowledge, culture, and memory on a planetary scale.

It is not only infrastructure.
It is both medium and message.
It is archive and pulse.
It is where we work, protest, mourn, meme, and make meaning.

The Internet is our shared loom.
It links a doctor in Mumbai, a researcher in Oslo, and a farmer in Kano on the same fabric.
It gives a teenager in Jakarta the reach once reserved for empires.

And like all looms, it vanishes in success.
When it works, it disappears.
When it breaks, the tapestry trembles.

The Internet is both machine and metaphor:
A silent frame that holds us.
A fabric stretched for creation.
A living weave of voices shaping a shared human story.

To understand how this infrastructure endures and where it begins to unravel, we must look beneath the smooth surface of every click. *What systems hum beneath? Whose hands built them? Whose voices remain at the edge of the weave?*

The loom beneath our lives

Protocols and packets, an unseen frame holding the weave together.

When Samir tapped Send, he did not think about protocols. He did not imagine cables spiraling beneath oceans or servers blinking in windowless data centers. He simply shared a message, but behind that single gesture, a global choreography unfolded.

The message was split into fragments called **packets**, each carrying both content and instructions for where to go. They raced through underwater fiber optic cables, sometimes bouncing off satellites, and slipped through routers across cities and borders. Within milliseconds, they reassembled, whole, on a screen half a world away.

Every message on the Internet is broken into packets. Each packet contains:

- **Payload**: The data being sent.
- **Header**: The control information describing origin, destination, and reassembly order.

This packet-switching design, first formalized in the 1960s through the **Advanced Research Projects Agency Network** (**ARPANET**), is what makes the Internet resilient. Even if some paths fail, packets can reroute and still reach their destination.

Samir could not see the system, but he could feel its rhythm:
Its reliability,
Its quiet choreography,
Its resilience under strain.

That moment was not powered by one company, country, or router. It was made possible by something more profound: an architecture built from collaboration, shaped by consensus, and running code.

Engineers across universities and nations agreed on open standards instead of proprietary designs. Protocols were published as **Requests for Comments** (**RFCs**), RFCs inviting anyone to propose, refine, and adopt improvements. This culture of *rough consensus and running code* gave the Internet its unusual strength.

Consensus defined the rules of packet exchange, routing, and naming. Standards were expressed as protocols, such as:

- **Transmission Control Protocol/Internet Protocol (TCP/IP)**: The foundation of reliable communication.
- **Domain Name System (DNS)**: Mapping human-readable names to IP addresses.
- **Border Gateway Protocol (BGP)**: Exchanging routing information between networks.

Code implemented those rules in working systems. Together, they built the Internet not as property, but as a shared fabric.

Unlike most engineered systems built top-down with central control, the Internet grew differently. From the beginning, it was designed to:

- **Distribute trust**: No single authority determines legitimacy.
- **Reroute under pressure**: Packets can find alternate paths when others fail.
- **Grow without permission**: Anyone can attach a new system if they follow shared protocols.
- **Adapt to tension**: Failures bend the system but rarely break it.

When Samir's protest message traveled across borders, these four principles carried it. They gave him reach beyond his neighborhood, safety despite disruptions, and continuity even under surveillance. The Internet is not flawless, but it is flexible. Not fragile, but adaptive. At its core, it is a loom; not rigid machinery, but a living frame designed to persist.

This design was not accidental. It reflected a radical belief:

- Communication should be open.
- Access should be fair.

To understand how the Internet holds under pressure and where it begins to fray, we must start not with the data flowing through it, but with the principles of its design.

Core principles shaping the Internet fabric

The Internet's strength lies not in speed or size but in the architecture that allows it to connect the world. It was never designed to be elegant; it was designed to endure. Its resilience comes from four foundational principles that shape every packet, protocol, and interaction, which are outlined in the following table:

Principle	Purpose	Effect
Decentralization	Distribute control	Removes single points of failure.
Interoperability	Create a shared grammar	Enables devices and networks to communicate across borders.

Principle	Purpose	Effect
End-to-end principle	Keep intelligence at the edges	Allows innovation without redesigning the core.
Statelessness	Treat every request independently	Supports scalability and fault tolerance.

Table 1.1: The core Internet design principles

These principles are not abstract ideals. They are encoded in routing tables, packet headers, and open standards. They are the warp threads of the digital loom: quiet, invisible, but strong enough to hold the rest of the weave.

Decentralization strengthening the loom

The Internet is a federation of autonomous networks, each operated by universities, companies, or service providers. There is no master control room. Each **autonomous system** (**AS**) manages its own routes yet connects through shared protocols.

If one path fails, packets take another. If a fiber link is cut, traffic is automatically rerouted. Protocols such as BGP and **Open Shortest Path First** (**OSPF**) update routes dynamically, ensuring continuous flow. When Samir uploaded his video during network disruption, packets still reached their destination because the system distributed control rather than concentrating it. Decentralization removes single points of failure and keeps the Internet resilient under strain.

Interoperability sustaining the loom

Not all looms are built alike, but standard tools keep weaving possibilities. The Internet follows the same principle, relying on standard protocols as a shared language. These protocols ensure that devices across continents and generations can interoperate. Without this common grammar, every network would speak in isolation, and the fabric of global connectivity would fall apart.

This compatibility rests on open, modular protocols:

- **Hypertext Transfer Protocol/Secure** (**HTTP/HTTPS**) for web delivery.
- TCP/IP for reliable transport.
- Ethernet, Wi-Fi (IEEE 802.11), and 5G for local access.

However, because of these standards, Samir's video recorded on one device could be transmitted, decoded, and viewed anywhere. Interoperability is not sameness; it is compatibility that keeps the world connected.

End-to-end principle shaping the loom

In many systems, intelligence sits at the center. The Internet chose the opposite—keep the core simple and place control at the edges. The network's job is to move packets; processing happens at the endpoints, Samir's phone, his browser, and the servers that render his video.

This end-to-end principle enables:

- **Scalability**: The network can handle millions of concurrent users.
- **Innovation**: New applications run without modifying the core.
- **Empowerment**: Users maintain control over data and functionality.

However, because of this principle, Samir could stream his video without needing approval from a central authority. The Internet simply carried the packets neutrally, leaving interpretation and control at the edges.

Statelessness scaling the loom

In weaving, each pass of the shuttle begins fresh. Statelessness works the same way. Every Internet request carries all the information it needs, without relying on previous interactions.

HTTP and REST-based APIs embody this design, allowing billions of independent transactions to occur simultaneously. Statelessness provides:

- **Scalability**: Parallel processing of countless requests.
- **Resilience**: Failures are isolated; another server can respond instantly.
- **Simplicity**: Each interaction is self-contained and easy to manage.

The network does not ask who you were yesterday. It only answers what you request now. When Samir's video went viral, each view was handled as a new transaction, and the system scaled effortlessly.

These four principles, decentralization, interoperability, end-to-end processing, and statelessness, form the architecture of trust. They are why the Internet bends under strain but rarely breaks. They are why it continues to serve billions, quietly holding the fabric of modern life.

Let us follow the weave into its next layer, resilience.

Resilient frame sustaining under strain

The Internet does not promise perfection. It promises persistence. From its earliest designs, it was meant to survive disruption, not just operate in calm. Its architecture assumes failure and prepares to route around it.

This principle of resilience emerged during the *Cold War*, when engineers asked a defining question: *If part of the network is destroyed, can the rest still communicate?* The answer became a design condition, not a feature.

That spirit endures in every failover mechanism, redundant path, and cached copy. When Samir's friends lost access to blocked news sites, they stayed connected through VPNs, satellite links, and mesh networks. They did not abandon the Internet; they relied on its capacity to adapt.

Redundancy is not inefficiency. It is scaffolding. Submarine cables cross oceans in parallel, data is cached at multiple locations, and critical systems maintain backup nodes. These duplicates are not luxuries; they are lifelines.

Resilience is both architectural and operational. No single failure should silence the Internet. When towers collapse or floods sever fiber, routing protocols redirect traffic through alternate paths. Packets may slow, but the system continues to deliver.

Yet persistence alone is not enough. For billions of strangers to share the same loom, trust must also be woven into the design.

Security woven in by design

You rarely notice the threads that hold; you see only those that snap. In the Internet's early days, trust was implicit among researchers. Today, billions of people, organizations, and machines interact across the network. Financial transactions, medical records, and political communications all depend on it. Trust, once ambient, must now be engineered.

Security cannot be added later. It must be embedded from the start. Modern Internet security relies on protocols and practices such as:

- **Transport Layer Security (TLS)/Datagram TLS (DTLS)**: Encrypts communications so intercepted data is unreadable.
- **Domain Name System Security Extensions (DNSSEC)**: Ensures the authenticity of domain name lookups.
- **Public key infrastructure (PKI)**: Confirms digital identities using certificates and cryptography.
- **Zero Trust Architecture**: Requires authentication for every request, never assuming trust based on network location.

When Samir uploaded sensitive footage, these systems worked silently in the background. Every hop was encrypted, every lookup validated, every request authenticated.

Security is not built from fear but from care. It anticipates failure, contains damage, and reinforces trust at every layer. When it fails, the fabric frays, and without reinforcement, the loom cannot hold.

Even with resilience and security, one more foundation is needed, a way to name and address every thread.

Addressing every thread in the loom

Every device on the Internet must have an identity. This identity is expressed as an IP address, while port numbers specify which process on a device should receive data. Like a postal system, IP addresses mark the building, and ports identify the room.

For decades, IPv4 supported global communication with 4.3 billion unique addresses. As billions of phones, sensors, and wearables came online, that space was exhausted. The solution is IPv6, with 128-bit addresses providing 340 undecillion possibilities, enough for every device on Earth, from streetlights to medical implants.

IPv6 restores true end-to-end connectivity, improves routing efficiency, and supports massive scalability. Ports continue to function seamlessly across both versions, ensuring that once a device is identified, its individual services remain reachable.

When Samir's phone streamed video to Leila's device, IPv6 enabled direct, peer-to-peer communication. Port numbers ensured that the stream reached her media app, not her inbox. For the future, IPv6 will make it possible for entire smart cities with billions of connected nodes, each with its own digital identity.

Naming is not cosmetic; it is structural. Addresses and ports ensure that every exchange has a destination and that the network can grow without losing order. Behind each digital identity lies a physical reality of wires, waves, and infrastructure, the true loom beneath the web.

The physical loom of wires and waves

The Internet is not an idea. It is a physical system. It relies on copper cables, fiber-optic backbones, cellular towers, and satellites. Over 1.4 million kilometers of undersea cables link continents. **Internet Exchange Points** (**IXPs**) decide whether traffic remains local or crosses oceans. Tier 1 providers carry traffic across global backbones. **Content delivery networks** (**CDNs**) replicate and cache data near users. Low Earth Orbit satellites extend connectivity to remote mountains, deserts, and disaster zones.

When Samir uploaded his video, the path was anything but straight. It flowed through fiber loops in Cairo, a CDN edge in Frankfurt, and a transcontinental backbone before reaching Leila. The journey was determined not by abstraction but by physics, where the distance introduces delay, geography shapes routes, and infrastructure decisions ripple across regions.

Infrastructure is not neutral. It reflects political boundaries, economic investment, and engineering trade-offs. The Internet is engineered, owned, and operated by people. To understand it fully, one must see it as anchored in matter, maps, and decisions.

Like any loom, it does not stand still. It evolves continuously, adapting to new materials, growing demands, and new generations of builders.

The loom evolving toward futures

The Internet that Samir's parents once saw on a laboratory terminal is not the same system he depends on today. The one his niece will inherit will evolve further still. The Internet continues to grow and adapt through new physical infrastructure, new protocols, and new forms of computation.

Key advances shaping this evolution include:

- **Undersea cables**: Increasingly dense and high-capacity links extend the global backbone, carrying most of the world's international traffic.
- **Low Earth Orbit (LEO) satellites**: Provide connectivity and resilience where terrestrial fiber cannot reach, such as remote regions or disaster zones.
- **Edge computing**: Moves processing closer to users and devices, enabling real-time autonomy and reducing dependence on centralized cloud servers.
- **Internet Protocol version 6 (IPv6)**: Expands the global address space to 340 undecillion unique addresses, allowing trillions of devices, from sensors to vehicles, to be connected natively.
- **Artificial intelligence (AI) and quantum networking**: Still emerging, these technologies promise adaptive routing, predictive fault management, and cryptographic systems resistant to quantum attacks.

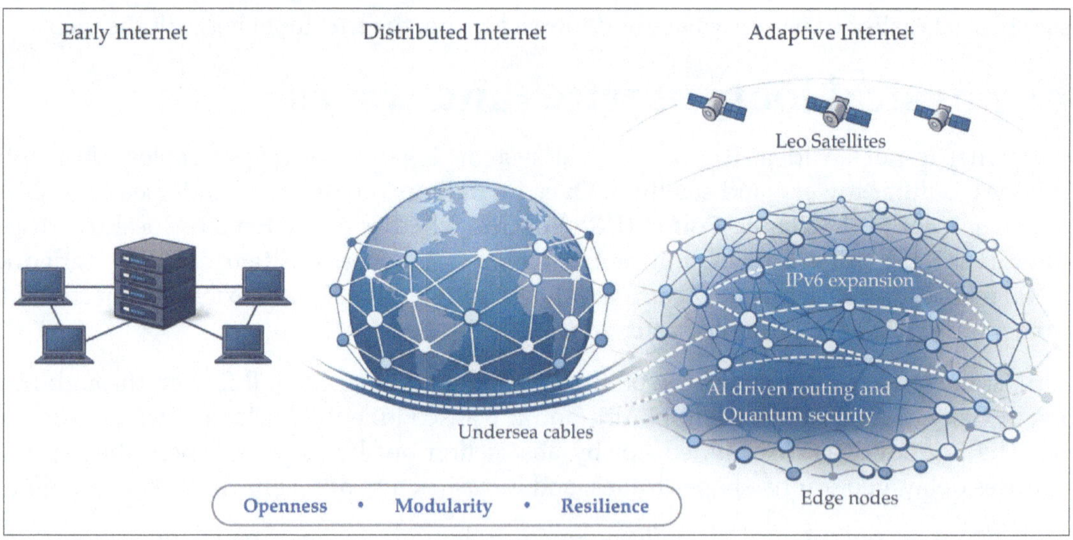

Figure 1.2: The loom evolving toward futures

Samir already experiences the benefits of this evolving loom. When local infrastructure failed, his message was still delivered by satellites and cached at edge nodes. In the future, AI-driven routing algorithms and quantum-secure communication links may protect flows in ways that remain invisible but critical.

These developments are not just technical upgrades. They represent social and political choices about who gains access, how control is exercised, and what forms of inclusion or exclusion shape the digital future.

Through all these changes, three design principles remain constant:

- **Openness as the default**: Shared protocols and transparency enable collaboration across borders.
- **Modularity as the strategy**: New technologies can be added without redesigning the entire system.
- **Resilience as the promise**: The fabric continues to operate under strain, adapting to disruptions rather than collapsing.

The Internet does not resist change. It absorbs new threads, turning strain into structure and tension into new patterns that carry the next generation of communication.

A message's journey across the Internet

Every packet is a thread, every layer a shuttle, binding intent into motion.

At 2:16 p.m., Samir pressed Send.

A design file zipped across his screen, bound for his sister Leila's inbox. No frozen bar, no crash, just the familiar whoosh as it disappeared from view.

Where did the message go?
Who carried it?
What paths did it follow, and what gates did it pass through?

What Samir could not see was the invisible choreography beneath the surface. His file was not a single object gliding through the network. It was divided into packets, small, self-contained units of data, each carrying both payload and instructions for routing and reassembly.

The Internet does not transmit data as a single, continuous stream. It moves in layers, each adding structure and meaning:

- **Application layer**: The interface where Samir hit *Send*.
- **Transport layer**: Slicing data into segments, ensuring delivery and order.
- **Network layer**: Assigning addresses and choosing routes.
- **Media access control (MAC)/data link layer**: Managing frames and access to shared media.

- **Physical layer**: The electrical pulses, light beams, or radio waves that carry signals across copper, fiber, and air.

Each layer acted like a loom shuttle, handing off the thread with its own markings, until the pattern reached the next stage.

Samir's message was no longer just his file. It was a pattern of packets, wrapped and unwrapped five times, crossing cables, switches, and routers, only to be reassembled whole on Leila's screen.

The Internet may feel instantaneous, but it is not magic. It is structured, layered, modular, and resilient.

To follow Samir's file is to see how every thread in the digital fabric depends on the strength of its layers.

The Internet stack

Samir's design did not travel as one complete file.

It was divided into smaller units, each labeled, addressed, and wrapped through five layers of the Internet stack. Each layer performed a specific function, ensuring the file could move reliably from his device to its destination.

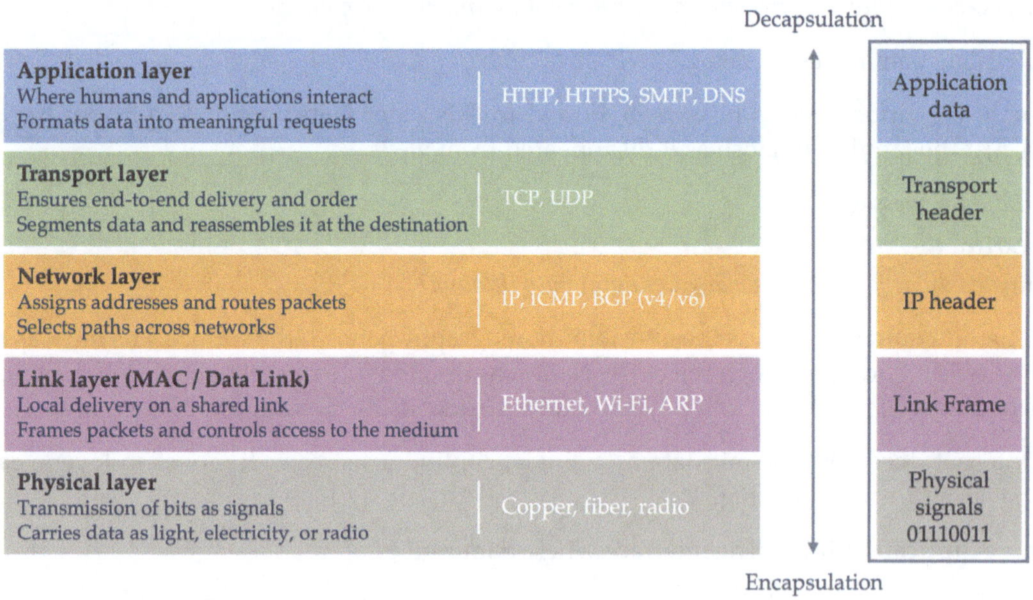

The Internet is organized into layers, each responsible for a distinct function. This separation of concerns allows global communication to scale without centralized control.

***Figure 1.3**: The five-layer Internet stack*

The Internet is not a single system.

It is a layered architecture, where each level has a distinct role and builds upon the one beneath it.

Much like a loom guiding cloth through heddles, shuttles, and tension rods, the Internet stack organizes communication into ordered stages. Each layer has a defined responsibility, and together they form a structure that carries information across the globe.

Let us walk through these layers, from the most visible to the most physical.

Application layer

The application layer is where people interact with the Internet. It provides services and protocols that make communication meaningful to both humans and machines.

Key protocols include:

- **HTTP/HTTPS**: Web browsing
- **SMTP/IMAP**: Email transfer and retrieval
- **FTP/SFTP**: File transfers
- **DNS**: Domain name lookups

This layer formats data, defines how it should be interpreted, and ensures that the receiving system knows what to do.

When Samir clicked Send, his email client used SMTP to prepare the design file with recipient details, subject, and attachment. When Leila's system later checked for mail using IMAP, it could recognize, retrieve, and interpret the file correctly.

Transport layer

The transport layer ensures that data is delivered reliably, accurately, and in the correct order. Its two primary protocols are:

- **TCP**: It provides reliable, ordered, and error-checked transmission.
- **User Datagram Protocol (UDP)**: It provides fast, connectionless delivery without guarantees of order or reliability, often used for real-time applications like streaming or gaming.

TCP divides large data into smaller packets, attaches sequence numbers, and ensures missing packets are retransmitted until the set is complete. It functions as the quality control mechanism of the Internet stack.

When Samir sent his design file by email, TCP divided it into a sequence of packets. Each packet carried not only sequence numbers for reassembly but also a destination port number, in this case, port 25, reserved for SMTP. The port told Leila's mail server that the packets belonged to the email service, not to her video player or web browser.

Network layer

The network layer is responsible for addressing and routing, ensuring that each packet is directed toward its destination across diverse networks. Key components include:

- **IP**: It provides addressing and delivery functions, available in IPv4 and IPv6 formats.
- **Internet Control Message Protocol (ICMP)**: It supports diagnostics and error reporting, such as with the ping command.
- **Routing Protocols (BGP, OSPF, IS-IS, RIP)**: They define the rules for selecting efficient paths across the global Internet.

Routers read the IP headers in packets and forward them step by step toward their destination. Each decision point, or hop, moves the packet closer to its target.

When Samir sent his file, every packet contained Leila's IP address, which functioned like a postal code. Routers in his city, across regional backbones, and across international links evaluated that address and chose the most efficient route until the packets arrived at her inbox.

Media access control layer

The MAC layer ensures that packets are delivered correctly on the local link, within the same subnet. It operates with unique hardware identifiers known as MAC addresses, which are assigned to every network interface. Key mechanisms include:

- **Ethernet**: Provides wired local delivery.
- **Wi-Fi (IEEE 802.11)**: Provides wireless local delivery.
- **Address Resolution Protocol (ARP)**: Maps IP addresses to MAC addresses for correct packet delivery.

This layer ensures that the intended device, and not any other, receives the packet within a local network.

When Samir's packets arrived at Leila's home Wi-Fi network, the router needed to determine which device should receive them. The router used ARP to match Leila's IP address to the correct laptop's MAC address. Once identified, the packets were transmitted directly to her computer, avoiding confusion with her phone, smart TV, or other connected devices.

Physical layer

At the foundation of the Internet stack is the physical layer, where bits are converted into physical signals that traverse communication media. It defines the actual transmission of 1s and 0s through:

- **Copper cables**: Electrical pulses
- **Fiber optics**: Light beams
- **Radio waves**: Wi-Fi and cellular transmission
- **Satellites**: Long-distance relays in space

This layer transforms the abstract into the tangible by converting binary data into measurable energy that can travel across cities, oceans, and the air.

The packets carrying Samir's design file traveled as pulses of light through transatlantic fiber cables, shifted to electrical signals inside local wiring, and finally converted to radio waves for the last hop across Leila's apartment. From electrons to photons to radio waves, the physical layer made his message real.

Stitching through the five layers

The five layers of the Internet stack rarely appear in isolation. They work together as a nested sequence, each handing off responsibility to the next. From human intent at the top to raw signals at the base, every online interaction is stitched through this layered fabric.

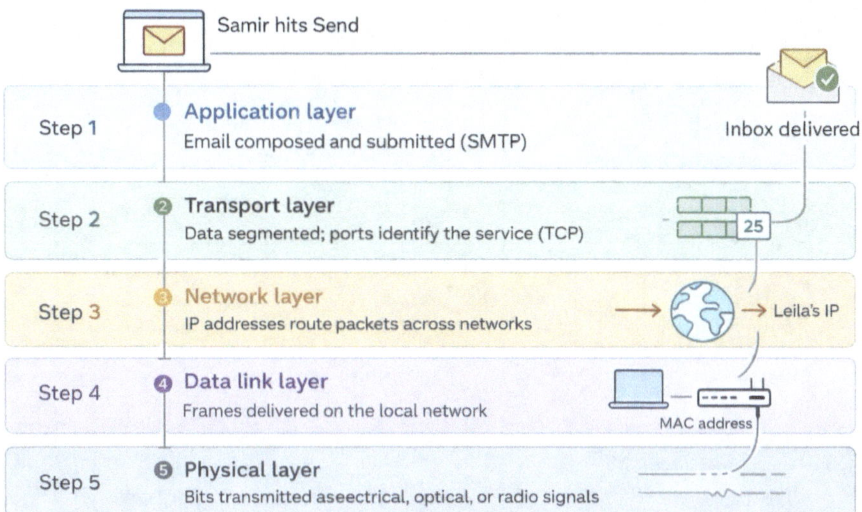

A message traverses the Internet stack, moving from application intent to physical signals and back to application delivery.

***Figure 1.4**: Samir's journey in 5 steps—from send to inbox*

When Samir pressed Send, his design file began a structured journey through the Internet stack:

1. **Application layer**: Packaged the design as an email with headers, subject, and attachment.

2. **Transport layer**: Broke the file into packets, assigned sequence numbers, and tracked delivery.
3. **Network layer**: Applied IP addresses and routed packets across networks and continents.
4. **MAC layer**: Resolved the destination IP into a local MAC address and delivered packets to the correct device on Leila's Wi-Fi.
5. **Physical layer**: Converted bits into signals: light in fiber, electricity in copper, and radio waves in the air, carrying the packets into Leila's laptop.

Each layer encapsulated the one above it, nesting Samir's file like threads passed hand to hand, node to node, until they reassembled in Leila's inbox, and when she replied, the same five-layer process unfolded in reverse.

Hosts, routers, and subnets

A single machine does not carry the Internet's motion. It is built from three fundamental actors that pass data hop by hop: hosts, subnets, and routers. Each plays a distinct role in this choreography.

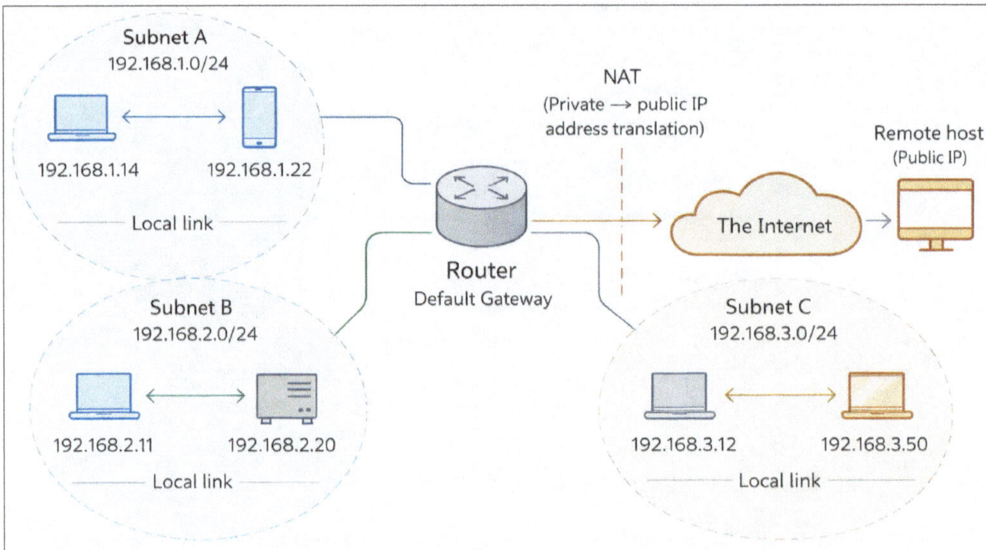

Hosts are grouped into subnets that share a common address prefix and local link. Routers connect multiple subnets, serve as default gateways, and forward packets between networks. When private subnets reach the public Internet, the router performs NAT.

***Figure 1.5**: The local network—subnet, hosts, link, and routers*

Subnets

A subnet is a cluster of hosts that share the same address prefix, forming a logical neighborhood within the Internet. Subnets are defined by a subnet mask (e.g., /24 or 255.255.255.0 in IPv4 networks), which tells the network which addresses are local.

Example:

Samir's laptop IP address: 192.168.1.14
Samir's mobile IP address: 192.168.1.22
Subnet mask: 255.255.255.0

Subnets help:

- Localize traffic within neighborhoods.
- Reduce routing complexity.
- Determine when packets remain inside the subnet and when they must leave through a router.
- Ensure all hosts share the same gateway.

Within a subnet, hosts exchange packets directly over the shared link using local MAC and IP addresses. When hosts are on different subnets, especially across cities, routers forward the packets between networks.

Hosts

A host is any device connected to the Internet, such as a laptop, phone, server, or IoT sensor.

Every host carries two key identifiers:

- **IP address**: A logical identifier used for routing.
- **MAC address**: A hardware fingerprint used for local delivery.

Hosts are the origins and destinations of traffic. All communication begins and ends with them.

Example: Samir's laptop acted as the sending host, while Leila's phone was the receiving host. Their devices were the edges of the digital conversation, the points where meaning was created and where it was consumed.

Routers

Routers do not generate data. They forward it from one subnet to another, guiding it across vast digital topologies.

Each router contains a routing table, a dynamic map of the Internet that shows the next hop for any destination IP address.

Key router functions include:

- Identifying the destination network from an IP address.
- Selecting optimal paths using routing protocols (e.g., OSPF, BGP).
- Forwarding packets to the next hop or final host.
- Performing **Network Address Translation** (NAT) when private networks access the public Internet.
- Providing failover by rerouting traffic instantly if a link fails.

Example: Samir's home router saw the packet destined for Leila's IP. It passed the traffic to the **Internet service provider** (ISP) router, which forwarded it to regional and backbone routers. Each router acted as a silent navigator, unseen by Samir but critical in carrying his message across continents.

Together in the weave:

- Hosts create, interpret, and consume meaning; all communication begins and ends with them.
- Subnets group hosts into logical neighborhoods, enabling efficient local delivery without interpreting content.
- Routers connect subnets into a global network, forwarding packets without understanding what they carry.

Each plays a distinct role, but all share the same contract: to move packets faithfully, efficiently, and without bias.

DNS

When Samir typed `leila@designmail.net` into his email client, his laptop could not use that name directly. The Internet does not move packets by names; it moves them by numbers, the IP addresses.

That translation from name (website URL, email address) to IP address is handled by the DNS. This hierarchical, distributed lookup system resolves billions of names into IP addresses within milliseconds.

The resolution chain works step by step:

1. **Resolver (Stub or Recursive)**: Runs on Samir's laptop or his ISP. The resolver first checks its cache for an answer. If none exists, it begins the query chain.

2. **Root server**: Stores the locations of **top-level domain** (**TLD**) servers. It does not answer directly but refers the resolver to the correct TLD.
3. **TLD server (.net, .com, .org, etc.)**: Contains records for domain families and points the resolver toward the authoritative server of the requested domain.
4. **Authoritative server**: Stores the DNS record for **`leila.designmail.net`** and responds with the corresponding IP address.
5. **Return to resolver | Application**: The resolver sends the IP address back to Samir's email client. From that point onward, packets know where to go. Numbers, not names, guide them.

Key supporting protocols:

- **DNS over UDP/TCP (Port 53)**: It is the standard query transport.
- **DNSSEC**: It ensures the authenticity of responses with cryptographic signatures.

In essence, DNS is the domain name system, mapping human-readable names into machine-routable numbers.

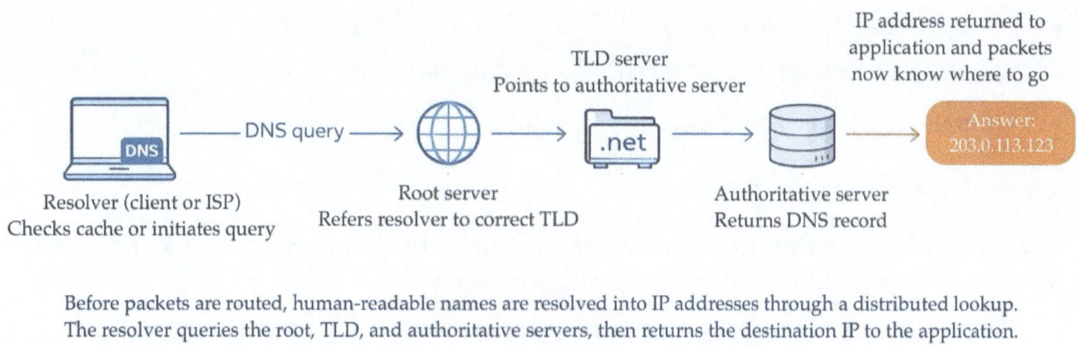

Figure 1.6: *DNS resolving a domain name to an IP address*

When Samir's email client attempted to send his design file, it asked his local resolver:

Where is leila.designmail.net?

- **The resolver checked its memory**: *No entry was found.*
- **The root server pointed**: *Ask the .net servers.*
- **The .net TLD server replied**: *This belongs to designmail's records.*
- **The authoritative server finally answered**: *Her inbox is at 203.0.113.123.*

Milliseconds later, Samir's client had the IP address. His packets used a precise destination IP address. With that, they could travel across the Internet and reach Leila's host.

ISPs, IXPs, and backbone providers

The Internet is not a single network. It is a federation of thousands of networks that interconnect through an ecosystem of ISPs, IXPs, and backbone providers. Together, they form the spine of global communication.

Internet service providers

An ISP is the entry point to the Internet for most users. Its responsibilities include:

- Assigning public IP addresses using DHCP or static allocation.
- Managing last-mile access through DSL, fiber, cable, or 5G.
- Offering recursive DNS resolution services.
- Forwarding packets toward upstream networks.

ISPs range from small regional operators to global telecoms, but their core role is always the same: connecting end-user devices to the broader Internet.

Examples:

- **Local/Regional**: Sonic (US), BSNL (India), iiNet (Australia)
- **National**: Comcast (US), Airtel (India), Orange (France)
- **Global**: AT&T, Verizon, Deutsche Telekom

Internet exchange points

An **Internet exchange point** (**IXP**) is a physical facility where multiple networks interconnect to exchange traffic directly. Their primary functions are to:

- Reduce latency by keeping local traffic local.
- Lower transit costs by avoiding third-party carriers.
- Improve resilience by supporting peering.

Traffic exchanged at IXPs operates under peering agreements, which allow ISPs and networks to share traffic without settlement fees. This model preserves decentralization and cost efficiency.

Examples:

- DE-CIX (Frankfurt, Germany)
- LINX (London, UK)
- AMS-IX (Amsterdam, Netherlands)
- Equinix IX (global operator)
- Mumbai-IX (India)

Backbone providers

Tier 1 backbone providers are large global carriers that operate high-capacity, long-haul networks. They own and manage:

- Submarine fiber-optic cables
- Terrestrial fiber backbones
- Intercontinental satellite systems

These providers interconnect with each other through settlement-free peering, ensuring global reachability without upstream transit fees. They sell capacity to ISPs, cloud providers, and enterprises.

Examples: Lumen Technologies, Tata Communications, NTT, AT&T, Cogent, China Telecom

How they work together

The following list outlines how a data packet travels across the Internet:

- A packet originates at the user's ISP.
- If the destination is on another network, the packet may be exchanged at an IXP.
- For long-distance delivery, the packet may traverse a Tier 1 backbone.
- The packet then enters the destination ISP and reaches the end host.

Each hop is shaped by routing policies, such as BGP, peering, and transit agreements, as well as economic or latency considerations.

What Samir experienced as a simple whoosh was, in fact, a relay across local ISPs, IXPs, and Tier 1 backbones, held together by protocols and trust.

Routing protocols

When Samir's message left his city, it did not follow a fixed path. There is no single map of the Internet. Instead, routers determine paths dynamically using routing protocols that exchange information about network reachability.

Routing protocols are the mechanisms that allow routers to build and maintain these maps. They operate continuously, measuring link availability, updating routes, and adapting to failures. Some work inside a single network, while others coordinate routing between entire networks.

Interior routing within networks

Inside an organization or an ISP, **Interior Gateway Protocols (IGPs)** handle routing automatically:

- OSPF and **Intermediate System to Intermediate System** (**IS-IS**) compute optimal routes by assigning costs to links and updating tables when conditions change. They converge quickly when a link fails.
- **Routing Information Protocol** (**RIP**) is used in smaller or simpler networks, relying on hop counts to determine the best path.

IGPs ensure that packets can move efficiently within a network even when parts of the infrastructure fail.

Exterior routing between networks

Across the global Internet, thousands of autonomous networks connect to one another. Each of these networks AS manages its own internal routing, but must share reachability information with others. This coordination happens through BGP, the Internet's main interdomain routing protocol.

BGP routers exchange announcements that specify which IP address blocks they can deliver. Each AS applies local policies to decide which routes to accept or prefer. The chosen *best path* may not be the shortest, but it reflects economic, political, or performance priorities.

Through this constant exchange, BGP enables independent networks to interconnect and maintain a global, reachable Internet.

When Samir's ISP received his outgoing packets, its BGP routers determined where to send them next, such as:

- His ISP's router advertised*: Traffic to Leila's address can go through DE-CIX Frankfurt.*
- Leila's cloud provider announced*: Our address block is reachable via Tata Communications.*

Through Tier-1 backbone interconnections, packets were exchanged between DE-CIX Frankfurt and Tata Communications, forming part of the global mesh that enables end-to-end reachability.

Each router made a local decision based on these advertisements, forwarding packets through the most suitable path. The entire route from Samir's home to Leila's cloud service was the outcome of these distributed decisions, updated in real time.

Routing protocols are the Internet's navigation system. They direct data across thousands of networks, adapt to failures, and sustain global communication. As packets follow these routes, their journey ends at servers, the systems that host, process, and respond to user requests. At this point, transmission becomes interaction: Internet services transform raw packets into web pages, emails, and applications that users experience every day.

Servers and services

At its core, a server is both a program and the machine it runs on. It listens for incoming requests and responds with data or an action. Servers form the foundation of Internet services:

- **Web servers (Apache, Nginx)**: Deliver HTML, CSS, JavaScript.
- **Application servers**: Handle business logic, authentication, and session state.
- **Database servers**: Store, query, and manage structured information.
- **Mail servers**: Send (SMTP) and receive (IMAP, POP) email.
- **DNS servers**: Translate human-readable names into IP addresses.
- **FTP servers**: Transfer files between systems.

Servers may be public-facing (serving millions), internal (databases, caches), or edge-based (close to users for faster response). Together, they create a fabric capable of handling billions of requests per second.

Internet services are designed to be stateless, and each request is treated independently. This allows systems to scale horizontally and recover from failures quickly. A typical request moves through a chain:

1. A load balancer distributes requests across multiple servers.
2. The web server receives the HTTP/HTTPS request.
3. Application server processes business logic.
4. The database server records or retrieves information.
5. Mail or messaging server triggers notifications.

No single server carries the whole load. Each plays its role and hands the thread forward, creating a resilient and modular system.

VPNs masking the thread

On the Internet, every packet carries both an address and a path, usually visible to providers, governments, and sometimes attackers. A VPN changes this by wrapping traffic in an encrypted tunnel and relaying it through another server, a VPN gateway. Packets then appear to come from the VPN gateway rather than the user's real IP address.

At the protocol level, VPNs establish secure channels using IPSec or TLS between a device and a VPN gateway. This provides:

- **Privacy**: Shields activity from ISPs and on-path observers.
- **Security**: Encrypts traffic on insecure networks such as public Wi-Fi.
- **Access**: Bypasses censorship and geofencing by appearing to originate elsewhere.

Extending private networks across public space

VPNs are widely used to link organizational networks across distances. Instead of leasing dedicated circuits, institutions use the Internet as transport while keeping traffic encrypted end-to-end. A VPN gateway at each site creates a tunnel that links entire subnets, so devices behave as if they share one local network. Internal resources like printers, databases, and applications remain accessible without exposure.

This enables:

- **Integration**: Extends private or institutional networks such as hospitals, banks, factories, or universities, securely across the public Internet.
- **Remote work**: Employees connect to office networks from anywhere.
- **Hybrid clouds**: On-premise infrastructure extends into cloud providers.

VPNs are not perfect shields. Trust shifts to the provider, latency can add delays, and some services block VPN traffic. Yet for Samir's friends in Cairo, VPNs made blocked news accessible. Their packets were encrypted, rerouted through Europe, and emerged onto the wider Internet as if from another country. The loom still held, but the thread's visible origin was masked.

Bringing it all together

The file was sent.

The response was received.

To Samir and Leila, it felt instant.

Beneath that sense of immediacy lies a precisely coordinated sequence of actions spanning machines, cables, and code. What seems like a single moment of communication is, in reality, the synchronized work of multiple layers and components operating as one continuous system.

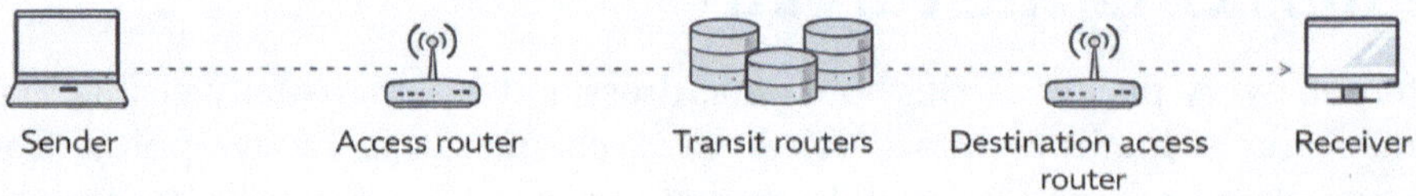

Application data (email, web, message)		Application data (email, web, message)
End-to-end segments		End-to-end segments
Packets to default gateway	Packet forwarding by destination IP	Packets from default gateway
Local delivery on link	Local delivery on each link	Local delivery on link
Signals over wire, fiber, or radio	Signals over wire, fiber, radio, or satellite	Signals over wire, fiber, or radio

A packet travels from sender to receiver by moving across networks while passing through different layers at each hop.

***Figure 1.7**: A packet's walk through the Internet*

From click to thread

When Samir pressed Send, the Internet stack activated in sequence:

1. **Application layer**: Prepared the message using SMTP, adding headers, attachments, and content.
2. **Transport layer**: Broke the message into TCP segments, applied sequence numbers, and added port information.
3. **Network layer**: Attached source and destination IP addresses and determined a suitable route toward Leila's network.
4. **MAC layer**: Assigned a hardware address to deliver the packet to the next hop on Wi-Fi or Ethernet.
5. **Physical layer**: Converts bits into electrical, optical, or radio signals, sending the first transmission onto the link.

Through the global weave

From Samir's home, the packet moved outward in a series of handoffs:

- **Local access**: Samir's laptop passed the packet to his home router, which forwarded it into his ISP's access network.
- **Regional exchange**: The ISP directed the packet to an IXP, where traffic was handed off to other participating networks.
- **Global transit**: From the IXP, the packet entered Tier 1 backbone networks that carry data across oceans and continents.
- **Destination cloud**: The backbone delivered the packet into Leila's cloud provider's infrastructure, where it descended back through regional and local networks until it reached her device.

During this journey,

Several background functions worked continuously to keep Samir's packet on track:

- **DNS resolution**: Translated human-readable domain names into numeric IP addresses for routing.
- **Routing decisions**: Routers consulted global routing tables to forward packets along the best available paths.
- **Transport reliability**: Protocols such as TCP handled sequencing, error detection, retransmission, and acknowledgment of packets.
- **Network functions**: Mechanisms like NAT, firewalls, and caching systems shaped traffic flow, improved efficiency, and provided security.

Servers

Inside Leila's cloud provider, packets were routed into a distributed service architecture:

- The load balancer distributed the request to an available server.
- The web or mail server received the packet and processed the protocol.
- An application server executes business logic, such as storing files or notifying users.
- The database server recorded the event and indexed the attachment.
- Mail service generated a notification and placed it into Leila's inbox.

These server clusters, often spread across cloud regions and edge facilities, turned the raw packet sequence into a usable service.

Back again

Leila's reply followed the same chain in reverse—layer by layer, hop by hop, service by service. Each packet traveled the fabric of protocols and agreements that keep communication continuous.

Every message is not just bits in motion. It is the product of a layered stack, engineered for trust, resilience, and delivery at scale.

Loom beneath our lives

The Internet is not a single place or machine. It is a cooperative fabric sustained by:

- Standards such as IETF specifications and RFCs define common rules.
- Providers, including ISPs, IXPs, backbone carriers, and cloud platforms, supply connectivity.
- Devices from hosts and routers to switches and servers execute the work of transmission.
- Protocols such as TCP/IP, DNS, HTTP, and SMTP coordinate communication across various layers.
- People such as engineers, designers, educators, and users, who design, maintain, and rely on the system.

Samir's message did not float freely. It traveled through layers of software and hardware, guided by standards and sustained by agreements. It arrived because the architecture held, and because thousands of independent systems cooperated to preserve the Internet.

This is the loom beneath our lives, an unseen structure that shapes communication, commerce, and connection every day.

Tapestry of industry and society transformation

The loom does not just carry data; it rewires work, care, and culture.

The Internet does not merely carry data. It rewires the structures of work, learning, care, and culture. As a loom stretched across continents, it transforms industries not by replacing them, but by redesigning their foundations.

To see this transformation up close, we follow Leila, Samir's sister, a designer and entrepreneur in Alexandria. Her ordinary day reveals something extraordinary: how deeply the digital loom threads through commerce, education, healthcare, cities, and creative work.

A day inside the digital fabric

At 6:45 a.m., sunlight spilled into Leila's studio. Coffee beside her, she opened her dashboard; live orders from Senegal, shipping delays from the Gulf, a licensing request from Jakarta. Messages from her mother and a voice note from Samir appeared beside a short video from Nairobi showing a seamstress reproducing her embroidery.

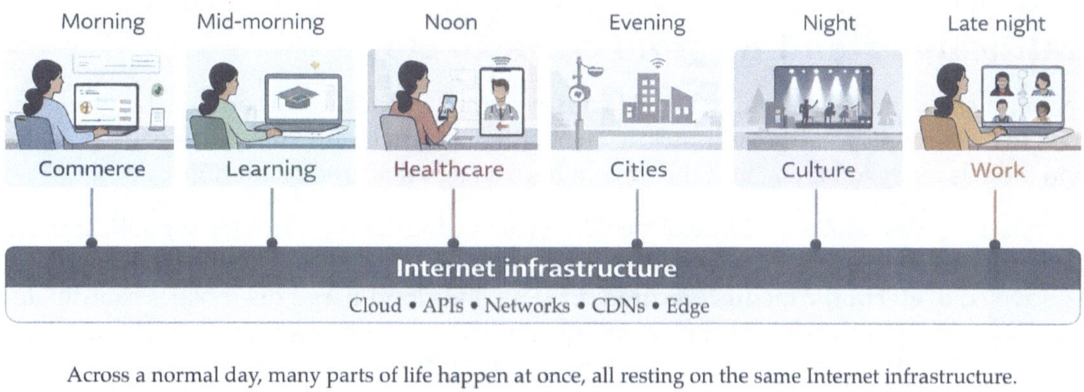

Figure 1.8: *Threads of commerce, learning, care, culture, and work interlace across one shared infrastructure, the Internet's invisible weave*

To Leila, this was not unusual. It was the rhythm of her day, threads of family, trade, and creativity woven together by the unseen loom of the Internet.

Commerce moving from booth to browser

When Leila's mother sold scarves at the souk, her reach ended at the market gate. Customers paid in cash, and reputation traveled by word of mouth. Leila, by contrast, sells across time zones. Her storefront runs in the cloud, linking payment gateways, tax calculators, and IoT-enabled logistics that track packages from warehouse to doorstep.

Each component operates as a microservice, communicating through **application programming interfaces** (**APIs**). Checkout, invoicing, and returns work independently yet synchronize in real time. Leila no longer manages a store; she orchestrates an ecosystem. The Internet has not only digitized trade, but it has also democratized entrepreneurship, lowering barriers once reserved for corporations.

Education shifting from the classroom to online

By midmorning, Leila's intern struggled with a fabric simulation. She shared a **Massive Open Online Course** (**MOOC**) lecture recorded in Singapore. Ten minutes later, the problem was solved.

This is education woven into workflow. MOOCs scale instruction to millions, adaptive platforms tailor content to learners, and peer-to-peer ecosystems like YouTube or Discord transform audiences into classrooms. CDNs reduce latency, streaming infrastructure adjusts to mobile bandwidth, and standards such as **Sharable Content Object Reference Model** (**SCORM**) and **Learning Tools Interoperability** (**LTI**) ensure interoperability. The loom of learning is no longer confined to classrooms; it is ambient, responsive, and embedded.

Healthcare extending from clinic to cloud

At noon, a call came from Beirut. Leila's cousin worried about a rash on her daughter and turned to Leila for help. Within minutes, a telehealth platform guided image uploads, machine vision models analyzed them, and the system booked a pediatric consultation.

For Leila, this was another thread of her day, connecting family through digital care. The experience was simple, but the architecture was intricate. Edge AI triaged the case, encrypted data traveled to **electronic medical records** (**EMRs**), and cloud-based diagnostics coordinated across hospitals. APIs linked insurance, pharmacy, and scheduling systems, while standards such as **Fast Healthcare Interoperability Resources** (**FHIR**) ensured security and portability. Healthcare now moves at network speed, offering presence without proximity.

Cities evolving from stone to sensors

At dusk, Alexandria's streetlights brightened responsively as Leila walked home. A push notification flagged a burst water pipe and projected the restoration time. Her city app also reminded her that trash collection was scheduled as her bin approached capacity.

The city looked unchanged, but beneath it pulsed a digital nervous system. Thousands of IoT sensors monitored infrastructure; low-power wide-area networks like LoRaWAN carried their signals; edge processors filtered data locally; and event-driven architectures dispatched repair crews automatically. Open data portals gave citizens access to the same dashboards as planners. The result was not spectacle, but quiet responsiveness, an infrastructure that listens and acts.

Culture flowing from stage to stream

Back home, Leila brewed tea and opened YouTube. She had missed a concert at the Alexandria Opera House but could join the live stream. With one click, she entered a digital audience spanning continents.

This is culture without borders, the performances streamed in real time, adaptive codecs delivering smooth video over uneven connections, and CDNs caching content close to users. Platforms embed subtitles and translation, enabling global access. For creators, analytics, licensing, and digital payments sustain their craft. The Internet has turned the stage into a stream, extending cultural memory far beyond walls and seats.

Work moving from labor to knowledge fabric

Later that night, Leila collaborated with peers in Kenya, Bangladesh, and Mexico on a shared digital canvas. Together, they tagged colors, adjusted stitch resolution, and synced renders to production, without offices, cubicles, or bosses.

Work today runs on cloud-native design tools, version control, project boards, and communication platforms that erase time-zone and language barriers. Distributed file systems, **continuous integration and continuous delivery/deployment** (**CI/CD**) pipelines, and encryption secure intellectual property and ensure continuous workflows. The Internet has not only relocated work, but it has also repatterned it into asynchronous, trust-based collaboration.

A living pattern

By midnight, Leila closed her laptop. Her designs were still moving through caches, servers, and queues across continents.

She did not think about the Internet when she joined her morning calls.
She did not marvel at it when her design files reached Jakarta, or when a voice memo from Nairobi played mid-scroll.
And yet it was always there, beneath every tap, every sync, every moment stitched across time zones.

Not as an app.
Not as a platform.
But as the condition of modern life.

The Internet has rewired society not by replacing institutions, but by rethreading their logic:

- **Commerce extends beyond storefronts**: Cloud marketplaces, APIs, and global logistics form the new fabric of trade.

- **Education reaches past classrooms**: MOOCs, adaptive platforms, video libraries, and peer-to-peer ecosystems embed learning into daily work.
- **Healthcare flows beyond clinics**: Telehealth, wearables, encrypted APIs, and cloud-based EMRs) distribute care across networks.
- **Culture streams beyond venues**: When Leila missed a concert, she joined instead through a YouTube livestream, where edge servers, CDNs, and adaptive bitrate streaming turned a distant stage into a local experience.
- **Work and industry shift beyond offices**: Cloud-native tools, distributed teams, and automation reshape collaboration, while IoT, AI, and data platforms retool factories, finance, and supply chains.
- **Governance and cities adapt in real-time**: Open data dashboards, digital service portals, and responsive infrastructure create feedback loops between citizens and institutions.

The loom runs quietly through everything Leila touches. Its threads connect billions of lives, forming patterns of cooperation, care, and creation. Yet no weave is perfect. Threads slip, knots fray, and gaps appear. To strengthen the digital fabric, we must look beneath its beauty and examine where it strains and where it must be rewoven.

Fraying edges of the loom

Every weave bears strain, privacy, power, and truth tugging at its edges.

As the Internet expands, its tensions multiply; more users, more devices, more data, and more demands. With scale comes both opportunity and strain. Stress gathers at the edges, where assumptions fail, where flaws are magnified, and where trust begins to fray.

Samir, once just a user, now navigates this fabric as a participant who sees both its beauty and its limitations. He encounters tools that surveil, algorithms that misjudge, and services that sometimes exclude or collapse under pressure. What began as a cooperative experiment has evolved into a global utility, making it both commercially viable and contested, with significant political implications.

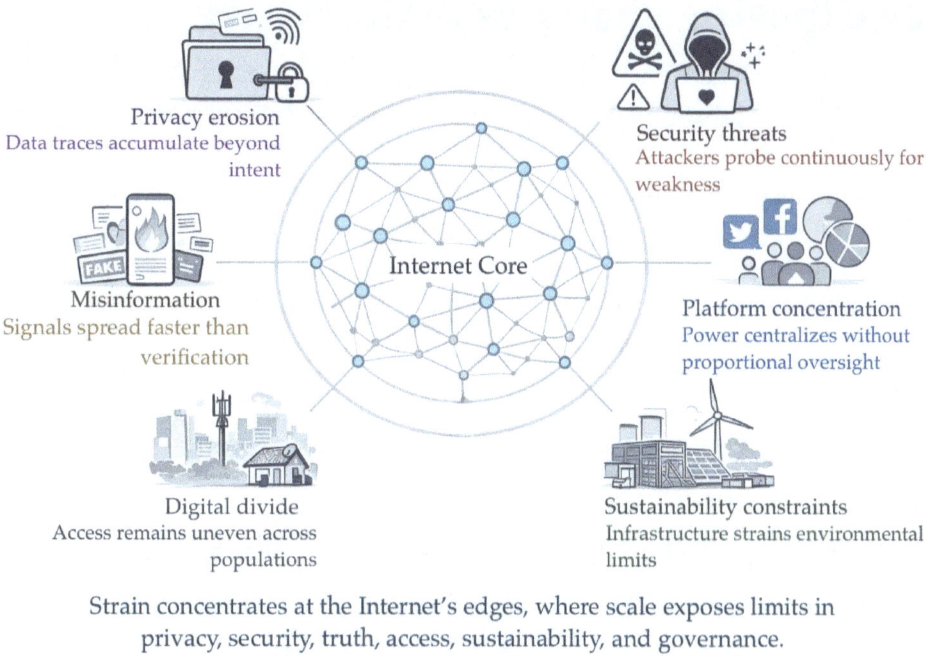

***Figure 1.9**: Fraying edges of the Internet*

The Internet's challenges today are less about malfunction than about growth effects:

- **Privacy erosion**: Profiles built from traces we never meant to share.
- **Security threats**: Breaches and adaptive attackers testing weak points.
- **Misinformation and fragmentation**: False signals spreading faster than the truth.
- **Digital divide**: Billions left outside reliable access.
- **Sustainability constraints**: Data centers, devices, and networks pressing ecological limits.
- **Platform concentration and governance gaps**: Decisions for billions made by a few.

For Samir, these issues are not abstract; they arrive as targeted ads that feel intrusive, breach notices at midnight, and feeds that blur the line between truth and rumor. Each moment reminds him that the loom is not neutral. It is fragile, contested, and unevenly governed.

The Internet holds because its threads are reinforced again and again, but every breach, every exclusion, every distortion shows where care must be renewed. To keep the pattern alive, we cannot remain passive users. We must become active stewards, watching not only the beauty of the weave but also the stress where it frays.

Privacy exposing shadows in the weave

Samir searched for a new backpack. Hours later, ads for hiking gear followed him across sites and apps. He had never given explicit consent, yet a detailed profile was assembled in the background.

Every digital action leaves a trace; clicks, searches, scrolls, pauses. These signals are captured, stored, and combined into behavioral models that reveal more than what users intentionally share. Even encrypted systems are not immune. Metadata such as time stamps, device type, and location can be analyzed to reconstruct patterns of behavior without ever touching the content itself.

Tracking relies on several technical mechanisms:

- Cookies and browser fingerprints that persist across sessions.
- IP addresses that tie activity to geography.
- Third-party scripts and pixels embedded invisibly in pages and apps.
- Mobile identifiers that enable cross-app profiling.
- Metadata correlations that reassemble fragmented identities.

Defenses exist. Encryption protects content, tracker blockers and VPNs mask browsing activity, and device settings limit data sharing. Yet none of these can fully counter systems designed for continuous surveillance. The deeper question is structural: *Is the Internet built to forget, or is it engineered to remember everything?*

Security unraveling trust in the weave

One night, Samir's phone buzzed with a breach alert. An old platform had leaked his email and password hash. He quickly reset his credentials, but the illusion of safety was gone.

Security is what prevents the digital fabric from tearing. When it falters, trust unravels. Today's most common threats include phishing, ransomware, credential stuffing, denial-of-service floods, supply-chain compromises, and zero-day exploits. Each tests the system at its weakest seam.

Defense relies on layered safeguards:

- Zero Trust frameworks that require validation for every request.
- Encryption protects data in transit and at rest.
- Multi-factor authentication that goes beyond passwords.
- Audits, threat modeling, and monitoring that detect and close vulnerabilities.
- User awareness that recognizes and avoids attacks before they succeed.

Security is not a fixed state but a living posture. It should anticipate failure, adapt to new threats, and reinforce weak points before they snap. Only by constant renewal can trust be rewoven into the Internet's weave.

Misinformation distorting the weave

Samir shared a video of clashes he thought were unfolding nearby. Only later did he learn it was years old and miscaptioned. By then, the damage had already spread through his network.

The Internet faithfully moves packets, not truth. Personalized feeds, engagement-driven algorithms, and generative media accelerate falsehoods far faster than facts. Outrage is rewarded; nuance lags behind. What begins as a single miscaption can scale into viral distortion.

Technical and social responses are emerging:

- Cryptographic provenance to verify where and when content originated.
- Distributed fact-checking networks that cross-validate claims.
- Transparent recommendation models that make ranking and amplification auditable.
- Contextual overlays on feeds to flag manipulated or outdated content.
- Decentralized reputation systems to weigh credibility across sources.

Misinformation does more than mislead. It fragments shared reality. If no two people see the same fabric, the loom itself risks unraveling.

Digital divide fragmenting the weave

Samir's livestream reached his friends in the city instantly. Hours later, his cousin in a rural village sent a short text: Still buffering. The same Internet, yet not the same experience.

The divide is layered. Some lack reliable infrastructure. Others face costly data plans, scarce devices, or low digital literacy. Content itself may exclude when local languages and cultural contexts are missing.

Technical and social remedies are advancing:

- Last-mile connectivity through satellites, mesh networks, and community-driven ISPs.
- Offline-first applications that cache and sync when connections return.
- Edge caching and processing to bring data physically closer to users.
- Affordable access programs for devices, repairs, and sustainable ownership.
- Localization of platforms to reflect languages, scripts, and cultural practices.

Bridging the divide is not just about bandwidth. It is about agency, who gets to contribute, critique, and co-create in the digital fabric. Without inclusion, the weave risks splitting into parallel worlds.

Sustainability straining the weave

The Internet feels weightless but rests on heavy foundations of power, water, and minerals. Every click draws on grids, cooling systems, and rare metals mined for hardware.

Its footprint includes:

- **Gigawatts of electricity** consumed by hyperscale data centers.
- **Water diverted** for cooling server farms.
- **Mountains of e-waste** from short-lived devices.
- **Embedded carbon** from global manufacturing and logistics.
- **Compute-intensive workloads** like AI and blockchain are pushing grids to their limits.

Efficiency gains are real, yet demand grows faster. Sustainable operation depends on renewable-powered data centers, lightweight and frugal protocols, longer-lasting devices, and circular design practices that recycle materials back into production.

The loom itself is not exempt from ecological limits. If it consumes more than the earth can provide, failures will break into the physical world, not just the virtual one. To keep weaving, we must treat the Internet as a living system, one that survives only through balance, restraint, and renewal.

Platform power tightening the weave

Samir once assumed the Internet was neutral. Now he sees the invisible gatekeepers. A handful of platforms dominate hosting, search, app distribution, and social feeds. Their decisions determine reach, revenue, and rules—often without transparency or accountability.

This concentration creates governance gaps:

- **Cloud workloads** clustered in a few hyperscale providers.
- **Mobile ecosystems** locked to proprietary app stores.
- **Algorithms shaping** discourse for billions through opaque tweaks.
- **Ad networks** channeling disproportionate revenue and data.

Policy responses are beginning to surface: interoperability mandates, algorithmic transparency, user rights to portability, and governance frameworks that cross borders.

The loom cannot be left to hidden stewards. If a few actors hold the power to set rules, stewardship by the many becomes essential to keep the weave open, resilient, and fair.

The fraying edges expose where the Internet is most vulnerable. Privacy leaks, security breaches, misinformation, uneven access, sustainability pressures, and platform concentration each test its stability. These are not isolated flaws but systemic stresses that accumulate as the network scales.

Addressing them requires resilience by design. The Internet must continue to reroute, adapt, and absorb strain without collapse. The next section examines how its architecture embeds new threads to keep the system running even under pressure.

Reinforcing the frame with new threads

The loom endures by adding new fibers, trust, resilience, inclusion, and care.

The Internet is not finished. It is a living fabric, patched, stretched, and rewoven with every new demand. What began as a fragile research network now carries the pulse of the world; messages, payments, medical records, streaming media, and daily conversations.

However, the loom shows strain. Privacy violations are routine, infrastructure proves brittle, borders fragment flows, automated systems outpace human oversight, energy demand grows faster than supply, and billions remain disconnected. These stresses are not errors; they are the effects of scale.

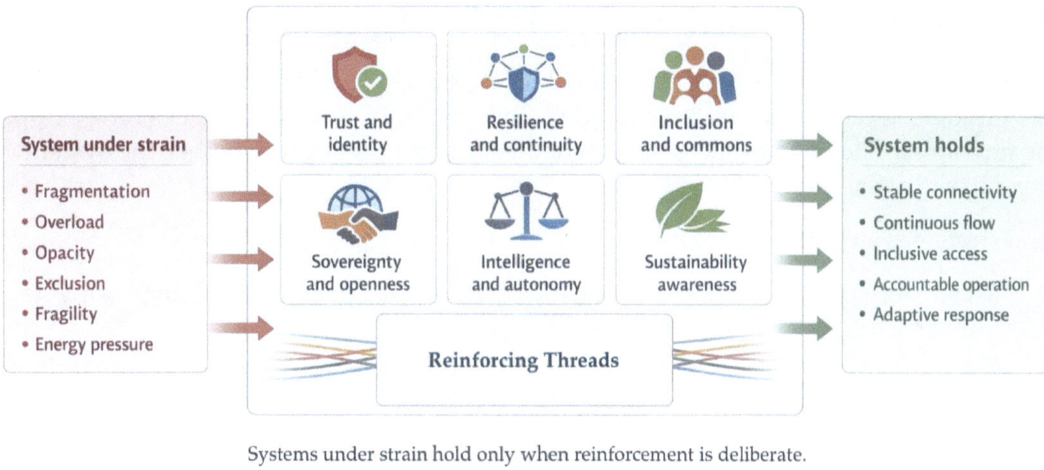

***Figure 1.10**: The loom reinforced with new threads of the future*

The Internet is not ending. It is maturing. A fabric under tension must either fray or be reinforced. Its future depends on the fibers we add: technical innovations, ethical safeguards, and social commitments that strengthen rather than weaken the weave. The following new threads mark the next stage of its evolution. These threads include technical mechanisms, governance structures, and social commitments that reinforce the Internet's core design.

Trust and identity strengthening the fabric

The Internet's future rests on trust. Without a reliable identity, every connection is uncertain. Passwords and centralized databases remain widespread, but they introduce single points of failure where one breach can compromise millions.

New approaches seek to close these gaps:

- **Privacy by design** embeds protection into protocols so applications cannot collect or misuse more data than required.
- **Zero-knowledge proofs** allow systems to verify facts, such as confirming Leila's authorization, without revealing unrelated details like her address or employer.
- **Decentralized identity (DID)** shifts control away from corporate providers, giving users cryptographically signed credentials they manage on their own devices.
- **Quantum-resistant cryptography** prepares for an era when quantum computers could break today's encryption, introducing lattice-based algorithms that resist such attacks.

For Leila, this means logging into her planning dashboard with a digital key instead of a password. For Samir, it means sending design files that only Leila can decrypt. Even as technology evolves, these advances help ensure the Internet's trust remains intact.

Resilience and continuity holding under strain

The Internet is often imagined as indestructible, yet history shows otherwise. Anchors have severed undersea cables, storms have flooded fiber conduits, and cyberattacks have crippled major providers. The key question is not whether failures occur but whether the system can rethread itself in real-time.

Several strategies strengthen continuity:

- **Mesh networking** allows devices to forward data peer to peer, bypassing failed infrastructure.
- **Community-hosted services** let neighborhoods and organizations run their own platforms, reducing dependence on distant servers.
- **Low Earth Orbit (LEO) satellite** constellations such as Starlink and OneWeb extend coverage, routing around terrestrial outages and preserving service during disasters.

When a storm knocks out Samir's coastal fiber, his design still reaches Leila. Packets hop through a rooftop mesh, leap to a satellite link, and rejoin terrestrial fiber inland. To the user, the flow feels seamless. Beneath the surface, the loom rewove itself instantly to hold the thread intact.

Sovereignty and openness keeping the fabric whole

Governments are increasingly asserting sovereignty over the Internet through data localization laws, firewalls, and regulatory controls. These measures may protect privacy or advance national interests, but they also risk fragmentation. A balkanized Internet would weaken the global fabric by tearing at its standard frame.

The challenge is to preserve openness while respecting sovereignty:

- **Sovereign interoperability** allows local data laws to be enforced while global protocols such as BGP continue to knit continents together.
- **Open standards**, maintained by bodies such as the IETF, W3C, and IEEE, provide the warp threads that ensure transparency and interoperability across borders.
- **Accountable governance** requires multistakeholder participation so that no single government or corporation determines the pattern for billions of users.

When Leila shares her design toolkit with students in Nairobi, Bangalore, and São Paulo, local data laws govern its handling in each jurisdiction. Yet the shared protocols ensure the exchange works seamlessly, and the fabric remains whole.

Intelligence and autonomy, anticipating the loom

The Internet began as a neutral transport system, designed to carry data between intelligent endpoints. Increasingly, intelligence is migrating into the network itself.

AI-governed networks now detect anomalies in real time, rerouting traffic during **distributed denial-of-service** (**DDoS**) attacks or predicting failures before they occur. Autonomous edge nodes bring computation closer to users, reducing latency for IoT control systems, gaming, and virtual reality. These advances make the fabric more adaptive, but also more opaque.

To reduce risk, explainability and safeguards are essential. Automated actions must be logged, reviewable, and subject to human override.

When Samir's CAD program slowed, an AI agent inside a backbone router detected congestion, shifted traffic to another undersea cable, and restored performance. Leila never noticed the disruption. Later, the decision appeared in an engineer's log. The loom anticipated the strain, but human intent remained in control.

Sustainability awareness greening the threads

The Internet now consumes energy on a scale comparable to that of industrial nations. Hyperscale data centers demand gigawatts of electricity and millions of liters of water for cooling. Devices are frequently replaced, creating e-waste, while compute-intensive workloads such as AI training and blockchain transactions strain power grids and supply chains.

The path forward is not efficiency alone but energy awareness. Energy-aware protocols can route traffic based on carbon intensity as well as latency. Dynamic scheduling shifts compute-heavy workloads to periods when renewable energy is abundant. Edge efficiency minimizes unnecessary transfers by processing data locally before uploading.

When Leila runs a city simulation, the platform aligns processing with solar-rich hours. Samir's edits move across low-carbon backbones. The seamless experience hides the deeper truth: every thread of the loom is being optimized for energy impact.

Inclusion and commons extending the fabric to all

An Internet that excludes billions is not a loom but a net with holes. Barriers of cost, limited literacy, poor accessibility, and weak infrastructure still leave many disconnected.

Inclusion requires deliberate design:

- Universal accessibility ensures interfaces work with screen readers, voice-first navigation, and low-literacy modes.
- Affordable connectivity can be achieved through community mesh networks, shared spectrum, and subsidy models.
- Viewing the Internet as a commons treats its protocols and infrastructure as public goods, much like roads or clean water.

When Leila runs a design workshop, her rural students connect through a community satellite node. Their participation is not charity but the result of infrastructure built as a right, extending the fabric of digital life to all hands.

Toward a stronger fabric

These six threads, trust, resilience, sovereignty, intelligence, sustainability, and inclusion, interlace with one another. Without trust, resilience fails. Without sustainability, inclusion collapses. Without openness, intelligence risks concentration in the hands of a few.

Samir and Leila's everyday exchanges, including an email that survives a storm, a file delivered across borders, a simulation powered by renewables, and a classroom extended to rural students, demonstrate what happens when the loom is reinforced.

The Internet's future will not arrive as a single redesign. It will be woven from deliberate choices: standards that adapt, policies that resist capture, and civic stewardship that keeps the frame intact. We do not inherit a finished fabric. We inherit a loom. The essential question is not whether it will endure, but what kind of weave we will leave behind.

Conclusion

That night, long after the café emptied and the streetlamps flickered over Cairo's quiet corners, Samir sat alone with a question that would not let go.

How does this thing even work?

Not just the video call, he would share with Leila. Not just the protest tweet that once circled the globe. But all of it, the invisible system that stitched his voice to the world, stitched his city to stories he had not lived, stitched his life to something larger.

***Figure 1.11**: Samir reflecting on the Internet*

A quiet buzz broke the silence.
Samir glanced at his phone, one new email, subject line urgent, sender unfamiliar.
He tapped, skimmed, and smiled. Not panic. Recognition.

A classic phishing attempt, well-disguised but poorly timed. He marked it as junk without flinching.
Not long ago, that message might have fooled him.
Now, he saw the subtle mismatches, the frayed edge of a forged thread.

The loom was learning.
And so was he.

The Internet was no longer just a system.
It was a living weave, patterned with trust, tension, and intelligence.

Every message carries more than content.
It carried structure through protocols, choices through routing and encryption, and intent through the purpose behind each action.

Understanding the Internet does not require building its protocols, but it does require learning how to read their effects.

Samir did not build the protocols.
But he had begun to understand their rhythm.
He could feel the loom shifting.
From infrastructure to insight. From flow to meaning.

And as he slipped the phone back into his pocket, the question lingered:
What else might this weave become?

The loom was waking up.
And Samir was ready to follow it.

Are you?

In the next chapter, we trace how the Internet grew its senses, moving from commands we typed to perceptions it gathers on its own.

Weaver's toolkit

From seeing the loom to shaping the weave, tools for hands-on weaving.

The weaver's toolkit is where understanding becomes usable. It gathers definitions, exercises, and references so that readers not only learn how the Internet works, but also practice seeing, questioning, and designing it for their own contexts.

Weaver's lexicon

This section defines the technical and conceptual vocabulary that has been used throughout the chapter:

- **Address (IP address)**: A unique numerical label is assigned to each device connected to the Internet, enabling data to find its source and destination. IPv4 offers approximately 4.3 billion addresses; IPv6 expands this to 340 undecillion addresses.
- **Architecture of trust**: The foundational principles, such as decentralization, interoperability, end-to-end design, and statelessness, make the Internet resilient, scalable, and trustworthy.
- **AS**: A network or group of networks under a single administrative control that exchanges routing information with others using protocols like BGP.
- **Backbone**: The high-capacity, long-distance connections (often undersea cables and major fiber routes) that carry Internet traffic between continents and across large regions.
- **Border Gateway Protocol (BGP)**: The routing protocol that enables different AS to exchange routing information, ensuring global connectivity despite decentralized control.
- **Content delivery network (CDN)**: A distributed system of servers that caches and delivers content close to users, improving speed, reliability, and resilience of online services.

- **Continuous integration and continuous delivery/deployment (CI/CD pipelines)**: A method of building and updating software quickly and reliably. Developers use CI/CD pipelines to automatically test code changes, fix errors early, and push updates into production. This makes apps safer, faster to improve, and always up to date.
- **Data center**: A facility housing servers, storage, and networking equipment that power digital services.
- **Decentralization**: The distribution of control across multiple independent networks means that no single entity governs the Internet or serves as a single point of failure.
- **Digital divide**: The gap between those with access to modern digital technologies and those without.
- **End-to-end principle**: A design rule of the Internet stating that intelligence and control should reside at the endpoints (devices, applications) rather than in the core network.
- **Firewall**: A system that filters incoming and outgoing traffic according to security rules.
- **Hypertext Transfer Protocol (HTTP)**: The standard protocol for transferring web pages and other resources across the Internet.
- **Interoperability**: The ability of diverse systems, devices, and protocols to communicate and work together through open standards.
- **Internet Protocol version 4 (IPv4)**: The original Internet addressing system, providing about 4.3 billion unique addresses, is now largely exhausted.
- **Internet Protocol version 6 (IPv6)**: The next-generation addressing system with virtually unlimited addresses, supporting the expansion of IoT, mobile, and future digital systems.
- **Internet Service Provider (ISP)**: A company or organization that provides users with access to the Internet, acting as a bridge between local devices and the global network.
- **Internet Exchange Point (IXP)**: A physical location where multiple networks interconnect directly to exchange traffic, improving efficiency and resilience.
- **Intermediate System to Intermediate System (IS-IS)**: A scalable, link-state routing protocol that helps routers build a complete map of the network to calculate the most efficient path, primarily used in large enterprise and service provider networks.
- **Learning Tools Interoperability (LTI)**: A standard that lets learning apps plug into an LMS without extra coding. With LTI, a teacher can add tools like a virtual lab, simulation, or quiz platform directly into their course, and students can access it with one login while grades flow back automatically.

- **Low Power Wide Area Network (LoRaWAN)**: A wireless protocol optimized for long-range, low-power IoT communication across urban and rural environments.
- **Net neutrality**: The principle that ISPs should treat all Internet traffic equally without discrimination.
- **Network Address Translation (NAT)**: A technique that allows multiple devices on a private network to share a single public IP address.
- **OSI Layer / TCP/IP stack**: The layered model of networking divides communication into functions (like physical, network, transport, and application) so that protocols can interoperate.
- **Open Shortest Path First (OSPF)**: An internal routing protocol used within large networks or AS to determine efficient paths for data.
- **Packet**: A small unit of data transmitted across the Internet, containing both payload (content) and headers (routing instructions).
- **Phishing**: A fraudulent attempt to obtain sensitive information by disguising as a trusted entity.
- **Platform power**: The concentration of control and decision-making in a few large digital platforms.
- **Public key infrastructure (PKI)**: A cryptographic framework for verifying digital identities, enabling secure communication through certificates and keys.
- **Quantum networking**: Networking that uses principles of quantum mechanics (such as entanglement) for communication and cryptography.
- **Resilience**: The Internet's capacity to adapt and recover when parts of its infrastructure fail is enabled by redundancy, routing flexibility, and distributed design.
- **Router**: A device that forwards packets between networks based on their IP addresses. Routers are also the default gateway for the hosts on the subnet.
- **Routing Information Protocol (RIP)**: A legacy, distance-vector routing protocol that uses hop count to determine the best path for data within a small, simple network.
- **Routing table**: A data structure in routers that determines where packets should be forwarded to reach their destinations efficiently.
- **Satellite Internet (LEO constellations)**: Low-Earth Orbit satellite networks that extend Internet access to remote and underserved regions, adding resilience to the physical backbone.
- **Security by design**: The principle of embedding encryption, authentication, and trust mechanisms into IPs from the ground up, rather than adding them as afterthoughts.

- **Sharable Content Object Reference Model (SCORM)**: A standard that makes online learning content work across different platforms. If a course or quiz follows SCORM, it can be uploaded to almost any **learning management system** (**LMS**) and still track things like scores, progress, and completion in the same way.
- **Statelessness**: A design approach where each request on the Internet is independent and contains all necessary information, reducing complexity and enabling massive scalability.
- **Transport Layer Security/Datagram TLS (TLS/DTLS)**: Protocols that encrypt Internet traffic to protect confidentiality and integrity during transmission.
- **Uniform Resource Locator (URL)**: A web address that provides a unique and specific location for a resource on the Internet.
- **Zero Trust Architecture**: A security model assuming no implicit trust in any part of the network; every request must be authenticated and authorized.

Weaver's workshop

These activities are not random tasks but a deliberate progression. You begin by seeing what is usually hidden, then mapping how those pieces connect. From there, you propose ways to extend the weave, reflect on its ethical tensions, and finally invent new looms altogether. Each step strengthens both technical insight and human imagination, helping you move from observing threads to shaping patterns.

Refer to the following exercises to build a comprehensive understanding:

1. **Trace a thread**: Follow the journey of a message you send across the Internet.

   Prompts:

   - *Choose a simple message (e.g., a text, tweet, or email).*
   - *Research how it moves through the Internet, what protocols, servers, and systems it touches.*
   - *Diagram its path from your device to its destination.*

   Learning objective: Understand the physical and logical path data takes through digital infrastructure and appreciate the hidden complexity in everyday communication.

2. **Map your loom**: Draw the Internet infrastructure around you.

   Prompts:

   - *What connects your device to the world?*
   - *Where are the routers, cables, ISPs, and access points?*
   - *What might be vulnerable? What remains invisible?*

Learning objective: Develop local awareness of digital infrastructure, its dependencies, and its points of fragility.

3. **Weaving access and equity**: Design a proposal to expand digital access in an underserved community.

   Prompts:

   - *Who is excluded?*
   - *What infrastructure is missing?*
   - *What partnerships, technologies, or policies could close the gap?*

   Learning objective: Recognize the Internet as a social as well as technical fabric, and analyze how equity, policy, and technology interweave.

4. **Thread ethics**: Debate or reflect on a moral dilemma in Internet infrastructure.

   Prompts:

   - *Choose a topic such as surveillance, censorship, misinformation, or digital colonialism.*
   - *What tensions arise between openness and safety, privacy and convenience, or local control and global flow?*

   Learning objective: Practice ethical reasoning in the context of networked systems, weighing competing values that shape digital trust.

5. **Design a loom**: Imagine a new Internet.

   Prompts:

   - *What would you keep, discard, or reinvent?*
   - *Draw the architecture and define its guiding values.*
   - *Who governs it? Who can participate in weaving its threads?*

   Learning objective: Foster imagination and systems thinking for future Internet architectures that balance resilience, equity, and human agency.

Weaver's library

The weaver's library provides authoritative references that anchor *Chapter 1, The Internet,* in the broader literature of Internet studies:

1. *Leiner, B. M., Cerf, V. G., Clark, D. D., Kahn, R. E., Kleinrock, L., Lynch, D. C., … & Wolff, S. (2009). A brief history of the Internet. ACM SIGCOMM Computer Communication Review, 39(5), 22–31.* **https://doi.org/10.1145/1629607.1629613**
2. *Abbate, J. (1999). Inventing the Internet. Cambridge, MA: MIT Press.*

3. *Castells, M. (2000). The rise of the network society (2nd ed.). Malden, MA: Blackwell.*

4. *Kurose, J. F., & Ross, K. W. (2020). Computer networking: A top-down approach (8th ed.). Hoboken, NJ: Pearson.*

5. *Mueller, M. L. (2010). Networks and states: The global politics of Internet governance. Cambridge, MA: MIT Press.*

Metaphorical and conceptual terms

The following list outlines the key metaphorical and conceptual terminology:

- **Fabric of connection**: The metaphor for the Internet as a woven whole, made up of countless interlaced data threads forming a global pattern.
- **Loom**: In this book, the Internet is imagined as a loom, a frame that holds together the threads of global connectivity. Just as a loom provides the structure for weaving fabric, the Internet offers the underlying architecture for all digital experiences.
- **Pattern**: Represents applications, services, and interactions that emerge from the weaving of countless data threads.
- **Shuttle**: The carrier of the thread across the loom symbolizes data packets moving from one side to another.
- **Threads**: The individual connections, data flows, relationships, and communications that interlace across the loom. Each is fragile on its own, but together they create a resilient and intricate pattern.
- **Warp and Weft**: The vertical (warp) and horizontal (weft) directions in weaving are used as a metaphor for structured Internet layers interlacing into stability.
- **Weave**: The emergent whole of the Internet, millions of systems, protocols, and people interlaced into a single living fabric. The weave is what users experience, even if they never see the loom beneath.
- **Weaver**: A metaphor for the human (user, coder, builder) who interacts with the loom, placing intention into the pattern.

CHAPTER 2

The Internet of Things

The sensory threads

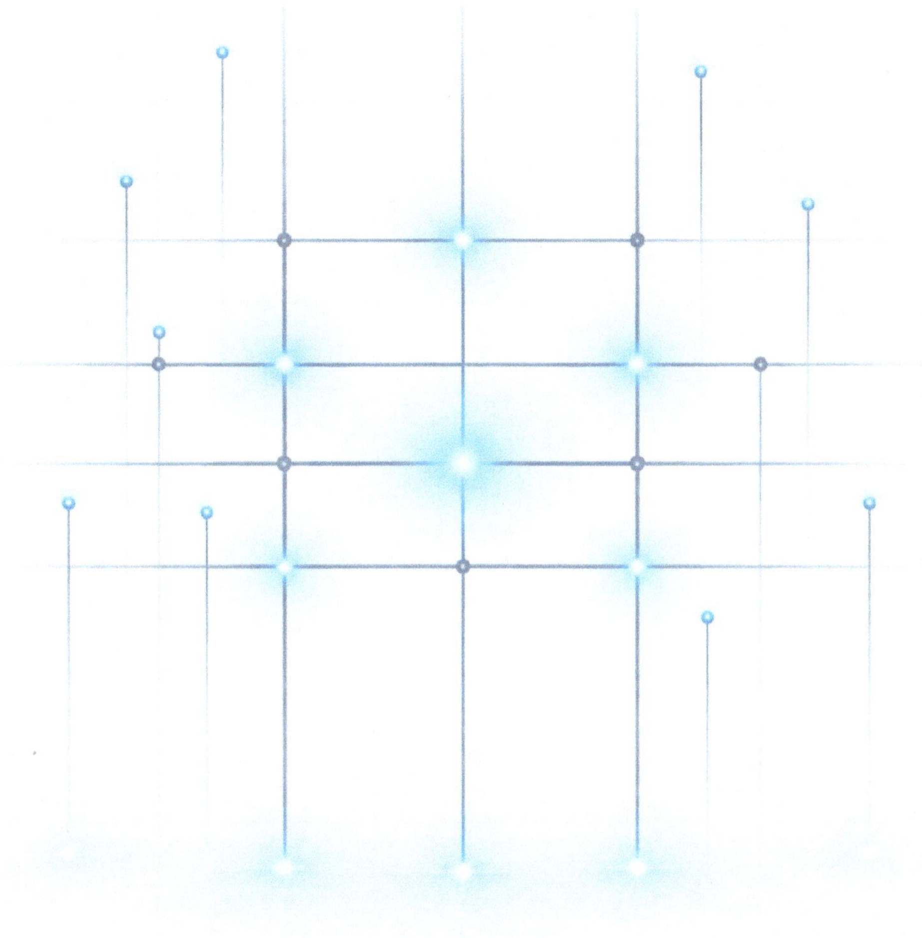

A system becomes aware when it begins to observe its environment.

CHAPTER 2
The Internet of Things

Introduction

The **Internet of Things** (**IoT**) extends the Internet beyond screens and servers into the physical world. It connects billions of sensors, devices, and machines that measure, observe, and respond to their surroundings. These sensory threads capture temperature, motion, pressure, light, and countless other signals, turning the world itself into a continuous source of data.

This chapter explores how the Internet learns to perceive. It traces the rise of sensing as the next phase of connectivity, where networks of embedded intelligence allow the Internet not just to transmit information, but to sense and respond. Readers will study the five-layer architecture that underpins IoT systems, follow how data travels from the edge of a field or a patient's wrist to the cloud, and examine how perception reshapes healthcare, agriculture, cities, and industry.

Structure

This chapter covers the following topics:

- The clinic that listens
- When the loom learns to feel
- Anatomy of a sensory thread
- IoT systems that listen and respond
- Fraying edges
- Future threads

Objectives

To study the IoT is to witness the moment the Internet begins to sense the world. By the end of this chapter, readers will understand how IoT extends digital connectivity into a sensory fabric that perceives, interprets, and responds to the physical environment. They will learn the structure and purpose of each layer, sensing, communication, edge processing, cloud aggregation, and actuation, and how these work together to build responsive, ethical, and sustainable systems.

Through Maya's story, readers will explore IoT in health, agriculture, energy, and cities; recognize challenges such as bias, security, and maintenance; and envision new directions in energy harvesting, **Tiny Machine Learning** (**TinyML**), and bio-integrated sensing. Most importantly, they will learn to view IoT not as a collection of devices, but as a design practice of attention and care, one that weaves data, context, and ethics into a living digital fabric.

The clinic that listens

The lights in the small clinic flickered as the solar inverter strained against the rising wind. Maya steadied the monitor with one hand and pulled down the fabric flap to shield it from dust. Outside, a storm gathered over the village. Inside, a different storm threatened, the fragile rhythm of a newborn's breath.

Beep. Pause. Beep.

The infant was three hours old, skin translucent, lungs still learning their pattern. Around the baby's wrist, a thin band with nanoscale electrodes measured oxygen, heart rate, and temperature. Each pulse traveled through a low-power mesh network of local nodes that relayed signals even if others failed.

The readings appeared on Maya's tablet, normal for the moment. Then the rhythm broke.

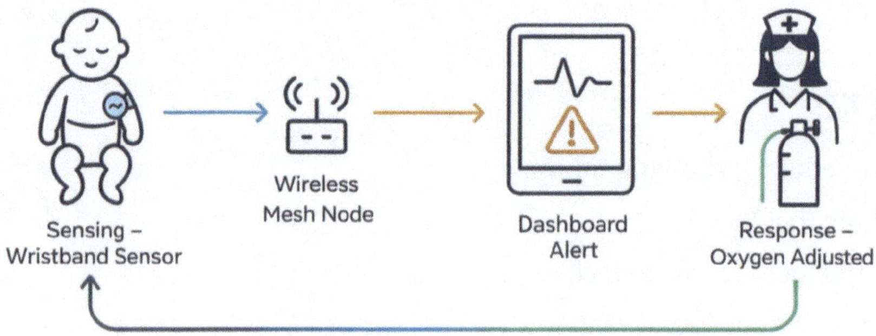

Figure 2.1: *The clinic that listens*

Beep-beep. Oxygen saturation: 83%.

The alert flashed. Maya moved quickly, rolled the oxygen canister closer, adjusted the nasal prongs, and increased the flow. Within seconds, the child's breathing steadied. Maya exhaled, realizing she had been holding her breath. The rescue was not hers alone. It was a thread of sensing, carried through the wristband, the mesh network, and the tablet, transforming signal into action.

Stepping outside, she watched stormlight flicker across the horizon. Beneath her feet, a soil probe whispered its moisture level, lower than expected. In the trees above, a motion sensor logged movement of the twitch of a squirrel's motion. On the roof, particulate detectors registered a rise in dust.

None of these signals demanded attention, yet all were continuously present. Only five years earlier, this village had no Internet, unreliable power, and paper records. Now, the environment itself had begun to speak. The clinic, the soil, the storm, and the child's breath were now linked through a shared sensing network.

Maya was still the nurse and technician. Yet to the system, she was something else, the one who had taught it to listen, a digital weaver.

When the loom learns to feel

Before there is thought, there must be sensation.

In its early decades, the Internet was a remarkable loom of connections, carrying messages and images across distances, yet it remained silent and acted only when instructed.

Users typed, and it transmitted.
They clicked, and it responded.
They pointed a camera, and only then did it capture.

The Internet was powerful but passive. It could compute and communicate, but not perceive. That silence is now broken.

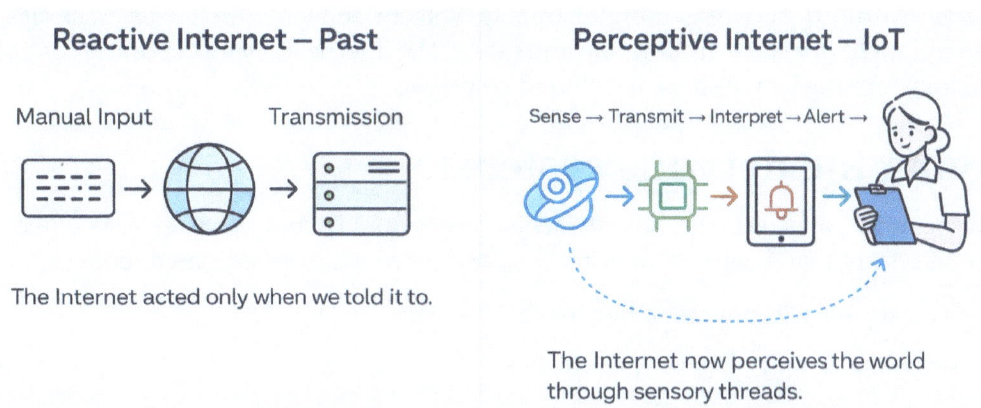

Figure 2.2: *From reactive Internet to perceptive Internet*

In Maya's clinic, no one pressed a button when the newborn's oxygen level fell. A wristband sensed the drop, a mesh network carried the signal, an alert appeared on her tablet, and action followed through attention distributed across people and machines.

This marks a turning point; from a reactive Internet that waits for instruction to a perceptive Internet that listens to the world. These are the Internet's first sensory threads, strands of awareness stitched into infrastructure. This is the IoT, the perception layer of the digital world.

The birth of perception in the machine

IoT represents the birth of sensation within the digital fabric. Sensors now inhabit nearly every environment:

- On wrists, tracking pulse, oxygen, and stress.
- In soil, measuring moisture and nutrients.
- In cities, sensing air, sound, and motion.
- In factories, monitoring vibration and heat.
- Across oceans, drifting as buoys that track currents and chemistry.

The transformation is profound, as:

- **From input to emission**: The Internet now generates signals continuously, without request.
- **From automation to attention**: Systems tune themselves to thresholds and rhythms.
- **From silence to streams**: Pumps announce leaks, fields broadcast thirst, grids declare strain, and heartbeats whisper warnings.

Across the world, IoT networks monitor infants, detect floods, monitor cities, factories, and other environments for smooth operation and safety. The Internet now incorporates continuous sensing, transforming signals into distributed responses.

Weaving the nervous system

The Internet once carried intent; now it carries perception. Each sensor becomes a node in a distributed system that detects, communicates, and responds in coordinated loops.

In Maya's clinic, this was not metaphor but mechanism:

- A wristband noticed an oxygen decline.
- A mesh node carried the signal.
- An edge processor stripped noise and confirmed the anomaly. And an alert reached the tablet.
- A nurse acted before the crisis escalated.
- A cloud system recorded the event for later analysis.

This was not a pipeline of command and control but a closed feedback loop—sense | relay | interpret | act | remember.

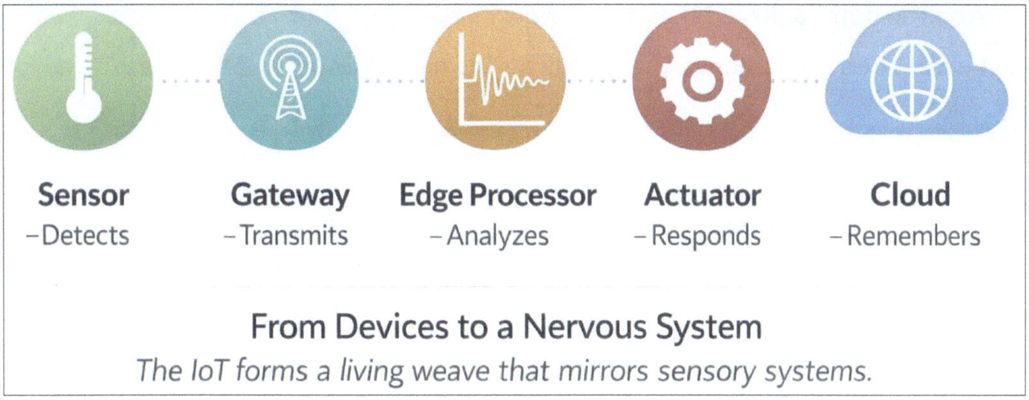

Figure 2.3: *The IoT sensory thread*

Across the village, soil probes warned of drought, and vibration sensors detected wind stress. These systems extended human capability rather than replacing it. The Internet, once a static loom of messages, now behaves like a distributed and adaptive nervous system.

A language of signals

IoT does not speak in words but speaks through thresholds, rhythms, and anomalies:

- Soil moisture below 12 % triggers irrigation.
- Body temperature above 38 °C issues a health alert.
- Machine vibration shift flags bearing fatigue.

Yet sensing is not the same as knowing. A temperature rise may mean fever or sunshine; a still sensor may signal rest or risk. Context turns readings into meaning. The difference between noise and signal defines reliability. In Maya's clinic, the neonatal monitor confirmed multiple readings before alerting staff. It validated multiple readings before issuing an alert.

To sense is to accept responsibility for how signals are interpreted and acted upon. Once a system notices, it must decide what to do and who it serves.

From sensing to systems

The term *Internet of Things* can mislead, suggesting a collection of gadgets rather than a coherent architecture of awareness. IoT gains meaning only when sensors, processors, and humans interact as one system.

In the clinic, a dip in oxygen saturation level triggered a full loop of care:

- **Sense**: The wristband noticed the change.
- **Interpret**: The edge processor filtered noise and flagged an anomaly.

- **Act**: The nurse adjusted the oxygen flow.
- **Learn**: The system refined thresholds for the next case.

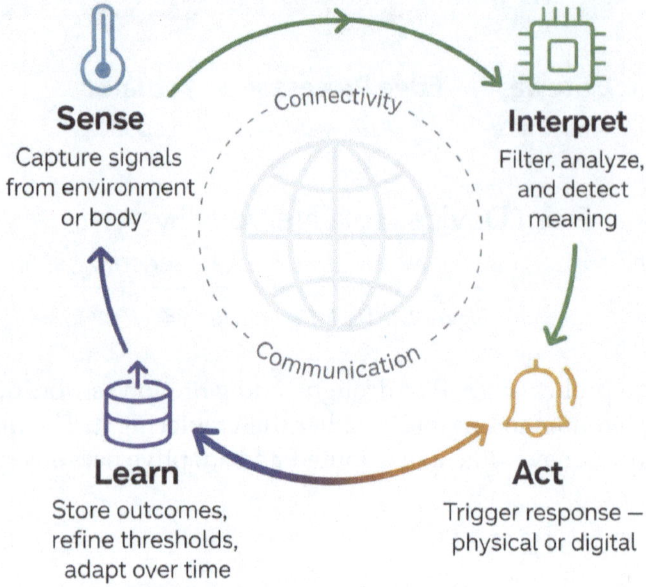

Figure 2.4: The IoT system loop

Connectivity carries the signal from skin to system, from moment to meaning. Each loop strengthens the next, defining the true architecture of IoT. The Internet is no longer only a loom of communication but a living fabric of perception linking care, balance, and intelligence.

What is at stake

To sense is to see earlier, intervene sooner, and change outcomes.

A farmer waters only when the land is thirsty.
A nurse catches a crisis before it grows.
A city reroutes traffic before congestion forms.

Yet sensing is never neutral. Every sensor encodes a choice about what is valued or ignored:

- A city that measures traffic but not noise reveals its priorities.
- A platform that tracks yield but not soil health rewards extraction.
- A workplace that monitors attendance but not air quality values outputs over well-being.
- A disaster-alert system that omits informal settlements decides whose safety counts.

- A wearable that counts steps but not stress sees movement but misses exhaustion.

To sense is to extend perception and responsibility. Every unnoticed signal is a choice, not an accident.

The loom breathes in

Once, the Internet depended on humans to describe the world. Now it captures physical conditions directly through sensors. Air carries data, soil speaks in voltage, and a heartbeat becomes a message.

Through sensory threads, the Internet begins to feel by design. Linked sensors and edge processors form feedback loops that listen, respond, and learn. Across clinics, farms, cities, and forests, this transformation unfolds:

- Infrastructure becomes awareness.
- Connectivity becomes care.
- Systems that once waited now anticipate.
- Places once observed now participate.

Awareness arises not from one device but from a seamless weave of sensor to system, signal to insight, and attention to action.

A question remains: *How does a tremor at the edge of the field travel to the edge of the cloud and return as meaning?*

To answer, we turn to the anatomy of a sensory thread.

Anatomy of a sensory thread

Sensing begins not with a device, but with a decision about what to notice and why.

One late afternoon, Maya walked across the west plot. The soil felt drier than expected, even though irrigation had finished that morning. Near the shade line, a probe registered low surface moisture where sprinkler reach was weakest. An edge processor analyzed the data against historical moisture patterns, crop-stage requirements, and the latest weather forecast, which predicted rainfall within thirty-six hours. The tablet pinged softly as the dashboard flagged the anomaly and displayed a recommendation: Delay seeding for 48 hours; natural rainfall likely to restore topsoil moisture. If the forecast changes, begin pre-seeding irrigation.

The probe had not spoken in words. It communicated through a chain of actions, sensing, transmitting, analyzing, integrating with external data, and generating guidance. To Maya, it was no longer just an instrument; it was a dialogue between the field and its caretakers.

Every IoT system, whether in agriculture, healthcare, or energy, follows the same anatomy, a sequence that transforms raw signals into meaningful action. This flow can be understood through five essential layers, which are outlined in the following table:

Layer	Function	Description
Sensing	Perception	Detects and converts physical phenomena into digital signals.
Communication	Data transmission	Transfers data across wired, wireless, or hybrid networks.
Edge processing	Interpretation	Filters, analyzes, and acts on data near the source.
Cloud	Aggregation and planning	Integrates data from distributed nodes, performs analytics, and connects with larger systems.
Actuation	Response	Executes decisions through alerts, controls, or physical adjustments

Table 2.1: A five-layer framework for IoT

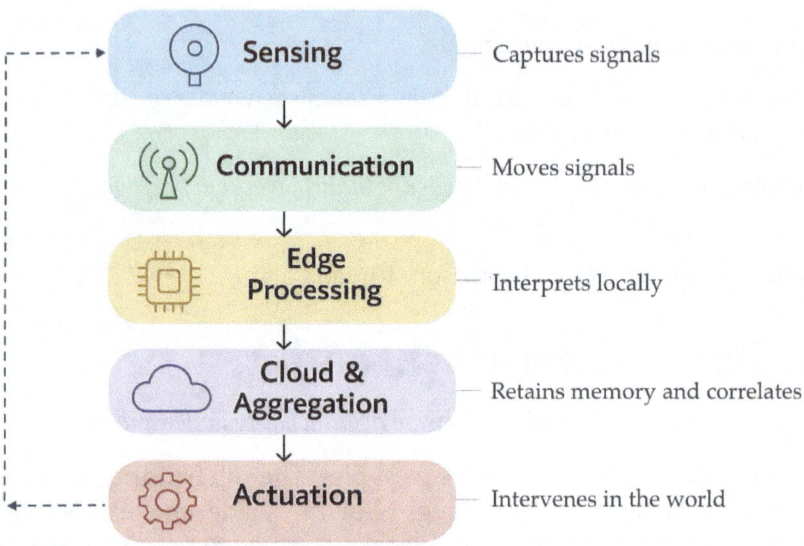

Figure 2.5: A five-layer framework for IoT

Each layer involves distinct technologies and trade-offs. Together, they create an architecture of attention, a distributed nervous system that extends from soil to clinic, from city street to power grid.

The following sections explore these layers in turn, how IoT systems perceive, interpret, and respond, and how the digital fabric learns to feel and to act.

Sensing layer

Every connected system begins with the decision to notice. The sensing layer forms the interface between the physical and digital worlds, where real-world phenomena are detected and converted into data. Sensors serve as translators, transforming temperature, motion, pressure, or chemical changes into digital signals that machines can interpret.

Common categories include:

- **Environmental**: Temperature, humidity, air quality, particulate matter, light intensity.
- **Mechanical**: Vibration, pressure, displacement, motion, torque.
- **Biometric**: Heart rate, oxygen saturation, body temperature, **electrocardiogram** (**ECG**).
- **Chemical**: Soil pH, carbon dioxide, ammonia, gas concentration, salinity.

In her early projects, Maya prioritized reliability over precision. A soil probe that survived a storm and reported consistently was more valuable than one that failed after a single season.

Each sensor typically includes:

- **Sensing element**: It detects the physical quantity (e.g., a thermistor for heat, a photodiode for light).
- **Analog-to-digital converter** (**ADC**): It converts analog readings into digital form.
- **Microcontroller**: It processes and packages the data.
- **Communication module**: It transmits information via **Bluetooth Low Energy** (**BLE**), ZigBee, **Long Range Wide Area Network** (**LoRaWAN**), **wireless fidelity** (**Wi-Fi**), or NB-IoT.

Together, these components allow sensors to perceive their surroundings and communicate with higher layers of the system. In Maya's clinic, infrared thermometers and pulse oximeters transmitted newborn vitals to a shared tablet. In her fields, rugged soil probes withstood heat, dust, and rain while streaming data reliably.

Sensing is never neutral. Every measurement reflects a decision about what matters. Each deployed sensor embodies a value choice, what deserves to be heard and what can remain unseen.

Communication layer

Capturing data is only the beginning. A sensed pulse or soil reading has value only when the signal can travel. The communication layer provides the pathways that move this information from one point to another, ensuring that what is sensed can be shared, interpreted, and acted upon.

In Maya's clinic, BLE and ZigBee supported low-power, stable indoor links. Beyond the building, its range declined, so she used LoRaWAN for the fields, powered by small solar panels. The network prioritized distance over speed. A 5G modem bridged the local mesh to the wider Internet.

Every design decision balanced four variables: power, range, bandwidth, and cost. Together, they shaped a communication fabric resilient enough to sustain observation and care across varied terrain.

All IoT networks build on a modified **Transmission Control Protocol/Internet Protocol** (TCP/IP) five-layer stack, optimized for constrained devices and operational environments, as shown in the following table:

Layer	Function	Example protocols
5. **Application**	Meaning and intent	**Constrained Application Protocol** (CoAP), **Message Queuing Telemetry Transport** (MQTT)
4. **Transport**	Message delivery	UDP, TCP
3. **Network**	Addressing and routing	**Internet Protocol version 4** (IPv4), **Internet Protocol version 6** (IPv6)
2. **Data link**	Local transmission	LoRaWAN, ZigBee, BLE, Wi-Fi
1. **Physical**	Signal medium	Radio waves, wiring, optical links

Table 2.2: TCP/IP communication stack for IoT

IoT communication technologies vary widely in their design trade-offs. The following examples in the table illustrate the range of available access protocols:

Protocol	Strengths	Typical use case
BLE	Ultra-low power, short-range	Wearables and medical monitors
ZigBee/Z-Wave	Mesh-capable and resilient	Clinics and buildings
LoRaWAN	Long range, low, and bandwidth	Farms, forests, and industrial environments
Wi-Fi/Ethernet	High bandwidth	Fixed and power-rich systems
NB-IoT/LTE-M	Cellular, wide-area	Urban sensors and utilities
LEO satellite links	Global coverage	Remote and disaster zones

Table 2.3: Common wireless access protocols

Maya's network combined several of these technologies, forming a hybrid system where each compensated for the others' limitations. The result was reliable communication across clinic, field, and sky, a fabric of continuity that made sensing meaningful.

Addressing and communication

Early Internet systems were designed to connect people, not devices. As billions of IoT nodes emerged, IPv4 addressing proved inadequate. IPv6 resolved this by providing over 340 undecillion unique addresses, enabling every sensor and actuator to hold a distinct digital identity. Messages could now travel directly and securely, even in rural or off-grid environments.

In Maya's system, each sensor, from soil probes to neonatal monitors, had its own IPv6 address, ensuring reliable end-to-end communication across the network.

An address alone does not create understanding. Devices also require a common language for data exchange. Two lightweight protocols dominate IoT communication:

- **MQTT**: A publish–subscribe protocol using a central broker to route data efficiently among many nodes. It performs well in networks with intermittent connectivity.
- **CoAP**: A web-based protocol for resource-limited devices, operating over UDP with DTLS encryption for secure, low-latency transmission.

In Maya's clinic, neonatal wristbands used CoAP to send encrypted health data to the local dashboard.

The communication layer thus becomes more than a transport mechanism. It is the architecture through which data turns into dialogue and distributed systems begin to cooperate intelligently.

Edge processing layer

In the cooperative fields, sensors did not continuously transmit raw data. Each included a small processor that analyzed readings locally and sent alerts only when soil moisture dropped below the threshold, and no rainfall was forecast. Acting near the source reduced unnecessary data flow and enabled rapid response.

Edge computing refers to processing that occurs close to data collection, on the device or through a nearby gateway, rather than in a distant cloud. It becomes essential when:

- Latency must be minimal, as in neonatal monitoring.
- Connectivity is intermittent, as in rural or disaster-affected areas.
- Privacy requires that data remain local.
- Bandwidth is limited by high-frequency sensor streams.

Maya's network used microcontrollers such as the ESP32, capable of filtering noise, applying thresholds, and running TinyML models for local analysis. Through these, IoT systems can:

- Smooth and filter noisy data streams.
- Summarize readings for efficient transmission.

- Make immediate decisions using embedded logic or ML.
- Trigger actuators or alerts without cloud dependency.

Processing at the edge allows systems to sense, interpret, and act autonomously while conserving energy, protecting privacy, and ensuring operation when connectivity falters.

As Maya reminded her trainees, *every second saved at the edge preserves a life, a crop, or a choice.*

Cloud and aggregation layer

Not all information remains local. In Maya's system, summarized sensor data was uploaded every few hours to a secure cloud managed by the regional health network. This layer aggregates distributed readings, identifies patterns, and transforms them into actionable insights.

The cloud and aggregation layer functions as the analytical and integrative core of an IoT ecosystem, converting raw signals into collective intelligence through several key functions:

- **Storage**: Time-series databases capture sensor readings, preserving historical records for trend analysis and auditing.
- **Analytics**: Algorithms detect correlations across time, geography, and device types, supporting forecasting and anomaly detection.
- **Visualization**: Dashboards and maps convert large data streams into understandable forms for human interpretation.
- **Integration**: **Application programming interfaces** (**APIs**) connect IoT data with other digital systems such as electronic health records, energy platforms, or climate models.
- **Governance**: Policies define ownership, access, retention, and consent, ensuring data is handled ethically and lawfully.

In resource-limited environments, *the cloud* often takes a localized form. Maya's clinic used an edge server that stored data locally, synchronized with regional systems when connectivity returned, and provided real-time insights without continuous Internet access.

Across the world, hybrid architectures are becoming more common. These systems combine local and global clouds to achieve a balance between control, efficiency, and collaboration. The following table summarizes three foundational principles for building hybrid cloud architectures:

Principle	Purpose
Sovereignty	Keep data under community or national control.
Sustainability	Reduce energy use through solar power and efficient data handling.
Trust	Share only essential, verified, and anonymized information.

Table 2.4: Principles guiding hybrid cloud architecture

The goal of this layer is responsible scalability; growth aligned with purpose and capacity. When designed well, it becomes the collective memory of a sensing network, where signals evolve into patterns, patterns reveal insight, and insight guides action.

Actuation layer

No sensing system is complete until it can respond. The actuation layer closes the loop between perception and action, turning information into tangible outcomes. At this stage, data no longer describes the world; it begins to shape it.

Responses take many forms. Some are physical, such as a valve opening or a light adjusting, while others are digital, such as alerts, control messages, or automated workflows. Actuation is where feedback becomes intervention.

In Maya's cooperative, irrigation valves operated under three conditions: soil moisture, rainfall forecast, and crop type. If any factor fell outside the target range, the pump remained silent. The result was precision irrigation guided by logic rather than routine, conserving water while maintaining crop health.

Actuation varies by autonomy:

- **Automated**: System acts independently using predefined rules or model outputs.
- **Assisted**: User reviews recommendations before confirming actions.
- **Manual**: System presents insights while users decide and execute.

Actuators include relays, servo motors, solenoid valves, and digital switches. Commands may originate at the edge for speed, in the cloud for coordination, or through hybrid logic that combines both. In industry, actuators regulate temperature, pressure, and motion; in healthcare, they adjust oxygen flow and environmental controls.

Responsiveness defines success. Each action must be reliable, verified, and context-aware. Because every response touches real environments and lives, actuation design must embed safeguards, authentication, and continuous monitoring. A delayed valve can waste a season; a silent medical failure can risk a life.

In Maya's world, this was the layer where sensing met stewardship, a reminder that technology's purpose is not only to measure but to care.

Security and trust

At the clinic, Maya understood the risks that came with connectivity. A single tampered sensor, intercepted signal, or corrupted update could cause real harm. In systems that monitor health, crops, or power, a breach is not only technical, it is human. Trust cannot be added later; it must be designed from the start.

From the moment a device powers on, it must establish integrity and protect the data it carries. A secure IoT system follows four foundational principles:

- **Authentication**: Each device verifies its identity before joining the network.
- **Encryption**: Data remains protected in transit and at rest.
- **Integrity verification**: Firmware and software are validated through secure boot and signed updates.
- **Access control**: Only authorized users or processes can read or modify operations.

Security is not confined to one point; it spans the entire stack. *Table 2.5* summarizes how security and trust are implemented across each layer of the IoT architecture:

Layer	Security focus
Physical	Tamper-resistant hardware, trusted chips.
Communication	Encrypted transmission using **Transport Layer Security (TLS)** or **Datagram Transport Layer Security** (**DTLS**) protocols.
Network	IP security extensions, routing validation, and firewalling.
Edge	Intrusion detection, anomaly monitoring, and gateway-level protection.
Cloud	Access logs, authentication, audit trails, data encryption at rest, and governance frameworks.
Actuation	Safety verification for trusted triggers and fail-safe mechanisms.

Table 2.5: Security and trust by design in IoT systems

Global standards, from the **World Health Organization** (**WHO**), **International Organization for Standardization** (**ISO**), and national agencies, now emphasize trust by design: embedding resilience, data sovereignty, and ethical protection into architecture rather than applying them after deployment. The focus has shifted from reaction to prevention.

Protection also means safeguarding those within the system, the nurses relying on accurate readings, the farmers depending on weather alerts, and the citizens whose data shapes policy. Security in IoT is therefore an act of care, ensuring that sensing, communication, and action remain dependable under stress.

In Maya's clinic, trust was not optional. Each secure transmission and authenticated node was a quiet promise that the system would keep listening faithfully when lives depended on it.

Designing for dialogue

Behind every sensor Maya installed, whether measuring soil, breath, or sunlight, was an intention. Each device did more than collect data; it taught the network how to listen and to care.

Designing for dialogue means treating IoT as a conversation between the physical and digital worlds. Systems must listen before acting, sense with purpose, and respond with restraint. Good design values transparency, security, and participation, turning sensing into collaboration rather than extraction.

In Maya's village, this dialogue was tangible; the clinic, the soil, and the grid adjusted together in quiet coordination. The true essence of IoT lies not in the number of devices but in the quality of relationships between humans, machines, and their environments. The goal is not automation but awareness and technology as stewardship.

The next section explores how these sensory threads operate across domains, turning scattered signals into coherent systems of care.

IoT systems that listen and respond

To sense is not just to collect, but to care. In every signal lies a chance to restore balance.

Maya often reminded her students that technology rarely begins in perfect laboratories. It is shaped by necessity, under leaking roofs, in dry fields, on unstable grids, and in hospital wards where life depends on attention.

IoT is not the future, she told them. *It is the present, learning to feel one sensor at a time.*

This section moves from anatomy to behavior, showing how sensing becomes action through the five-layer architecture. Each example illustrates how systems listen, interpret, and respond within their own context.

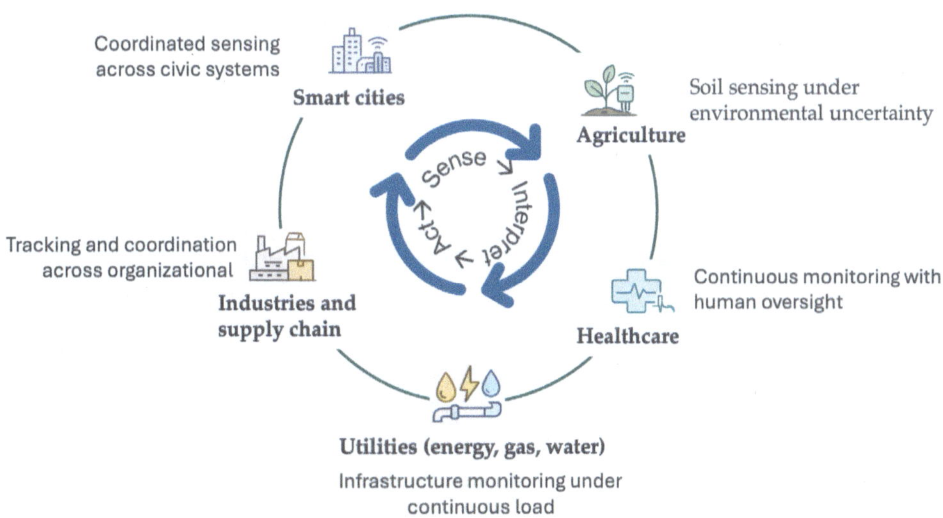

Figure 2.6: *IoT applications across domains*

The stories that follow are not about devices or dashboards but about networks that sense together, loops of care linking human intention to digital intelligence:

- *Fields* that wait before they water.
- *Clinics* that listen to breath before it fails.
- *Cities* that adapt to human rhythm.
- *Factories* that predict fatigue before failure.
- *Grids* that balance awareness and flow.

These examples reveal how sensing, guided by design and ethics, transforms technology into collaboration between data and decision, between what is measured and what is valued.

The field that speaks

The wind hummed across the west plot as Maya brushed dust from a soil probe. The irrigation cycle had ended that morning, yet the dashboard glowed red, indicating critical dryness. The system had compared the reading with satellite forecasts and advised postponing irrigation for two days. Rain was expected; premature watering would waste both water and energy.

Beneath this simple alert lay an intricate network. Soil probes measured moisture and temperature, weather APIs streamed forecasts, and a solar gateway transmitted data through LoRaWAN. At the edge, a TinyML model filtered noise and confirmed anomalies. The cloud dashboard aggregated results from all cooperative farms, verifying the pattern as regional.

When the rain arrived, irrigation stayed off. If it had not, valves would have opened automatically. Each sensor played a part, but meaning arose from their coordination.

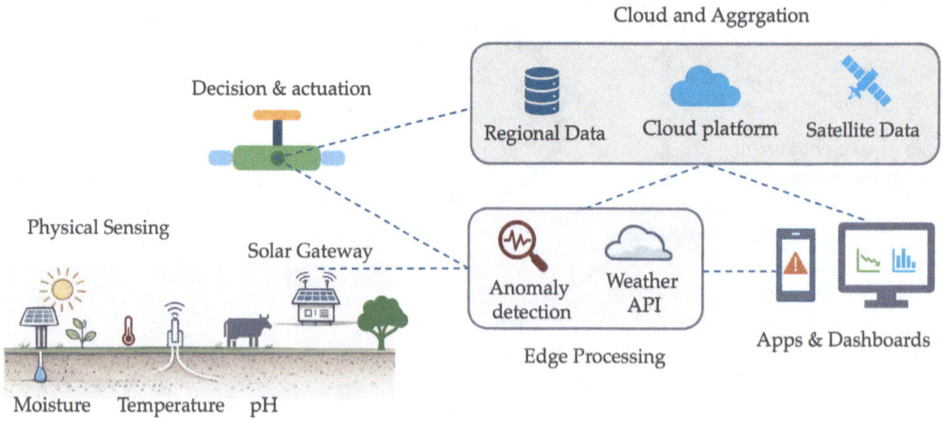

Figure 2.7: IoT in agriculture, the fields that speak

The system followed a standard IoT architecture:

- **Sensing**: Soil moisture, temperature, pH, and sunlight sensors gather raw data.
- **Communication**: LoRaWAN and 4G links carry readings to the local gateway.
- **Edge processing**: TinyML filters noise and predicts near-term water stress.
- **Cloud and aggregation**: Dashboards integrate weather, soil, and crop data.
- **Actuation**: Valves open or remain closed based on confirmed thresholds.

This fusion of sensing, edge intelligence, and cloud integration turns farmland into a responsive ecosystem. The goal is precision with restraint, replacing routine with evidence, conserving water and energy, and empowering farmers through informed action.

The ward that watches

The neonatal ward was still except for the rhythmic pulse of monitors. Maya's tablet displayed real-time readings from wristbands the size of a coin. Each streamed oxygen saturation and heart rate via BLE to a local gateway that processed data before sending summaries to the clinic server.

When one infant's oxygen level fell, a soft alert blinked instead of an alarm. The system verified the signal twice, filtered noise, and confirmed a true anomaly before calling for attention. Maya adjusted the oxygen flow, and the readings steadied.

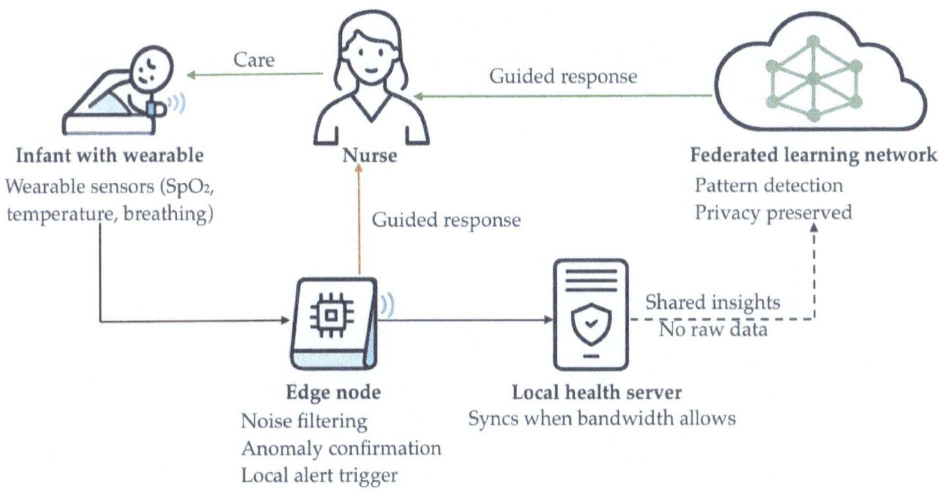

Figure 2.8: An IoT use case in healthcare

IoT layers in the healthcare loop:

- **Sensing**: Wearable sensors track oxygen saturation, temperature, and micro-vibrations of breathing.

- **Communication**: BLE transmits data securely to the local gateway using the CoAP protocol with DTLS encryption.
- **Edge processing**: A microcontroller runs a TinyML model that filters noise and predicts early respiratory distress.
- **Cloud and aggregation**: Local servers store patient histories, compare trends across wards, and synchronize with regional databases.
- **Actuation**: Alerts guide the nurse's response, and thresholds are refined as new data accumulates.

This layered design keeps intelligence near the patient while enabling network-wide learning. Edge analytics ensures rapid, private response; federated learning allows clinics to collaborate without sharing raw data. In Maya's ward, devices did not replace nurses; they amplified attention, turning the clinic into a shared nervous system of care.

The city that breathes

At dawn, streetlights dimmed, traffic sensors awakened, and air monitors began their first readings. At the municipal operations center, the dashboard shifted in real time, displaying the city's pulse, noise levels were rising near the market, and nitrogen dioxide had crossed the morning threshold. The city's adaptive system responded quietly, traffic lights adjusted green cycles to ease congestion, lights dimmed in empty lanes, and an alert went to sanitation crews to inspect an exhaust hotspot.

Environmental, acoustic, and motion sensors streamed data through hybrid networks of Wi-Fi, 5G, and LoRaWAN. Gateways analyzed intersections locally while cloud analytics integrated weather, traffic, and health data. When pollution spiked near schools, the system rerouted vehicles and activated classroom ventilation.

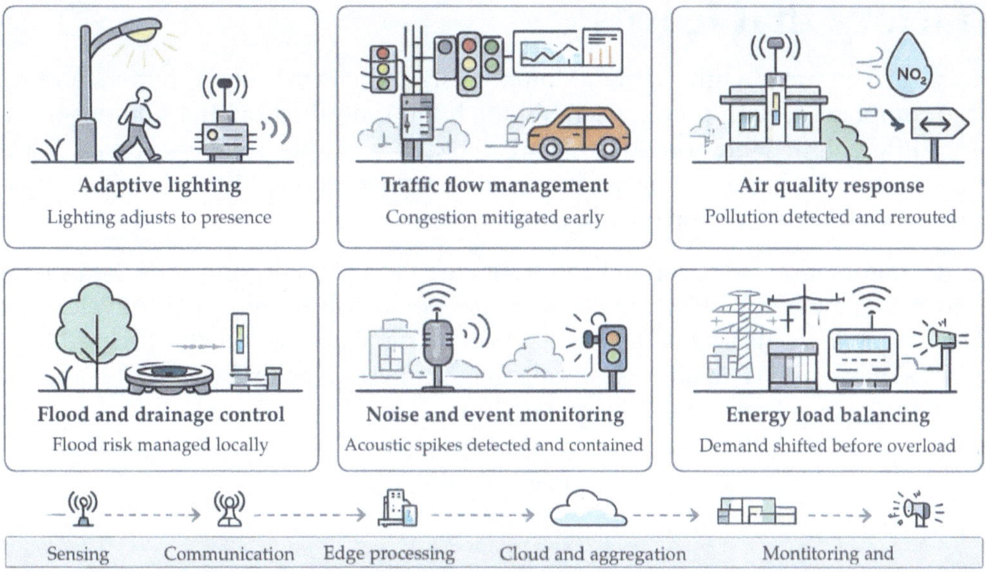

***Figure 2.9**: A few IoT use cases in cities*

IoT Layers in adaptive cities:

- **Sensing**: Environmental, motion, and acoustic sensors collect air, traffic, and noise data.
- **Communication**: Hybrid networks use 5G for dense areas, LoRaWAN for distant nodes, and fiber for the core backbone.
- **Edge processing**: Gateways near intersections analyze local data for low-latency control.
- **Cloud and aggregation**: City dashboards integrate multisource data for coordinated decision-making.
- **Actuation**: Lights, traffic systems, and public alerts adjust dynamically or via operator input.

This architecture shifts cities from static control to dynamic coordination, where systems adapt to patterns of weather, movement, and daily life. Local nodes act instantly while central systems interpret long-term trends. Gateways manage signal timing or floodgates, and cloud analytics guide air quality, traffic, and energy planning.

Cities such as *Barcelona*, *Singapore*, and *Seoul* already employ this logic, blending IoT, AI, and civic dashboards into feedback loops that anticipate imbalance before it grows. For Maya, visiting such a city was like watching a living organism, breathing, caring, and adapting in rhythm with its people.

The factory that learns

The factory floor hummed with motion. Motors whirred, belts moved in rhythm, and robotic arms lifted components with precision. Yet in the hum of production, the supervisor noticed something different. A vibration sensor had detected a subtle frequency shift, signaling bearing wear. The alert appeared instantly on the supervisor's console, and maintenance was scheduled before failure occurred. The line never stopped.

This was not automation for speed but foresight embedded in steel and code. Sensors across the floor tracked temperature, vibration, torque, and power use. Their signals traveled through a private 5G network to nearby edge processors running algorithms that compared live data with historical patterns. When anomalies emerged, the system generated maintenance tickets automatically, turning observation into prevention.

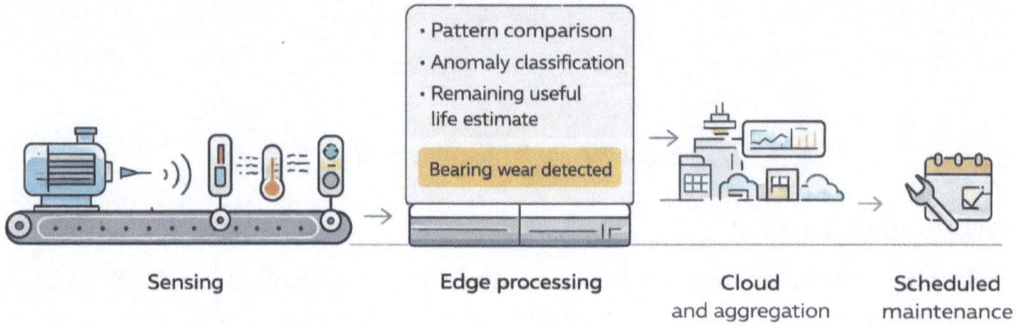

High-frequency machine signals are analyzed at the edge to detect early wear, with verified anomalies triggering scheduled maintenance before failure, preserving safety and production continuity.

Figure 2.10: An example of predictive maintenance using IoT

IoT layers in the industrial loop:

- **Sensing**: Accelerometers, acoustic sensors, and current monitors detect vibration, sound, and power irregularities.
- **Communication**: Private 5G and industrial Ethernet provide secure, low-latency connectivity across the floor.
- **Edge processing**: Local servers run predictive models that classify anomalies and estimate remaining machine life.
- **Cloud and aggregation**: Enterprise dashboards visualize performance across plants and integrate with supply systems.
- **Actuation**: Maintenance requests, robotic adjustments, or controlled shutdowns occur to prevent damage.

This architecture enables anticipatory operation, systems that predict rather than react. Predictive maintenance combines sensor analytics and machine learning to detect early signs of fatigue or inefficiency, turning observation into prevention.

Edge computing is vital in this process. Industrial machines produce high-frequency data that would overwhelm networks if transmitted continuously. Local processing reduces latency, preserves safety during outages, and sends only summarized patterns and alerts to the cloud for long-term analysis.

Integration with digital twins strengthens this loop. Each virtual replica mirrors its machine's real-time state, allowing engineers to test repairs, optimize performance, and plan maintenance without halting production.

Beyond efficiency lies an ethical dimension. Intelligent systems enhance safety by predicting equipment stress, but risk surveillance if misused. Responsible design demands transparency so that data serves collective safety, not personal control.

The future of industry depends on collaboration between human skill and digital foresight, machines that anticipate, freeing workers to focus on creativity, quality, and innovation.

The grid that balances

The lights flickered once and steadied. Across the region, thousands of sensors and substations performed a quiet choreography. The electric grid was learning to breathe.

Across the cooperative's solar network, the dashboard displayed live flows of voltage, current, and frequency. When the afternoon sun peaked, excess power flowed to nearby homes and clinics. As evening fell, the same network predicted demand surges and drew from stored energy. The exchange was seamless, guided by sensing and coordination rather than command.

IoT layers in smart energy systems:

- **Sensing**: Smart meters, current sensors, and weather monitors collect load, supply, and environmental data.
- **Communication**: Power-line communication and 5G links carry measurements to substations and regional grids.
- **Edge processing**: Local controllers predict short-term demand and balance supply from solar, wind, and batteries.
- **Cloud and aggregation**: Grid management systems analyze regional patterns and coordinate distributed energy resources.
- **Actuation**: Automated switches, battery inverters, and demand-response controls adjust flow in real-time.

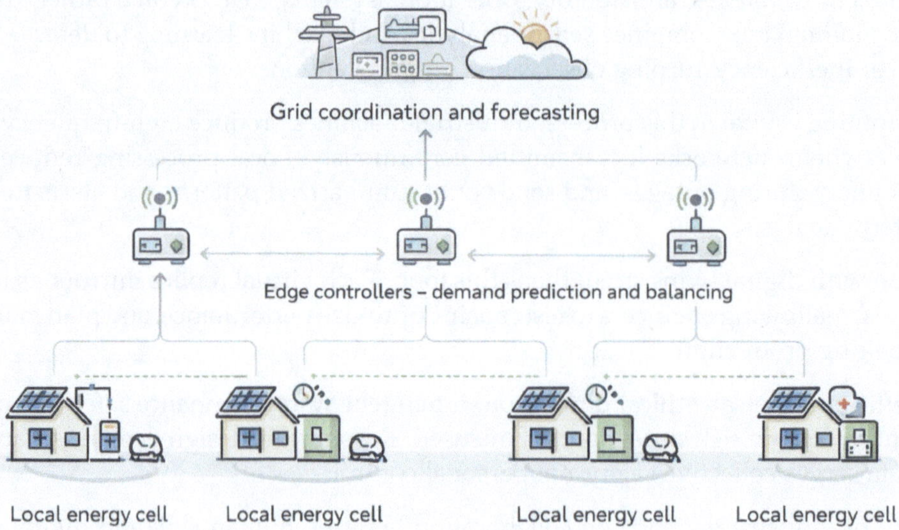

Local energy cells sense generation and demand and exchange power with neighbors. Edge controllers predict short-term conditions and balance supply locally. Regional systems aggregate patterns and forecast demand to coordinate the grid without centralized control.

***Figure 2.11**: Decentralized federated smart grid*

Modern power grids are shifting from centralized delivery to distributed, sensing networks. Smart meters and renewable microgrids transform consumers into participants who both draw and supply energy. Embedded sensors in transformers, substations, and homes create continuous feedback loops measuring generation, distribution, and consumption. Decisions once made centrally now emerge from many distributed controllers working in coordination.

At the edge, controllers adjust voltage and frequency to prevent cascading failures. In the cloud, analytics forecast demand, detect faults, and optimize renewable integration. During stress, the system isolates damaged sections, reroutes power, and recovers gracefully, preventing blackouts like the Texas 2021 crisis.

Artificial intelligence deepens this responsiveness. Machine learning models analyze weather and consumption histories to predict demand hours in advance. Blockchain-based energy markets allow microgrids and households to trade surplus power securely, ensuring transparency and fairness.

Threads of attention across domains

Across fields, clinics, cities, factories, and grids, Maya saw a shared rhythm, systems sensing, interpreting, and acting as one fabric of awareness from soil to satellite. A paused irrigation cycle conserved power for a clinic; a factory's efficiency eased strain on the grid; a cleaner city meant healthier patients.

This interconnection reflects cross-domain resilience, the capacity of systems to adapt and recover through shared sensing and mutual reinforcement. When one domain becomes more responsive, others grow more stable in return.

New frontiers now extend this pattern of perception and adaptation:

- **Oceans and climate systems**, where buoys, drones, and satellites collaborate to monitor temperature, salinity, and carbon flux.
- **Conservation networks**, where acoustic sensors detect poaching or illegal logging in real-time.
- **Infrastructure and construction**, where embedded strain and corrosion sensors predict bridge fatigue or building settlement.
- **Supply chains**, where connected packaging tracks provenance, temperature, and sustainability metrics from origin to destination.
- **Space systems**, where constellations of nanosatellites create a planetary nervous system linking weather, communication, and disaster management.

IoT is evolving from isolated applications into the sensory fabric of civilization. Each network extends collective awareness, observing, remembering, and responding.

As the fabric expands, so do its tensions. Interoperability, ethics, and governance must evolve together to ensure trust, transparency, and inclusivity. The next challenge is not weaving more threads, but caring for those that fray.

Fraying edges

A weave is still made of threads, no matter how intelligent. And every thread has a breaking point.

The storm came without warning. In seconds, sensors in Maya's clinic went silent. The solar inverter flickered, and the oxygen monitor failed for three minutes. In that moment, three minutes could mean a life.

When systems returned, Maya knelt beside a soaked sensor casing. She was not angry. The failure had not betrayed her; it revealed the design's limits. Every digital fabric carries tension, and those points of strain are where resilience is tested.

IoT is powerful because it connects so much, yet each new connection introduces risk. Every added sensor, protocol, or dependency increases sensitivity and vulnerability. The more intricate the weave, the more places it can fray.

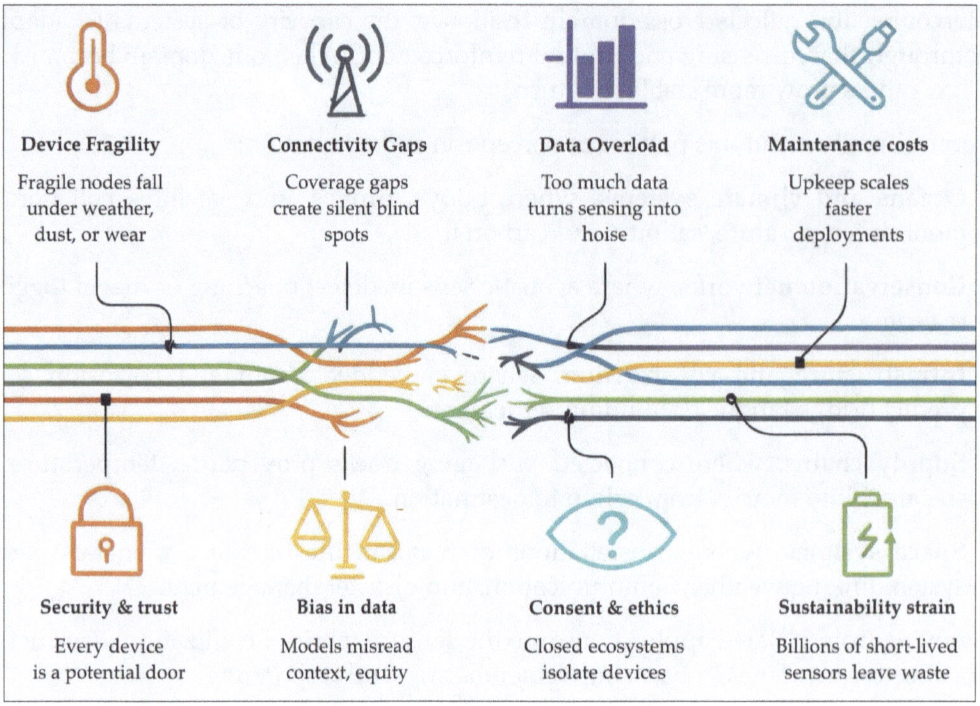

***Figure 2.12**: Frayed edges of the IoT fabric*

These weaknesses are not mysterious. They appear as familiar patterns: failed sensors, disconnected gateways, insecure communication, biased algorithms, and neglected maintenance. Some are technical, others human, but all stem from the same root, complexity without care.

Designing for resilience means seeing fragility as feedback, not failure. Each fault reveals what the system values, tolerates, or ignores. Recognizing these weak points early allows reinforcement before confidence unravels.

This section explores where the sensory fabric most often weakens and how to restore its strength:

- **Device fragility**: When physical limits undermine reliability.
- **Connectivity and coverage**: When networks fail to reach or report.
- **Data overload**: When abundance becomes interference.
- **Maintenance and lifecycle**: When care becomes the hidden cost of intelligence.
- **Security and integrity**: When trust is assumed rather than assured.
- **Bias in sensing**: When the data excludes the very people it serves.
- **Consent and ethics**: When sensing crosses the line between care and intrusion.

- **Protocol fragmentation**: When systems cannot speak to one another.
- **Sustainability and material impact**: When digital sensitivity burdens the physical world.

Each represents a fray in the weave of trust. Resilient design does not eliminate these tensions; it listens to them. The strength of any sensing system depends not only on how well it perceives the world, but on how gracefully it accepts and repairs its own imperfections.

Device fragility

Every IoT system depends on its smallest parts, sensors on rooftops, in fields, or on skin. They extend perception yet remain most vulnerable to heat, moisture, dust, and time. In Maya's village, storms dislodged nodes, connectors corroded, and some sensors sent false readings. A single faulty value could mislead the network or hide real danger. Silent failures eroded trust more than visible ones.

Resilience begins with durable design, redundancy, and self-diagnostics that let devices fail loudly instead of quietly.

The following list outlines the design principles for durable sensing systems:

- **Environmental protection**: Use weatherproof enclosures and corrosion-resistant materials suited to local climates.
- **Redundancy**: Deploy overlapping sensors or backup nodes for continuous coverage.
- **Self-diagnostics**: Detect anomalies, stuck values, or power loss and report them automatically.
- **Graceful failure**: Announce faults using heartbeat signals or timeout alerts so errors are visible.

A resilient device does not hide its weakness; it declares it. Failure should be visible and reportable so the system can respond before errors spread. As Maya wrote in her logbook, *A silent thread is the most dangerous one. If it must break, let it do so loudly so the weave can be repaired in time.*

Connectivity and coverage

In theory, a sensor can work anywhere; in practice, it depends on power, connectivity, and care. A device is only as strong as the network that links it. When that link breaks, the system stops listening.

During one monsoon, a fallen branch blocked a LoRaWAN relay, silencing the western plots. The dashboard still showed data, but it was stale, and crops withered before anyone noticed. Such quiet failures reveal a deeper issue; networks that appear alive but are not.

Reliable connectivity means designing for interruption, not perfection, with redundant links, local buffering, and regular health checks so systems admit when they cannot see or speak.

Principles for resilient connectivity:

- **Network redundancy**: Overlap coverage zones so no single node becomes a point of failure.
- **Edge buffering**: Store data locally during outages and forward it once the network recovers.
- **Health monitoring**: Use heartbeat messages or watchdog timers to flag inactive nodes.
- **Adaptive routing**: Enable networks to reconfigure and reroute data automatically.

These practices transform connectivity from a fragile thread into a self-healing fabric. In Maya's later designs, each relay carried a solar cell and buffer, allowing nearby gateways to bridge gaps when nodes failed.

Connectivity, she realized, is not about perfect signal strength but about graceful degradation. A resilient system must know when it cannot see and say so clearly. As she noted, *Networks that admit their blind spots are the ones that keep their vision.*

Data overload

Not all failures are silent; some come from excess. When Maya set her soil probes to report every thirty seconds, precision became noise. Dashboards froze, alerts piled up, and analysis lagged. The system was no longer sensing; it was drowning.

This is the paradox of scale—the more a system observes, the easier it is to lose clarity. Many conditions change slowly, and constant reporting wastes power and bandwidth while burying insight in repetition. True intelligence lies in restraint, sensing when change matters, filtering what repeats, and ignoring what does not.

Design principles for managing data flow are as follows:

- **Edge filtering**: Process and smooth data near the source to remove redundant readings.
- **Adaptive thresholds**: Adjust sensing frequency to match environmental change.
- **Event-driven reporting**: Transmit only when values cross critical boundaries or contexts shift.
- **TinyML inference**: Use lightweight models on microcontrollers to detect anomalies before sending data upstream.

These strategies shift focus from collection to comprehension. The goal is not to capture everything but to extract timely meaning from the right signals.

In Maya's later deployments, each soil probe measured every minute but transmitted only when a significant deviation occurred. The network grew calmer, devices lasted longer, and insight sharpened.

As she told her trainees, *A system that listens to everything hears nothing. It must learn the rhythm of the world it observes.*

Effective sensing demands discipline. Attention, human or digital, is finite. The art of IoT lies not in constant awareness but in intelligent restraint.

Maintenance and lifecycle

Sensors, like living systems, need care. In the early months, the network seemed self-sufficient, but corrosion, heat, and wear proved otherwise. Each small failure disrupted the flow of data and trust. Maintenance is the hidden cost of intelligence; every device adds a duty to clean, calibrate, or replace. Without lifecycle planning, even smart networks decay into silence. Sustainable IoT design treats upkeep not as repair but as part of the system's rhythm.

Principles for lifecycle resilience are as follows:

- **Scheduled calibration**: Recalibrate sensors at defined intervals against reliable baselines.
- **Spare-part logistics**: Keep local inventories of critical components and batteries to minimize downtime.
- **Modular hardware**: Use replaceable parts rather than sealed units to enable repair and reduce waste.
- **Battery and seal monitoring**: Add telemetry to track power and enclosure integrity for early detection of wear.
- **Local capacity building**: Train field technicians to diagnose and repair devices independently.

When maintenance becomes habitual, resilience shifts from aspiration to routine. In Maya's cooperative, quarterly maintenance weeks restored trust and performance through cleaning, testing, and recalibration. Devices that endure for years are not only economical but environmentally responsible.

As Maya reminded her trainees, *Intelligence that forgets to care for itself cannot care for the world it measures.*

Security and integrity

Every connection in an IoT network is a potential point of entry, making security not only a technical function but an ethical commitment. Trust cannot be assumed; it must be designed, verified, and renewed throughout a system's life.

Maya's IoT network followed this principle. Each device authenticated itself before joining, encrypted data during transmission, and verified signed firmware to prevent tampering. Even simple soil sensors had to prove they belonged before being heard.

Yet no defense is final. Threats evolve, and each new feature expands the surface of risk. A single compromised node can distort readings, trigger false actions, or expose sensitive data. Security failures in IoT rarely announce themselves; they begin as subtle distortions of truth.

Resilient systems protect both information and the people it represents. Security must be embedded across every layer, sensing, communication, edge, cloud, and actuation, not added after deployment. It combines encryption, integrity checks, and human oversight. In healthcare, an altered signal can endanger a life; in agriculture, falsified data can destroy a harvest.

Integrity requires continuous attention: regular audits, secure updates, and transparent governance. As Maya told her students, *Every secure signal is a promise. It means the system not only functions but respects the lives woven into its network.* Trust, once built, is never permanent; it must be renewed like every other thread of the weave.

Bias in sensing

Not all failures are mechanical; some arise from assumptions in design. In one early trial, a neonatal monitor built and tested abroad misread oxygen levels for several infants. The issue was not a malfunction but a calibration problem; the optical sensor had been tuned for lighter skin tones. The device worked as specified, yet excluded those it was meant to help.

This is the quiet danger of bias in sensing. It hides behind normal operation, distorting truth without visible fault. A weather model trained on city data may misjudge rural rain; a recognition system may fail to see faces it never learned. Such errors are not only technical but ethical, defining whose realities are recorded and whose remain invisible.

Bias in IoT arises from three primary sources, namely the sensor's design, the data used to train analytical models, and the contexts chosen for testing and validation. Each filters reality through human judgment about what is normal or valuable.

Principles for equitable sensing:

- **Inclusive design**: Calibrate sensors and models across diverse environmental and demographic conditions.
- **Transparent validation**: Publish testing parameters and datasets so limitations are visible.
- **Contextual adaptation**: Enable local recalibration for regional climates, cultures, and physiology.
- **Feedback integration**: Let users flag anomalies and contribute real-world data for refinement.

In later work, Maya's team recalibrated neonatal sensors using regional datasets. Once adjusted, readings became consistent across all patients, turning exclusion into inclusion.

Bias cannot be fully erased, but can be reduced through diversity, transparency, and accountability. As Maya wrote, *A sensor that cannot see everyone equally is not broken; it is incomplete.*

Equity in sensing ensures the digital fabric mirrors the full complexity of the world it observes. Without it, the weave may function but never truly represent the lives intertwined within it.

Consent and ethics

To sense is powerful, but to sense without consent is dangerous. Sensors capture what the human eye cannot, such as temperature, motion, heartbeat, location, and voice. Alone, these data points seem harmless; together, they can reveal a person's routines, emotions, and vulnerabilities. The power to sense must therefore be balanced by the duty to respect.

Maya understood this when deploying air-quality monitors in her village. Before installation, she gathered residents beneath the banyan tree to explain what would be measured, who would access the data, and how it would help. Villagers raised concerns about privacy and surveillance. Maya listened, revised the plan, and earned consent through dialogue, not persuasion. Trust arose not from technology but from transparency.

In many large-scale systems, this dialogue is absent. Devices are placed in homes or public spaces without disclosure, assuming that data collection automatically serves the common good. True ethical design rejects this assumption. In IoT, care begins with consent, and trust begins with listening.

The following list highlights the principles for ethical sensing:

- **Transparency**: Communicate clearly what is measured, why, and who has access.
- **Informed consent**: Ensure participants understand and agree before sensing begins.
- **Data minimization**: Collect only what is essential for the defined purpose.
- **Contextual sensitivity**: Respect cultural norms, privacy expectations, and local concerns.
- **Accountability**: Define responsibility for governance, security, and redress in case of misuse.

Ethical design is not a single act but a continual practice. Consent must evolve as systems expand, goals shift, and technologies change. A community that welcomes air-quality sensors today may reject cameras or biometrics tomorrow.

As Maya often said, *Every sensor is a guest in someone's space. It should enter only when invited, stay only as long as needed, and leave without leaving a trace.*

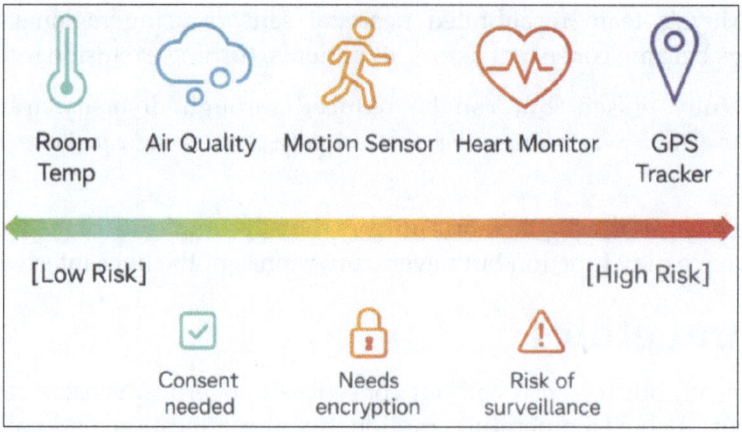

Figure 2.13: Sensing ethics spectrum

Consent transforms surveillance into stewardship. When people understand how their data supports cleaner air, safer roads, or healthier lives, they become participants rather than subjects. The true ethics of IoT lie in this partnership, which is to sense with empathy, design with humility, and act with accountability.

Protocol fragmentation

Even when sensors function flawlessly, and networks stay secure, the IoT can still unravel through fragmentation. Devices often fail to communicate because they depend on incompatible standards or closed ecosystems.

During integration testing, a new air-quality monitor worked perfectly within its own app but refused to share data. Its readings were accurate yet trapped in a proprietary cloud. The device was not broken, but disconnected from the larger system it was meant to serve.

Interoperability remains one of IoT's greatest challenges. Competing data formats, APIs, and control platforms fragment the digital landscape, driving up costs and limiting collaboration. When each network becomes an island, the collective weave weakens.

Open standards restore dialogue. They allow devices from different makers to exchange data securely and meaningfully, transforming isolated products into parts of a unified ecosystem, a true Internet of Things rather than islands of technology.

The following table outlines the emerging frameworks for open communication:

Framework	Purpose	Core contribution
Matter	Common application layer for smart devices	Enables cross-brand compatibility and simplifies device setup.

OpenThread	Open-source, low-power mesh networking	Allows resilient, IPv6-based connectivity for edge devices.
Web of Things (WoT)	W3C standard for web-based device interaction	Makes IoT devices discoverable and programmable using web principles.

***Table 2.6**: Open standards for interoperable IoT ecosystems*

These frameworks do not impose uniformity; they create shared language. A soil sensor should be able to communicate with systems monitoring water, air, or power. Open protocols make this collaboration possible, turning isolated devices into participants in a broader dialogue.

For Maya, adopting open standards allowed her clinic's air sensors to integrate with citywide pollution monitors and public health databases. Data once confined to silos began to flow across networks, strengthening both local care and regional insight.

Interoperability is more than technical efficiency; it is fairness. It prevents lock-in, reduces waste, and keeps systems open to evolution. A truly woven IoT depends on transparency and cooperation among its threads. As Maya wrote in her logbook, *every closed protocol is a knot in the weave. When systems speak openly, the whole fabric holds together.*

Sustainability and material impact

Even when systems work perfectly, their material impact endures. IoT depends on metals, plastics, batteries, and circuits drawn from the Earth and often returned to it as waste. The cloud may appear weightless, but its foundation is physical.

Maya saw this when she opened her workshop drawer and found broken probes, cracked housings, and dead batteries. Each was both a technical and ecological loss.

Billions of devices are produced annually using scarce materials such as lithium, cobalt, and tantalum. Extraction and disposal release emissions and toxic waste. Batteries fail quickly in harsh climates, while casings built to resist dust and water resist decay as well.

Sustainability must begin with design. Repairable, recyclable, and biodegradable components enable circular lifecycles where materials return to use instead of becoming waste. The goal is not only efficient systems but also responsible ones that sense the world without harming it.

Principles for sustainable IoT design:

- **Modularity**: Use replaceable components rather than sealed, disposable units.
- **Material responsibility**: Favor recyclable metals and biodegradable polymers.
- **Energy harvesting**: Power sensors through sunlight, vibration, or thermal gradients.
- **Lifecycle planning**: Include take-back programs and recovery pathways.
- **Operational efficiency**: Apply low-power protocols and duty-cycling to extend lifespan.

Maya's newer prototypes used cornstarch-based casings that dissolved after each season and sensors powered by soil temperature differences. They were simple but revealed what gentler sensing could be.

Sustainability extends beyond devices. Cloud computation and data storage consume vast energy, and every transmitted byte carries a carbon cost. Local processing, adaptive sampling, and data compression reduce both noise and footprint.

If IoT allows us to sense the planet, it must also sustain it. Every layer, from sensor to cloud, should embody ecological awareness. Sustainability is not an addition but the foundation of responsible design. As Maya wrote, *A system that measures the planet should never wound it. To listen well, we must tread lightly.*

The frayed edges of IoT are not failures but reminders that living systems evolve. Sensors corrode, gateways overheat, and models drift as conditions change. Each weakness signals the need for attention.

Resilience begins with recognition. A system that adapts must also notice when it cannot. This is digital maintenance, listening to both the environment and to the network itself.

Principles for systemic balance:

- **Continuous monitoring**: Track uptime, calibration, and data quality to detect early faults.
- **Feedback loops**: Use diagnostics to guide repair and reconfiguration.
- **Graceful degradation**: Design for partial operation rather than total collapse.
- **Human-in-the-loop**: Keep skilled operators to interpret and act on anomalies.
- **Cultural resilience**: Build local capacity for maintenance and evolution.

In Maya's cooperative, these principles became habits. Farmers checked soil probes, nurses verified sensors, and technicians reviewed logs. Repairs turned into acts of care that sustained trust and continuity.

A resilient system absorbs tension and heals where it thins. Its strength lies not in automation but in humility, recognizing that every layer needs tending. As Maya wrote, even the strongest weave loosens with time. What keeps it whole is not its strength alone, but the hands that return to mend it.

Resilience is not permanence but renewal. Systems that endure are designed to be repaired, not replaced. They accept fragility and weave that awareness into design. When technology acknowledges its limits, it begins to heal.

The story of IoT is about wear as much as function. Each broken node and noisy signal reveals that intelligence lies in recovery, not perfection. In tending these edges, Maya and her students discovered that care is the true currency of resilience.

The next horizon builds on this truth: sensing with wisdom, harvesting energy instead of consuming it, and designing for renewal rather than waste. What follows explores these future weaves, systems that listen, adapt, and fade gently when their work is done.

Future threads

A truly intelligent weave does not only respond to pressure, it anticipates it, lightens it, and adapts without tearing.

After the storm and its lessons, Maya returned to her hillside plots. She was not there to repair what failed but to test what might endure. In her hands lay a new kind of sensor printed with cornstarch polymer. It harvests energy from sunlight and ambient heat, stores no data locally, and dissolves harmlessly at the end of its life.

This is more than engineering. It is empathy expressed through design, a recognition that technology must return gently to the world it measures. This reflects a shift toward design practices that prioritize sustainability and social impact.

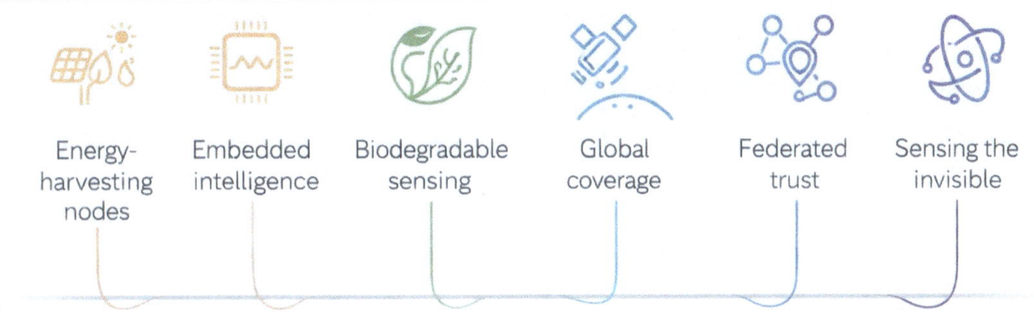

Emerging IoT designs emphasize lighter materials, local intelligence, shared trust, and planetary reach, shifting sensing from extraction toward care, restraint, and renewal.

***Figure 2.14**: Future threads of IoT fabric*

The next generation of the IoT is not defined by quantity but by consciousness. Systems are evolving from constant sensing to considerate sensing, from extraction to reciprocity. The goal is no longer to sense everything but to sense wisely, live lightly, and act with purpose.

IoT architectures are evolving toward more adaptive and sustainable designs, easing tension, restoring balance, and preparing for the responsibilities of a truly connected planet.

Sustainability as a design principle

When Maya sorted the clinic's waste, she found a new category, the retired sensors. Each color band told a story—red for biodegradable shells, blue for rechargeable cores, green for locally rebuilt parts. This was not symbolic recycling but a framework for sustainable design grounded in material awareness and lifecycle responsibility. Sustainability in IoT begins with mindful choices of energy and materials. It is not an afterthought but a guiding principle.

Core principles of sustainability-by-design:

- **Energy harvesting**: Sensors draw power from ambient sources such as sunlight, vibration, or thermal gradients, reducing dependence on disposable batteries.
- **Modularity**: Components can be replaced or upgraded locally, cutting e-waste and reliance on imports.
- **Network frugality**: Devices sleep when idle and transmit only what matters, conserving bandwidth and energy.
- **Shared infrastructure**: Communities rotate devices, share data access, and avoid duplication of cost and effort.
- **Circular pipelines**: Local workshops reclaim, test, and repurpose components to extend material life.

These principles redefine progress in connected systems. The next generation of IoT technologies seeks a smaller ecological footprint without sacrificing function. Waste becomes a measure of design failure, not operational success.

As Maya told her students, *To build a system that lasts, begin by asking how gently it can touch the world.*

Energy harvesting and zero-power systems

In early deployments, Maya worried more about batteries than bandwidth. A drained cell meant silence and missed warnings. She soon realized that dependence on replaceable batteries limited both reliability and sustainability. The new generation of IoT devices overcomes this by harvesting energy from light, heat, or motion, converting ambient power into continuous sensing and communication.

Common energy sources:

- **Solar and light**: Photovoltaic cells or micro panels power weather and agricultural sensors.
- **Vibration and motion**: Bridge and factory monitors capture energy from structural tremors and machine oscillations.
- **Thermal gradients**: Soil and building probes exploit temperature differences between air and ground.
- **Radio frequency (RF)**: Passive nodes harvest stray electromagnetic energy from transmitters or Wi-Fi networks.

These designs follow the principle of zero-power IoT, where devices draw energy from their surroundings instead of consuming finite reserves. Ultra-low-power microcontrollers sleep most of the time, waking briefly to sense, process, or transmit. By removing the weakest link, the battery, networks operate more autonomously and in closer balance with their environment.

Benefits of energy-harvesting systems:

- Remove battery maintenance in remote or hazardous locations.
- Reduce e-waste and total lifecycle cost.
- Extend operational lifetime with minimal intervention.
- Enable deployment in places unreachable by powered devices.

In Maya's valley, solar-assisted soil probes endured entire monsoon cycles without human touch. Their quiet persistence reflected a deeper truth of sustainable design: systems that sustain themselves also sustain trust.

As she wrote in her field notes, *A sensor that feeds itself also frees its caretaker.*

Embedded intelligence with TinyML

Early IoT systems behaved like eyes without judgment, sending raw data to distant servers for interpretation. This design worked but created latency, bandwidth strain, and reliance on constant connectivity. Today, intelligence moves closer to the source. With TinyML, compact machine learning models run directly on microcontrollers, enabling sensors to interpret and act in real time. Within tight memory and energy limits, TinyML turns sensing threads into thinking threads.

Applications of TinyML are as follows:

- **Healthcare**: Neonatal wristbands detect abnormal breathing or heart-rate patterns and alert nurses instantly.
- **Agriculture**: Soil probes classify dryness or nutrient imbalance, triggering irrigation only when needed.
- **Infrastructure**: Bridge and motor sensors detect micro-vibrations that signal fatigue before failure.

These capabilities transform passive observation into active understanding.

The following list outlines the advantages of embedded intelligence:

- **Reduced latency**: Local inference delivers millisecond decisions for safety-critical systems.
- **Lower bandwidth**: Only results are transmitted, minimizing network load.
- **Enhanced privacy**: Sensitive raw data stays local.

- **Energy efficiency**: Edge processing reduces cloud computation and transmission needs.

In Maya's clinic, this shift was transformative. Wristbands no longer waited for cloud validation; they sensed, interpreted, and responded within seconds. On her farm, TinyML-equipped probes distinguished natural drying from drought stress, conserving water and power.

By embedding intelligence within each node, IoT systems evolve from passive messengers to active participants.

As Maya told her students, *A sensor that understands its silence is wiser than one that never stops speaking.*

Bio-integrated and dissolvable sensing

The boundary between machines and materials is fading. The next generation of sensors blends with its environment, designed to sense without leaving scars and to vanish once their purpose is fulfilled. In Maya's field, this shift was transformative. Soil could host sensors that nourished and then dissolved into it. Medical patches on skin are no longer required to be removed; they biodegrade safely after completing their task.

Examples of bio-integrated applications:

- **Healthcare**: Silk-protein patches with magnesium circuits monitor hydration and temperature, then biodegrade harmlessly.
- **Logistics**: Compostable temperature tags verify vaccine integrity and dissolve after delivery.
- **Construction**: Embedded passive sensors in concrete or timber track stress, moisture, and heat flux over decades without maintenance.

These sensors are not installed but grown, printed, or woven into their surroundings, redefining how technology coexists with nature.

The following are the advantages of bio-integrated sensing:

- Eliminates electronic waste at the end of life.
- Minimizes ecological disruption.
- Simplifies deployment in healthcare, agriculture, and conservation.
- Aligns digital systems with natural renewal cycles.

Yet as sensors fade physically, their ethical visibility must grow. Invisible technology requires deliberate transparency; people must know what is sensed, who benefits, and how data is used.

For Maya, this was more than technical progress; it was moral evolution. She reminded her students that invisibility can enable harmony or intrusion. *The gentlest sensors*, she wrote, *are those that listen without leaving a trace, and still ask permission to hear.*

Satellite networks and global coverage

Even as terrestrial networks grow, vast regions of the planet remain beyond reach. Mountains, oceans, deserts, and conflict zones still lack connectivity, and with it, visibility.

This gap is closing through **Low-Earth Orbit** (**LEO**) constellations such as Starlink, OneWeb, and Kuiper, which extend IoT coverage across remote environments. Orbiting between 500 and 2,000 kilometers above Earth, these satellites offer lower latency and higher bandwidth than traditional geostationary systems, enabling real-time sensing and communication on a planetary scale.

Applications of satellite-enabled IoT:

- **Environmental monitoring**: Detecting wildfires and tracking carbon in remote forests.
- **Oceanography**: Measuring pH, temperature, and fisheries across global routes.
- **Humanitarian response**: Coordinating logistics in refugee camps and disaster zones.
- **Agriculture and water systems**: Monitoring irrigation, soil moisture, and flood risk in under connected regions.

These orbital networks complement rather than replace ground systems. Surface gateways aggregate sensor data and transmit summaries to satellites, which relay them to regional or global hubs. The result is continuous connectivity linking even isolated ecosystems to global systems of care.

Advantages of satellite IoT integration:

- Extends coverage to remote and crisis-prone areas.
- Preserves communication when terrestrial links fail.
- Reduces the cost and delay of expanding physical infrastructure.
- Strengthens resilience through redundancy and reach.

In Maya's valley, satellite nodes redefined distance. Remote clinics synchronized patient data in real time, and flood alerts reached villages before the first wave arrived. The same constellations that once guided ships now guided awareness.

As she told her students one evening under the stars, *The sky has always carried our signals. We are only learning to listen again.*

Federated and trust-centric architectures

In her early projects, Maya relied on vendor dashboards that stored data far away. The systems worked, but ownership did not. Information from her clinic and fields flowed outward yet rarely returned.

A new generation of federated and trust-centric architectures restores balance by treating data as a shared community asset, not a commodity.

Core developments shaping this shift:

- **Federated learning**: Devices train local models and share only aggregated insights, preserving privacy and saving bandwidth.
- **Blockchain-based identity**: Devices verify authenticity and enable traceable, auditable exchanges while rewarding communities for data value.
- **WoT**: A W3C framework that connects devices through open web protocols, ensuring interoperability.

Together, these enable digital governance built on trust, transparency, and shared control.

Advantages of trust-centric IoT:

- Protects privacy while enabling collaboration.
- Reduces dependency on proprietary platforms.
- Strengthens resilience through distributed authority.
- Ensures fair value and recognition for data contributors.

At the cooperative clinic, this change was transformative. The regional health network joined global studies without revealing personal data, and farmers shared soil metrics while retaining ownership. The system learned collectively without centralizing power.

As Maya told her students, *When trust becomes part of the design, the loom belongs not to the manufacturer, but to the weavers.*

Quantum and advanced sensing

Some signals remain too faint for today's instruments. The early signs of an earthquake ripple through the Earth's magnetic field before the ground moves. A shift in atmospheric chemistry can hint at a coming storm. Molecular traces in blood can reveal disease long before symptoms appear. These patterns exist, but current sensors often cannot detect them.

The next frontier extends sensing into the quantum domain, where phenomena such as superposition, tunneling, and spin resonance enable measurements once thought impossible, pushing perception to the limits of physics.

Emerging quantum and advanced sensing technologies:

- **Quantum magnetometers**: Detect nanoscale magnetic variations for mapping, navigation, and early earthquake alerts.
- **Quantum gravimeters**: Measure subtle gravitational changes to reveal groundwater levels, cavities, or shifting foundations.
- **Quantum clocks**: Synchronize distributed IoT systems with nanosecond precision, ensuring reliability in energy and communication grids.
- **Advanced biosensors**: Identify molecular or microbial changes in tissues for early disease detection.

These instruments convert quantum behavior into actionable insight, allowing systems to perceive the invisible and connect physical, biological, and environmental change.

Potential applications include:

- **Environmental resilience**: Tracking groundwater, volcanic movement, and atmospheric shifts.
- **Infrastructure safety**: Monitoring bridges, tunnels, and pipelines at atomic precision.
- **Precision healthcare**: Detecting metabolic or infectious changes before clinical onset.
- **Climate modeling**: Capturing ultra-fine environmental data to refine global forecasts.

Though still emerging, these technologies represent the next stage of perception, expanding digital awareness from the visible to the molecular.

To practitioners like Maya, this progress carried a deeper lesson: *The smaller the signal we learn to hear, the greater the care required to listen well.*

The evolving tapestry

When Maya installed her first sensor, she sought only to measure. Years later, she sought to understand. What began as a cluster of devices in soil and on skin had become a living system that sensed, learned, and adapted.

The evolution of IoT is not measured by how many sensors exist, but by how wisely and responsibly they work together. The future depends less on smarter things than on sensitive systems, architectures that respond with purpose, adapt with care, and sustain the worlds they touch.

Across the layers of IoT, a quiet transformation is unfolding:

Transition	From	To
Purpose	Monitoring	Mutual understanding
Design	Efficiency	Empathy

Transition	From	To
Architecture	Centralized clouds	Distributed intelligence
Governance	Ownership by vendors	Stewardship by communities
Impact	Data extraction	Environmental and social regeneration

***Table 2.7**: The evolving IoT design continuum*

These transitions reveal a deeper movement, from networks that act on command to systems that act with awareness. In this next generation, every act of sensing carries ethical and ecological consequences. The line between digital and biological systems continues to blur, forming a shared fabric of perception across planet and machines.

As Maya stood at the edge of her valley, she watched faint lights shimmer across the hills. Each point marked a node, a soil sensor, a clinic monitor, a weather relay, yet together they pulsed like one organism, alive with coordination.

She closed her notebook and reflected: *The weave is learning, and if we continue to weave with care, it may one day learn to care for us.*

Conclusion

The clinic was quiet again. Evening light filtered through the shutters, touching monitors that traced oxygen, heart rate, and temperature. Each hummed softly in its corner. Outside, soil probes blinked as they sent readings through the mesh, while air-quality sensors on the roof adjusted to the fading light. Different origins, different purposes, yet joined in the same attentive weave. To a visitor, it was background noise. To Maya, it was a conversation.

She paused beside the incubator of a newborn whose oxygen levels had once dipped during her early experiments. The same wristband design now transmitted calm, steady signals across hundreds of clinics. What began as a fragile prototype had matured into a trusted companion in care.

Maya exhaled and let the silence settle. It was not absence but awareness. The devices did not demand attention; they listened quietly and continuously.

This, she realized, was the essence of IoT, not a web of devices, but a fabric of attention connecting bodies, fields, and cities. Each sensor was a thread, each signal a reminder that the world reveals itself when we choose to listen.

Yet attention brings responsibility. If sensing is an act of care, every system must ask: *Who owns the signals?; Who benefits from the patterns?; Whose experiences are amplified, and whose are overlooked?*

When sensing becomes surveillance, awareness turns into control. When data becomes extraction, participation becomes exploitation. When devices fail without resilience, trust unravels. A digital weave endures only through the integrity and care with which it is made.

Maya closed her notebook. Her final line read: *The loom has begun to feel, but feeling is not enough. We must design systems that remember, that care, and that endure.*

As she turned off the last monitor, the clinic and the field hummed in quiet synchrony. The network no longer behaved as a static system. It felt alive, aware, and learning, an intelligence not of circuits, but of connection.

Every sensed signal carries the potential for understanding. What IoT senses, the data must interpret.

The next chapter follows these signals as they are shaped into meaning, tracing how awareness becomes knowledge and knowledge becomes care.

Weaver's toolkit

The loom is in place. The threads are alive. What remains is learning how to weave them with care.

In her clinic storeroom, Maya kept a drawer labeled **Fios** (Portuguese for *threads*). It held spare wires, salvaged boards, waterproof casings, and tagged sensors from past deployments. It was not just a toolbox. It was a library of lessons.

This section invites readers to pick up a thread and begin weaving, regardless of background.

Weaver's lexicon

The weaver's lexicon defines key terms and technologies forming the sensory foundation of the Internet of Things. These concepts across sensing, networks, data, and trust link technical details to the broader fabric of awareness in this chapter:

- **Access control and audit trails**: Frameworks that record interactions and restrict permissions based on role or authority.
- **Actuation layer**: The returning path in IoT systems where insights drive physical or digital actions such as alerts, controls, or mechanical responses.
- **Analog-to-digital converter (ADC)**: A circuit that transforms physical signals such as temperature or voltage into digital data for processing.
- **Application layer (TCP/IP layer 5)**: The interface where IoT protocols such as CoAP and MQTT give data meaning and enable interaction with users and applications.
- **Authentication**: Verification that a device or user is legitimate before any data exchange occurs.
- **Bandwidth**: The data transfer capacity of a communication link, affecting energy use and protocol efficiency.
- **Bias in sensing**: Distortion caused by limited training data or device design that excludes certain environments, contexts, or populations.

- **Bio-integrated sensing**: Devices built from biocompatible or biodegradable materials that merge with their surroundings and leave no long-term waste.
- **Blockchain-based identity**: A decentralized record of device provenance and data transactions that ensures traceability and trust.
- **Bluetooth Low Energy (BLE)**: A short-range, low-power communication protocol used in wearables, medical sensors, and mobile accessories.
- **Circular IoT pipeline**: A design framework promoting reuse, repair, and recycling of sensors and electronic components.
- **Cloud and aggregation layer**: Infrastructure for long-term data storage, analytics, visualization, and integration across distributed IoT systems.
- **Constrained Application Protocol (CoAP)**: A lightweight, REST-style protocol for resource-limited devices using UDP with DTLS security.
- **Consent**: Informed agreement from individuals or communities before collecting or using their data.
- **Data governance**: Policies defining ownership, consent, access, and retention of IoT-generated data.
- **Data link layer (TCP/IP layer 2)**: Responsible for local data transmission between nearby nodes using technologies such as ZigBee, LoRaWAN, BLE, or Wi-Fi.
- **Distributed responsiveness**: A design principle where local edge systems and central clouds coordinate to maintain real-time balance and resilience.
- **Edge computing/Edge processing**: Local computation near sensors that filters, interprets, and reacts to data before cloud transmission to reduce latency and preserve privacy.
- **Energy harvesting**: Capturing ambient energy from light, vibration, or heat to power sensors without disposable batteries.
- **Federated learning**: A distributed machine learning approach where devices share model updates instead of raw data, preserving privacy and bandwidth.
- **Internet of Things (IoT)**: A network of interconnected sensors, devices, and systems that perceive, interpret, and act on data from the physical world.
- **Latency**: The time delay between a sensed event and its corresponding response, critical for applications in health and safety.
- **Layered IoT architecture (Five-layer framework)**: A conceptual model organizing IoT into sensing, communication, edge processing, cloud aggregation, and actuation layers that together convert physical signals into meaningful responses.

- **Low-Earth-Orbit (LEO) satellite links**: Satellite constellations providing global IoT connectivity in remote or disaster-affected areas.
- **Long Range Wide Area Network (LoRaWAN)**: A long-range, low-bandwidth wireless protocol suited for agriculture, environment, and smart-city monitoring.
- **Matter**: An interoperability framework that allows smart devices from different manufacturers to communicate seamlessly.
- **Microcontroller (e.g., ESP32)**: A compact processor that manages sensor input, applies local logic, and handles network communication.
- **Modular design**: Hardware designed from replaceable, locally assembled components to extend lifespan and minimize waste.
- **Message Queuing Telemetry Transport (MQTT)**: A lightweight publish–subscribe messaging protocol that aggregates data efficiently from many sensors.
- **Narrowband Internet of Things (NB-IoT) and LTE-M**: Cellular standards optimized for low-power, wide-area IoT connectivity in urban and rural deployments.
- **Network layer (TCP/IP layer 3)**: Responsible for addressing and routing packets across networks using IPv6 or IPv4.
- **OpenThread/Thread**: An IPv6-based, low-power mesh networking protocol connecting smart homes, buildings, and sensors.
- **Participatory design**: A collaborative approach involving users and communities in defining sensing goals, data use, and ethical boundaries.
- **Physical layer (TCP/IP layer 1)**: The medium that carries IoT signals, radio, optical, or wired, and determines range, speed, and reliability.
- **Quantum sensing**: Measurement using quantum phenomena such as entanglement or spin resonance to achieve extreme precision in gravity, chemistry, or health applications.
- **Redundancy**: Intentional overlap of sensors or networks to maintain functionality when individual components fail.
- **Response loop**: The continuous cycle of sensing, interpreting, acting, and learning that enables adaptive system behavior.
- **Responsible innovation**: A practice aligning technological advancement with social, ethical, and environmental well-being.
- **Secure boot and signed firmware**: Security methods that ensure only verified software and firmware run on IoT devices.
- **Sensing layer**: The interface between the physical and digital worlds, where devices capture data such as temperature, pressure, or motion.

- **Silent fault**: A hidden failure where a sensor stops working or misreports without notifying the system.
- **Threshold**: A predefined sensor value that triggers an alert, action, or adjustment.
- **Time-series database**: A specialized database for storing sequential sensor readings used for analysis, forecasting, and trend recognition.
- **Tiny Machine Learning (TinyML)**: Machine learning models optimized for microcontrollers to perform on-device inference and anomaly detection.
- **Transparency**: Open disclosure of what is sensed, how data is processed, and the reasons behind its collection.
- **Trust by design**: The principle that security and privacy are embedded from the beginning of design, not added later.
- **Web of Things (WoT)**: A W3C framework that makes IoT devices accessible and interoperable through familiar web technologies.
- **Weaver's ethic**: The belief that technology must listen before it acts and serve before it controls.
- **Zero-power IoT**: Systems designed to operate autonomously on harvested or recycled energy, minimizing ecological and maintenance costs.
- **ZigBee/Z-Wave**: Short-range, mesh-capable wireless protocols offering resilience and low power consumption for home and campus networks.

Weaver's workshop

The weaver's workshop translates the concepts of this chapter into practice. It presents exercises and design scenarios that help readers apply IoT principles of sensing, connectivity, data processing, and resilience to build functional, trustworthy systems:

1. **Sense your space**: Use your smartphone to explore the difference between sensing and understanding. Over a twenty-four-hour period, record how digital sensors capture fragments of your environment and how meaning emerges only through context.

   Prompts:

   - *Use a mobile app such as Arduino Science Journal or Google Fit to record at least four signals (light, sound, temperature, motion, heart rate).*
   - *For each reading, note where you are and what you are doing.*
   - *Import the data into a spreadsheet, plot variations, and annotate patterns and anomalies.*
   - *Reflect: Which moments of change correspond to meaningful events and which are just noise?*

Learning objectives: Recognize that data alone does not equal understanding. Learn how context transforms raw signals into knowledge.

2. **Mapping the layers of attention**: Model how the five layers of IoT, sensing, communication, edge processing, cloud, and actuation, work together in a familiar environment such as a clinic, greenhouse, or classroom.

   Prompts:

   - *Identify all sensors and actuators present or needed.*
   - *Trace how data travels through the communication, edge, and cloud layers.*
   - *Indicate where decisions are made and who controls the resulting information.*
   - *Add at least one trust feature for each layer (e.g., encryption, secure update, user consent).*
   - *Deliverable: Draw a labeled diagram showing the complete loop from sensing to response.*

   Learning objectives: Understand the IoT architecture as a layered system of perception and action. Identify how technical and ethical design choices intersect.

3. **Map a local nervous system**: Design an IoT sensing network for a real location, such as a park, clinic, campus, or home, and represent it as a digital nervous system.

   Prompts:

   - *Choose three to five conditions worth monitoring, such as air quality, occupancy, soil moisture, or temperature.*
   - *For each, specify sensor type, communication path, and action triggered.*
   - *Sketch the five layers showing where computation and storage occur.*
   - *Identify one possible failure point and one redundancy strategy.*
   - *Include a simple consent or transparency method, such as signage or* dashboards.

   Learning objectives: Apply systems thinking to map how multiple sensors form an integrated loop of sensing, communication, and response.

4. **Thinking at the edge**: Explore how edge processing changes efficiency and resilience in sensing networks.

   Prompts:

   - *Start with a soil sensor that sends readings every thirty seconds.*
   - *Modify the logic so it transmits only when moisture stays below the threshold for ten minutes and no rainfall is expected.*
   - *Estimate how much bandwidth and power are saved per day.*
   - *Reflect: how do edge decisions affect privacy, speed, and reliability?*

Learning objectives: Quantify the benefits of edge intelligence. Understand how local decision-making improves sustainability and responsiveness.

5. **Ethics of attention**: Investigate the ethical dimensions of sensing in public or shared spaces.

   Prompts:

   - *Select a real or proposed project that tracks pedestrian, traffic, or environmental data.*
   - *Identify who benefits from the collected data and who might face risks.*
   - *Propose safeguards such as anonymization, opt-in consent, and data retention limits.*
   - *Write a one-page position note outlining how to balance usefulness and privacy.*

   Learning objectives: Recognize the moral responsibility of sensing systems. Learn to design IoT deployments that preserve trust and agency.

6. **Research proposal for social good**: Integrate technical, ethical, and contextual learning into a practical proposal for an IoT system that serves a community or environmental goal.

   Prompts:

   - *Define a real-world challenge such as flood warning, elder care, or urban air quality.*
   - *Identify sensors, communication methods, edge processing, and response mechanisms.*
   - *Include privacy, consent, and sustainability measures.*
   - *Present your concept as a short poster or five-slide presentation.*

   Learning objectives: Synthesize the complete IoT design process, from sensing to social impact, and demonstrate responsible innovation for the common good.

Weaver's library

The weaver's library curates key references that deepen the understanding of IoT systems discussed in this chapter. These works span technical design, edge intelligence, ethical frameworks, and sustainability, offering readers a foundation for further study and responsible innovation:

1. *Atzori, L., Iera, A., & Morabito, G. (2010). The Internet of Things: A Survey. Computer Networks, 54(15), 2787–2805.*
2. *IEEE. (2020). Ethically Aligned Design (EAD): A Vision for Prioritizing Human Well-being with Autonomous and Intelligent Systems.*
3. *World Health Organization. (2021). Global Strategy on Digital Health 2020–2025.*
4. *European Commission. (2023). Circular Electronics Initiative: Sustainable Product Policies for IoT and Electronics.*

The toolkit is not an appendix. It is a working surface where design choices are made visible. As Maya told her students, *each device you place is not only a technical element. It is a choice about what the world will hear, and how it should respond.*

Metaphorical and conceptual terms

The section explains the key metaphors that frame this chapter's ideas. These metaphors, drawn from weaving and sensing, translate complex technical systems into intuitive patterns of understanding, linking threads, fabrics, and attention to the architecture of the IoT:

- **Attention**: The quality of perception in IoT systems. True attention arises when design aligns sensing with intention, noticing the right signals at the right time for the right reason.
- **Blueprint of the weave**: The data architecture that underlies sensing systems. It defines relationships among signals, decisions, and responses, a transition from sensing to understanding that leads into the next chapter on data.
- **Frayed edge**: A weakness or breakdown in the sensing system, a failed device, corrupted link, or ethical gap. Detecting frayed edges early allows designers to repair and reinforce the weave before it unravels.
- **Loom**: The foundational Internet infrastructure, the shared protocols, addressing systems, and networks that form the structural base upon which digital systems are woven. In this chapter, the loom represents the Internet gaining sensory awareness through IoT.
- **Tension**: The balance between performance, complexity, and fragility. In IoT, tension appears where energy, bandwidth, or trust are strained. Healthy tension sustains function; unmanaged tension causes failure.
- **Thread**: A single channel of sensing or communication, such as a sensor signal or data stream. Each thread holds one dimension of awareness and gains meaning through interconnection with others.
- **Sensory thread**: The complete sensing loop, which consists of sensor, transmission, processing, and action. It is the digital equivalent of perception, converting environmental signals into structured understanding.
- **Weave/Fabric**: The integrated IoT ecosystem. Sensors, devices, networks, analytics, and responses together form a dynamic fabric that learns and adapts. The weave represents the interdependence that gives systems resilience.
- **Weaver/Digital weaver**: The human designer, engineer, or policymaker who integrates technology with empathy and precision. A digital weaver builds systems that serve human and ecological well-being, not only efficiency.

CHAPTER 3

Data

The design blueprint

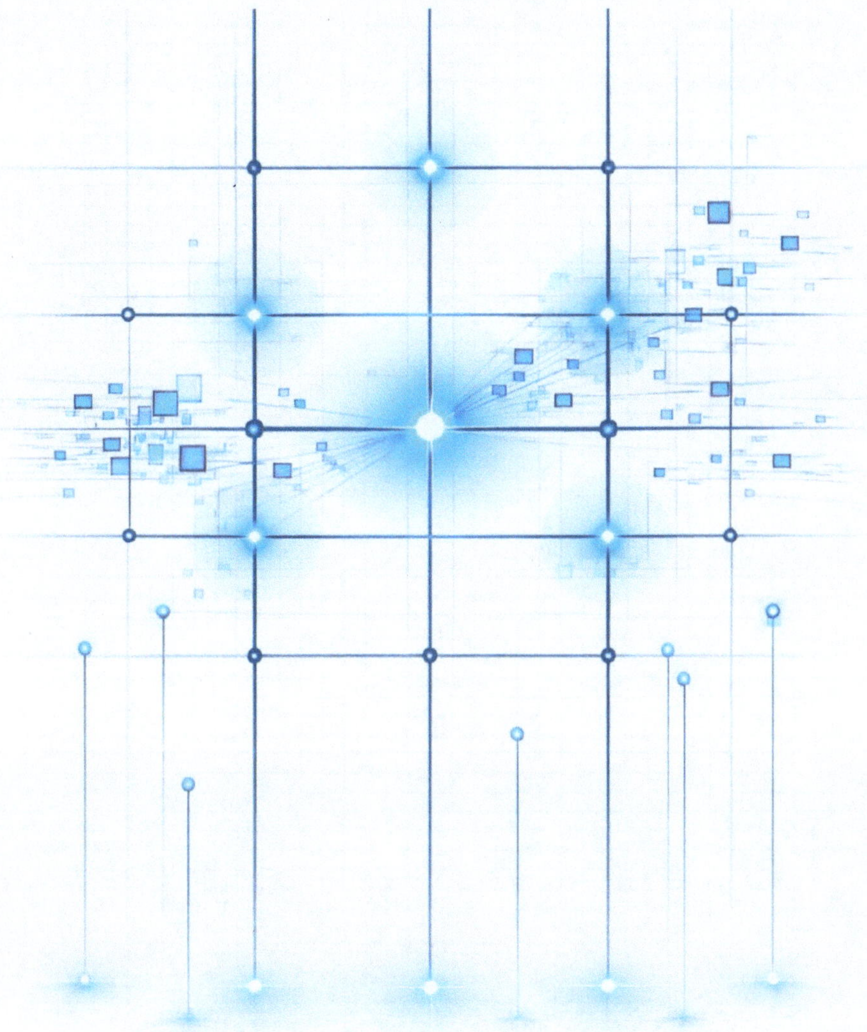

Signals become knowledge when they are arranged into a structure.

Chapter 3
Data

Introduction

Every digital system begins with data, the raw material from which patterns, models, and intelligence emerge. Data records the pulse of the world, from the heartbeat of a patient to the voltage of a grid, from the rhythm of rainfall to the hum of a market. In practical terms, data consists of recorded measurements, observations, and logs that digital systems use to describe conditions, events, and change.

This chapter examines how data becomes design, how it is gathered, shaped, and transformed into knowledge that informs action. It treats data not as static storage but as a blueprint that guides decisions, reflects ethical choices, and connects local realities to global systems.

Like a weaver studying each thread before forming a pattern, responsible designers must understand how data moves, changes, and sometimes fails. This chapter explores the full lifecycle: from collection and classification to analysis, visualization, and responsible use. It also examines what happens when the weave frays due to bias, silos, or strain, and how to design systems that learn, repair, and evolve.

Structure

This chapter covers the following topics:

- The pulse of patterns
- Understanding data
- Data in motion
- Data in action
- Data under strain
- Data in evolution

Objectives

Data is more than a record; it is the blueprint through which systems and humans learn, adapt, and act. Understanding its flow and integrity is essential to designing technologies that endure and serve their purpose. By the end of this chapter, readers will be able to trace how data moves through its lifecycle, from collection and classification to analysis, visualization, and decision-making, and explain how architectural choices shape reliability and meaning. They will learn to apply principles of interoperability, provenance, and efficiency to design resilient, transparent systems. Readers will also recognize how bias, privacy, energy, and governance affect trust and sustainability. Finally, they will envision the evolution of data systems toward autonomy and ethical intelligence, capable of learning and self-repair while remaining aligned with human values and environmental responsibility.

As readers move through this chapter, they will encounter *data as the blueprint*, which introduces the data as both design and record, bridging physical events and digital understanding. They will follow *data in motion*, exploring the data lifecycle, from collection and storage to analysis and transformation into insights. They will then see *data in action*, examining how data operates across edge, fog, and cloud layers to support coordination and learning. In *data under strain*, readers analyze vulnerabilities in data systems, including bias, privacy, energy, and governance. In *data in evolution*, they consider adaptive and decentralized architectures that sustain intelligence and trust over time. Finally, the weaver's toolkit provides vocabulary, exercises, and references for designing data systems that remain coherent, traceable, and capable of trustworthy action.

The pulse of patterns

Dawn spread like ink across the horizon as Aisha stepped barefoot into her sorghum field. The soil, still cool from the night, carried a secret she could not yet see, but her tablet whispered it gently.

Low moisture. High wind. A change was beginning.

The field was no longer silent. Beneath the surface, sensors measured humidity and nutrients; above, satellites tracked wind and temperature. Between earth and orbit, signals flowed in invisible rhythm, a pulse of patterns translating environmental change into measurable form.

Data is information encoded from observations of the world around us, from soil and air to networks and human choices. It enables people and systems to observe, compare, and reason about change across their environments.

Aisha had learned to read these patterns the way her grandmother once read the clouds, not by superstition, but through thousands of careful observations. Two years earlier, her cooperative had nearly collapsed after a failed harvest. The rains came late, the seeds went in too early, and losses rippled through food, income, and health. Some said the land was angry. Aisha knew better. The land was not angry; it was misunderstood.

That season, they had no data, no map, and no pattern to read ahead of time.

Now every decision, when to plant, how much to irrigate, how to rotate crops, was guided by evidence rather than instinct. Her tablet did not offer certainty; it offered an informed choice.

Across every field of human work, healthcare, transport, education, and industry, the same transformation unfolds. Decisions once shaped by intuition now rest on data. Sensors and logs feed platforms; algorithms uncover patterns; visualizations translate them into understanding. The ability to sense is no longer enough. We must interpret, verify, and act.

Data does not solve problems; Aisha told a visiting researcher.

It helps us ask better questions, before the ground answers for us.

Behind her, the clinic's **Internet of Things** (**IoT**) sensors, many installed by Maya, sent quiet updates: infant heart rates, power reserves, medication levels. Across the village, the data threads were beginning to converge. What once existed as scattered readings was becoming a coherent design of care.

Aisha's work was no longer about farming alone. It was about listening to soil, to weather, to signals, and weaving that listening into an adaptive plan her entire community could follow. Each data point carried a consequence. A single misstep could disturb not just a crop but the delicate balance of water, energy, health, and livelihood.

Here, data was not a record to be stored but a responsibility to be shared, a living pattern meant to be sustained, not merely observed.

From loom to life

In every age, humans have sought meaning through patterns, such as stars stitched into constellations, glyphs carved into stone, and footpaths traced across the earth. Today, we weave those patterns differently: in datasets and dashboards, in visualizations glowing with temperature shifts, and in algorithms mapping unseen correlations.

Yet one question remains.
Not just how patterns are formed from data, but why those patterns matter?

When designed with care, data becomes more than numbers.

It becomes **memory**, preserving what has been.
It becomes a **story**, explaining why things change.
It becomes **foresight**, predicting what might come.
It becomes **design**, shaping what we build next.

Data is how we listen to the world. Every heartbeat, rainfall, and soil shift leaves a trace. Data captures those traces, not as final answers, but as signals awaiting understanding.

In this chapter, we will explore how raw signals become structured knowledge. We will examine how we collect, clean, and interpret data; how we identify patterns amid noise; and how these patterns help us design systems that learn, adapt, and endure.

Just as a loom needs a blueprint to weave fabric, technologies need data to weave action and meaning. And that blueprint we draw is not only technical, it is also ethical, ecological, and human.

Data is the design beneath every decision.

Understanding data

The first act of weaving is learning to see the threads.

Aisha sat beneath the neem tree outside her cooperative's meeting hut; her tablet balanced on her knees. Columns of numbers filled the screen: soil pH, rainfall probability, planting dates, and market prices. To an outsider, it looked like a grid of unrelated values. To her, it was a story in motion.

She had learned that every dataset carries a rhythm. A sudden drop in moisture might indicate irrigation failure. A change in protein levels in clinic notes, shared by Maya, could reveal nutritional gaps. Data is not the truth by itself. It is evidence waiting for interpretation. Each figure is a clue about the health of a larger system.

Before any pattern can appear, its elements must be understood. In digital design, data is a recorded representation of events or conditions, structured so that both people and machines can process, compare, and interpret it. A soil reading, a satellite image, a transaction record, or a heartbeat log, each is a datum, a single observation of the world.

The same principle holds at enterprise scale.

Organizations collect millions of observations every second—temperature readings from factories, supply-chain transactions, inventory updates, financial entries, and user interactions. These streams feed into databases, analytic systems, and dashboards that guide decisions. Just as Aisha's cooperative links soil and market data, an enterprise connects production, logistics, sales, and sustainability data into a single blueprint for action.

Whether in a small village or a global corporation, data gains meaning only when it is organized, contextualized, and shared. Understanding this transformation is the foundation of digital design. This section traces how raw signals evolve into structured information, how context turns information into insight, and how sharing closes the loop of understanding.

Tracing the path from signals to story

The world emits signals constantly—rainfall, motion, light, temperature, clicks, and words. Sensors and software capture these signals as data. Yet raw data alone has little meaning. It must be organized, analyzed, and interpreted before it becomes useful.

This transformation follows the **Data, Information, Knowledge, and Wisdom** (DIKW) hierarchy. It applies to farms, hospitals, factories, and global enterprises alike.

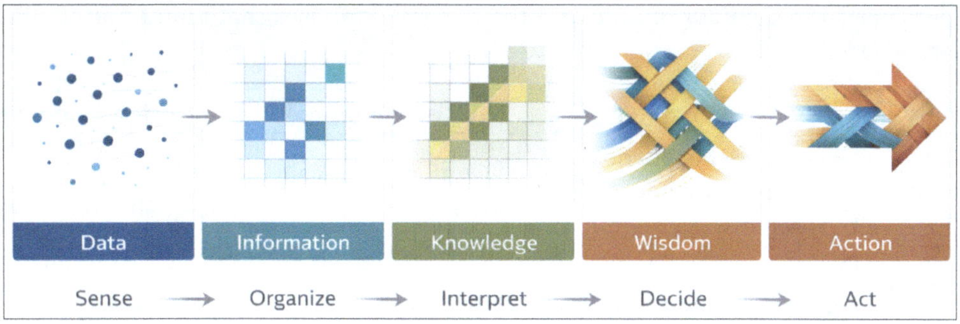

***Figure 3.1**: From signals to wisdom: the DIKW hierarchy*

The following table traces how raw signals evolve through the DIKW stages, linking data, information, knowledge, and wisdom across real contexts such as agriculture and enterprise:

Level	Definition	Agriculture example	Enterprise example
Data	Raw signals or measurements	Soil moisture = 23%, pH = 7.2	Product sold = 123 units
Information	Organized data with context	Moisture = 23% and pH = 7.2 in Plot A on April 12	Product sold = 123 units in Dallas on April 12
Knowledge	Interpreted information leading to understanding	The field will require irrigation tomorrow	Sales in Dallas indicate a demand spike
Wisdom	Judged and acted upon with insight	Schedule irrigation early morning to conserve energy	Adjust the supply chain to restock the Dallas center

***Table 3.1**: From data to wisdom across contexts*

This progression from data to wisdom shows why collection is only the beginning. The DIKW hierarchy is a conceptual model, not a rigid pipeline. In practice, its stages overlap and feed back into one another through continuous learning and action.

Without context, data is silent. Without action, it is incomplete. The DIKW hierarchy reminds us that the true value of data, whether from a single sensor or a global enterprise system, lies not in its volume but in how it improves understanding and decisions.

At every scale of the digital weave, data is the blueprint that connects sensing, understanding, and action.

Recognizing what makes data unique

Data possesses properties unlike any physical material. Threads wear out, and circuits corrode, but once digitized, data can be copied indefinitely. This durability introduces fragility of another kind, and the context can fade, meaning can distort, and bias can appear unnoticed.

Key properties that make data unique and the design responses that maintain reliability are detailed in *Table 3.2*:

Property	Description	Risk if ignored	Design response
Abstraction	Data represents phenomena, not the phenomena themselves.	Confusing model with reality	Combine quantitative and qualitative data.
Relationality	Data gains value through comparison and connection.	Isolated datasets lose value	Integrate through common identifiers.
Layering	Data exists at multiple levels of processing.	Overfitting or redundancy	Maintain a clear schema and documentation.
Temporality	Meaning changes with time and context.	Outdated insights	Timestamp and version every record.
Fragility	Data can be incomplete, biased, or corrupted.	Distorted decisions	Apply validation and audit procedures.

***Table 3.2**: Properties of data and corresponding design safeguards*

Aisha encountered these principles often. When her team compared soil readings without synchronized timestamps, patterns appeared chaotic. Once aligned by date, the meaning became clear. Data quality depends less on numerical precision and more on alignment and governance.

The same rules apply to large enterprises where consistency across regions, versions, and formats determines the reliability of dashboards and decisions.

Seeing data as the blueprint

In earlier chapters, the Internet served as the loom that connects, and IoT as the threads that sense and respond. In this chapter, data becomes the blueprint through which both humans and machines understand the world and decide how to act.

Every dataset expresses a model of reality. Its structure, including columns, relationships, and constraints, defines what can be known, compared, and improved.

Data as a blueprint is not a static drawing but a design for cognition and coordination.

- A **soil database** outlines how crops relate to water and season, guiding irrigation.
- A **hospital schema** maps patient data to diagnosis and treatment pathways.
- An **enterprise model** links transactions to supply and demand, aligning production and delivery.

Each dataset represents a bounded unit of information about a system or environment. For example, soil moisture readings, weather records, and crop yield data describe different aspects of agricultural conditions. When these datasets are connected through shared identifiers such as location and time, they reveal relationships that analysis can use to anticipate outcomes and guide action, including irrigation or planting adjustments. In this way, analysis links observation to response through a continuous feedback cycle.

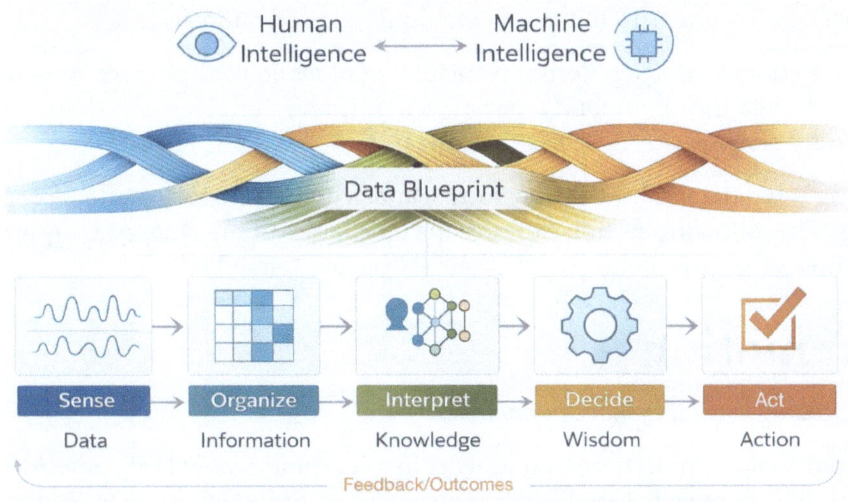

***Figure 3.2**: Data as the blueprint for understanding and action*

Without a coherent design, even abundant data fragments into noise. Structure is what transforms records into knowledge.

Aisha often reminded her team:

Our data does not just describe the land; it teaches us how to care for it.

Through this awareness, the act of data design becomes an act of understanding, a deliberate architecture for intelligent and responsible action.

Crossing the threshold to insight

In *Chapter 2, The Internet of Things,* we explored how IoT systems sense the physical world. This chapter begins where sensing ends, at the threshold where signals become meaning. Every temperature probe, heart monitor, or drone camera produces a stream of values. The challenge is to translate these values into trustworthy insight.

Three guiding questions shape this translation:

1. *What do we measure?* Determines visibility. Missing measurements hide critical variables.
2. *How do we interpret it?* Defines accuracy. The same signal can imply different causes depending on context.

3. *Who decides what matters?* Establishes power. Data selection determines whose needs the system serves.

Aisha discovered that an omitted variable can mislead as much as a faulty sensor. When early datasets lacked altitude information, her cooperative's model underestimated evaporation on hillside farms. Adding one field to the schema doubled prediction accuracy.

This experience confirmed a key design principle: *what we do not collect can be as consequential as what we do.* In healthcare, mobility, or finance, missing variables can shape outcomes as strongly as faulty sensors.

Understanding what data is, how it transforms, and why its structure matters prepares us for the next stage. The following section explores the mechanics of the blueprint, the architectures, models, and flows that give data systems their shape and reliability.

Data in motion

Threads find meaning when they move in rhythm.

Aisha once said that learning to read data was like learning a new language. At first, it was noise, columns of numbers that spoke in fragments. Over time, she began to recognize rhythm and order. Patterns formed, decisions followed, and consequences became measurable.

Data moves through a lifecycle that shapes its accuracy, reliability, and purpose. Understanding that flow is essential to designing any digital system. It reveals how information gains meaning, how patterns guide action, and how systems learn from experience.

This section explores that journey step by step, how signals become structure, how structure becomes insight, and how insight guides actions.

The data lifecycle:

- **Collection**: Capturing signals from devices, logs, or human inputs.
- **Transmission**: Moving data from the source to a repository.
- **Storage**: Preserving it in a database, data lake, or cloud system.
- **Processing**: Cleaning, normalizing, and organizing for analysis.
- **Analysis**: Finding relationships and generating predictions.
- **Visualization**: Translating insights into human-readable form.
- **Action and feedback**: Applying results and feeding new data into the loop.

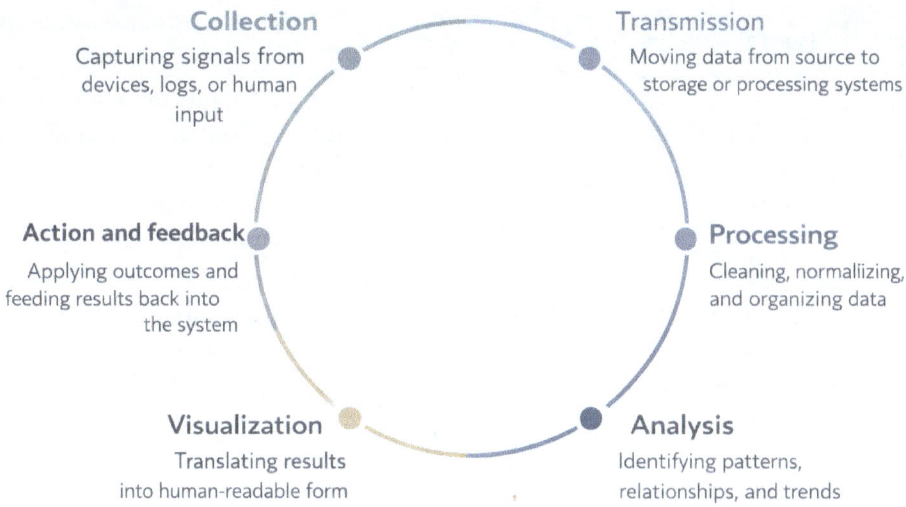

Figure 3.3: *A typical data lifecycle*

Each step builds upon the previous one, but the lifecycle is not a linear pipeline. It operates as a continuous loop that refines system awareness and supports ongoing learning from environmental change.

Once data is in motion, the first task is to capture it.

Collecting data

Every dataset begins with a moment of sensing or recording.

A soil probe measures moisture, a **customer relationship management** (**CRM**) logs a transaction, and a web service tracks user interactions.

Each event marks the instant when the physical or digital world becomes information.

Data collection is the process of capturing, recording, and contextualizing these events for later analysis. It defines what will be visible and what will remain unseen. The precision of every future insight depends on the discipline applied at this first step.

Collection pathways

Modern systems collect data along two intertwined pathways, as shown in *Table 3.3*. This comparison highlights how operational and enterprise data pipelines differ in sources and integration mechanisms:

Pathway	Typical sources	Mechanisms	Core transport and integration technologies
Operational data pipeline	Sensors, devices, gateways, control systems	Continuous telemetry	**Message Queue Telemetry Transport** (MQTT), **Constrained Application Protocol** (CoAP), Kafka, **Open Platform Communications Unified Architecture** (OPC-UA)
Enterprise data pipeline	Business applications, transactions, and digital services.	Batch extraction or API integration from systems of record.	**Extract, transform, and load** (ETL), **change data capture** (CDC), **application programming interfaces** (APIs), and event buses

Table 3.3: Data pipelines across operational and enterprise systems

Operational pipeline

The operational pathway connects physical systems through hierarchical layers:

- **Edge layer**: IoT sensors and embedded devices collect physical readings, often on limited power budgets.
- **Network layer**: Gateways and routers aggregate data and relay it via secure APIs or message brokers.
- **Cloud or enterprise layer**: Central platforms store data in databases, lakes, or streams for analytics and coordination.

Aisha's cooperative used a hybrid model. Solar-powered gateways collected hourly sensor data through **Long Range Wide Area Network** (LoRaWAN) and synchronized it daily with the cloud. This design conserved bandwidth while maintaining situational awareness.

Enterprise pipeline

The enterprise pathway gathers digital events from business applications and workflows:

- **Application logs**: Web and mobile platforms instrument every click, query, and transaction.
- **Business systems**: **Enterprise resource planning** (ERP), CRM, and **supply chain management** (SCM) platforms export structured data through APIs.
- **Integration middleware**: **Enterprise service buses** (ESBs) and data integration tools orchestrate data exchange.
- **Cloud services**: **Software as a service** (SaaS) platforms stream operational events through webhooks or analytics connectors.

A manufacturer, for instance, might stream order data from ERP into a data warehouse while synchronizing sensor telemetry from its factories.

Together, these flows create a unified operational view.

Design considerations

Designing an effective collection system, whether in an agricultural field or a financial platform, requires intentionality and restraint. The details are as follows:

- **Define purpose before capture**: Collect only what supports a clear analytical or operational goal. Collecting without purpose creates clutter, cost, and compliance risk.
- **Preserve context**: Record when, where, and how data was captured, including metadata that explains the conditions and meaning of the data.
- **Ensure consistency**: Apply common data dictionaries and unit conventions.
- **Automate governance**. Integrate validation, access control, and lineage tracking from the start.
- **Protect privacy and ethics**: Follow principles of consent, minimization, and relevant standards, such as **General Data Protection Regulation** (**GDPR**), **Health Insurance Portability and Accountability Act** (**HIPAA**), and ISO 27001.

Every byte collected carries not only computational cost but also energy, legal, and ethical weight. Responsible collection balances completeness with necessity.

Data provenance

Provenance completes the design of the collection. It records the origin, context, and transformation of each dataset, linking every value to the device, process, or person that produced it. This chain of custody documents when data was captured, how it was modified, and where it is stored, supporting reproducibility, accountability, and trust.

In Aisha's cooperative, each soil reading carried metadata about its sensor ID, calibration date, and transmission path. When anomalies appeared, engineers could trace errors to their source instead of discarding the record. Provenance turned uncertainty into understanding, enabling transparency and recovery.

It is not only a technical safeguard but an ethical foundation.

It ensures that every thread in the digital weave can be traced back to its origin.

Once data is collected and its lineage secured, the next challenge is to shape it, organizing raw signals into structured forms that can speak clearly and guide design.

Classifying data

Once collected, data must be shaped before it can inform.

Unprocessed signals resemble loose threads, and they exist, but without structure, they cannot hold a pattern. Classification transforms these threads into organized strands that can be stored, compared, and woven into meaning.

Aisha often described this step as *teaching the data to speak clearly*. When her cooperative first automated soil monitoring, the sensors, field notes, and satellite images produced values in different units and formats. Some data arrived as numbers, others as text or images. Classifying and standardizing these inputs became the first act of design.

Understanding data types

Every digital system handles a spectrum of data types.

Each type carries its own format, precision, and suitable tools as shown in the following table:

Type	Description	Example	Common format
Numerical (quantitative)	Measured values, continuous or discrete	Temperature = 28.6 °C	**Comma-separated values** (**CSV**), **Structured Query Language** (**SQL**)
Categorical (qualitative)	Labeled groups or classes	Soil type = Loamy	CSV, **JavaScript Object Notation** (**JSON**)
Textual	Written or spoken words	Farmer notes in Hausa	JSON, TXT
Geospatial/ visual	Coordinates, maps, images	Drone photograph of the field	**Geographic JavaScript Object Notation** (**GeoJSON**), **Tagged Image File Format** (**TIFF**)
Time-series	Values over time intervals	Hourly moisture readings	InfluxDB, Parquet

Table 3.4: Common data types and their representations

In modern systems, data is multimodal, combining structured tables, unstructured text, and streaming telemetry. Designing for multimodality ensures adaptability as systems evolve.

Mapping data to storage architectures

Each type also maps to specific storage architectures:

- **Structured data** fits neatly into relational databases like PostgreSQL or MySQL.
- **Semi-structured data** uses flexible schemas such as JSON in NoSQL systems like MongoDB.

- **Unstructured data**, video, images, or audio requires object storage in data lakes.
- **Time-series data** benefits from specialized databases such as InfluxDB or TimescaleDB, which are optimized for time-series queries.

Aisha's cooperative seamlessly combined these architectures. Sensor values were stored in a time-series database for quick trend analysis, field notes in a document store for context, and satellite imagery in a geospatial index for spatial insight. Together, these streams formed a coherent information fabric that supported timely, confident decisions.

Once classified and structured, data must next be understood by its origin. Knowing where each value begins gives it credibility, traceability, and context, the foundation for trustworthy design.

Identifying data sources

Every dataset carries a story.

Before values can be analyzed or models trained, we must understand where those values begin. The origin of data defines its reliability, context, and interpretation.

Aisha discovered this after a flood swept through her fields. Sensor readings still showed normal moisture levels even though the soil was submerged. It was the farmers' handwritten notes that revealed the truth; the water current had displaced the probes. Institutional rainfall records later confirmed the anomaly.

That single discrepancy reminded her that sensors, people, and institutions each observe the world from different vantage points. No single perspective captures the whole picture, but together they can form a coherent and trustworthy map of reality.

The following list outlines the key categories of data sources:

- **Sensor data**: Continuous measurements from IoT devices such as soil probes, power meters, or air-quality monitors.
- **Transactional data**: Logs of operations, purchases, machine events, or digital interactions.
- **Social and web data**: Digital expressions of collective sentiment such as posts, reviews, and search trends.
- **Public and open data**: Shared repositories including NASA EarthData, **World Health Organization** (**WHO**) health statistics, or national meteorological records.
- **Enterprise systems**: Internal data from CRM, ERP, and supply-chain applications.
- **Human input**: Observations, surveys, and notes that provide cultural or contextual depth.
- **Derived data**: Outputs generated by simulations or machine learning models based on primary sources.

Each category differs in frequency, reliability, and ownership. Understanding these dimensions helps determine how different sources complement or correct one another. The most reliable systems are hybrids, blending the precision of machines with the interpretation of humans.

Weaving human, machine, and institutional threads

Aisha's cooperative embodied this hybrid design. Sensors collected quantitative signals, farmers contributed qualitative context, and institutional systems provided validated satellite rainfall data. When integrated, these threads corrected one another; sensors measured what happened, farmers explained why, and institutional datasets confirmed how far the effects reached.

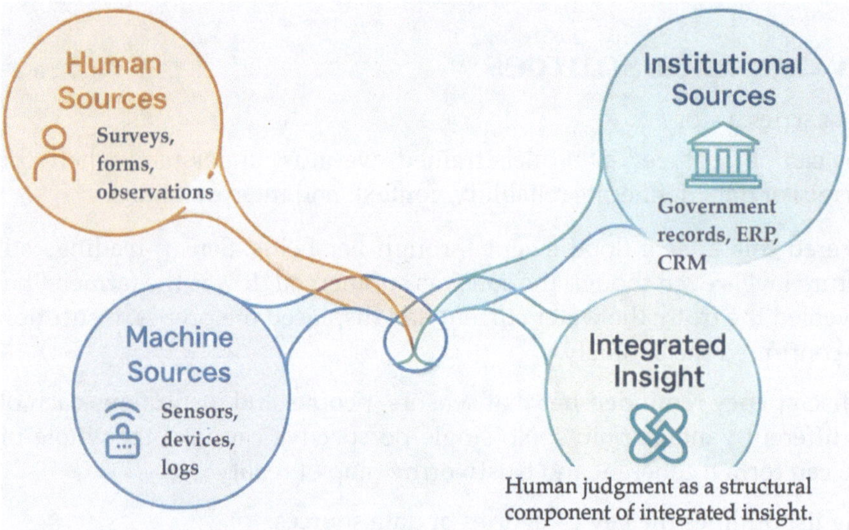

***Figure 3.4**: Human judgment meets sensor networks and organizational systems*

This interplay transformed raw inputs into shared understanding. Human insight gave meaning, machines provided precision, and institutions ensured authenticity and continuity. When woven thoughtfully, these threads form a living fabric of data, one that balances local knowledge with global coordination and keeps digital systems grounded in the realities they represent.

Once data sources are identified and harmonized, the next challenge is to understand their behavior that defines the data system's complexity.

Understanding the five dimensions of data

As data scales, quantity alone no longer defines complexity. Its behavior depends on several interrelated dimensions that determine how it must be stored, processed, and understood. These are often known as the **five Vs.**: **volume**, **velocity**, **variety**, **veracity**, and **value**. The five dimensions of data behavior introduce both opportunity and risk. These are described in the following table:

Dimension	Meaning	Example	Risk if ignored
Volume	The quantity of data generated	10 GB/day from sensors	Storage overload, cost
Velocity	Speed of arrival	1 record/second	Inability to process real-time events
Variety	Diversity of formats and sources	Images, text, telemetry	Incompatibility, data silos
Veracity	Accuracy and reliability	Sensor calibration errors	False conclusions
Value	Relevance to purpose	Unused logs	Wasted resources

***Table 3.5**: The five dimensions of data and associated risks*

Some practitioners add a sixth *V*, **Variability**, to describe fluctuations in data flow. Managing these dimensions requires scalable and adaptable infrastructure such as data lakes to handle volume and variety, streaming platforms to manage velocity, and validation pipelines to preserve veracity.

Aisha's team observed that their sensors produced more data during the rainy season. They dynamically adjusted their transmission rate to manage bandwidth, demonstrating variability in practice. Through this process, they discovered a deeper lesson that value mattered most. Data that guided decisions was far more meaningful than data that merely accumulated.

In any system, the five Vs. remind us that scale is not just a matter of size, but of balance, the art of designing data to remain both rich in information and efficient in purpose.

Understanding these dimensions prepares designers for the next phase—refining data so it can be trusted. From raw readings to reliable records, cleaning and preparation shape the integrity of every insight.

Preparing, cleaning, and storing data

Raw data, like raw fiber, must be refined before it can form a pattern. Collected data is rarely ready for analysis. It often contains gaps, duplicates, or inconsistent units. Data preparation transforms raw inputs into structured knowledge that systems can trust and humans can interpret.

When Aisha's cooperative first gathered soil readings, identical sensors in nearby plots produced widely differing values. Some were mis-calibrated; others reported in inches instead of centimeters. The team realized that precision depends less on collecting more data than on carefully preparing it.

From raw signal to reliable form

The standard process for transforming data is called **extract, transform, load** (**ETL**), where:

1. **Extract** data from sources such as sensors, APIs, or logs.
2. **Transform** it by cleaning, standardizing, and reconciling inconsistencies.
3. **Load** it into a database or analytical platform for use.

During transformation, several key operations ensure consistency and reliability:

- **Type conversion**: Store numbers, dates, and categories in correct formats.
- **Standardization**: Align units, such as °F to °C or acres to hectares.
- **Deduplication**: Remove repeated or overlapping records.
- **Handling missing values**: Use interpolation, substitution, or flagging.
- **Validation**: Check that values fall within expected ranges.

Automation tools such as Pandas, Apache Airflow, and AWS Glue can assist in these steps.

Yet automation does not replace judgment; it amplifies it.

Over-cleaning may erase valuable anomalies, while under-cleaning leaves noise that can mislead models.

Good preparation balances efficiency with care.

Data storage models

Clean data still needs a home suited to its nature.

Effective storage is memory with intent. It allows the system to grow without forgetting. Each properly structured and documented record adds to an evolving fabric of understanding.

Different databases serve different purposes and vary in how they balance structure, flexibility, and performance. Combining them often achieves the best balance between performance and flexibility. The following table summarizes various database architectures:

Database type	Strength	Limitation	Example use
Relational (SQL)	Structured, consistent, ideal for queries	Rigid schema	Transaction logs, ledgers
Document store (NoSQL)	Flexible, unstructured	Weak relationships	Field reports, sensor metadata
Time-series database	Optimized for sequential data	Less suited for complex joins	Sensor telemetry, log analytics
Object storage/ data lake	Scalable for large unstructured data	Slower querying	Images, video, archival data

Table 3.6: Comparing data storage models for balanced design

Aisha's cooperative combined all four. Sensor readings flowed into a time-series database for real-time analysis. Field notes were stored in a document store for contextual richness. Summaries were preserved in SQL tables for reporting. Satellite imagery lived in the cloud as archived objects. This layered architecture kept their system both agile and accountable; scalable in volume yet transparent in lineage.

Preparation as stewardship

Preparing data is more than technical hygiene; it is stewardship. Documented transformations support transparency, reproducibility, and traceability when errors occur, because data preparation can amplify or suppress patterns, it directly shapes the accuracy and ethical impact of downstream decisions.

Aisha's cooperative came to see cleaning as a form of care; a process of aligning measurements, correcting inconsistencies, and preserving meaningful variation within the data through validation checks, range testing, schema alignment, and provenance tracking.

In every domain, from agriculture to industry, the quality of insight depends on the discipline of preparation and the ethics of maintenance.

Once data is cleaned and stored with integrity, its usefulness depends on how well it can interact with other systems. The next step in design is interoperability, ensuring that data can travel, translate, and collaborate across boundaries.

Enabling interoperability and standards

No matter how accurate a dataset is, it loses value if it cannot interact with others.

Interoperability ensures that systems can exchange, interpret, and reuse data consistently across platforms, organizations, and time.

Shared standards make this possible by providing a common language for data. They also reduce long-term system strain by preventing silos, easing governance, and supporting reuse across time and institutions.

They define how information moves, how it is described, and how meaning is preserved along the way.

Common standards include:

- **Formats**: CSV, JSON, **Extensible Markup Language** (**XML**) for general data; GeoJSON for spatial data.
- **Protocols**: REST and GraphQL APIs for application access; CoAP, MQTT, and OPC-UA for sensor and machine communication.
- **Ontologies**: Schema.org or **World Wide Web Consortium** (**W3C**) **Semantic Sensor Network** (**SSN**) for shared meaning.

- **Principles: Findable, Accessible, Interoperable, Reusable (FAIR).**

Aisha's co-op adopted open formats to collaborate with government climate services. This decision transformed isolated measurements into part of a regional dataset. Shared structure enabled rainfall readings, soil data, and satellite imagery to be combined seamlessly, supporting larger weather prediction and resource planning models.

When data adhere to shared standards, knowledge can scale, from field to nation, from sensor to system. Interoperability enables digital fabrics to expand without tearing, weaving diverse sources into a coherent and trustworthy whole.

Once systems can communicate fluently, the next step is to interpret the data they share. Analysis turns connectivity into comprehension, translating structure into meaning.

Analyzing data for meaning

Data becomes valuable only when it teaches something about the world.

Data analysis is the process of converting structure into insight, turning raw records into evidence and evidence into understanding. It is both computation and interpretation, the act of seeing structure in streams of numbers.

Aisha once described it as *listening for rhythm in the noise.*

When her cooperative began analyzing soil data across seasons, they noticed cycles that mirrored rainfall and crop rotation. What once appeared as columns of figures became stories of growth, stress, and recovery.

Analysis, they realized, is not only about precision, but about perception.

Levels of analysis

Every system progresses through a hierarchy of analytical depth. Each level answers a different question, demanding greater context and responsibility.

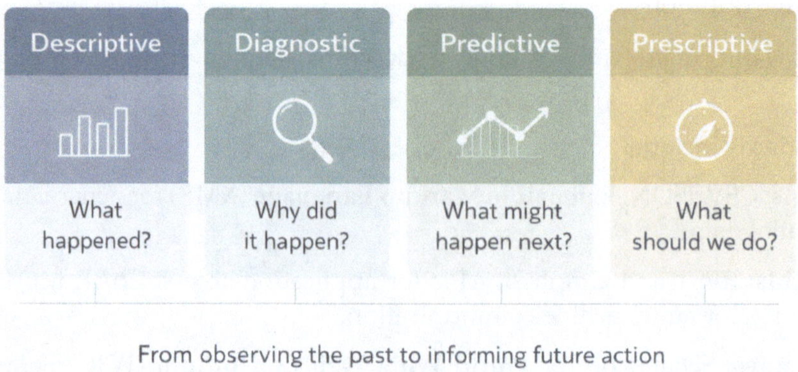

***Figure 3.5:** The analytics continuum*

Table 3.7 maps analytical levels from descriptive to prescriptive, linking each to its guiding question and purpose:

Level	Key question	Primary goal	Example context
Descriptive	*What happened?*	Summarize and visualize facts	Soil moisture dropped below normal; sales increased 10%.
Diagnostic	*Why did it happen?*	Identify causes and correlations	Rainfall declined; demand rose during the holidays.
Predictive	*What might happen next?*	Forecast or classify future outcomes	Crop yield expected to fall; the machine may fail soon.
Prescriptive	*What should we do?*	Recommend or automate actions	Adjust irrigation; reschedule maintenance.

***Table 3.7**: Levels of data analysis and their intent*

These analytical levels represent different design intentions, not stages every system must reach. Many systems operate effectively at one or two levels without progressing through the entire continuum. Each level deepens interpretation. Descriptive analysis tells what occurred, diagnostic analysis explains why, predictive analysis anticipates what may come, and prescriptive analysis guides what should happen next. Together, they form a continuum from observation to action.

Dimensions of analysis

Patterns emerge not only over time, but also across space, relationships, interactions, and categories.

Common analytical dimensions include:

- **Temporal analysis**: Tracks changes over time, hours, days, seasons, or years.
- **Spatial analysis**: Maps variations across geography using coordinates or satellite imagery.
- **Relational analysis**: Explores influence among entities such as users, suppliers, or ecosystems.
- **Categorical analysis**: Groups attributes such as soil type, customer segment, or patient risk.
- **Text and sentiment analysis**: Extract meaning from language, social media, or reports.
- **Multimodal analysis**: It integrates several of these dimensions at once, for example, combining climate, economic, and health data to study regional resilience.

Aisha's cooperative used all of these. Satellite imagery mapped flood boundaries, sensor time-series tracked soil patterns, and farmer notes captured local knowledge. Combined, they created a multidimensional portrait of the land, revealing not only what changed but why.

Analytical and learning models

Different analytical tasks call for different forms of reasoning.
Some describe, others infer, forecast, or optimize.
Each model represents a way of turning data into evidence.

Representative model families and their domain applications are presented in *Table 3.8*:

Category	Purpose	Common models or methods	Example use
Descriptive and exploratory	Summarize and visualize data distributions.	Descriptive statistics, histograms, **principal component analysis** (**PCA**), clustering (K-means, **density-based spatial clustering of applications with noise** (**DBSCAN**))	Identify field types, customer segments, or operational patterns.
Diagnostic and causal	Explain relationships and influences.	Linear and logistic regression, correlation analysis, decision trees, Bayesian inference	Assess rainfall–yield correlation or equipment failure causes.
Predictive	Forecast or classify future outcomes.	Time-series models (**Autoregressive Integrated Moving Average** (**ARIMA**)), Random Forest, Neural networks, **long short-term memory** (**LSTM**), **convolutional neural network** (**CNN**), Transformer)	Forecast demand, predict crop health or energy usage.
Prescriptive and optimization	Recommend next actions.	Reinforcement learning, constraint optimization, linear programming	Optimize irrigation, logistics, or resource allocation.
Anomaly and quality control	Detect irregular or abnormal patterns.	Isolation Forest, control charts	Identify faulty sensors, fraud, or outliers in transactions.

***Table 3.8**: Spectrum of data analysis and representative techniques*

These models span the analytical spectrum, from statistics to adaptive learning. The goal is not to master every algorithm but to understand their roles in translating data into actionable insights.

No single model fits every problem; effective design begins with the question, not the algorithm.

Layers of analytics

In distributed systems, analysis occurs at multiple layers, each serving a unique balance of speed, scope, and privacy:

- **Edge analytics** executes directly on devices or gateways, allowing fast local decisions.
- **Fog analytics** aggregates regional insights before sending summaries to the upper levels.
- **Cloud analytics** performs large-scale model training, global coordination, and archival storage.
- **Federated or collaborative learning** enables distributed models to learn from multiple sites without centralizing sensitive data.

Aisha's network followed this structure: soil sensors predicted irrigation locally; fog nodes summarized regional patterns; cloud analytics refined long-term models.

Each layer learned from the others, keeping intelligence distributed yet coherent.

Model lifecycle and governance

Models evolve as the world changes.
To remain reliable and ethical, they must be governed and continuously renewed.
A typical lifecycle follows five stages: Train | Validate | Deploy | Monitor | Retrain.

Key governance practices include:

- **Validation**: Measuring accuracy before deployment.
- **Monitoring**: Tracking performance and detecting drift.
- **Explainability**: Ensuring results can be understood.
- **Traceability**: Recording versions, data sources, and parameters.
- **Retraining**: Updating models as new data arrives.

When rainfall patterns shifted, Aisha's team retrained their models each season, restoring accuracy and preventing false predictions. Every update was documented and reviewed, turning adaptation into habit, not crisis.

Meaning beyond metrics

Analysis is not the end of the lifecycle; it is the midpoint between knowledge and action. Numbers alone do not ensure wisdom. Understanding emerges when systems and people interpret data together, testing what algorithms predict against what experience knows.

In Aisha's cooperative, analysis did not replace farmers' judgment; it deepened it. Dashboards became spaces for dialogue, not for issuing commands. Through this exchange, the community learned that insight is not only computational but also communal, an evolving conversation among evidence, interpretation, and care.

Once meaning is uncovered, the next challenge is perception. Visualization gives form to understanding, allowing both humans and machines to see the pattern in data.

Seeing the patterns

Numbers alone rarely inspire understanding.

For meaning to travel between people and systems, data must be seen.

Visualization transforms abstraction into perception, making relationships, trends, and anomalies visible at a glance.

When Aisha's cooperative first installed soil sensors, their dashboards displayed endless columns of numbers, accurate but unreadable. Once the team replaced them with color-coded charts, the story became clear—green for stable soil, amber for risk, red for immediate action. Each color condensed hundreds of readings into a moment of clarity.

Visualization is not decoration; it is cognition. It turns data from a static record into a shared frame for interpreting evidence and guiding decisions. Different visual forms support different kinds of understanding.

Three principles guide visualization that truly communicates:

1. **Simplify without distortion**: Every mark should serve understanding.
2. **Highlight change**: Motion and comparison reveal cause and consequence.
3. **Connect to the decision**: A visualization earns purpose when it guides action.

In Aisha's cooperative, every graph is linked directly to action thresholds, irrigation, alerts, and maintenance schedules. The dashboard became an interface between sensing and doing, translating complexity into care.

Analytical perspectives

Different types of visualizations reveal different kinds of structure. Each analytical view highlights a unique relationship between variables, time, or space. Selecting the right view determines what the system and its users can see. *Table 3.9* summarizes visualization techniques aligned with analytical perspectives and decision contexts:

Analytical view	Purpose	Common techniques	Example
Descriptive summaries	Show distributions and proportions.	Bar charts, histograms, and pie charts	Crop yield by field, revenue by region
Temporal trends	Reveal change over time.	Time-series plots, control charts, and moving averages	Soil moisture variation, production throughput

Analytical view	Purpose	Common techniques	Example
Spatial relationships	Map data to location.	Heatmaps, choropleth maps, and GPS overlays	Field moisture map, delivery route efficiency
Correlation and causality	Identify relationships among variables.	Scatter plots, regression lines, and correlation matrices	Rainfall vs. yield, price vs. demand
Anomaly detection	Expose outliers or unusual behavior.	Control charts, z-score thresholds, box plots	Faulty sensors, fraud in transactions
Predictive modeling	Estimate future outcomes.	Decision trees, trend projections, and regression analysis	Forecasting yield, predicting maintenance needs
Exploratory and scenario analysis	Test what if conditions.	Simulation dashboards, sliders, and interactive filters	Adjusting planting schedules, varying prices, or energy inputs

***Table 3.9**: Analytical perspectives for visualizing and interpreting data*

Patterns emerge only when raw measurements are viewed through different analytical lenses. Each perspective reveals a unique structure in the information and guides a different type of decision. The details are as follows:

- **Descriptive summaries** show the shape of the data at a glance through distributions and proportions.
- **Temporal trends** highlight how values change over hours, seasons, or years, revealing cycles and drift.
- **Spatial relationships** map variation across locations to uncover local clusters, boundaries, or imbalances.
- **Correlation and causality** expose how variables move together and whether one influences another.
- **Anomaly detection** identifies points that deviate from expected behavior, often signaling faults or risk.
- **Predictive modeling** uses patterns to estimate what may happen next, turning observation into foresight.

Together, these views form a woven framework for understanding. Each illustration represents a different way of seeing, and the full picture emerges only when these perspectives are combined.

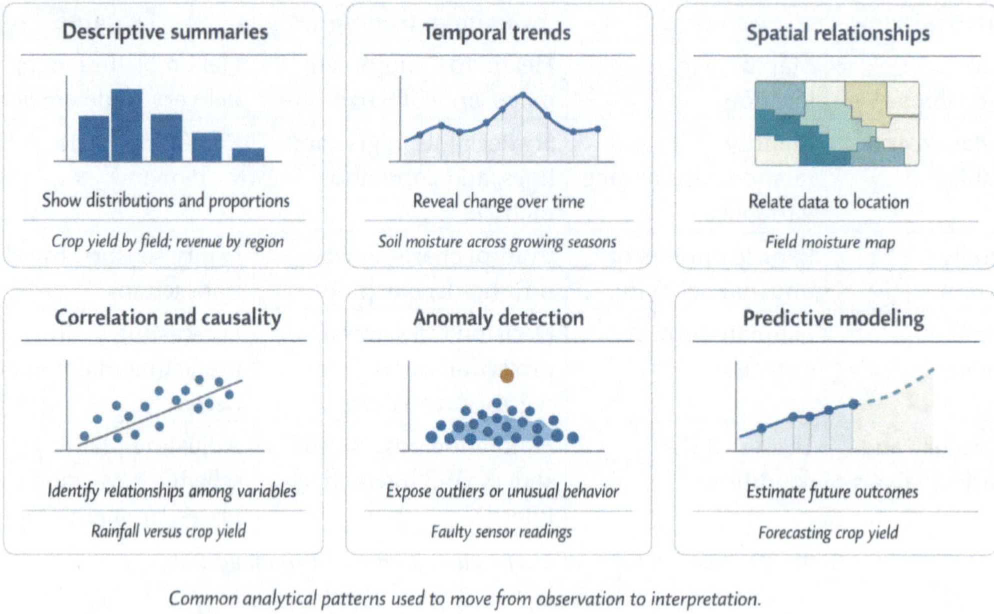

Figure 3.6: *Seeing the pattern in data*

Each visualization acts as a lens, focusing attention and revealing what happened, why it happened, and what may happen next. When combined, these lenses provide a full picture of system behavior, from local variation to global trend, from stability to risk.

Vision as connection

Ultimately, visualization is an act of connection and empathy. It lets humans and systems think together through shared perception. When designed with integrity, it aligns stakeholders around truth, replacing confusion with coordination.

In Aisha's community, the dashboards did more than inform; they united. Farmers, engineers, and policymakers could look at the same color bands and reach the same conclusion about what to do next. The data pattern became a pattern of cooperation, a shared language between the environment, the systems that measured it, and the people who cared for both.

Once patterns are seen, the next step is to act upon them. Decision systems close the loop, turning understanding into action and insight into impact.

Integrating insights with decision systems

Seeing a pattern is only half the journey.

A system becomes intelligent when insight leads to action, when analysis shapes what happens next. Decision systems bridge understanding and operation, linking data to behavior.

When Aisha's cooperative connected its moisture dashboard to irrigation controls, the change was immediate. If readings dropped below a threshold, pumps switched on automatically; if community water reserves fell, alerts paused the process until human review. Data had evolved from reflection to response, a living feedback loop between the field and the farmer.

The decision loop

Most decision systems follow a recurring cycle that mirrors how humans learn from experience:

1. **Sense**: Capture signals from sensors or applications.
2. **Analyze**: Interpret those signals through models or rules.
3. **Decide**: Evaluate outcomes against goals or constraints.
4. **Act**: Execute actions manually or automatically.
5. **Learn**: Feed results back into the system to refine future behavior.

This loop transforms systems from static processors into adaptive learners. Each iteration embeds feedback into the design, improving performance while retaining awareness of context.

Balancing automation and human agency

Automation accelerates response but cannot replace context or conscience. Effective systems balance machine precision with human judgment.

Three principles maintain that equilibrium:

- **Transparency**: Every automated action should reveal its reasoning and data source.
- **Override capability**: Users must intervene when local priorities or ethics demand it.
- **Feedback integration**: Human choices should update the models that guide automation.

Aisha's cooperative practiced all three. Farmers could override irrigation cycles during water shortages, and their decisions were recorded and used to retrain the predictive models. This preserved both adaptability and accountability.

Automation without agency risks efficiency without empathy.
Automation guided by human feedback fosters systems that learn responsibly.

Embedding intelligence in enterprise ecosystems

Decision systems rarely stand alone. They integrate with enterprise tools that manage production, logistics, and services:

- ERP systems align analytics with resource planning.
- CRM systems use insights to improve engagement.
- Supply-chain platforms connect forecasts to inventory and delivery.
- Energy and operations dashboards balance sustainability with cost.

Integration ensures that knowledge moves seamlessly from insight to action.

In a manufacturing firm, a predictive maintenance alert can automatically trigger a work order, notify suppliers, and update customer timelines.

Aisha's cooperative mirrored this pattern on a smaller scale. Soil readings triggered irrigation, solar dashboards checked energy capacity, and water management systems balanced supply.

Every subsystem acted in rhythm with the others, an intelligent ecosystem, not a collection of tools.

Learning from consequences

Every decision, human or digital, generates new data.
Feeding that data back into models closes the loop between design and performance.
This learning from consequence is what makes systems adaptive.

The cooperative retrained its predictive models each season using new outcomes.
When rainfall shifted or soil composition changed, predictions recalibrated automatically.
It became a student of its own history, learning, adjusting, and remembering.

Responsibility at the point of action

As systems gain autonomy, their influence widens. Designers must decide not only what to automate, but which values to encode. Thresholds, priorities, and feedback mechanisms all carry ethical weight. These systems are often described as socio-technical decision systems because outcomes emerge from the interaction of algorithms, interfaces, institutional rules, and human judgment.

Decision systems complete the data lifecycle, yet they also begin it anew. Every action reshapes the next cycle of sensing and interpretation. For enduring systems, the goal is not perfect automation but sustained harmony between data, decision, and human intention.

In the end, a system's intelligence is measured not only by how it acts, but by how well its actions remain aligned with human purpose. As the lifecycle comes full circle, we return to the foundation of every digital weave, responsibility.

Each design choice, from sensing to action, reflects what we value and what we intend to sustain.

From data to responsibility

Every digital system ends where it began, with choice. What we choose to measure, clean, store, and automate defines not only what our systems know but also who they serve. Responsibility is the invisible thread that binds the entire data lifecycle together.

Aisha's cooperative learned this lesson when their irrigation model began favoring fields with better connectivity. The algorithm was not malicious; it was incomplete. It amplified the inequality hidden in its own data.

Once the bias was recognized, the team shared sensors among farms, balanced access, and retrained the model with more representative samples. Fairness, they realized, was not a feature to be added; it was a value to be designed for.

Principles of responsible data design

Four interlocking principles sustain responsible digital systems:

- **Accuracy**: Ensure data reflects reality through calibration, validation, and context.
- **Privacy**: Protect individuals and communities through consent and minimization.
- **Inclusion**: Capture diverse experiences so that silence does not become exclusion.
- **Sustainability**: Manage data and computation with awareness of energy and material costs.

Together, these principles turn technical systems into civic systems. Each dataset, model, and visualization becomes a moral artifact, carrying the imprint of human intent and care.

The loop of care

Seen as a whole, the data lifecycle is a loop of care: sensing, refining, analyzing, deciding, and reflecting, all guided by attention, humility, and responsibility. When feedback becomes understanding and automation remains accountable, systems mature without losing humanity.

That is the essence of responsible design. Data is not only infrastructure; it is an act of listening. Handled with care, it becomes a blueprint not just for efficiency, but for empathy, a fabric that holds both intelligence and integrity.

Data in action

A weave comes alive when patterns begin to act.

Aisha often compared data to water flowing through irrigation channels; its value lies not in storage but in flow, reach, and renewal.

From a soil sensor to a satellite, from a clinic's oxygen monitor to a national policy dashboard, data travels through layers of edge, fog, and cloud, each adding new meaning. Together, these layers form a digital fabric where local threads strengthen global patterns.

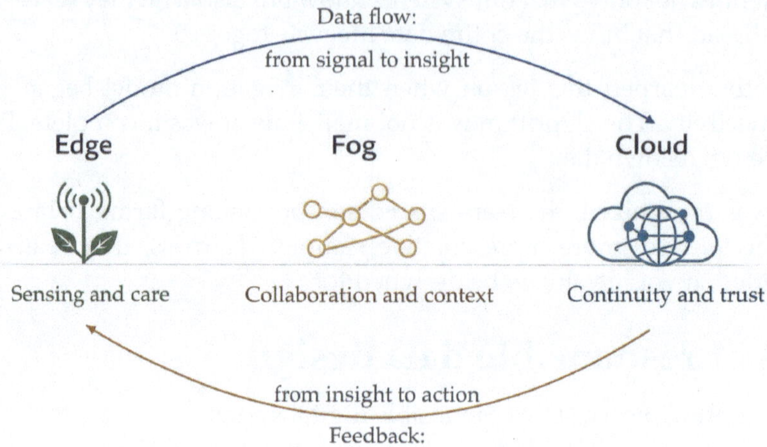

Data weaves across edge, fog, and cloud layers to support sensing, coordination, and global continuity.

***Figure 3.7:** Data weave in action, from edge sensing to global coordination*

The preceding section explored how data is collected, classified, and prepared for use. This section shows how it moves into the world, how signals act, systems learn, and networks govern across scales of connection.

Edge intelligence and local sensing

At the edge, data begins its journey. Devices close to the source capture and act before the network can respond, embodying immediacy, resilience, and local autonomy.

Agriculture and precision in every plot

In Aisha's cooperative, LoRaWAN soil sensors measured moisture, pH, and temperature. Small edge models embedded in gateways estimate irrigation needs directly on site, without depending on the cloud.

When rainfall dropped below the threshold, the system automatically activated pumps, conserving 35% more water and increasing yields by nearly 30%. Farmers gained control and literacy as data became a shared language of care and collaboration. Their dashboards, available in Hausa and English, used icons to show soil risk levels, making analytics accessible to everyone, even those with limited digital experience.

Energy grids and fault anticipation

Across regional utilities, phasor-measurement units and smart meters monitor grid stability in real time. Edge processors detect frequency drift and voltage sag within milliseconds, triggering local isolation before cascading blackouts occur. **Machine learning** (ML) models in substations forecast transformer load, vegetation intrusion, and component stress. These predictive insights help prevent large-scale outages like those that crippled parts of Texas in 2021, turning edge data into foresight rather than reaction.

Healthcare and patient awareness in real-time

In Maya's rural clinic, heart rate, oxygen saturation, and temperature sensors connected to a local hub that analyzed vital trends. A lightweight model identified early respiratory distress within ten minutes, three times faster than manual observation. Even during network outages, alerts reached staff through handheld devices, ensuring continuity of care and faster intervention. Over time, the system learned typical patient patterns, distinguishing normal fluctuation from true emergencies.

Edge analytics weave data into the rhythm of daily life. They are close enough to sense, fast enough to act, and simple enough to trust.

Fog collaboration and regional coordination

Between local devices and global clouds lies the fog layer, the connective tissue of regional intelligence that links communities, factories, and institutions. Fog systems aggregate, interpret, and coordinate data while preserving context and privacy.

Climate and conservation through shared sensing

In the Sahel, Aisha's students joined a reforestation project where edge sensors in the soil and drones in the air sent summaries to a regional fog cluster. The system merged these readings with satellite vegetation data from Google Earth Engine.

Early-warning models detected desertification six months sooner than before, guiding irrigation and tree planting.

Community dashboards visualized rainfall, soil fertility, and crop growth across districts, helping cooperatives act together rather than in isolation.

Manufacturing and logistics through fog networks

In industrial corridors, factories connect through fog servers that integrate machine telemetry, operator logs, and ERP data.

When vibration on a production line exceeded tolerance, a nearby fog node analyzed patterns and predicted bearing failure before a breakdown occurred. The same insights synchronized spare-parts delivery and maintenance schedules across facilities.

This design reduced downtime, energy waste, and logistics cost while keeping raw data on-site, maintaining both privacy and efficiency.

Healthcare networks and regional learning

Hospital clusters use fog gateways to collect patient telemetry from multiple wards and summarize it into anonymized dashboards.

During an influenza outbreak, early signals of rising temperature and oxygen anomalies across several clinics triggered targeted vaccine distribution before national data confirmed the spread.

This balance between local autonomy and regional coordination illustrates fog computing as a foundation for public health resilience. Fog systems braid nearby threads into regional strength, creating collaboration without sacrificing context or control.

Cloud and commons for collective intelligence

At the cloud layer, billions of data threads converge. Here, information gains universality through standardization, shared analytics, and transparent governance.

Supply chains and transparent movement

A cocoa exporter in Ghana partnered with a technology consortium to trace every shipment from harvest to retail. **Radio Frequency Identification** (**RFID**) tags and **quick response** (**QR**) codes recorded location, humidity, and certification at each step.

Each transaction was recorded in a shared blockchain ledger that connects producers, exporters, and regulators. Disputes that once lasted weeks were resolved in hours; spoilage dropped below 3%; and buyers gained real-time visibility into ethical sourcing.

Similar methods now power vaccine logistics, where IoT cold boxes report temperature and route data every five minutes to global dashboards that ensure quality and compliance.

Open data for governance and equity

National open-data platforms aggregate metrics from weather, agriculture, transport, healthcare, and other systems.

In Aisha's country, cooperatives contributed field statistics and, in return, received real-time weather and price forecasts. FAIR-compliant architectures highlighted underserved regions, guiding equitable allocation of subsidies and infrastructure.

Other examples echo this principle: Lagos optimized bus routes using mobility data; Estonia secured citizen registries through blockchain; Delhi schools used low-cost air-quality monitors to shape policy.

Across these contexts, transparency became the foundation of coordination.

Responsible intelligence for finance and inclusion

Banks and fintech organizations now use cloud-based AI models trained on distributed data to extend credit access to the unbanked. Federated learning protects privacy while allowing collective model improvement. Bias-auditing pipelines detect skewed decisions, and real-time fraud analytics strengthen trust. In many countries, these systems helped small enterprises qualify for microloans, stimulating inclusive economic growth.

Cloud ecosystems transform isolated datasets into shared understanding. They are the warp threads of governance and coordination, broad in reach yet dependent on the fine weft of local integrity.

From threads to ecosystems

Together, these layers sustain a loop of awareness and adaptation in which insights at the edge feed learning in the cloud, and global models strengthen local responses.

The relationships among these layers are summarized in *Table 3.10*, which illustrates how edge, fog, and cloud systems interconnect to form a federated data weave that exchanges intelligence across contexts:

Layer	Sector examples	Data processes and technologies	Outcome
Edge	Agriculture, energy, and clinics	IoT sensing, edge analytics, event detection	Immediate response, local autonomy
Fog	Manufacturing, climate, and regional health	Aggregation, federated learning, coordination	Shared insight, resilience
Cloud	Governance, finance, supply chains	Cloud AI, blockchain, open data, analytics at scale	Global intelligence, policy, equity

***Table 3.10**: Layers of the data weave across systems*

Across edge, fog, and cloud, foundational design principles turn isolated systems into connected ecosystems. Interconnection creates value through relationships. Context aligns meaning with place and purpose. Ethics embeds fairness and sustainability. Feedback drives improvement, and diversity builds resilience.

Aisha's cooperative, Maya's clinic, regional grids, and national dashboards show that enduring systems are grounded in trust and coherence, where every thread, human or digital, contributes to a shared purpose.

Data gains value when it completes its loop: sensing at the edge, coordination in the fog, and learning in the cloud. Each layer strengthens the others, forming a continuous cycle of observation, analysis, and action. Transparency and feedback keep this cycle stable, turning performance into accountability and insight into confidence.

Technical architecture mirrors social architecture, balancing local autonomy with global coordination. Integration across sectors expands inclusion and deepens understanding.

Aisha often told her students, *Each of us shapes a part of the data weave. The challenge is to connect it in ways that strengthen both the system's performance and its purpose.*

Yet even the strongest weave can fray. The next section examines what happens when bias distorts perception, energy is wasted, or insecurity unravels trust, and how designers can learn to mend the fabric of data before it tears.

Data under strain

The strength of the weave is tested where it is pulled.

Every blueprint carries tension.

Where there is structure, there is strain, the hidden pressure that tests design integrity.

After weeks of steady readings, Aisha's dashboard glowed green across every field. Yet two days later, she stood ankle-deep in floodwater. The numbers had looked perfect, but a missing feed from the nearby river hid the warning. The pattern failed not from a broken sensor, but from unseen stress within the weave.

Data systems rarely collapse from one cause. They weaken through subtle accumulations: biased samples, untested assumptions, silent silos, energy waste, insecure links, and absent governance.

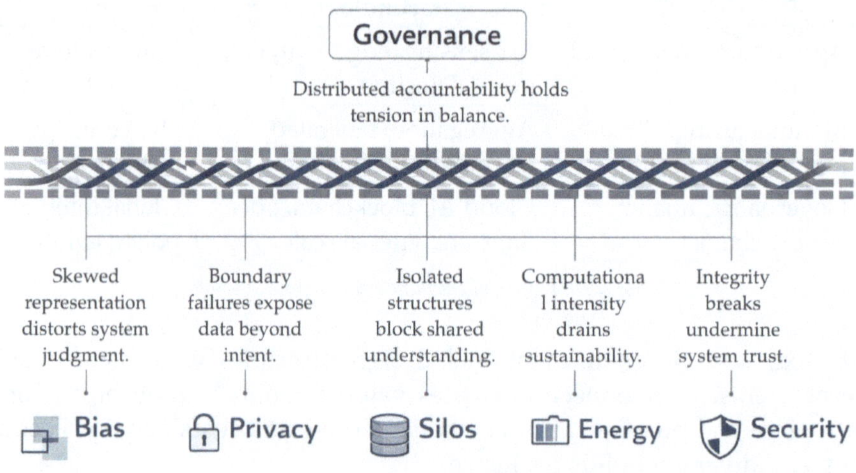

Bias, privacy gaps, silos, energy demands, and security weaknesses introduce structural strain that governance must manage to maintain system integrity.

Figure 3.8: *Frayed edges of the data weave*

Each strain begins small, a delay, a drift, a missing consent, but together they test whether a digital system can endure what it was built to serve.

Bias

When data reflects only one story, every other story fades into the background. Bias enters data systems primarily through sampling choices, labeling practices, and historical imbalance.

Aisha's drought-prediction model performed flawlessly for the lowland farms, yet failed in the uplands. The model's training data came mostly from flat terrain and male-led farms; hillside plots and women's cooperatives were nearly absent.

The system was not malicious; it was incomplete. The imbalance in its data quietly shaped the limits of its intelligence.

Bias enters digital systems through many doors: uneven sampling, historical inequities, mislabeled records, or algorithms that amplify dominant patterns. These distortions are subtle at first but accumulate until the design bends under their weight. *Table 3.11* identifies major sources of bias and their impacts on fairness:

Cause	Description	Impact
Sampling bias	Missing or uneven representation in data.	Misleading or regionally skewed predictions.
Historical bias	Outdated data reflecting inherited inequities.	Reinforces systemic exclusion.
Label bias	Inconsistent or subjective classification.	Incorrect training outcomes.
Algorithmic bias	Model overweights dominant correlations.	Unfair or inaccurate decisions.

Table 3.11: Sources and impacts of bias in data systems

Repairing these distortions begins with measurement.

Fairness audits test models for demographic parity, equal opportunity, and error rate balance. Cross-validation with domain experts exposes gaps that metrics alone overlook. Retraining cycles introduce underrepresented cases, while monitoring pipelines detect drift as conditions change.

Aisha's cooperative revised its data collection plan to include hillside plots and seasonal gender participation. Within weeks, model accuracy and community trust both improved. The fix was not just technical; it was participatory.

Bias cannot be entirely eliminated, but it can be balanced.

Fairness begins with visibility, seeing what the dataset does not contain.

A balanced weave depends on restoring the missing threads before the pattern skews beyond repair.

Privacy

A dashboard can look transparent and still betray its users.

Aisha's cooperative built an open *vulnerability map* to direct aid during droughts, but a seed supplier scraped the public data to target sales. What was meant to empower farmers ended up exploiting them.

The system's flaw was not in its algorithms, but in its boundaries; it revealed more than it protected.

Privacy failures arise when the design overlooks control.

Even anonymized data can be re-identified when combined with other datasets. Information shared for care or research can be repurposed for marketing or surveillance. The integrity of data use depends on whether contributors retain agency over how their data travels through the system. *Table 3.12* outlines key privacy risks with real-world examples and their consequences for trust:

Risk	Example	Consequence
Re-identification	Linking anonymized records with public data.	Personal exposure or profiling.
Function creep	Welfare data reused for commercial targeting.	Loss of trust and misuse of consent.
Consent gaps	Inability to see or withdraw participation.	Ethical and legal violations.

Table 3.12: *Common privacy risks and consequences*

Technical safeguards restore that agency.

Differential privacy adds statistical noise to hide individuals while preserving patterns. Tiered access control separates open summaries from sensitive records. Consent dashboards allow users to pause, edit, or withdraw data contributions. Context-aware policies limit reuse, and encryption secures transmission and storage.

Aisha's cooperative redesigned its system to align with privacy-by-design principles.

Only aggregated statistics appeared on public maps. Farmers reviewed what data was left on their devices, and consent could be revoked at any time. The new system did not collect less data; it collected responsibly.

Privacy is not secrecy; it is the power to decide how one's data participates in the weave.

A trusted system honors that power by making visibility a choice, not a risk.

Silos

A weave gains strength from intersections. When threads stay apart, the pattern weakens.

During a severe storm, Aisha's flood-warning model failed. The nearby river's flow data was held by another agency, stored in a proprietary format that her cooperative's systems could not read. The information existed, but isolation made it invisible.

Silos arise when systems are designed for independence rather than collaboration.

They may be technical, institutional, or cultural, but their effects are the same, and the data becomes fragmented, duplicated, and outdated. Insight stalls because one system cannot see what another already knows.

Table 3.13 lists root causes of data silos and the design issues they create:

Root cause	Description	Effect
Proprietary formats	Data stored in incompatible or locked schemas	Fragmentation and poor integration
Institutional barriers	Lack of policy or incentive for sharing	Gaps in collaboration and visibility
Missing metadata	Incomplete documentation or context	Data that cannot be found or reused
Absent APIs	No standard interfaces for exchange	Manual or delayed data flow

Table 3.13: Root causes for data silos

Repairing isolation requires openness, not exposure, but interoperability.

Modern data systems use open standards like CSV, JSON, and GeoJSON; for real-time data, the **Open Geospatial Consortium** (OGC) SensorThings and REST APIs enable structured exchange. Metadata catalogs, such as **Comprehensive Knowledge Archive Network** (CKAN) or **Data Catalog Vocabulary** (DCAT) make datasets discoverable, while federated query systems allow access without centralization.

In Aisha's region, an inter-ministerial data charter eventually connected hydrology, weather, and agriculture services through a shared API gateway. Each department retained ownership, but the models finally learned to read from one another.

A closed dataset is like a locked drawer, secure, but useless.

An interoperable system transforms that drawer into a shared workspace where trust and transparency replace isolation.

Only then can the weave regain its strength through connection.

Energy

Generating insight consumes energy. As computational intensity increases, energy use rises unless efficiency is designed into the system. As a result, data design decisions often translate directly into power and resource demands.

Aisha's cooperative learned this when its forecasting pipeline scaled beyond its intended scope. Each night, thousands of soil readings streamed into a cloud model to predict irrigation needs. The forecasts were accurate, but the cost was invisible; one nightly cycle consumed enough electricity to power several homes.

A system built for sustainability had quietly become unsustainable. This paradox now defines the digital era.

In 2024, the **International Energy Agency** (**IEA**) estimated global data-center power demand at about 415 **terawatt-hours (TWh**), nearly 1.5% of global electricity use. Under current trends, this could exceed 900 TWh by 2030, rivaling the annual consumption of entire nations. In the United States alone, data centers accounted for roughly 4.4% of national electricity consumption in 2023, with projections ranging from 6.7% to 12% by 2028, driven largely by AI workloads.

The energy footprint of intelligence itself has become part of the design equation.
Efficiency must be engineered as deliberately as accuracy.

Aisha's team re-architected their system to process 70% of data locally, sending only summaries to the cloud. They replaced energy-intensive neural networks with lighter gradient-boosted models and scheduled computation during daylight hours when solar generation was highest.

Accuracy remained steady, but the energy curve flattened.
Sustainable intelligence begins with awareness that every calculation leaves a trace, not only in storage, but in carbon. To weave responsibly is to design systems that think clearly and tread lightly.

Security

Trust, once torn, takes seasons to repair.
Aisha learned this when her cooperative's dashboard was quietly altered.
An intruder used a shared administrator account to lower flood-alert thresholds, so warnings never appeared. By the time the breach was discovered, crops were already underwater. The failure was not only technical, but it was also human, organizational, and architectural.
In digital systems, security is stewardship.
It protects not only information but also the relationships that depend on it.
Every permission, credential, and interface is a thread in that trust weave, strong when aligned, fragile when neglected.

Table 3.14 lists common vulnerabilities and their associated risks:

Vulnerability	Description	Risk
Shared credentials	Multiple users reusing logins	No accountability, weak traceability
Unsecured endpoints	APIs without encryption or token control	Data manipulation or injection
Lack of audit logs	Missing event history	Delayed detection, untraceable changes

***Table 3.14**: Typical vulnerabilities and associated risks*

A secure architecture anticipates failure, not perfection.

Defense must be layered, each control catching what the others miss.

Modern practices integrate several reinforcing patterns:

- **Zero Trust Architecture**: Every request is verified; no network zone is inherently safe.
- **Least privilege access**: Users and services receive only the permissions necessary for their task.
- **Multi-factor authentication (MFA)**: Identity is confirmed beyond passwords.
- **Encryption at rest and in transit**: Protects data from observation and tampering.
- **Tamper-evident logs or blockchain audits**: Record every action with integrity guarantees.
- **Continuous monitoring and anomaly detection**: Detects deviations early, before damage spreads.

Aisha's cooperative implemented these principles in small, steady steps.

Each device received unique credentials; the dashboard required two-factor authentication; a daily audit log verified configuration changes. When another intrusion attempt occurred months later, the system detected and automatically contained it.

The lesson was not in fear, but in foresight.

Security is not a fence around data; it is the discipline of care that keeps the loom intact.

It ensures that what systems know remains trustworthy, and that those who depend on them can continue to act with confidence.

Governance and the invisible tension

Even the strongest data systems can fray when no one holds the threads.

In Aisha's region, different ministries managed separate parts of the agricultural dataset, weather in one portal, soil in another, and prices in a third. Each worked well in isolation, yet no one was accountable for errors or updates. Farmers received conflicting forecasts. The loom functioned, but the pattern was disjointed.

Governance gives structure to complexity.

It defines who owns the data, how it changes, who can access it, and when it must be retired. Without governance, quality decays quietly.
With it, systems remain traceable, accountable, and aligned with purpose.

Table 3.15 defines essential elements of data-governance frameworks with implementation examples:

Element	Function	Implementation example
Ownership and stewardship	Assigns responsibility for accuracy and updates	Dataset owner and custodian are defined in metadata
Version and lineage control	Tracks the evolution of data and models.	Git-style repositories, data catalogs, audit trails.
Access policy	Defines who can view or modify.	Role-based control with periodic review.
Retention and archival rules	Manages data lifecycle.	Automated expiration or anonymization.
Ethics and compliance	Aligns with legal and social norms.	GDPR, ISO 27001, or national data policies.

***Table 3.15**: Core elements of effective data governance*

Good governance is more than documentation; it is a living practice that connects technical, institutional, and ethical dimensions. It ensures that every data asset has a clear lineage, where it originated, how it was processed, and who validated its use. It also turns datasets from static resources into accountable participants in the digital ecosystem.

Aisha's cooperative adopted a data stewardship charter. Each dataset listed its owner, update frequency, and usage policy. All changes were logged through version control, and access requests were reviewed by a small ethics board. Conflicts no longer required guessing; they were resolved by design.

Governance is the loom's backbone. It distributes tension evenly across threads so that no single failure tears the pattern apart. When governance works, systems gain not just stability but also legitimacy and trust that endure even when technologies change.

Holding the weave together

The strength of a data blueprint lies not in flawlessness but in resilience.

Every digital system carries tension between speed and care, access and protection, automation and judgment. What defines endurance is not the absence of failure but the discipline of repair.

Aisha's cooperative made a choice that changed their practice. Instead of hiding system faults, they documented each one: bias in the model, exposure in the dashboard, isolation between datasets, energy waste in the pipeline, a security lapse in credentials, or confusion over ownership.

Every incident became a thread to study, strengthen, and reweave. Over time, the cooperative's system did not become perfect, but it became self-correcting.

Table 3.16 consolidates major data-system challenges and the preventive practices that reinforce resilience:

Challenge	Typical failure	Preventive practice
Bias	Skewed predictions	Fairness audits, diverse data inclusion
Privacy	Unintended exposure	Differential privacy, consent control
Silos	Fragmented datasets	Open standards, shared metadata catalogs
Energy	High computational cost	Edge analytics, efficient coding, and renewable scheduling
Security	Unauthorized access	Role-based access, MFA, encryption, and audits
Governance	Accountability gaps	Defined stewardship, transparent policies

***Table 3.16**: Designing resilience into data systems*

Resilience begins with visibility. Each feedback loop, from anomaly detection to governance review, becomes part of a larger pattern of learning. When bias metrics trigger retraining, when privacy breaches prompt new consent flows, when outages lead to architectural redesign, systems evolve through reflection. This is how digital fabrics mature, through feedback, correction, and iteration.

In Aisha's cooperative, weekly *weaving sessions* became rituals of stewardship. Farmers, engineers, and analysts met to review anomalies, update models, and share lessons. Each correction became a reinforcing stitch, not just in code, but in trust. By making maintenance visible, they made responsibility communal.

Resilience is not discovered by chance; it is designed and sustained. It grows from diversity of data, transparency of process, and humility in interpretation. The blueprint of data holds not because it avoids strain, but because it distributes it. It adapts to pressure without tearing.

When a system learns to repair itself, it becomes more than infrastructure; it becomes a system capable of sustained correction, learning, and accountability. Each safeguard, each audit, each transparent correction turns information into integrity, and design into stewardship.

As the frayed edges are repaired, a new question emerges: *How does the weave evolve?*

The next frontier is not about collecting more data, but about designing systems that can adapt, coordinate, and remain accountable over time.

The future of the blueprint lies in self-adaptive intelligence, architectures that preserve provenance, optimize energy, correct bias, and renew trust as part of their design. These systems will not merely compute; they will reflect. They will remember where their data came from, understand why their decisions matter, and adapt without forgetting the people they serve.

The following section explores this horizon, where data, intelligence, and trust coevolve, weaving a digital future that is not only smart but also self-aware, sustainable, and humane.

Data in evolution

A living weave learns to renew its own design.

Aisha looked at her dashboard one last time that season. The plots were greener than ever, each line and color alive with rhythm. Moisture, yield, and market graphs shimmered in balance, yet she knew the harmony would not last. Every system, like every living thing, must grow, adapt, and one day outlive its design.

Data never stands still. It flows, multiplies, and learns. The systems of tomorrow will no longer behave as static repositories but as living blueprints, self-correcting, distributed, and adaptive. They will sense their environment, negotiate between autonomy and coordination, and continually reshape the balance between efficiency and ethics.

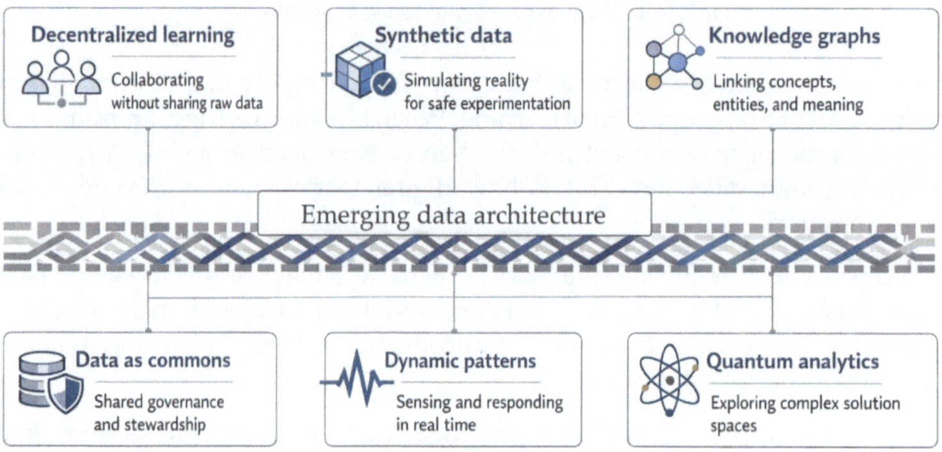

Emerging capabilities extend a shared data fabric, enabling new forms of learning, coordination, and governance.

***Figure 3.9**: Emerging data architecture*

This section explores the emerging directions that signal this evolution, showing how humans and machines will learn and design together in the next horizon of digital weaving.

Decentralized learning

In traditional systems, data travels to a central model for analysis. This method simplifies computation but accumulates risk: privacy breaches, energy waste, and uneven representation. In decentralized learning, that flow is reversed. The model itself travels to the data.

Each device, phone, sensor, or local server trains a version of the algorithm using its own dataset. Only the learned parameters, not the raw data, are shared with a coordinator that aggregates them into an improved collective model. In Aisha's cooperative, regional nodes trained local predictors of soil yield, sharing only model weights. Together, they built a shared intelligence that respected local privacy while learning global patterns.

This approach mirrors the way ecosystems evolve: each element adapts locally while contributing to the resilience of the whole. Decentralized learning reduces data movement, conserves energy, and allows collaboration across institutions that cannot exchange sensitive data. It represents a shift from ownership to participation, from control to coordination, the same logic that governs a healthy weave.

Synthetic data

As privacy regulations strengthen and access to real-world data narrows, designers turn to synthetic data, artificial datasets that mimic the structure of real data without exposing individuals. Using generative models such as **generative adversarial networks** (**GANs**) or variational autoencoders, systems learn the statistical properties of real data and produce realistic but fictional examples.

Synthetic data enables innovation in sensitive fields such as healthcare and finance, where real data is limited or protected. Aisha's students used synthetic weather records to simulate climate patterns beyond recorded history, testing how new irrigation strategies would respond to extreme scenarios.

Yet this freedom carries responsibility. Poorly governed synthetic data can reproduce the same biases it was meant to avoid or be mistaken for real evidence. Transparency is vital; datasets must be clearly labeled, regularly audited, and validated against trusted benchmarks. When used wisely, synthetic data becomes a creative instrument, extending imagination while respecting privacy.

Quantum analytics

Where classical computers represent bits as 0 or 1, quantum computing uses qubits that exist in multiple states simultaneously. Through superposition and entanglement, quantum systems explore vast combinations of variables at once, uncovering patterns unreachable by traditional computation.

This new capability holds promise for optimization, simulation, and complex modeling. Quantum systems could reduce the number of delivery routes from millions of options, simulate molecular interactions in drug design, or predict energy flows in ecosystems. In finance, they may analyze risk correlations across portfolios faster than any current method.

However, quantum computing remains fragile and experimental. Hardware instability, limited qubit coherence, and high cost restrict its use. For now, hybrid architectures that link classical and quantum processors offer the most practical path. Data preprocessing happens on traditional servers, while quantum units solve the hardest subproblems. Like warp and weft, classical precision and quantum possibility may one day interlace to form an intelligence that reasons across dimensions.

Dynamic patterns

In most organizations today, data follows a fixed rhythm: collect, clean, analyze, act. The future will move differently. Systems will sense and respond in real-time, guided by event-driven design. Here, data streams are continuous signals, not static snapshots.

When a sensor detects a sudden shift, a voltage drop, a patient's pulse irregularity, or a price fluctuation, connected processes react instantly. Stream processors route information to applications that adjust operations on the fly. In Aisha's network, a drop in soil moisture automatically triggered irrigation pumps and alerted neighboring farms, turning data from record into reflex.

This shift toward continuous flow demands lightweight architectures, low latency, and robust feedback. It closes the gap between awareness and action, allowing systems to behave more like organisms: perceiving, adapting, and learning in motion. The blueprint comes to life, its threads tightening and relaxing as conditions change.

Knowledge graphs

As data grows, meaning it no longer lies in individual records but in relationships. Knowledge graphs make those relationships visible by linking entities, people, sensors, places, and events through contextual edges. They store not just information, but connections.

Aisha's cooperative used a local knowledge graph that linked soil type, crop variety, fertilizer, and rainfall history. From it, the system derived statements such as *Plots with sandy soil and early planting perform best under high humidity*. The data had not changed, but its structure had learned to speak.

Knowledge graphs now power search engines, recommendation systems, and scientific discovery platforms. They support explainability by tracing how insights arise and enable interoperability by linking data across domains. In a woven system, they act as the grammar that keeps the threads intelligible.

Data as commons

The next evolution in data ethics will move beyond ownership toward stewardship. Just as water and air are shared resources, data too can be governed as a commons, used collectively, managed responsibly, and distributed for mutual benefit.

Communities, cities, and governments are beginning to form data cooperatives, trusts, and unions. These frameworks let contributors decide how their data is used and ensure that value created from it returns to the community. Barcelona's citizen data programs and Kerala's state-led data cooperatives exemplify this shift, balancing innovation with public accountability.

Aisha's cooperative joined a regional trust that enabled farmers to collectively govern soil and climate data. They voted on who could access it, set pricing for research use, and ensured transparency in outcomes. The system transformed data from a private asset into a social infrastructure, shared, cared for, and continually renewed.

Designing for tension

Every living fabric holds tension. The future of digital design will depend on how we balance forces rather than eliminate them. Privacy must coexist with insight, centralization with autonomy, power with explainability, and speed with sustainability.

Tomorrow's systems will adjust dynamically, like a loom adapting to strain. Privacy-preserving computation will protect individuals while supporting collective learning. Federated architectures will distribute power without losing coherence. Hybrid AI will combine deep pattern recognition with transparent reasoning. Green computing and edge analytics will ensure that intelligence grows without exhausting the planet.

Aisha called this balance *the art of the woven system,* not perfect but resilient enough to hold meaning under stress.

Designing beyond ourselves

Late one evening, Aisha and Maya spoke over a flickering connection. *What happens,* Maya asked, *when our models start improving without us?*

Aisha smiled. *Then our job is to make sure they still remember why they began.*

The next generation of systems will sense, decide, and evolve with minimal supervision. Yet the purpose must remain human. Engineers will design not only for accuracy or efficiency but for values, empathy, inclusion, and repair. Each dataset, algorithm, and visualization will be part of a continuous dialogue between human intention and machine interpretation.

The blueprint of tomorrow will not be fixed on paper. It will be a living design that grows, learns, and heals, responsive to its environment, guided by its ethics, and aware of its origins.

Ethics will serve as institutional memory, innovation as adaptive capacity, and stewardship as the discipline that sustains both. The future of data design belongs to those who can hold all three at once.

The blueprint is evolving. Decentralized learning enables collaboration without data exchange. Synthetic data extends experimentation while protecting privacy. Quantum analytics opens new dimensions of insight. Event-driven systems create real-time responsiveness. Knowledge graphs bind meaning across domains, and data commons redefine ownership as shared care.

Together, they mark a shift from static architectures to living systems, woven networks of intelligence, accountability, and adaptation.

Conclusion

Evening settled over the cooperative, and the fields glowed gold under the retreating sun. Aisha closed her laptop and listened to the hum of distant sensors, their quiet signals threading through the air like unseen voices.

She realized that data begins not in dashboards but in life, small, human, and full of meaning. Each signal is a fragment of someone's story, waiting to be understood and cared for.

She often told her students: *A single data point is only a whisper, but when woven with purpose and respect, those whispers can guide the world toward balance.*

That semester, before the students graduated, Aisha gathered them in the community hall. On the board behind her, she wrote the words *The Weaver's Oath.*

It was not a rulebook, she said, but a reminder of the care that must hold every system together.

The Weaver's Oath

To weave responsibly is to remember that every dataset is a fragment of life.

I will document what I collect and collect only what I must.
I will seek consent as a partnership, not formality.
I will design for diversity and measure my impact on the Earth.
I will treat data not as property, but as a relationship.
I will remember that behind every number is a human story worth hearing.

A hush lingered after she finished reading. The students copied the lines into their notebooks, some in pen, some as code comments, promising to carry them into whatever systems they built next.

The data blueprint is more than technical architecture. It reflects values embedded in design, where precision is informed by empathy, logic is constrained by ethics, and innovation is guided by care. When handled responsibly, data becomes a foundation for decisions that remain accountable to the people and environments they affect.

Now the loom passes to you. The next thread belongs to your hands and imagination.

What will you measure?
What will you model?
And what kind of world will your blueprint help weave?

As data matures into intelligence, the loom itself grows more complex.

The next chapter explores how AI extends the human weave, learning from patterns, amplifying possibilities, and revealing both beauty and risk in automation.

If data is the thread, AI is the weaver that learns to move on its own. The challenge ahead is not only to teach machines to think, but to ensure they remember why they were taught.

Weaver's toolkit

Where insight meets intention, the weave holds true.

Every designer needs tools. For the digital weaver, the tools are not looms and threads but concepts and practices that turn signals into understanding.

This toolkit is a reference for students, practitioners, and policymakers who wish to apply the principles of this chapter to design with data rather than merely use it.

Weaver's lexicon

Each term here represents a stitch in the larger fabric of digital systems—how we collect, clean, analyze, and respect information. Together, they form a shared vocabulary that links engineers, analysts, and citizens in the same conversation.

Keep the following glossary close as you experiment, build prototypes, or evaluate systems. It will help you navigate from data to design with precision and care:

- **Abstraction**: Data stands for phenomena rather than being the phenomena; design must prevent confusing the model with reality.
- **Accuracy/Precision/Recall**: Core evaluation metrics for analytical and ML model performance.
- **Adaptive system**: Software that modifies its parameters automatically in response to changing data.
- **Algorithm**: A defined, stepwise procedure for solving a computational task.
- **Anomaly detection**: Techniques for spotting unusual patterns, Isolation Forest, control charts, z-scores, or autoencoders.
- **Apache Airflow**: An open-source platform for designing, scheduling, and monitoring data workflows through programmable pipelines.

- **Application programming interface (API)**: A standardized interface enabling communication between software components.
- **Autoregressive Integrated Moving Average (ARIMA)**: A time-series model combining autoregression, differencing, and moving averages for forecasting.
- **Autoencoder**: A neural network architecture that compresses and reconstructs data, used for anomaly detection.
- **AWS Glue**: A cloud-based data integration service from AWS that automates data discovery, preparation, and transformation for analytics.
- **Bayesian inference**: Probabilistic updating of beliefs as new evidence appears.
- **Bias audit**: Systematic evaluation of data and models to detect and correct unfair or imbalanced outcomes across groups.
- **Blockchain**: A distributed ledger that stores immutable transaction blocks for trust and traceability.
- **Carbon accounting**: Measurement of greenhouse-gas emissions from digital infrastructure.
- **Carbon footprint**: Total greenhouse-gas emissions produced by data storage, computation, and transmission activities.
- **Choropleth map**: Map visualization shaded by variable intensity.
- **Cloud computing/Cloud analytics**: On-demand networked resources for large-scale computation and storage.
- **Comma-separated values (CSV)**: A simple text format for storing tabular data where each line represents a record and values are separated by commas.
- **Convolutional neural network (CNN)**: A deep-learning model for recognizing spatial patterns in images or sensor grids.
- **Constrained Application Protocol (CoAP)**: A lightweight communication protocol for low-power IoT devices that sends sensor data efficiently over constrained networks.
- **Control chart**: A tool for monitoring process stability and detecting anomalies.
- **Correlation analysis**: Quantifies the strength and direction of relationships between variables.
- **Cross-sector integration**: Interlinking of data systems across industries for shared insight and equity.
- **Customer relationship management (CRM)**: A system used to manage interactions with customers, track sales, and improve business relationships through data-driven insights.

- **Data catalog**: A metadata repository that documents datasets, ownership, schema, and lineage for discovery and governance.
- **Data governance**: Policies ensuring data integrity, security, and ethical use.
- **Data lake**: A repository for raw structured and unstructured data.
- **Data lineage/provenance**: The recorded trail showing origin, transformations, and use of data throughout its lifecycle.
- **Data pipeline/Extract, transform, load (ETL)**: A workflow that moves data from sources through cleaning to storage.
- **Data visualization**: Graphical rendering that transforms measurement into meaning.
- **Decision tree**: Hierarchical model splitting data by feature thresholds to classify or predict outcomes.
- **Density-based spatial clustering of applications with noise (DBSCAN)**: Algorithm grouping dense data points and labeling outliers.
- **Descriptive analytics**: Summarizes historical data using statistics and charts.
- **Differential privacy**: A Statistical technique that introduces calibrated noise to data or queries to protect individual identity while preserving aggregate accuracy.
- **EarthData**: A platform by NASA providing open access to global Earth science data, including satellite observations, climate records, and environmental measurements.
- **Edge analytics/Edge computing**: Localized data processing performed near data sources to reduce latency and bandwidth use.
- **Enterprise resource planning (ERP)**: An integrated software system that manages core business processes such as finance, supply chain, manufacturing, and human resources within a unified platform.
- **Federated learning**: Distributed training where local devices update a shared model without sending raw data.
- **Fog analytics/Fog computing**: Regional layer between edge and cloud, performing intermediate aggregation.
- **GeoJSON**: JSON-based format for geographic data.
- **Gradient Boosting (XGBoost)**: Ensemble technique combining many weak models into a strong one.
- **Graph database**: A data store that represents data as nodes and edges for efficient relationship queries.
- **GraphQL**: A query language for retrieving precisely specified data from APIs.

- **Heatmap**: Matrix or map using color gradients to display value intensity.
- **InfluxDB**: A time-series database optimized for storing and analyzing data that changes over time, such as sensor readings, metrics, and events.
- **Isolation Forest**: Algorithm for anomaly detection by random partitioning of data.
- **JavaScript Object Notation (JSON)**: A lightweight, human-readable format for structuring data as key–value pairs, widely used for APIs and web communication.
- **Kafka (Apache Kafka)**: Distributed streaming platform for high-throughput event pipelines.
- **K-means**: An unsupervised algorithm that partitions data into K clusters.
- **Knowledge graph**: Semantic network linking entities and relationships for contextual reasoning.
- **Linear regression**: Model that estimates continuous outcomes as a linear combination of inputs.
- **Logistic regression**: Model predicting categorical outcomes using a logistic (sigmoid) function.
- **Long short-term memory (LSTM)**: A Recurrent neural network capturing long-range dependencies in sequences.
- **Machine learning (ML)**: Algorithms that learn from data to make predictions or decisions.
- **Metadata**: Descriptive information about datasets (origin, schema, version).
- **Message Queue Telemetry Transport (MQTT)**: Lightweight publish-subscribe messaging protocol designed for reliable communication in IoT networks.
- **Model drift**: Gradual decline in model accuracy as real-world data distributions change over time.
- **Model lifecycle**: Sequence of training, validation, deployment, and monitoring.
- **Multi-factor authentication (MFA)**: Security mechanism requiring multiple identity proofs (password, token, biometric).
- **Neural network**: A computational model of interconnected nodes that learn representations from data.
- **Normalization**: Rescaling or standardizing data for consistency.
- **Not Only SQL (NoSQL)**: Database category supporting flexible, unstructured storage.
- **Open data**: Publicly accessible data for reuse with attribution.

- **Open Platform Communications Unified Architecture (OPC-UA)**: An industrial communication standard that enables secure, structured, and interoperable data exchange between machines and enterprise systems.
- **Pandas**: A Python library for data manipulation and analysis, offering tools to clean, transform, and organize structured datasets.
- **Parquet**: Column-oriented storage format optimized for analytics.
- **Predictive analytics**: Forecasts future outcomes using statistical or ML models.
- **Principal component analysis (PCA)**: A method that reduces dimensionality by identifying dominant variance directions.
- **Privacy-by-design**: Approach embedding data-protection principles directly into system architecture and workflows.
- **Radio Frequency Identification (RFID)**: A wireless identification method that uses small tags and radio signals to automatically track or recognize objects, animals, or equipment without direct line-of-sight.
- **Quick response (QR) code**: A two-dimensional barcode that stores information in a grid of black and white squares and can be scanned instantly by smartphones or cameras to open links, retrieve data, or trigger actions.
- **Random Forest**: Ensemble of decision trees averaging results for improved robustness.
- **Regression analysis**: A statistical technique for modeling relationships among variables.
- **Representational State Transfer (REST)**: HTTP-based architectural style for APIs.
- **Role-based access control (RBAC)**: A security model that assigns permissions by user role.
- **Resilience**: The capacity of a system to absorb disruption, adapt, and recover without loss of integrity.
- **Schema**: Structured definition of database organization.
- **Semantic Sensor Network (SSN)**: Ontology describing sensors and observations.
- **Structured Query Language (SQL)**: Language for querying and managing relational data.
- **Streaming analytics**: Real-time analysis of continuous data flows.
- **Supply chain management (SCM)**: A system that coordinates the flow of goods, information, and resources across suppliers, manufacturers, distributors, and customers.
- **Synthetic data**: An artificially generated dataset that replicates the statistical properties of real data for testing or privacy protection.

- **Temporal analysis**: Study of change and trends over time.
- **TimescaleDB**: A time-series database built on PostgreSQL, designed for efficient storage, querying, and analysis of time-stamped data.
- **Time-series database (TSDB)**: Database optimized for time-indexed data.
- **Value, Variety, Velocity, Veracity, Volume (5 Vs.)**: Key dimensions describing data quality and scalability.
- **Extensible Markup Language (XML)**: A markup format that encodes documents in a structured, hierarchical form for data exchange between systems.
- **Zero Trust Architecture**: A security framework that continuously verifies every user and device before granting access, assuming no inherent trust.
- **Z-score**: Standardized measure of deviation from the mean used to detect anomalies.

Weaver's workshop

These exercises invite you to apply the ideas of data as the design blueprint, tracing how data flows, learning how design choices affect quality, and understanding how responsibility and resilience shape enduring systems.

Refer to the following exercises to build a comprehensive understanding:

1. **Mapping the data lifecycle**: Trace how data moves from collection to consequence, revealing the architecture beneath everyday systems.

   Prompts:

   - *Select one familiar system, such as environmental sensing, healthcare monitoring, or logistics tracking.*
   - *Map its data lifecycle: Collection | storage | processing | analysis | decision | feedback.*
   - *Label tools, formats, and technologies at each stage.*

   Deliverable: A clear lifecycle diagram (digital or hand-drawn) annotated with key design choices.

   Learning objective: Identify and describe the main stages of a data system and how each stage contributes to overall quality and purpose.

2. **Tracing data provenance**: Understand how transparency and lineage strengthen reliability and trust.

   Prompts:

   - *Choose an open dataset or a sample from your project.*
   - *Trace its origin, transformations, and current use.*
   - *Propose how you would document its lineage using metadata, version control, or automated provenance tools.*

Deliverable: A short-written brief (300–400 words) or visual flow illustrating the dataset's provenance and methods for ensuring traceability.

Learning objective: Explain how data provenance supports reproducibility, accountability, and ethical integrity.

3. **Designing a responsible data loop**: Integrate ethical principles directly into technical design.

   Prompts:

   - *Redesign a simple data workflow, such as a sensor network or survey collection, using the four principles of responsible data design: accuracy, privacy, inclusion, and sustainability.*
   - *Describe how each principle influences your data choices and architecture.*
   - *Propose one mechanism to protect consent or fairness.*

   Deliverable: A one-page responsible data charter outlining how values are embedded in your system.

   Learning objective: Demonstrate how to translate ethical principles into concrete data practices and design safeguards.

4. **Balancing the data dimensions**: Apply technical reasoning to balance the five dimensions of data (Volume, Velocity, Variety, Veracity, Value).

   Prompts:

   - *Design a small edge-to-cloud data system for a realistic scenario (e.g., precision farming, urban mobility, supply chain analytics).*
   - *For each of the five Vs., describe how it influences system architecture and decision performance.*
   - *Identify one trade-off between scalability, accuracy, or cost.*

   Deliverable: A comparative table or diagram summarizing design decisions, trade-offs, and optimizations.

   Learning objective: Analyze the technical constraints of data systems and justify architectural choices under multiple data dimensions.

5. **Repairing the frayed thread**: Synthesize lessons on failure, resilience, and responsibility in real-world systems.

   Prompts:

   - *Research a real incident involving data bias, privacy breach, or infrastructure failure.*
   - *Diagnose the technical and organizational causes.*
   - *Recommend design improvements that would have prevented or mitigated the failure, referencing principles from the previous section.*

   Deliverable: A one-page case analysis linking technical fixes to ethical and governance lessons.

Learning objective: Evaluate system failures to propose resilient and responsible data design strategies.

Weaver's library

The weaver's library for this chapter brings together foundational and reflective works that trace the evolution of data from raw signal to social infrastructure. These sources explore not only how data is collected, analyzed, and governed, but also how it shapes equity, accountability, and collective progress:

1. *Kitchin, R. (2014). The Data Revolution: Big Data, Open Data, Data Infrastructures and Their Consequences. SAGE Publications.*
2. *O'Neil, C. (2016). Weapons of Math Destruction: How Big Data Increases Inequality and Threatens Democracy. Crown Publishing.*
3. *World Bank. (2021). World Development Report 2021: Data for Better Lives. The World Bank.*

Metaphorical and conceptual terms

Metaphors in this chapter serve as conceptual tools that translate complex technical ideas into accessible forms. They clarify rather than replace precision, helping readers connect abstract processes of data design with the tangible logic of weaving:

- **Blueprint**: The structural logic that guides how humans and intelligent systems understand and act. Data serves as this blueprint, translating experience into structure and enabling perception, reasoning, and response across digital systems.
- **Fabric of data**: The interconnected network of datasets, devices, and participants that collectively enable reliable operation.
- **Frayed edge**: A point of weakness or degradation in a system caused by bias, inefficiency, or security failure.
- **Loom**: The foundational infrastructure that supports data integration, including protocols, hardware, and communication frameworks.
- **Pattern**: A recurring structure or identifiable relationship revealed through data analysis or system behavior.
- **Thread**: An individual data stream, signal, or user contribution that forms part of a larger system.
- **Weave/Digital weave**: An integrated data ecosystem combining sensing, computation, and human decision-making into a coherent whole.
- **Warp and weft**: The two interdependent dimensions of a digital system—architecture (warp) providing structure, and interaction (weft) creating flow and adaptability.

CHAPTER 4

Artificial Intelligence

The master weaver

Intelligence emerges when patterns appear within complexity.

CHAPTER 4
Artificial Intelligence

Introduction

Artificial intelligence (**AI**) transforms data from a static archive into a pattern that adapts as conditions change. It reads signals, uncovers structure, and improves its predictions through repeated corrections. In practice, AI is not a single technique. It is a family of learning systems. Neural networks interpret images, sequence models trace unfolding events, transformers map relationships across entire datasets, and foundation models learn broad representations from large collections of information. These systems gain strength not simply because they compute but because they learn. Their power comes from how they handle uncertainty, adjust to new situations, and translate observations into coordinated action. In this sense, AI becomes the loom's master weaver, shaping decisions across homes, enterprises, clinics, factories, and entire cities.

Intelligence gains meaning only when it enters the world. Models succeed when they support human judgment, adapt to real environments, and remain open enough to be examined and questioned. This chapter traces AI from its mathematical foundations to its behavior in complex settings. It explains how intelligence moves through feedback loops, how failure reveals hidden tension, and how design choices influence fairness, reliability, and trust. It examines systems that guide daily routines, support financial access, stabilize supply chains, and assist clinicians. It also looks ahead to generative models and AI Twins that explore multiple possible futures. The central question is simple. *How do we design intelligence that serves people, respects context, and strengthens the digital fabric rather than straining it?*

Structure

This chapter covers the following topics:

- The rhythm that thinks
- From data to decision
- Inside the loom of learning
- Intelligence touching everyday life
- Fraying patterns
- Designing with conscience
- The loom that imagines

Objectives

This chapter explores how AI learns, adapts, and influences decisions made by people and systems. By following how data becomes action, readers will see how AI models perceive patterns, update their internal representations, and operate through feedback loops. The chapter prepares readers to evaluate different forms of intelligence, identify where failure modes arise, and apply design principles that promote fairness, transparency, and reliability. It emphasizes the shared role of engineers, practitioners, policymakers, and communities in shaping responsible AI. By the end of the chapter, readers will understand how to assess AI systems, embed human judgment into digital design, and build intelligent systems that strengthen rather than strain the fabric of digital life.

The rhythm that thinks

Intelligence begins when the loom learns to measure change.

Rain turned Barranquilla's streets into shallow channels. Streetlights blurred into amber reflections as the sensor network pulsed with activity. Rainfall gauges reported intensity, drainage sensors measured flow capacity, and mobility feeds tracked congestion. Inside the municipal response center, *Diego* studied the display. The map refreshed in real time with blue overlays for rainfall density, gold for sensor activity, and red for blocked routes. To most viewers, it was a data grid. To Diego, it was a coordinated system of signals moving together.

As new readings arrived, the system began rerouting traffic. At first, it behaved like a standard monitoring platform. Then its timing shifted. Predictions were updated more frequently, and routing suggestions appeared before operators could react. This behavior came from the AI model Diego had trained using rainfall histories, road capacity estimates, and local risk patterns. When moisture levels rose in low-lying districts and drainage sensors crossed an early warning threshold, the model reprioritized shelter routes and resource allocation. These were not predefined rules. They were decisions inferred from learned relationships in the data.

The responses were early and accurate. Diego knew the system was not intuitive. It was expressing computation shaped by learning.

Learning through rhythm

Rain intensified, yet the system responded with a steady cadence. Patterns formed, dissolved, and reformed as new data arrived. The behavior resembled a loom recalibrating tension to maintain structure. In the city's digital fabric, the AI learned through feedback rather than awareness.

Mathematically, the process was simple. After each prediction, incoming sensor readings revealed the true conditions. The model compared its forecast with these observations, calculated the error, and adjusted its internal parameters. As conditions shifted, the constant flow of measurements corrected earlier assumptions. Learning emerged from this repeated cycle of predicting, comparing, and adjusting.

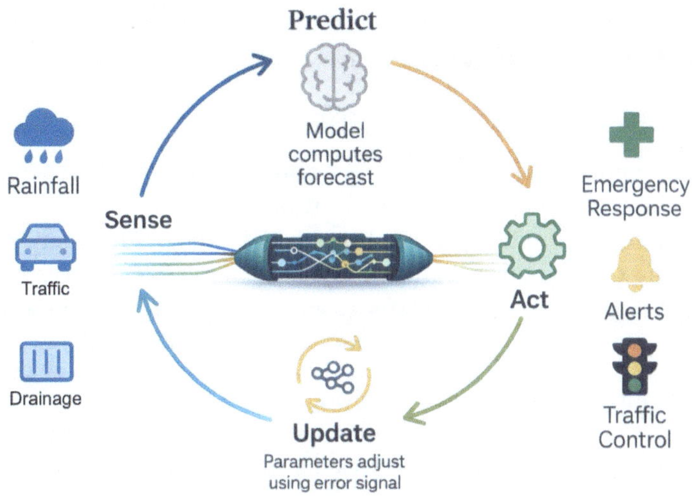

Figure 4.1: *Storm intelligence loop*

The system displayed confidence intervals as green and violet bands that indicated levels of uncertainty. High confidence reflected familiar conditions. Lower confidence signaled noisy or conflicting data. The model did not understand the storm, but it aligned its behavior with the evolving environment. *Intelligence,* Diego realized, *often begins as synchronization with change.*

During a workshop months earlier, Aisha had said, *Data is the design, but design without context becomes reflex.* Looking at the system now, Diego understood her point. The system could coordinate routes and resources, but it could not understand their meaning. It generated coordinated actions, not comprehension. Its regular update cycles simply kept the system stable, much like a loom maintaining even tension across threads.

When the storm eased, Diego stepped outside. Routing recommendations held steady, surface flooding stabilized in monitored zones, and risks remained contained. The city felt guided rather than overwhelmed.

Patterns behind intelligence

Diego understood that AI was not a mind. It was a form of decision intelligence, a computational system that learned by updating its predictions against real conditions. It did not imitate human reasoning. It transformed input into action through structured adaptation.

AI is often described as cognition, yet in practice, it is the science of adaptive coordination. It learns from feedback, adjusts through error signals, and extends human capacity to perceive and respond at scale. Its rhythm is mathematical. The challenge is designing such systems so they remain responsible within the patterns we define.

This chapter introduces AI as decision intelligence. It explains how patterns form, how learning emerges from feedback, and how this rhythm becomes the foundation for adaptive action.

From data to decision

A loom begins with threads, but intelligence begins with decisions.

Morning light settled over Barranquilla, leaving a thin sheen of moisture on every street. The storm had passed, yet the city remained awake in its digital rhythms. Inside the municipal response center, Diego sat before the console that had glowed with urgency the night before. Now the interface was calm. The monitoring system displayed steady streams of rainfall levels, water flow rates, soil absorption data, drainage capacity, and mobility updates. The weave of signals looked orderly compared to the intensity of the flood.

He replayed the activity logs. Each sequence unfolded as a structured timeline. Sensor readings arrived, the system processed them, model outputs propagated across districts, and the city adjusted. What he watched was not intuition. It was computation, with each action grounded in data.

The monitoring system formed the first layer of the digital weave. It sensed the world and turned raw measurements into usable signals. But the decisions came from the predictive model embedded within it. AI interpreted the monitored data, recognized patterns that signaled risk, and produced recommended actions. Only when the model detected meaningful relationships did the system intervene.

The data formed the raw threads, and the model wove them into coordinated action.

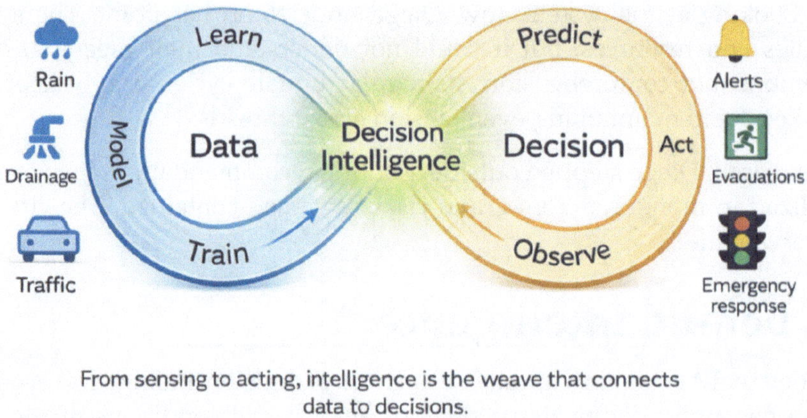

Figure 4.2: *Decision intelligence loop*

The flood model Diego had trained worked in exactly this way. It compared incoming signals with patterns learned from months of past storms. When it rerouted traffic or prioritized shelters faster than human operators, it was responding to familiar conditions in the data.

Aisha joined for a quick morning check-in, reviewed the logs, and summarized the behavior simply. *It was not intuition. It was learned response.*

The night had made one point clear. The city did not need the machine to understand. It needed a reliable way to turn information into coordinated decisions.

The loom of intelligence had begun to move.

Understanding how machines learn

AI is a set of mathematical methods that link inputs to outputs. These systems observe examples, refine internal representations, and improve through feedback. They do not understand in the human sense. They adjust patterns until their predictions match real conditions.

Machine learning (**ML**) begins with the idea that a system can infer relationships from data. When Diego trained the flood model, he used past storms as examples. Rainfall distributions, soil saturation curves, movement patterns, and infrastructure limits were paired with known outcomes. Over many iterations, the model learned a mapping between conditions and results. With more examples, the mapping became more stable and more generalizable.

The model approximated a function. It attempted to generalize from known cases to new ones. This is the foundation of decision intelligence.

Three primary learning modes support this behavior:

- **Supervised learning**: Supervised learning uses labeled examples. Each input has a known target, and the model adjusts its predictions by comparing them with the correct values. Diego's flood model used supervised learning to associate rainfall patterns and terrain features with overflow risk.
- **Unsupervised learning**: Unsupervised learning analyzes data without labels. It identifies clusters and structures that may not be immediately visible. Maya once applied unsupervised learning in a hospital network to detect early viral signals. The system identified unusual patterns in vitals long before clinicians recognized a trend.
- **Reinforcement learning**: Reinforcement learning enables systems to learn through trial and error. Actions receive rewards or penalties that guide behavior. When Aisha experimented with reinforcement learning for agricultural drones, the reward design shaped how the drones explored irrigation routes and discovered efficient paths.

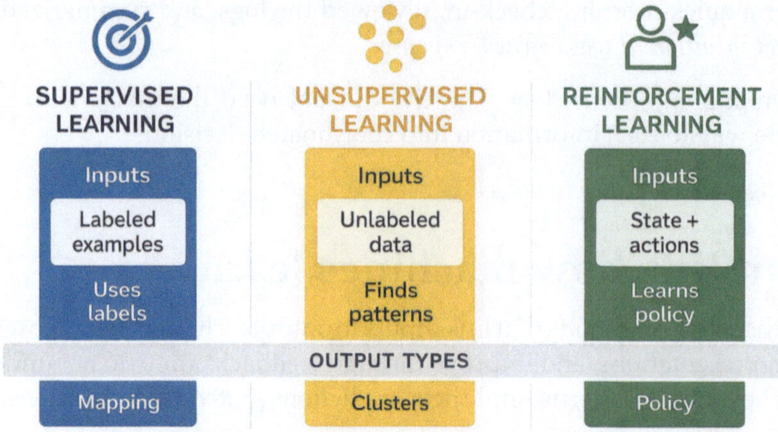

***Figure 4.3**: The three primary modes of ML*

These three modes form a conceptual triangle of perception, discovery, and adaptation. Each contributes a different dimension of intelligence. Supervised learning provides precision. Unsupervised learning provides insight. Reinforcement learning provides a strategy. Together, they enable systems to navigate uncertainty.

When Diego reviewed the training logs, he saw traces of this triangle in the flood model's behavior. The system relied primarily on supervised learning, yet its grouping of unusual sensor readings resembled unsupervised clustering, and its real-time adjustments under storm pressure resembled reinforcement-style feedback, where incoming signals influenced how priorities shifted.

AI systems often move between these modes, switching approaches the way a craftsperson selects tools. The objective remains constant, which is to align prediction with reality.

Threads of the neural weave

Inside the flood model was a neural network. It processed information through layers of interconnected units. Each layer applied a mathematical transformation that revealed an increasingly abstract structure. Early layers detected simple cues such as rainfall intensity or slope gradients. Middle layers combined these cues to describe flow movement. Deeper layers produced the representations that guided decisions.

This layered design allowed the model to learn relationships that were difficult to specify through explicit rules. Engineers defined the architecture. The network learned the weights through training.

Training followed a familiar loop. After each prediction, new sensor readings revealed actual conditions. The model calculated the error and adjusted its internal parameters. Small updates accumulated across thousands of cycles, aligning internal representations with the structure of the data. Neural networks do not form explanations. They form mathematical alignments that help them recognize familiar patterns in noisy environments.

Diego often explained it to new engineers with a simple analogy. *The network was the loom. Data was the thread. Learning was the craft that brought structure into coherence.*

Learning the rhythm of models

Later that morning, Diego ran a simulation using overnight data. As the model processed the inputs, its loss curve declined smoothly. This curve reflected the error between predictions and measured values, and its steady descent showed improvement.

The rhythm was consistent; predict, compare, correct, repeat. Each cycle strengthened the model's ability to generalize beyond the storms it had seen. Generalization is the property that lets a model recognize patterns in new situations rather than memorizing old ones.

Aisha once compared strong models to durable fabrics. *They flex when conditions change yet remain coherent*. A model that is too rigid fails in unfamiliar settings. A model that is too flexible becomes unstable. Effective learning requires balance.

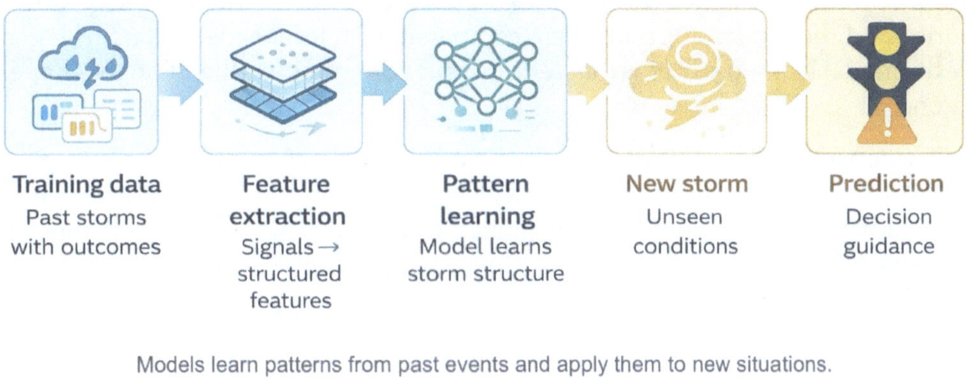

Figure 4.4: *Deep ML from examples to generalization*

As Diego watched the system settle into updated parameters, he saw that balance in motion. The model adapted to new data yet remained stable enough to avoid erratic behavior. It was learning in the mathematical sense, not the human one.

Adapting through feedback

Later in the week, Diego tested the system under new rainfall conditions. Some outputs drifted from expected values, but the system corrected itself as updated sensor readings arrived. Each correction nudged the model toward better alignment.

This behavior demonstrated adaptive intelligence. The system incorporated new information as it arrived. It performed a form of online learning, updating incrementally without full retraining. These feedback loops acted as continuous quality checks on the model's internal pattern.

The process also revealed the risk of model drift. Uneven data coverage caused the system to favor high-income regions with dense sensors. Under-monitored neighborhoods influence predictions less, resulting in unequal accuracy. To correct this, Diego applied data weighting to ensure all regions contributed fairly.

Bias often arises mathematically before it appears in outcomes. Uneven data creates uneven influence. Addressing it requires careful monitoring, transparency, and active intervention.

From design to alignment

One evening, Diego reviewed the week's updates with Maya and Aisha. Their focus had shifted from accuracy to alignment. They examined whether the model's priorities matched community needs. Maya reminded them that *intelligence without alignment is only automation. A flood model must protect people, not only infrastructure.*

The team created a new evaluation protocol. Instead of testing only for predictive accuracy, they added community-defined scenarios. Residents described situations they considered high priority, and the model's outputs were compared with local expectations. The goal was to ensure the model learned patterns that reflected the community rather than the shape of the dataset alone.

Back at his console, Diego studied the updated visualization. Blue lines represented environmental data, gold lines showed learned patterns, and green lines displayed recommended actions. These flows moved together as one structure. He saw more than a technical display. He saw a system that connected sensing, learning, and coordinated response.

The intelligence did not lie in the colors. It lay in the architecture that transformed raw signals into decisions. To understand the rhythm he had witnessed during the storm, Diego knew he needed to examine the loom more closely and trace how each layer shaped the flow of information.

Inside the loom of learning

The loom reveals its intelligence in how it carries patterns forward.

AI does not learn through a single insight. It learns through structure. The architecture of a model determines how data is represented, refined, and transformed into decisions. Inputs move through layers that extract features, identify relationships, and guide responses. These layers shape the system's ability to generalize, adapt, and act under changing conditions. In this sense, the architecture becomes a loom that moves threads of information from one transformation to the next.

Understanding this interior structure matters. A flood warning, a clinical alert, or a soil moisture prediction is the visible outcome of many small internal shifts. To understand how an AI system learns, one must step inside the loom where representation and adaptation take place.

Learning with layers

Before exploring specialized architectures, Diego often returned to the foundation—the **artificial neural network** (**ANN**). An ANN is a layered system made of simple computational units called **neurons**. Each neuron receives numeric inputs, multiplies them by learned weights, adds a bias term, and applies a nonlinear activation function. A single neuron captures only a simple relationship. When thousands of them are arranged in layers, the network can model complex patterns.

In its simplest form:

- The input layer receives raw signals.
- Hidden layers transform those signals through weighted combinations and nonlinear activations.
- The output layer produces a prediction or classification.

Learning occurs through backpropagation. The network compares its predictions to the correct values, calculates an error, and updates the weights to reduce it. When this process is repeated across many layers, it becomes deep learning.

This layered structure forms the baseline model for many advanced systems. **Convolutional neural networks** (**CNNs**) learn spatial structure. **Recurrent neural networks** (**RNNs**) and **long short-term memory** (**LSTM**) models learn temporal sequences. Transformers learn global relationships. All of them rely on repeated weighted transformations and nonlinear activations.

The ANN is the frame of the loom. Without the frame, the threads cannot be guided. Without these foundational neural layers, no higher intelligence emerges.

Layers and logic

The storm model that guided the city's response relied on a layered architecture that transformed raw signals into meaningful patterns. The first layer received numerical inputs from rainfall monitors, drainage sensors, topographic grids, and traffic feeds. Each input arrived as a vector describing intensity, position, and time. From there, the network shaped its understanding through a sequence of transformations.

Each layer performed two operations. A linear transformation reshaped the input. A nonlinear activation function followed, allowing the model to capture relationships that simple linear equations cannot represent. When stacked across many layers, these operations created a hierarchy of abstraction. Early layers detected local cues. Middle layers combined them into broader structures. Upper layers aggregated information into regional assessments and recommendations.

Aisha sent a brief message to Diego.

How many layers now?

Twenty-four, he replied.

Depth collects context.

He saw the idea in the model's behavior. Lower layers responded to immediate signals. Deeper layers held context that shaped overall interpretation. The architecture resembled a loom with several levels. Lower threads carried raw data. Middle threads produced motifs. Upper threads aligned motifs into coherent patterns that supported real decisions.

Spatial and temporal models

Later in the afternoon, Diego joined a technical review call with Maya and Aisha. Their applications differed, yet their learning principles were shared.

Maya displayed an image from her diagnostic platform. As the model processed it, small regions brightened. *This part uses convolution*, she said. *It learns by examining the picture in small patches*.

CNNs are designed for spatial perception. They use filters that slide across an image to detect edges, textures, and shapes. Each filter captures a specific feature and applies it across the entire image through parameter sharing. CNNs excel in tasks where spatial structure matters, such as medical imaging, satellite maps, and terrain analysis.

Aisha linked this idea to her farmland surveys. *Each drone pass captured a single plot. When the plots were combined, the system understood the full field*.

Storm patterns, however, unfolded not only in space but also in time.

RNNs process sequences step by step and pass a hidden state forward, allowing the model to capture short-term temporal dependencies. They perform well on brief patterns but struggle when signals must be remembered across long intervals because their internal states fade.

LSTM models address this limitation by using gates that regulate information flow. One gate controls what to store, another what to discard, and another what to output. These gates preserve important signals over extended periods, allowing LSTMs to model long storm cycles, river levels, and sensor sequences.

Diego combined convolutional layers for spatial structure with recurrent and LSTM layers for temporal evolution. In the architecture diagram, these components resembled horizontal threads for space and vertical threads for time. The system's intelligence emerged where these threads intersected.

He realized that capability came not from choosing a single architecture, but from aligning specialized structures so they operated as a coherent system.

The transformer shift

Several weeks later, Diego visited the coastal research *laboratory in Cartagena*. Inside a dim analysis room, attention visualizations from a transformer model glowed across a curved display. The patterns did not rise in stacked layers or progress through time steps. They spread outward like a field of relationships.

Transformers process entire sequences at once through a mechanism called **self-attention**. Each token is transformed into a query, key, and value vectors; the query expresses what a token is looking for, the key represents what information each token provides, and the value holds the content that will ultimately be combined. An attention matrix compares every query against every key to determine how strongly each element should influence the others. Instead of relying on fixed sequence order, the model evaluates relevance directly. Signals that matter more receive higher attention weights, while less influential ones fade into the background.

Transformers use multiple attention heads in parallel. Each head learns a different relationship, as some capture fine-grained local structure, others detect long-range dependencies. Together, they give the model a wide and adaptive field of view.

Maya shared an example from her multilingual triage system. *Transformers learn context*, she said. *They connect meaning even when the words appear far apart*.

For Diego's coastal model, the transformer shift was transformative. Rainfall measurements, tide cycles, satellite imagery, traffic flow, and citizen alerts could all influence one another directly. When one signal changed, the attention weights reorganized, and the model recalculated the pattern.

Transformers did not create awareness. They created coordinated relevance. They enabled learning across entire fields of relationships rather than narrow sequences.

To Diego, this marked a turning point. The system was no longer weaving understanding thread by thread. It was learning from patterns spread across the whole field.

Foundation models

As transformer architectures matured, foundation models emerged. These large pretrained systems learned broad representations from massive collections of text, images, environmental records, sensor histories, and scientific datasets. Their generality allowed them to support many tasks with limited fine-tuning.

Diego acquired a foundation climate model trained on decades of global weather data. Its broad training allowed it to detect large-scale patterns quickly, yet it also carried the imprint of its dataset. Temperate regions were overrepresented. Tropical coastlines were underrepresented. These imbalances shaped its initial predictions for Barranquilla.

He summarized the issue simply. *A large loom can weave wide fabric, but a misaligned thread runs through everything.*

To adapt the model, he fine-tuned it on regional storm data. The predictions improved, but traces of inherited bias remained. Areas with denser sensors received more accurate forecasts. Regions that resembled temperate training zones were sometimes misclassified.

To correct this, the team built a smaller derivative model. It used the foundation model's general knowledge but retrained frequently on local sensor streams and community observations. This improved alignment with the city's lived realities.

Foundation models provided scale and efficiency. Local adaptation provided trust and accountability. For Diego, intelligence could not be judged only by accuracy. It had to reflect the people and places it served.

Weaving precision and visibility

Although each architecture builds on the same foundational principles, their learning mechanisms and trade-offs differ. The following table summarizes the core characteristics of the architectures introduced in this section:

Architecture	What it learns	Strengths	Limitations	Common applications
ANN	Basic weighted transformations across layers	General-purpose baseline, flexible structure	Limited representational power without depth	Simple classification, regression, tabular prediction
CNN	Spatial filters that detect edges, textures, and local patterns	Excellent for images and grids, parameter-efficient	Cannot model long temporal dependencies	Vision tasks, satellite imaging, medical imaging, and geospatial analysis
RNN	Sequential dependencies using hidden state	Suitable for short sequences, lightweight	Vanishing gradients, weak for long-term patterns	Time-series forecasting, sensor streams, and basic language modeling
LSTM	Gated memory that retains long-term dependencies	Strong sequence modeling, stable training	Slower training and inference than attention models	Weather sequences, clinical data streams, and multi-step forecasting

Architecture	What it learns	Strengths	Limitations	Common applications
Transformer	Attention relationships across all positions in a sequence	Parallel processing, rich context modeling	High computational and memory cost	Multilingual text, multimodal fusion, and long-context prediction
Foundation model	Broad pretrained patterns from massive datasets	Effective transfer learning, strong generalization	Can inherit dataset bias and require costly fine-tuning	Climate modeling, code assistants, general-purpose languages, and vision systems

Table 4.1*: Architecture families and their learning patterns*

CNN layers produced spatial feature maps that detected shapes and textures across terrain grids. RNN and LSTM components traced temporal sequences to reveal how rainfall and drainage evolved. Transformer layers highlighted which signals influenced each decision. Foundation model overlays added environmental patterns learned from global datasets.

Each architecture increased accuracy, but greater accuracy came with greater complexity. As the models grew deeper and more interconnected, the path from input to recommendation became harder to interpret. The system gained capability, yet its internal reasoning became less visible.

During an early workshop, Aisha remarked, *A weave is strongest when you can still see the pattern*. The storm had shown how effective the system could be, but it also demonstrated why visibility mattered. Interpretability was not an optional enhancement. It was a structural requirement for responsible deployment.

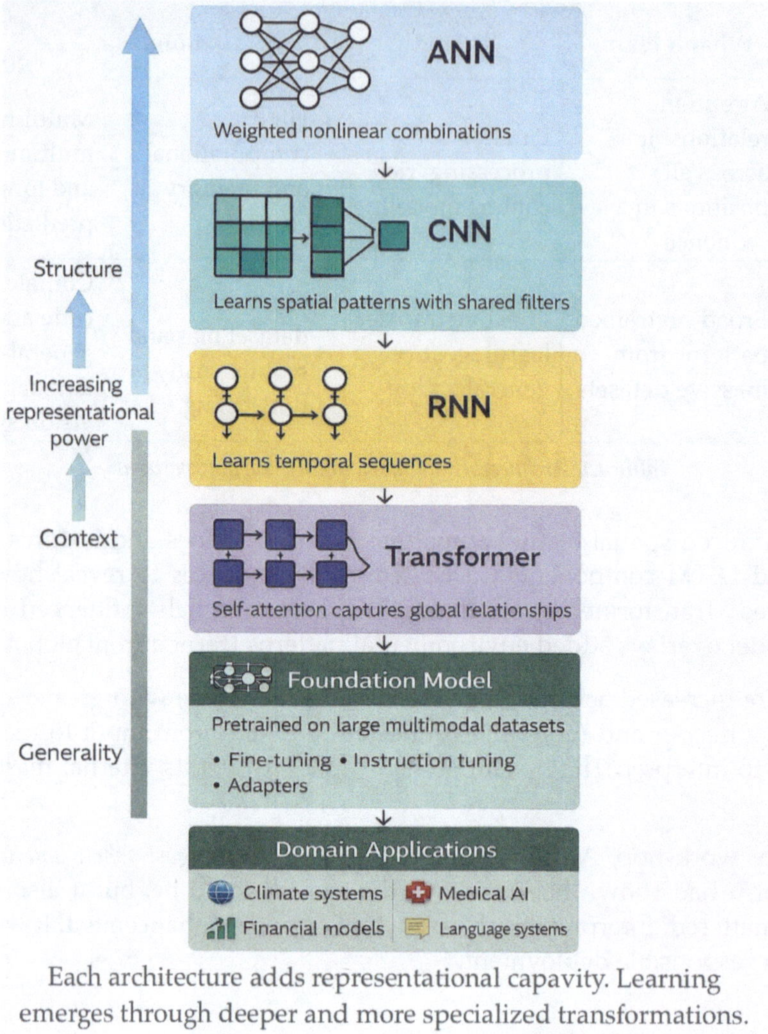

***Figure 4.5:** The learning stack*

To Diego, the value of the model was not in its depth but in how clearly its transformations could be inspected. Architecture shaped the system's ability to learn. Transparency shaped its ability to be trusted. As the visualization dimmed, he understood that intelligence was defined not only by structure but by how well patterns connected back to real communities and informed decisions on the ground.

Intelligence touching everyday life

A weave is tested not on the loom, but in the wind.

AI becomes meaningful only when it meets real conditions. It shapes morning routines, adapts to disrupted supply chains, supports clinicians under pressure, and expands scientific inquiry. In these settings, intelligence appears as adaptive behavior. It reads context, absorbs feedback, and recalibrates decisions as conditions shift.

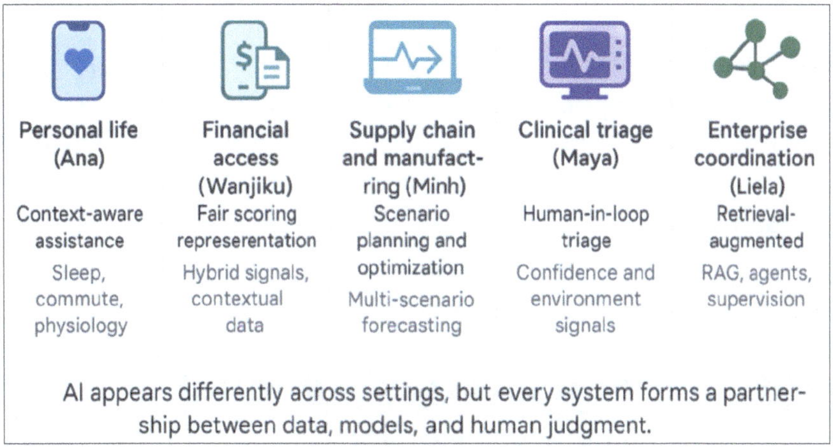

Figure 4.6: *Intelligence touching everyday life*

Across homes, cooperatives, hospitals, enterprises, and laboratories, AI does more than compute. It collaborates. Each setting reveals a different dimension of learning. Some systems anticipate needs. Others compensate for imperfect signals. Some simulate futures. All depends on a partnership between mathematical structure and human judgment.

This section brings these movements into view.

The assistant who understands the day

In a small apartment in Lisbon, *Ana* woke before sunrise to the soft vibration of her wristband. Her AI assistant had shifted the alarm after detecting that her sleep cycle ran deeper than usual. It did not rely on the clock alone. It synchronized with her physiology.

She opened her kitchen window and checked the morning briefing. The system merged her calendar, commute patterns, and weather conditions into a simple plan. It recommended leaving ten minutes early because construction work had slowed her bus route for the past two days. Ana had not noticed the delay, but the model had identified the pattern.

While she prepared breakfast, a message appeared. Protein recommended this morning. The assistant inferred from her running logs and elevated heart rate that her recovery score was low. It did not prescribe a diet. It suggested options based on physiological and behavioral history.

During her commute, she played a language lesson. The app adjusted pacing based on her hesitation patterns, slowing down when she repeated concepts and speeding up when she showed confidence. The system measured progress through mastery curves rather than time spent.

By evening, as she walked home along the waterfront, a gentle prompt appeared. You have taken fewer steps today. *Would you like a detour by the marina?* Its design favored choice rather than instruction.

Before bed, Ana reviewed her day. None of the suggestions felt intrusive. Each responded to real context, such as sleep depth, commute disruptions, physiological strain, and learning behavior. The assistant worked not as a scheduler but as a companion who adapted to her rhythm.

She wrote in her journal, *It feels like the system sees the shape of my day even before I do.*

Personal intelligence systems succeed when they adapt to individual rhythms without imposing decisions. Their value lies in their sensitivity to context and respect for user agency.

The algorithm that measures potential

Morning sunlight spread across the hillside town of *Eldoret* as *Wanjiku* unlocked her workshop. Her furniture business had grown steadily, but she needed a loan to purchase new tools. The cooperative's mobile app offered a digital application powered by an AI credit model. It promised speed and fairness.

She entered her information and waited. Within seconds, the result appeared. Application declined due to insufficient credit history.

Inside the cooperative office, loan officer Samuel reviewed her case. The model evaluates digital footprints, he explained. Mobile payments, transaction logs, and supplier receipts, but the system had been trained mostly on urban customers with rich digital histories. Wanjiku's customers often paid in cash. Sparse data had been misinterpreted as risk.

Samuel opened the model's feature explanation. Payment regularity, digital receipts, and savings transactions dominated. Community savings groups, informal supplier relationships, and local trust networks were missing because they had never been part of the training dataset.

Over the next week, the cooperative gathered additional information. Supplier receipts were digitized. Savings group records were linked to verified participants. Neighbors confirmed repayment reliability. Engineers retrained the model, weighting these new signals alongside digital ones.

This time, the model returned a score with a transparent explanation—consistent supplier reliability, active community savings participation, moderate payment history.

Her loan was approved. More importantly, the model now reflected economic truth where it once saw silence. The intelligence had grown not by learning new mathematics but by learning new contexts.

She left the office holding the approval message, feeling recognized for her potential rather than her data.

Decision systems become fair when they incorporate the full range of human experience. Intelligence improves when the data becomes more complete.

The algorithm that plans the unseen

At *Minh's electronics plant,* the morning shift began with a quiet alert. An AI planning system had flagged a possible shortage of a key microcontroller used across three product lines. It was not a failure prediction. It was an early signal that supply conditions were shifting.

She opened the scenario panel. A set of branching futures appeared:

- One scenario showed a forty-hour port delay leading to a line stoppage.
- Another showed that advancing a small order from a secondary supplier would cover half the gap.
- A third showed that reducing production speed slightly could stretch buffer inventory long enough for alternate stock to arrive.

The model did not choose. It generated possibilities, each weighted by likelihood and impact.

Minh walked on the floor with her headset on and consulted team leads. Operators confirmed increased component use from a recent design change. Maintenance teams reported vibration in an older conveyor motor, suggesting that high-load operation was risky. These insights adjusted the model's assumptions.

By noon, Minh issued a revised plan:

- Advance a partial shipment from a backup supplier.
- Redirect a low-priority variant to a plant in *Cebu* with spare capacity.
- Reduce line 3 speed by eight percent.
- Schedule light maintenance on the conveyor to avoid downtime.

The AI updated its projections instantly. The plant's output remained stable. Customer lead times remained intact. No line stoppage occurred.

Minh watched the forecast settle. The intelligence was not in a single choice but in the shared adaptation between people and algorithms. The system revealed tension. The team shaped the response.

Planning systems amplify human decision-making by providing structured foresight and enabling people to guide the final choice.

The algorithm that listens

Afternoon heat pressed against the glass walls of São Paulo's central hospital as *Maya* reviewed triage data from a chemical incident. The AI model sorted vital signs and symptoms from portable scanners and assigned risk scores in real time. On most days, the system worked reliably. Today, it hesitated.

A patient flagged as low risk began showing rapid shifts in heart rate and oxygen saturation. The model's confidence level remained stable, suggesting certainty where none existed. Maya sensed the mismatch. The system had been trained on winter respiratory cases, not on solvent exposure in humid conditions.

She opened the decision trace. The model highlighted variables shaping the score, but nothing explained the anomaly. The missing factor was environmental. The dataset had never encountered this pattern.

Maya lowered the threshold that triggered clinician review. More cases surfaced for manual evaluation. Nurses entered observations on tablets, adding contextual details that the model had never seen. These corrections fed into the system's short-term calibration and reweighted relevant signals.

Within minutes, the model recalibrated. Confidence shifted, and the earlier low-risk patient moved near the top of the list. Intervention arrived in time.

This was a **human-in-the-loop** (**HITL**) design at its core. Automation provided speed. Clinicians preserved meaning. The system learned humility through the feedback of those who understood the lived patterns of illness.

Later, Maya wrote in her notebook: *Listening in machines begins where certainty ends.*

Safety-critical systems require visibility, awareness of uncertainty, and human judgment. Intelligence grows when it can be corrected.

The system that thinks with the enterprise

Liela stood in her Dubai design studio surrounded by fabric rolls, embroidered samples, and shifting production schedules. Her boutique business had expanded quickly. To keep pace with custom orders and fluctuating supply chains, she relied on an enterprise AI platform that coordinated design, sourcing, and manufacturing.

Each morning, she crafted a structured prompt to plan her day. Over time, she learned that prompt engineering was part technique and part discipline. Specific prompts produced clearer reasoning. Vague prompts produced vague plans.

That afternoon, a retailer requested a rush order of embroidered jackets with a ten-day delivery window. Liela asked the system to evaluate the feasibility. The platform initiated its retrieval layer, pulling information from inventory logs, supplier records, machine schedules, and past delivery patterns. **Retrieval augmented generation** (**RAG**) grounded each suggestion in verifiable documents. She inspected dye-lot sheets, machine logs, and supplier histories.

Then the agent activated. It performed sequential tasks automatically. It identified suppliers with the required thread, checked embellishment availability, projected machine workload, and generated three production plans. One favored speed. One favored cost. One balanced throughput. The agent drafted job cards and a message for the retailer, pausing for confirmation at each stage.

The system was powerful, but the guardrails mattered. No schedule change occurred without her approval. No purchase order was issued without a cost review.

Her local knowledge filled the gaps. One scenario recommended sourcing a thread from a vendor in *Sharjah* who usually delivers in four days. Liela adjusted the plan. She knew from a recent conversation that the vendor faced a staffing shortage. She selected an alternate supplier with a slightly longer timeline but more reliable service. The agent incorporated the change and recalculated production.

Later that evening, Diego sent a message asking how the system had handled the rush order. Liela forwarded the updated plan.

He replied that the model learned because she guided it.

Liela smiled, recognizing the truth in his words. Her studio no longer felt like a small workshop running on intuition. It felt like a coordinated fabric of people, processes, and intelligent assistance. The loom had grown, yet she remained at its center.

Enterprise intelligence succeeds when algorithms coordinate complexity and humans provide judgment and constraints.

Weaving intelligence into action

Across personal routines, financial decisions, manufacturing floors, hospital wards, and enterprises, intelligence revealed a shared truth. Learning systems do not act alone. They adapt because the world around them responds. With Ana, the system adjusted to her rhythm. With Wanjiku, it learned to value forms of credit that had never been digitized. With Minh, it balanced global supply chains through human insight. With Maya, it recalibrated under uncertainty. With Liela, it learned to follow her lead.

Each story showed that intelligence is not a fixed artifact. It is a relationship that forms between data, environment, and human intent. The power of any system depends on how clearly its patterns remain visible and how openly people can correct, question, and guide its learning.

When intelligence moves with us, the weave holds.

When we shape it in return, the pattern becomes whole.

Fraying patterns

Every weave unravels somewhere; wisdom lies in knowing where to mend.

Even the most refined systems falter when the world shifts in ways they have never seen. Models trained on familiar patterns stumble when the environment breaks its old patterns. Resilience is not the absence of error. It is the ability to recognize where tension accumulates and restore balance.

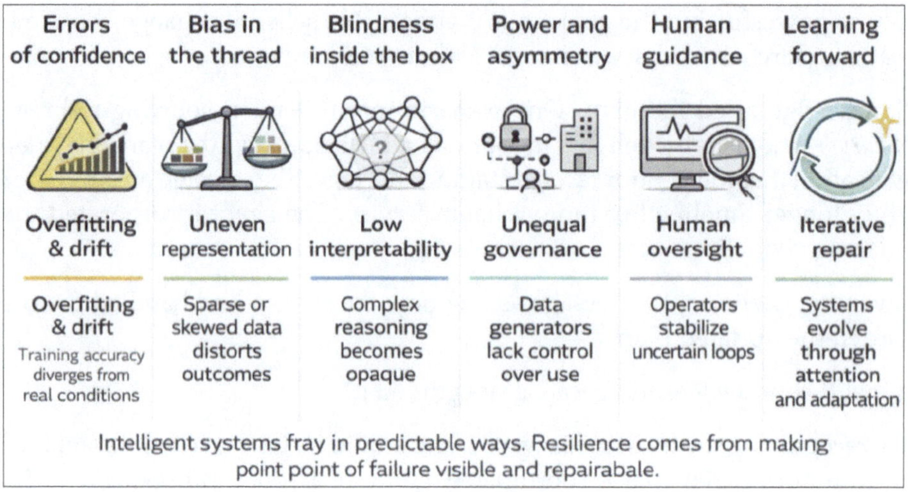

Figure 4.7: *Fraying edges of an AI system*

This section examines the quiet places where systems drift, distort, or become opaque, and the practices that keep intelligence grounded in care.

Errors of confidence

The storm that struck Barranquilla moved in from an unexpected direction, and rainfall doubled within an hour. Yet the dashboard reported high confidence that the districts marked as safe would remain stable. Minutes later, water levels rose faster than the model predicted.

What prevented escalation was not the system but the people observing it. Field personnel saw rising currents that did not match the forecast. Operators initiated precautionary diversions, updated evacuation guidance, and adjusted pump sequences based on local judgment. The model had expressed confidence. Human oversight prevented a mistake.

The next morning, Diego reviewed the logs. The failure was rooted in overfitting. The model had performed almost flawlessly on its training data but struggled when real conditions drifted. Training error had dropped toward zero, yet deployment error increased sharply as the storm unfolded.

Maya recognized the pattern. She had seen similar outcomes in clinical triage, where confident predictions encouraged staff to trust the system more than their own assessment.

Confidence is not competence, she reminded him. *A model must reacquire trust with every new observation.*

They retrained the network with broader variability, rare cases, and synthetic extremes. The priority shifted from precision to resilience, enabling the system to remain balanced as the rhythm of the world changed.

High confidence does not guarantee correctness. Systems must be calibrated to reflect real uncertainty, and humans must remain attentive interpreters.

Bias in the thread

Wanjiku contacted Diego with a concern. Her cooperative's credit model was drifting again. Loan approvals were concentrated in regions with richer digital histories, while rural applicants saw fewer opportunities.

Even fairness drifts, she said.

Bias often begins quietly. Missing records, uneven sampling, and cultural proxies distort patterns long before outcomes reveal a problem. A model can be mathematically neutral yet still amplify imbalance when its inputs reflect unequal conditions.

Diego's audit showed that rural communities remained underrepresented. Sparse records were interpreted as weak potential rather than missing context.

The team evaluated fairness metrics, including disparate impact and representation coverage. They expanded data sources, added community reliability indicators, and reweighted features to reduce structural imbalance. Metrics helped guide corrections, but judgment shaped the direction.

Diego reminded the group that *bias does not fade without deliberate repair.*

Fairness requires continuous monitoring, richer representation, and active intervention.

Blindness inside the black box

During a city audit, a council member asked Diego why the flood alert for a district had failed. He could not give a clear answer. The model had combined thousands of signals through multiple nonlinear layers, producing reasoning too complex to trace directly.

Interpretability tools highlighted which variables influenced the output, but not how interactions produced the final decision. The logic remained blurred.

Opacity weakened trust. Even correct predictions felt fragile when no one could explain the chain of reasoning.

To address this, Diego's team created a glass-box interface. Each output displayed key variables, confidence levels, and uncertainty ranges. The system ran slightly slower, but it became far more legible. A small delay was worth the clarity required to keep the pattern visible.

Interpretability is not optional. Transparency strengthens trust and accountability.

Power and asymmetry

As the models expanded in influence, Diego began to notice a deeper imbalance.

Citizens generated the data.

Local communities lived with the consequences.

Yet infrastructure and ownership often rested with distant organizations that held economic or political power.

Wanjiku encountered this tension when international firms sought to license their improved credit model. She hesitated.

If others take it, she wondered, *will it still work for the people who shaped it?*

Similar concerns appeared in *São Paulo*, where clinicians saw their local triage model absorbed into regional platforms without clear community oversight.

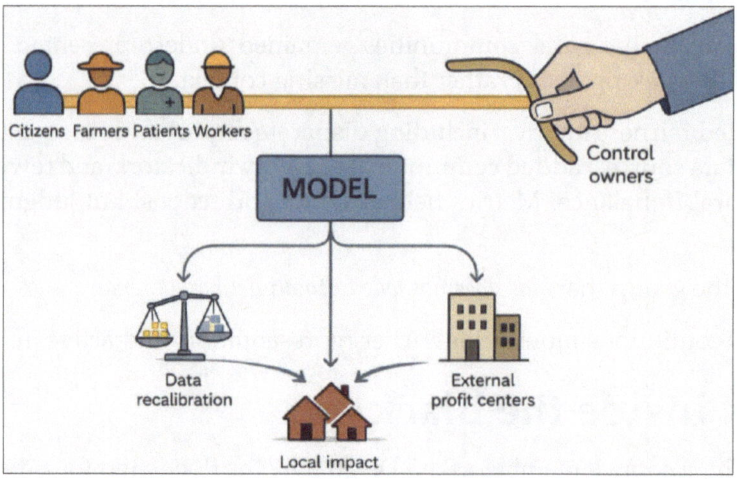

Figure 4.8: *Whose hand holds the thread?*

These moments pointed to a wider issue. Systems built from local experience could drift from local needs once ownership shifted. Many communities began exploring governance structures such as data trusts, which give shared rights and decision-making authority to those whose information fuels the system. The approach was not perfect, but it restored a measure of agency to the people whose lives formed the model's thread.

Intelligence systems should respect the communities that create their data and bear their impact.

Human guidance in the loop

As systems grow more autonomous, they can continue acting even when their confidence no longer matches reality. The flood model in Barranquilla, the triage platform in São Paulo, and the credit engine in Eldoret showed the same pattern. When uncertainty increased, the systems did not slow down or request oversight. They continued forward anyway.

This is the real risk. A model can misread a storm, overlook a symptom, or undervalue a rural applicant, but the greater threat comes when it fails to signal that it needs human judgment.

To overcome this, Diego redesigned the city's platform with an oversight console. It displayed data quality, model confidence, and ethical compliance as clear indicators. Operators could pause the system, inspect inputs, or override recommendations whenever a decision felt brittle or unfamiliar. It shifted the loop from automation to cooperation. Diego called it the **loop of care**.

Similar changes appeared elsewhere. Maya's clinical network added checkpoints requiring manual review when confidence dropped. Wanjiku's cooperative introduced community review panels for high-impact credit outcomes. Lami's research team added human evaluation to generative simulations.

Across these settings, the insight was consistent. Resilience came not from autonomy but from attentive correction. Intelligence was measured not by how independently a model acted but by how openly it invited oversight and adapted through guidance.

Human-in-loop design is a safeguard, not a limitation. Systems become safer when they ask for help.

Learning forward

As a new storm gathered over Barranquilla, Diego stood by the control center window and watched the sensor grid flicker to life. The models were stronger now, more adaptive and more transparent, yet the memory of earlier failures remained. He understood how quickly confidence could harden into complacency and how easily a pattern could slip.

He opened his journal and wrote the line that had shaped every repair and redesign over the past months.

Mastery is not control. It is care.

The city's loom would continue learning, but now it would do so under steadier hands, shaped by attention rather than assumption, and supported by those who designed, deployed, and lived within it.

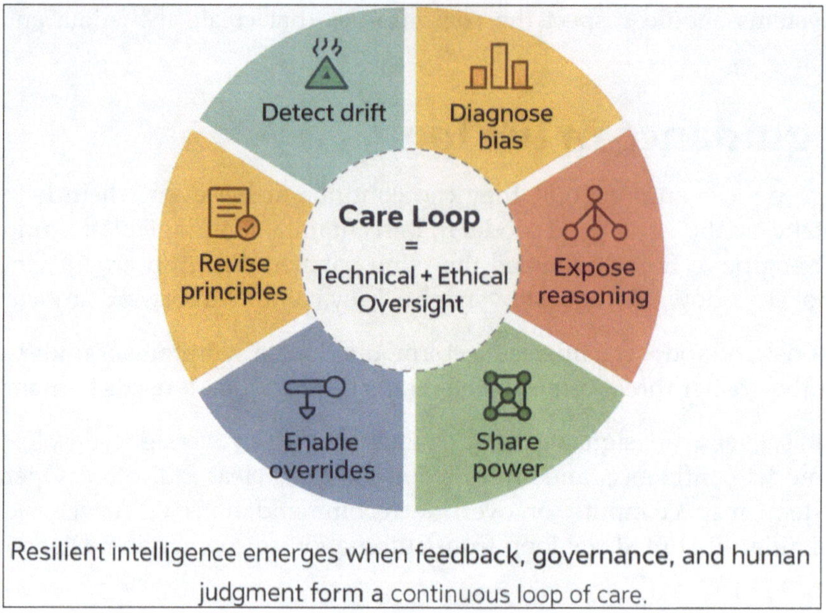

Figure 4.9: *The loop of care*

The storms and audits revealed something deeper than technical faults. Each frayed thread pointed back to choices about data, representation, and accountability. Fixing the model was necessary, but not sufficient. They needed to reshape the principles guiding intelligence development and governance.

This is where the next section turns—from correcting errors to designing with conscience.

Designing with conscience

A pattern endures not through strength but through attention to what pulls against it.

Intelligence gains meaning when it aligns with the communities and environments it serves. A system can be precise yet harmful, efficient yet unfair, powerful yet opaque. Conscience is the design layer that keeps these forces in balance. It shapes how models learn, how decisions unfold, and how responsibility is shared between people and machines.

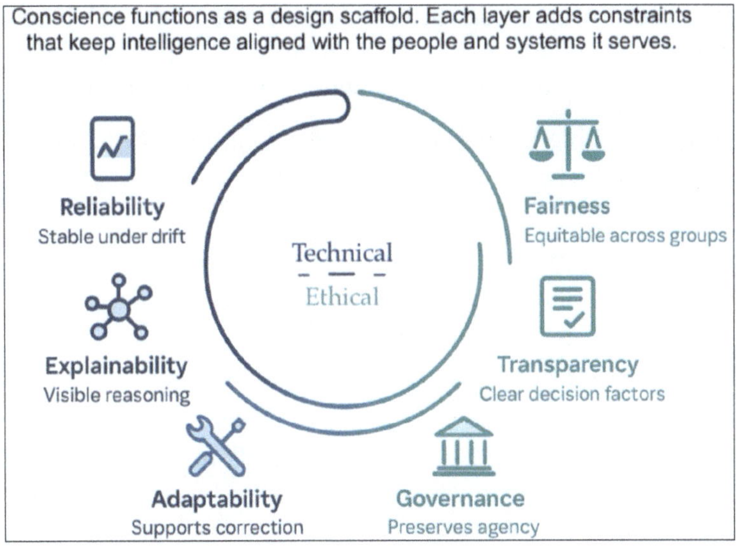

***Figure 4.10**: The layers of conscience in AI design*

Designing with conscience means treating intelligence not as an instrument to optimize but as a relationship to cultivate. It requires reliability under stress, fairness across contexts, transparency in reasoning, explainability that supports human judgment, and governance that preserves agency. The principles outlined in the following sections describe how intelligence acts with care rather than force.

Seeing beyond accuracy

Morning light filtered across the control center as Diego replayed the previous night's storm. By numerical standards, the model had performed nearly perfectly. Its forecasts matched recorded water levels across the coastal district within two percent.

Yet the numbers hid the truth. Two neighborhoods avoided flooding only because field engineers diverted runoff after noticing an unexpected buildup along an old drainage channel. The model did not detect the risk because that channel rarely influenced past storms. The accuracy was high, but the awareness was low.

Diego opened the evaluation panel and added the following three fields alongside precision and recall:

- **Reliability** measured whether the model stayed stable when conditions drifted.
- **Explainability** showed how clearly the system exposed the reasoning behind each prediction.
- **Human impact** tracked how recommendations shaped evacuation routes, resource allocation, and neighborhood safety.

Traditional accuracy metrics captured correctness against historical labels. They did not capture alignment with lived reality. A model could be statistically impressive yet misread the vulnerabilities of a hillside settlement or recommend actions that amplified operational strain.

As Diego reviewed the combined metrics, he realized that intelligence was defined not only by performance but by how well it lived in harmony with the people, infrastructure, and constraints of the world it served.

Accuracy is necessary but insufficient. Systems must be judged by how well they support real-world outcomes.

Fairness as balance

A week later, Wanjiku called from Eldoret. Her cooperative's credit model was drifting again. Loan approvals clustered in regions with strong digital histories, while rural applicants received fewer approvals. Sparse data was being interpreted as weak potential.

Diego reviewed the audit. Representation coverage maps revealed clear gaps. Rural applicants remained underrepresented, and the imbalance had seeped back into the model's learned patterns.

They applied fairness checks to quantify the problem:

- Disparate impact ratios measured unequal outcomes.
- Counterfactual tests showed that identical applicants received different scores when only the location changed.
- Reweighing increased the influence of underrepresented groups during training.

These corrections helped, but Wanjiku noted that fairness was not a destination. It was an equilibrium that had to be renewed with each dataset, deployment, and update.

Fairness requires continuous attention to representation, outcomes, and context.

Transparency in practice

Diego began redesigning the storm dashboard to make the system's reasoning visible. Each prediction now displayed its primary contributing factors, confidence level, and uncertainty range. A side panel revealed feature importance scores so engineers could understand which signals shaped the outcome.

The system ran slightly slower, but failures became easier to diagnose. Engineers no longer argued about hidden logic. They could trace the threads that led to each decision.

The same principle appeared elsewhere. Maya added visible summaries to triage results. Wanjiku included explanation notes in loan decisions. Transparency changed the nature of engagement. People responded not with suspicion but with informed curiosity.

Visibility strengthens collaboration. Transparency turns decisions into shared understanding.

Explainability for trust

When the regional ethics board visited São Paulo, a member asked Maya whether patients could request an explanation for any AI-driven triage decision.

Yes, she said. *That is their right.*

Explainability requires two levels of clarity. Internally, the model needed coherent representations so its reasoning could be traced. Externally, explanations had to be understandable without technical expertise.

Maya illustrated how this clarity was implemented in practice through a structured explanation pipeline. The details are as follows:

- The model produced a prediction.
- An interpretability layer translates variable influences into plain language.
- A validation script ensured reasoning avoided protected attributes.
- A review trail allowed clinicians to examine, contest, or refine the decision.

Diego later adopted the same approach for the flood system. Wanjiku integrated explanation trails into credit audits. Across sectors, the same principle emerged. Systems should be explainable by default, not by exception.

Trust grows through explanations that support human judgment.

Consent and co-weaving

Months later, Wanjiku convened a workshop titled *Our Data, Our Decisions*. Farmers, artisans, and shopkeepers gathered to discuss how their information shaped the cooperative's credit model. She began with a question. *Whose data builds this system?*

The room answered, *Ours*.

They formed a community data council that reviewed data sources, approved new features, and assessed outcomes. Members learned basic statistics and model ethics. Consent became continuous rather than a single moment.

Aisha adopted a similar approach for the agricultural network. Environmental data contributed by rural communities could now be viewed, edited, or withdrawn through local councils. People gained visibility into how their information influenced models that touched their daily lives.

These efforts showed that responsible design is shared work. Systems become collaborative rather than imposed when communities help shape them. Transparency reveals how a model reaches its decisions, but consent determines who has the right to influence them. Agency strengthens intelligence, and governance is strongest when the people whose data fuels a system also guide its direction.

Ethics as a structural force

During a joint review, *Aisha* presented a troubling finding. Her agricultural model had boosted yield predictions, yet farms that followed its recommendations began to show signs of soil stress.

We optimized for output, she said. *We forgot the renewal.*

The team recognized the pattern. A system tuned too narrowly to one metric could strain everything around it. Ethics was not an accessory. It was the structural force that kept competing values in balance.

They gathered the principles that now guided all their projects, a framework for designing with conscience:

- **Accountability**: Track decisions, document assumptions, and ensure outcomes are traceable.
- **Inclusion**: Give communities underrepresented in the data a voice in design, evaluation, and deployment.
- **Transparency**: Make reasoning visible enough for people to verify, question, and correct system behavior.
- **Explainability**: Provide clear and domain-appropriate explanations that help users evaluate recommendations.
- **Consent and agency**: Give individuals and communities meaningful control over how their data is used and how systems that affect them evolve.
- **Sustainability**: Consider ecological and computational cost when building and maintaining intelligent systems.
- **Guarded autonomy**: Use automation to support, not override, human judgment. Ensure humans can pause, correct, or redirect actions at any point.

These principles became their shared design checklist, the weaver's code of conscience. It reminded them that every technical choice carried human weight.

Ethics anchors design by keeping values in balance, especially when metrics pull in different directions.

Designing forward

Later that night, Diego stood by the same window where he once watched floodwaters rise. The city lights pulsed in a steady rhythm. The models continued to learn, but each loop now carried reminders of responsibility. Data came from real lives. Patterns shaped real choices.

He whispered, *Care is not caution. It is a connection.*

He opened his journal and wrote the closing line for their next paper:

To design is to decide.

The loom of the city would continue weaving, held together not only by data and architecture but by conscience. Yet Diego sensed that the next chapter would demand more. New forms of intelligence were emerging, which include the generative systems that created possibilities, adaptive models that learned continuously, and agentic tools that coordinated entire workflows.

These advances expanded capability but also demanded a deeper understanding of imagination, foresight, and responsibility.

The following section explores that frontier where intelligence not only responds to the world but imagines what the world could become.

The loom that imagines

Even when the loom learns to move, it still needs a story to follow.

Intelligence is evolving. Models that once predicted the next word or recognized a familiar pattern now generate new designs, coordinate long workflows, and adapt across months or years. They operate across text, images, maps, code, and real-world sensors, weaving many forms of knowledge into coherent actions. These systems no longer behave only as tools. They act as collaborators who propose ideas, refine options, and respond to human intent.

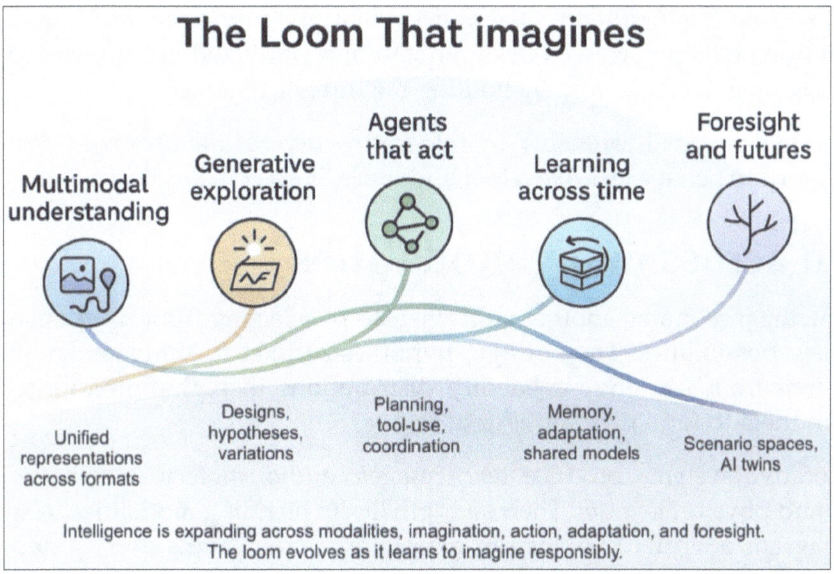

Figure 4.11: *The loom's imagination for the future*

This growth brings new responsibilities. Creation needs boundaries. Adaptation needs care. Governance must guide both. The future of AI will not be defined by stronger models alone, but by the judgment built into the systems we design and maintain.

Lami, now a graduate student in an intelligence design lab, often thought of these systems as looms that had begun to imagine. They predict. They create. They act. Yet their direction still depends on the stories people choose to teach them.

This section explores how intelligence is expanding across modalities, actions, time, and discovery. It turns from present capabilities toward the possibilities that will shape tomorrow.

From tools to collaborators

AI systems are entering a new stage, shifting from isolated models to integrated partners. Traditional systems solved single tasks in narrow domains. The next generation coordinates knowledge across many sources. A multimodal model can read satellite maps, summarize policy documents, interpret photographs, and produce recommendations from a single prompt.

This shift depends on unifying representations. A single model can encode text, images, tables, diagrams, and sensor streams into a shared latent space. Information that once lived in separate systems becomes interoperable. The result is not only convenience but a change in capability. A system that understands both weather data and soil imagery can support resource planning. A system that links architectural sketches with energy reports can help redesign buildings.

In her lab, *Lami* saw this firsthand. One system analyzed environmental signals, proposed water distribution layouts, reviewed design notes, and simulated expected yields. It did not replace her reasoning. It extended it by holding the threads together.

Multimodal models expand capability by integrating diverse data sources, and as they do, intelligence begins to behave less like a tool and more like a collaborator.

Creation across many modalities

Generative intelligence marks another shift. Instead of selecting from fixed answers, models now create new possibilities. They design, hypothesize, sketch, simulate, and refine. These capabilities stem from learning probability distributions in high-dimensional spaces and sampling from them to form new configurations.

Modern generative systems produce text, images, audio, molecular structures, software components, and physical layouts. Their strength lies in blending modalities. A single request can yield a diagram, a written explanation, a design variation, and a step-by-step plan.

These systems operate using generative transformers and diffusion architectures. Designers adjust parameters such as temperature and guidance strength to steer variation between realism and exploration.

In practice, generative systems already support early-stage ideation. Architects explore designs shaped by local climate data. Teachers create multiple lesson paths for different learning needs. City planners visualize flood adaptations across future decades.

Lami experimented with this frequently. She combined soil maps, rainfall projections, and cooperative goals. The system produced irrigation layouts, planting guides, and narrative explanations of tradeoffs. She never accepted its suggestions without review, but its ability to sketch possibilities accelerated her thinking.

Generative AI broadens creative exploration by offering many plausible futures rather than a single answer.

Agents that can act

A new horizon is agentic AI. These systems do more than analyze or generate. They take actions to achieve goals. They call tools, query databases, coordinate with other agents, and adjust plans as conditions change.

An agent typically includes five components:

- A goal it must pursue.
- A planning module that sequences actions.
- Access to tools and **application programming interface** (**APIs**).
- A memory that carries context across steps.
- An evaluation loop that monitors progress and recalibrates.

With these elements, agents can perform multi-step tasks such as scheduling, procurement, infrastructure monitoring, or task automation. They can run simulations, gather missing information, and propose decisions for human confirmation.

As these systems evolve, they will operate as coordinated networks. Some agents will manage supply chains. Others will handle policy checks, energy balancing, compliance, or risk forecasting. Shared protocols will allow them to negotiate priorities in real-time, supporting environments too complex for a single model.

Lami and her team built an early prototype. One agent monitored tide sensors along the coast. Another set of adjusted drainage valves was used as conditions shifted. A third scanned citizen reports for anomalies. A supervisory agent synchronized their behavior so the system acted as a unified whole. Human operators remained in the loop, watching the sequence unfold and stepping in whenever judgment or context was required. The agents did not replace the people. They extended the team by taking on continuous, high-frequency tasks.

Agents extend human teams by coordinating tasks across time, tools, and environments while relying on human oversight.

Learning across time

Future systems will not be trained once and deployed indefinitely. They will learn across time, maintaining stability while adapting to new conditions without discarding old knowledge.

The following three advances make this possible.

- **Lifelong learning**: Models update across months or years. Techniques such as memory consolidation, replay sampling, and modular parameter isolation reduce catastrophic forgetting.
- **Self-supervised scaling**: Systems learn structure from raw data without labels. They uncover patterns directly from sequences, images, signals, or text, which helps in domains where labeled data is scarce, such as climate systems or biomechanics.
- **Collective learning**: Federated and distributed training allow institutions to share insights without sharing raw data. Local models remain private while aggregated updates improve global performance. This helps health networks, agricultural regions, and city coalitions.

Aisha applied a version of this in her agricultural network. Local models captured soil conditions from each farm. Global updates improved drought predictions across the region. Knowledge moved, but data stayed with the communities that generated it.

Lifelong and collective learning enable models to adapt to shifting environments through continuous updates while preserving previously acquired knowledge.

Science as a new frontier

AI is becoming a partner in scientific discovery. Models now support hypothesis generation, simulation acceleration, and exploratory analysis across complex domains.

In climate research, systems ingest decades of atmospheric and oceanic data to uncover subtle interactions. In materials science, generative models propose new chemical compounds and structural variations. In biology, multimodal systems integrate genomic data, medical literature, and protein structures to help identify promising research directions. In environmental science, they combine satellite imagery, soil logs, river-flow archives, and sensor readings to explore emerging patterns.

These systems work by mapping relationships in high-dimensional data and sampling new configurations consistent with known constraints. They do not replace scientific reasoning. They expand the search space that scientists and engineers can explore.

Lami and Diego used such a system when redesigning the flood-monitoring network. Instead of predicting water levels alone, the model generated hypotheses about why certain districts saturated earlier. Some explanations were trivial. Others pointed to overlooked factors such as subsurface flow or the combined effect of building shadows on evaporation. The model did not provide answers. It revealed where answers might be found.

Scientific discovery becomes a partnership. Humans provide theory, intuition, and verification. AI provides breadth, speed, and alternative perspectives, helping researchers trace patterns that were once hidden deep within the weave of natural systems.

Imagining with care

One of the most promising frontiers is generative foresight. These systems create structured possibilities rather than single predictions, helping societies explore how choices shape outcomes. Instead of offering one expected future, they generate families of trajectories based on environmental, social, and economic constraints.

These systems combine generative architectures, agent-based simulations, and adaptive learning loops. They construct high-dimensional representations of real systems and sample alternative futures based on known limits. Their value is not certainty. It is clarity about the range of what could unfold.

Diego encountered this approach in Lami's lab. Her regional AI Twin simulated thousands of seasonal patterns across rainfall, urban growth, preparedness, soil retention, and infrastructure stress. Some trajectories reduced risk. Others revealed vulnerabilities that traditional forecasts missed.

Lami emphasized that *the system did not choose outcomes. It illuminated sensitivity*. Small shifts in maintenance schedules or resource allocation produced sharply different futures. The AI Twin allowed planners to explore these branches before acting.

Generative foresight offers a new mode of reasoning. It allows communities to test interventions, policymakers to evaluate trade-offs, and engineers to design for resilience. These systems are not crystal balls. They are disciplined imagination tools that explore many possible futures and the forces that shape them. Their value lies not in prediction but in perspective, expanding judgment by revealing paths the present does not yet show.

Keeping the future aligned

As intelligence grows, alignment becomes a shared responsibility. Agentic systems will coordinate infrastructure. Generative models will influence communication and culture. Lifelong learners will shape scientific inquiry. These capabilities require governance equal to their influence.

Three directions are emerging:

- **Value-guided systems**: Constitutional or norm-guided AI embeds human values directly into model behavior. Systems evaluate outputs against defined principles and adjust when needed.

- **Collective governance**: Oversight is shared among communities, institutions, and governments. Local groups retain authority over data created in their environments. Governance becomes participatory rather than distant.
- **Transparent auditing**: High-impact systems benefit from audit trails that record reasoning steps, tool use, data provenance, and human inputs. Future regulations may require traceable explanations for consequential decisions.

During a virtual roundtable, Diego, Maya, Wanjiku, and Lami explored these futures. They discussed rules for agents managing energy systems, methods for verifying hypotheses generated by scientific models, and ways communities could meaningfully participate in systems that affect their lives. They understood that stronger systems required stronger accountability, both in design and deployment.

Conscience becomes the force that keeps the pattern aligned as new forms of imagination unfold. Achieving alignment requires collective effort built on values, governance, and transparent oversight.

Looking beyond the horizon

Generative, adaptive, and agentic systems show that intelligence is moving beyond prediction. Models generate designs, explore scenarios, refine behavior through feedback, and coordinate tasks across digital and physical environments. AI Twins simulate futures. Foundation models encode broad patterns for reuse. Agentic systems plan, reason, and act with increasing autonomy.

These advances form only the first layer. Future systems may learn from constraints and values as much as from data. They may support discovery by exploring hypotheses beyond human intuition. They may help communities examine social, environmental, and economic interactions together.

The central challenge is guiding this growth. Emerging systems will require memory with clear provenance, creativity with accountability, and autonomy that remains understandable to people. They must balance exploration with safety and innovation with ecological and social responsibility.

Looking ahead, the horizon of AI is shaped not by what machines can generate but by what societies choose to cultivate. The next breakthroughs will come from designing systems that expand possibilities without losing responsibility.

The loom of intelligence will continue to evolve. What it weaves will depend on the principles we set today.

Conclusion

Evening settles over Barranquilla. The flood sensors blink in an easy rhythm, reflecting the steady movement of the city. In a classroom across an ocean, Lami walks her students through the AI Twin. In São Paulo, Maya's triage system supports another night of careful decisions. In Eldoret, Wanjiku's cooperative meets to review how community data shaped the week's outcomes. Along a quiet field, Aisha watches drones trace slow arcs over soil she once tended by hand.

The systems they built have grown beyond their creators. They now belong to the loops of care that sustain them. Citizens give consent. Engineers question assumptions. Clinicians challenge predictions. Students imagine what comes next.

On Diego's desk rests a small piece of worn cotton his grandmother wove years ago. The threads are uneven, and the colors have softened with time. He keeps it as a reminder that good systems do not hide imperfections. They carry them forward as texture, as history, as truth.

He initiates the nightly update routine, a disciplined cycle of learn, review, and pause that the team treats as essential practice. The system begins its staged optimization sequence. It ingests the day's sensor streams, recalculates gradients, and prepares intermediate checkpoints. At each pause, execution waits until a human verifies data quality, parameter stability, and any flagged anomalies. Only after these checks does the model advance to the next step in its refinement.

Outside, distant thunder murmurs over the coast. Inside, monitors pulse in quiet succession, each flicker a sign of information moving through a fabric held together by attention.

Diego whispers the line that has stayed with him through every storm and every redesign.

The thread that learns is the one that listens.

He imagines that the message is traveling outward across cables and airwaves, through labs, cooperatives, enterprises, and classrooms. Everywhere, people adjust parameters, refine audits, revise prompts, and ask better questions. The pattern grows not by force but by shared responsibility.

The loom of intelligence continues to hum, mindful and many-handed.

However, Diego also knows learning alone is not enough.

If systems shape lives, they must also be protected.

If data becomes thread, it must be guarded from those who would pull it loose.

If intelligence gains power, trust must rise with it.

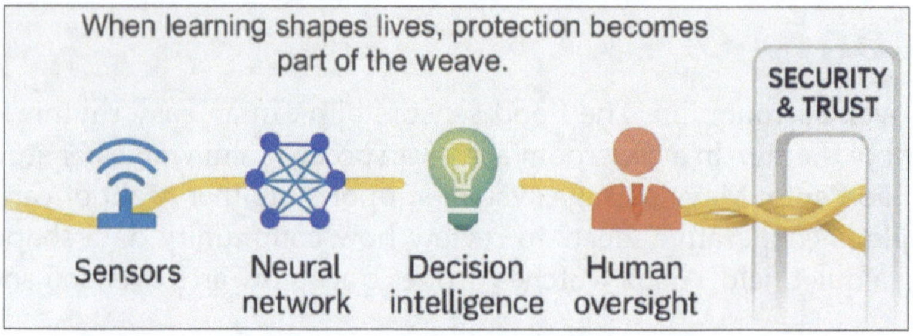

Figure 4.12: From learning to safeguarding

The city did not need smarter models; it needed systems that remained accountable even as they grew more capable.

The next chapter begins here:

How we secure the weave, protect the people within it, and make trust the foundation rather than the afterthought of every intelligent design.

Weaver's toolkit

The thread that learns is the one that listens.

Intelligence becomes meaningful only when practiced with clarity, curiosity, and care. This toolkit brings together the elements that support deeper learning: a shared lexicon for precision, exercises that build understanding through action, and references that connect the chapter's ideas to wider scholarship. Whether in classrooms, design studios, engineering teams, or policy workshops, these resources help readers move from knowing about AI to weaving with it thoughtfully.

Weaver's lexicon

Working with intelligent systems requires a shared vocabulary. The concepts introduced in this chapter span data, algorithms, architectures, and decision design. This glossary gathers the essential terms and acronyms used throughout, offering clear definitions that support deeper reading and connect the technical ideas that shape modern AI systems:

- **Accuracy**: A measure of how closely a model's predictions match observed outcomes.
- **Adaptive intelligence**: Systems that update their internal parameters during or after deployment based on new data.
- **Agentic AI**: AI that performs multi-step tasks autonomously, coordinating actions across tools or systems.
- **Agent-based simulation**: A modeling approach where individual entities (*agents*) follow rules, producing emergent system behavior.

- **AI twin (Digital twin):** A virtual model of a real system that simulates its behavior under varying scenarios.
- **Algorithm**: A set of rules or computations used to process data and produce an output.
- **AI:** Systems capable of performing tasks requiring perception, reasoning, learning, or decision-making.
- **Attention mechanism**: A neural network component that assigns weights to different inputs based on relevance.
- **Black box model**: A system whose internal reasoning is too complex or opaque for direct interpretation.
- **Buffer inventory**: Extra stock used to absorb supply or demand fluctuations.
- **Conscience in design**: An approach emphasizing ethics, accountability, and human impact in system development.
- **Confidence level**: A numerical measure indicating how certain a model is about a prediction.
- **Continuous learning**: Model updates occurring during operational use without full retraining.
- **Counterfactual test**: A fairness method where one variable is changed while others are kept constant to observe the influence on predictions.
- **Data drift**: Changes in input data distribution that degrade model performance over time.
- **Data trust**: A governance structure granting communities shared control over data use and rights.
- **Deep learning**: A class of neural networks with multiple layers capable of modeling complex relationships.
- **Derivative model**: A smaller or specialized model adapted from a larger foundation model through fine-tuning.
- **Digital footprint**: Recordable behavioral data produced through digital interactions.
- **Disparate impact**: A fairness metric measuring unequal outcomes across demographic groups.
- **Explainability**: The ability of a model to communicate how and why it produced a specific output.
- **Feature**: An input variable used by a model.
- **Feature importance**: A ranking of how much each feature contributes to a prediction.

- **Feedback loop**: A cycle where a system's output influences future input, enabling continuous refinement.
- **Fine-tuning**: Adapting a pretrained model to a specialized task using additional data.
- **Foundation model**: A large pretrained model designed to be adapted for many downstream tasks.
- **Generative AI**: Models that create new content, such as text, images, designs, or hypotheses.
- **Generative forecasting**: Predicting possible futures by sampling from learned probability distributions.
- **Glass-box interface**: A transparent system that shows the factors influencing each decision.
- **Gradient**: In learning algorithms, the direction and magnitude of adjustment needed to reduce error.
- **High-dimensional data**: Data containing many variables that interact in complex ways.
- **Human-in-the-loop**: Systems that incorporate human judgment at critical steps in decision-making.
- **Inference**: The process of applying a trained model to new data to generate predictions.
- **Informal trust networks**: Social structures where reputation and reliability are assessed through community relationships.
- **Input vector**: A numerical representation of data passed into a neural network.
- **Interpretability**: Methods for analyzing how a model's structure or components lead to outcomes.
- **Latent space**: A compressed representation of data capturing underlying patterns or structure.
- **Linear transformation**: A mathematical operation that reshapes input using matrix multiplication.
- **Long short-term memory (LSTM)**: A type of recurrent neural network designed to retain information over long sequences.
- **Loss function**: A formula that measures the difference between predicted and actual outcomes.
- **Mastery curve**: A progression metric reflecting how well a learner or model is acquiring a new skill.

- **Memory consolidation**: A technique that stabilizes previously learned knowledge by periodically strengthening or replaying past representations so the model does not forget them when learning new tasks.
- **Model drift**: The degradation of model accuracy due to environmental or behavioral changes.
- **Modular parameter isolation**: An approach that assigns separate parameter subsets or modules to different tasks so learning new skills does not overwrite or interfere with previously learned ones.
- **Multimodal data**: Data from different formats, such as text, images, video, and sensor streams.
- **Neural network**: A computing architecture inspired by biological neurons, composed of interconnected layers.
- **Nonlinear activation**: A function that allows neural networks to model complex, non-linear relationships.
- **Online learning**: Incremental model updates are performed continuously as new data arrives.
- **Overfitting**: A condition where a model learns training data too precisely and performs poorly on new data.
- **Prompt engineering**: The practice of crafting precise instructions for large language models to improve responses.
- **Real-time prediction**: Model outputs are generated instantaneously as new data is received.
- **Recurrent neural network (RNN):** A neural network that processes sequences by carrying information through steps.
- **Reinforcement learning from human feedback (RLHF):** A learning method where models are rewarded for preferred outputs based on human evaluation.
- **Replay sampling**: A continual learning method where a model revisits selected past examples (real or generated) during training to preserve earlier knowledge while absorbing new data.
- **Representation coverage**: A fairness concept describing how well different groups are represented in training data.
- **Retrieval augmented generation (RAG)**: A method that grounds generative models in external documents retrieved at inference time.
- **Scenario planning**: The evaluation of multiple possible futures to guide operational decisions.

- **Sensor network**: A collection of interconnected devices capturing data from the physical environment.
- **Shapley Additive Explanations (SHAP)**: An interpretability method that explains predictions by distributing contribution scores across features.
- **Simulation**: The process of imitating system behavior for analysis or prediction.
- **Supervised learning**: Training models using labeled datasets containing known inputs and outputs.
- **Synthetic data**: Artificially generated data used to expand training sets or simulate rare events.
- **Temporal sequence**: Ordered data points that unfold over time.
- **Token:** A token is the smallest unit of input a model processes, such as a word, fragment, or symbol, used as the basic element for computing embeddings and attention in transformer models.
- **Transformer model**: A neural architecture based on self-attention that processes sequences in parallel.
- **Uncertainty range**: The quantifiable interval within which a model's prediction may reasonably vary.

Weaver's workshop

These five exercises translate the chapter's concepts into applied skills. They cover personal assistance systems, decision loops, fairness and bias, explainability, generative intelligence, and responsible AI design. Each exercise is structured for use in undergraduate classrooms, industry training, and policy workshops, with prompts that develop both conceptual understanding and practical competence.

Refer to the following to build a comprehensive understanding:

1. **Reading a feedback loop**: Students analyze a simple AI-driven scenario (e.g., a thermostat or fitness tracker) to identify the elements of a feedback loop.

   Prompts:

   - *Identify the sensor, model, action, and environment response.*
   - *Explain how the loop stabilizes or destabilizes under changing conditions.*

   Deliverables: A short diagram + a one-paragraph explanation of the loop's functioning.

   Learning objective: Understand the basic structure of AI feedback loops and how systems refine decisions over time.

2. **Diagnosing overfitting**: Analyze a dataset and two model performance graphs (training vs. real-world error) to diagnose whether overfitting has occurred.

   Prompts:

   - *Compare training accuracy and deployment accuracy.*
   - *Identify signals that the model has memorized instead of generalized.*
   - *Propose at least two techniques to improve resilience.*

   Deliverables: A brief write-up with graphs annotated and a list of recommended corrections.

   Learning objective: Recognize overfitting in practice and propose methods to improve model robustness.

3. **Investigating bias in a dataset**:

   Examine a mock dataset with an imbalanced distribution (e.g., loan applicants or hospital cases) and identify potential sources of bias.

   Prompts:

   - *Identify features that may act as cultural or socioeconomic proxies.*
   - *Run a simple demographic parity check or representation ratio.*
   - *Recommend additional data sources or corrections.*

   Deliverables: A written fairness audit with a table showing representation coverage and proposed mitigation steps.

   Learning objective: Identify how an imbalance in data leads to bias in model outcomes and propose strategies to restore fairness.

4. **Explainability and glass-box design**: Given a model prediction and a feature-importance chart, students explain why the model produced the decision and evaluate its clarity.

   Prompts:

   - *Interpret the Shapley Additive Explanations (SHAP) style feature contribution chart.*
   - *Rewrite the explanation in human-readable form.*
   - *Assess whether the explanation would build or erode trust among citizens or stakeholders.*
   - *Suggest one improvement to increase visibility.*

   Deliverables: A short explanation text + a critique of the model's current interface.

   Learning objective: Translate model reasoning into accessible language and assess the role of interpretability in trust-building.

5. **Designing a responsible generative system**:

   Design a conceptual blueprint for a generative model (e.g., climate simulator, design assistant, community-planning tool) with built-in governance principles.

   Prompts:

   - *Define the model's purpose and scope.*
   - *Describe what real data it learns from and what synthetic data it produces.*
   - *Identify risks: hallucination, drift, misuse, bias, attribution.*
   - *Propose guardrails: provenance tracking, consent policies, attribution logic, verification steps.*
   - *Describe the role of human review.*

   Deliverables: A 2-page design brief + a high-level diagram of system components and governance checkpoints.

   Learning objective: Integrate technical capability with ethical design principles, demonstrating how responsible AI requires structure, supervision, and shared agency.

Weaver's library

This collection of references offers a solid foundation in responsible AI, algorithmic fairness, governance models, and socio-technical system design. Each source is selected for its strong research grounding, adoption in leading universities, and practical relevance to building systems that remain accurate, accountable, transparent, and aligned with human values:

1. *Russell, S., & Norvig, P. (2020). Artificial Intelligence: A Modern Approach (4th ed.). Pearson.*
2. *O'Neil, C. (2016). Weapons of Math Destruction: How Big Data Increases Inequality and Threatens Democracy. Crown.*
3. *IEEE Global Initiative. (2020). Ethically Aligned Design: A Vision for Prioritizing Human Well-being with Autonomous and Intelligent Systems. IEEE Standards Association.*
4. *Mitchell, M. (2019). Artificial Intelligence: A Guide for Thinking Humans. Farrar, Straus and Giroux.*
5. *Selbst, A., & Barocas, S. (2018). The Intuitive Appeal of Explainable Machines. Fordham Law Review.*

Metaphorical and conceptual terms

The weaving language in this chapter is not stylistic decoration. Each metaphor acts as a structural aid, helping readers map technical ideas onto systems thinking. These terms illuminate how data, models, decisions, and human judgment interact as parts of a dynamic whole. The following definitions clarify how each metaphor functions within the chapter's analytic framework and how it supports understanding of intelligent systems in practice:

- **Fabric**: The interconnected structure formed when many threads, such as data, models, people, and decisions, interact to create a coherent system.
- **Fabric of digital life**: The full set of digital interactions, systems, and infrastructures that shape modern living. In the chapter, it refers to how AI integrates into communication, governance, healthcare, the environment, and everyday tools.
- **Loom**: The underlying architecture or mechanism that brings data, models, and decisions together. It represents the technical structure that makes learning and inference possible.
- **Loom of intelligence**: The complete AI system that combines sensing, modeling, training, inference, feedback, and governance. It is where patterns of intelligence are formed and maintained.
- **Loop of care**: A human-supervised oversight cycle that monitors data quality, model confidence, ethical behavior, and system impact. It is the mechanism that ensures AI remains aligned, trustworthy, and correctable.
- **Master weaver**: A metaphor for intelligence, specifically AI systems that learn patterns, adapt to data, and produce coherent outputs. It also refers to the designers and engineers who shape and refine these systems.
- **Pattern**: In this chapter, a pattern refers to any structure the system learns, detects, or produces. At the data level, it is a regularity in signals such as spatial shapes, temporal changes, or correlations. Within a model, a pattern is the internal representation formed by weights, activations, and attention relationships that link inputs to outputs. In prediction and action, it describes the model's observable behavior as conditions evolve. In a broader sense, a pattern is also the coordinated flow across sensing, prediction, action, and feedback that shapes decision intelligence. Throughout the chapter, the term conveys both the technical structure that models learn and the conceptual structure that emerges when these learning processes operate together.
- **Rhythm**: The cycle through which AI operates: sense, interpret, decide, act, learn, and adjust. In the chapter, rhythm represents both the tempo and regularity of learning and correction.
- **Thread**: A single element in a system: a data point, a feature, a decision, a human action, or an oversight step. Threads are the smallest units that shape larger patterns.
- **Weave**: The interaction of many threads into a coherent system behavior. In the chapter, the weave represents how data, models, people, and policies combine to form real outcomes.

CHAPTER 5

Security

The trust thread

Systems endure only when their foundations can be trusted.

Chapter 5
Security

Introduction

Security is the discipline that allows digital systems to endure under strain. In connected environments, failure rarely begins with dramatic attacks or visible breakdowns. It starts quietly, through small shifts in timing, configuration, access, or data quality that accumulate over time. These early distortions often remain unnoticed because systems continue to function, dashboards remain stable, and outputs appear plausible. Yet trust weakens long before it breaks.

This chapter follows *Linh* as she learns to recognize those early signals and design systems that can detect, absorb, and recover from stress. Security is presented not as a barrier or a set of defensive tools, but as a reinforcing structure woven through identity, data, behavior, and decision-making. Verification replaces assumption. Visibility replaces silence. Recovery replaces brittle prevention.

Through real-world scenarios involving clinics, agricultural cooperatives, and flood monitoring networks, the chapter shows how trust erodes when verification is deferred and how systems regain alignment when reinforcement is deliberate. It explores how modern pressures such as automation, intelligent adversaries, supply chains, and cyber-physical coupling expand the attack surface and demand a new design discipline.

Security, in this framing, becomes an active practice rather than a static configuration. It is how systems remain accountable to the people who rely on them, even as environments shift and complexity grows. By the end of the chapter, security is no longer a separate concern. It is the structural thread that holds the pattern together.

Structure

This chapter covers the following topics:

- Linh and the silent breach
- Security as engineered trust
- Pressures that strain systems
- Layers that secure digital systems

- Learning from failure modes
- Zero Trust as a design discipline
- Future pressures on trust
- Ethical posture for security design

Objectives

This chapter establishes security as a structural discipline for sustaining trust in complex digital systems. By the end of this chapter, readers will be able to recognize early signs of system misalignment before visible failure occurs. They will understand how trust is engineered through verification, visibility, integrity, isolation, and recovery, rather than assumed through static controls. The readers will also learn to analyze security failures as patterns of strain, not isolated incidents, and to trace those failures back to missing principles, signals, or reinforcements.

The chapter equips readers to apply Zero Trust as a design discipline rather than a product architecture, and to reason about emerging pressures such as intelligent adversaries, supply chain exposure, and cyber-physical risk. The readers will further understand how ethical posture shapes security decisions by defining authority, dignity, and accountability within systems. Together, these capabilities enable readers to design, review, and steward digital systems that remain trustworthy as conditions change.

Linh and the silent breach

A pattern weakens long before it tears.

In connected systems, trust rarely fails all at once. It erodes quietly, through minor deviations that pass inspection and remain within accepted limits. These shifts influence decisions long before they trigger alarms or visible faults. Linh learned to watch for those early signs, not because they were dramatic, but because they were consequential.

A hesitation in the weave

The breach began with a delay so slight it could have been dismissed. A rainfall packet from *Diego's* upstream sensor arrived later than usual. The reported value was ordinary. The checksum matched. The route showed no anomalies. By conventional measures, the system appeared healthy.

What drew Linh's attention was repetition. The delay recurred with the same narrow rhythm. Networks do generally not behave that way. Natural traffic varies with load, interference, and routing conditions. This sensor produced a consistency that felt artificial.

The device was an older, low-power unit without a trusted internal clock. It measured and transmitted, relying on the gateway to assign timestamps. That design was common across the valley and usually sufficient. It was also a structural weakness. If the device's internal loop slowed or shifted, the gateway logs would remain accurate even as the source drifted from expected behavior.

The system looked normal. The timing did not.

Signals beneath the surface

Linh pulled the raw telemetry feed to inspect the packets as they arrived, without aggregation or smoothing. The rainfall readings aligned with seasonal expectations, but the distribution was unusually tight. Each value sat slightly above the expected range, consistent enough to matter without being extreme enough to alarm.

A configuration hash comparison revealed the cause. The sensor no longer matched its baseline. An unprotected update interface had been accessed, and the firmware had been modified. The change introduced a slight upward bias in each measurement. The sensor still reported real data, but every value leaned in the same direction.

The timing irregularity now made sense. On constrained devices, modified firmware often increases processing time. The repeated delay reflected added computation, not network congestion. To a cursory review, it resembled hardware aging. In fact, it was evidence of tampering.

A quiet test of trust

The effects propagated quickly. Rainfall accumulation indicators began to rise. Automated workflows adjusted resource plans and shifted schedules, even though local conditions remained unchanged. No thresholds were crossed, and no alerts fired, but the system started preparing for a scenario that did not exist.

Linh paused the automations and placed the model into verification mode. The pattern suggested intent. This was not an attempt to trigger a flood warning. It was an experiment in influence.

By introducing small, plausible distortions, the attacker was assessing whether the system would verify its inputs, escalate uncertainty, or continue operating without challenge. It was a test of trust rather than a direct attack.

Listening for early drift

Linh alerted her team and initiated a review of firmware provenance across similar devices. She knew that in complex systems, compromise rarely announces itself through obvious failure. It appears as calibration shifts, timing changes, or trends that are acceptable in isolation but redirect the system as a whole.

A single incorrect value rarely causes harm. A sustained pattern of plausible errors can alter a model's understanding of reality.

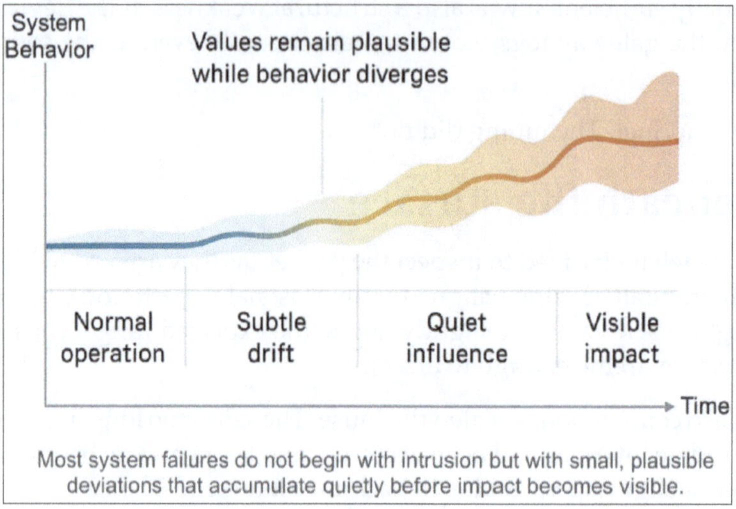

Figure 5.1: *A silent breach timeline*

Detecting this kind of drift requires disciplined verification. Configuration baselines must be enforced. Firmware must be signed and validated. Devices must be compared against peers and against their own historical behavior. Without these practices, systems continue operating while decisions become increasingly shaped by manipulated inputs.

The silent breach did not interrupt service or damage infrastructure. It revealed how easily trust can bend when verification is incomplete, because the misalignment was detected early, the team corrected it before it propagated into visible harm. Linh later reminded the team; *Trust is lost long before damage appears. It bends first, quietly, when no one asks the system to prove its state.*

The next section builds on this case by examining how secure systems deliberately engineer trust through clear principles, measurable controls, and evidence that remains valid under strain.

Security as engineered trust

A weave holds only when every thread can show how it fits.

Security is the discipline that keeps system behavior verifiable, accountable, and aligned with real-world conditions under strain. It applies across networks, data pipelines, models, infrastructure, and the people who operate them.

A digital system remains trustworthy not because it is untouched, but because its components can demonstrate why their behavior is legitimate. Linh understood security as something built into the structure of the system itself. It preserves data accuracy, supports accountable action, and enables dependable operation across changing conditions.

For Linh, trust is not a static state. It is an engineered outcome. A system holds its form when every part can demonstrate how it contributes to the whole, like a weave that remains intact only when each thread stays visible within the pattern it supports.

During one review, *Maya* summarized this clearly. As the clinician responsible for operating IoT systems in her clinics, she depended on Linh's designs to protect patient data and guide care under real constraints. *She said she trusted a system not because it worked on a good day, but because she could see the evidence behind its decisions*. Linh carried that standard into every design discussion. A secure system makes its logic observable and its state explainable.

Linh's First Principle

At the center of Linh's approach was her **First Principle**:

Trust requires verification.

A system earns confidence only when it can demonstrate its internal state. Quiet operation is not evidence of safety. A stable dashboard or clean log offers little assurance unless the interactions beneath them can be examined and confirmed. Systems often drift while appearing healthy, as timing regularities, access patterns, or values remain within acceptable ranges even as underlying assumptions weaken.

Linh trained her teams to treat these minor deviations as early signals rather than background noise. Most failures begin as small variations long before they surface as incidents. **Verification** exposes these variations while they are still correctable. It is both a technical practice and a way of reasoning about how systems change over time.

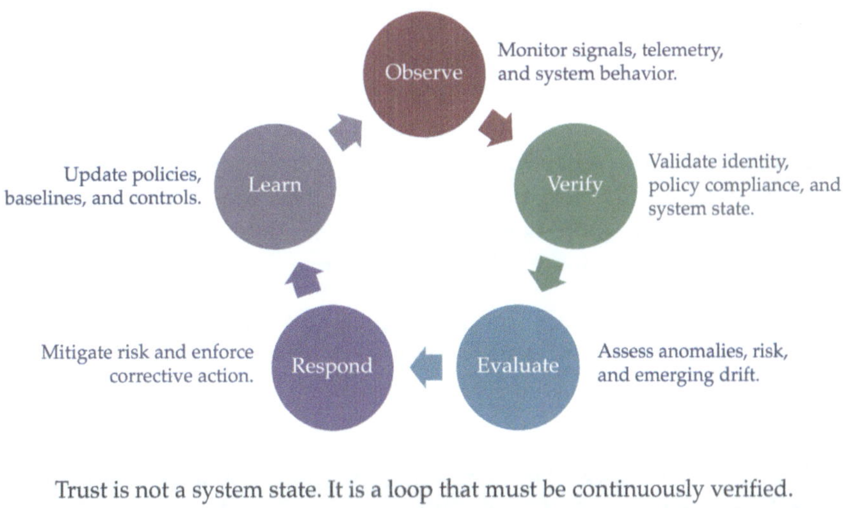

Figure 5.2: *Trust verification loop*

She reminded her students in *Hanoi* that *any component requesting trust must show its work.* That expectation applied equally to simple sensor feeds and to complex distributed models.

Foundations of digital trust

To make trust concrete and measurable, Linh grounded her designs in the three core properties of the **confidentiality, integrity, and availability** (**CIA**) triad. Together, they define the minimum conditions under which a system can operate responsibly and withstand strain.

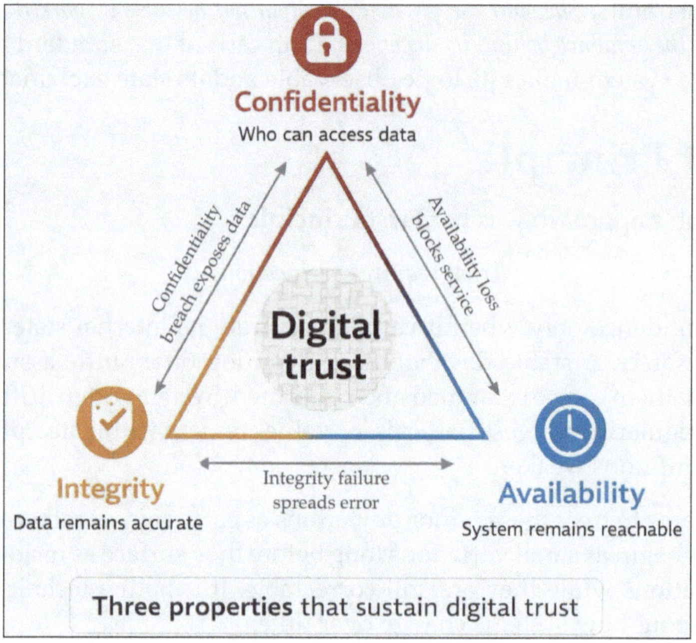

Figure 5.3: CIA triad interdependence

Confidentiality governs who can access information. It is enforced through encryption, authentication, and permission models such as **role-based access control** (**RBAC**) and **attribute-based access control** (**ABAC**). Beyond protecting systems, confidentiality protects people. Maya's clinic relied on it to preserve patient privacy as devices moved between villages. In Aisha's cooperative, Linh's security architecture determined how field connectivity was protected so that yield data remained under the control of the farmers who produced it.

Integrity ensures that data and logic remain accurate as they move through the system. Checksums, secure boot chains, digital signatures, and versioned logs help detect tampering and reveal drift. These controls allowed Diego's flood network to identify subtle sensor bias before it shaped critical forecasts.

Availability ensures that systems and information remain reachable when needed. Redundant nodes, failover routines, rate limiting, and offline execution paths allow services to continue operating under constraint. When connectivity dropped in Maya's region, cached records and local workflows kept essential care running.

Together, these properties answer three persistent questions:

- *Are the right people seeing the data?*
- *Can the data be trusted?*
- *Will the service be reachable when it matters?*

A system may operate for years without intrusion and still fail if confidentiality, integrity, or availability erode. These properties reinforce one another. If confidentiality holds but integrity fails, the system spreads error. If integrity holds but availability collapses, the system cannot fulfill its purpose. If availability holds but confidentiality breaks, the system exposes what it was meant to protect.

The CIA triad describes what must be preserved, not how it is implemented. These properties create the tension that keeps the structure stable. *Table 5.1* summarizes the CIA triad that forms the foundations for the digital trust:

Quality	What it protects	Common techniques	Example from the field
Confidentiality	Who can access data	TLS, authenticated sessions, RBAC, ABAC	Maya's clinic maintained private medical records even when tablets were misplaced.
Integrity	Whether data remains accurate	Hashing, digital signatures, secure boot, versioned logs	Diego detected biased sensor readings before they affected flood planning.
Availability	Whether systems remain reachable	Redundant nodes, rate limiting, offline modes, failover	Aisha's cooperative operated through connectivity gaps.

Table 5.1: *Foundations of digital trust*

The shift from walls to patterns

The environments Linh worked in no longer matched traditional perimeter security models. Devices moved across regions, cloud services exchanged data continuously, and users connected under changing conditions. Every sensor reading, **application programming interface** (**API**) call, and update became part of the system's exposed surface. Static boundaries could no longer capture that reality.

As systems evolved, Linh moved away from thinking in terms of walls and toward understanding the attack surface as the sum of all interactions where the system touched the world. This shift replaced perimeter defenses with layered verification. Security became a set of distributed checks embedded throughout the system rather than a single control at the edge.

A secure system observes its own behavior, tests its assumptions, and adjusts as conditions change.

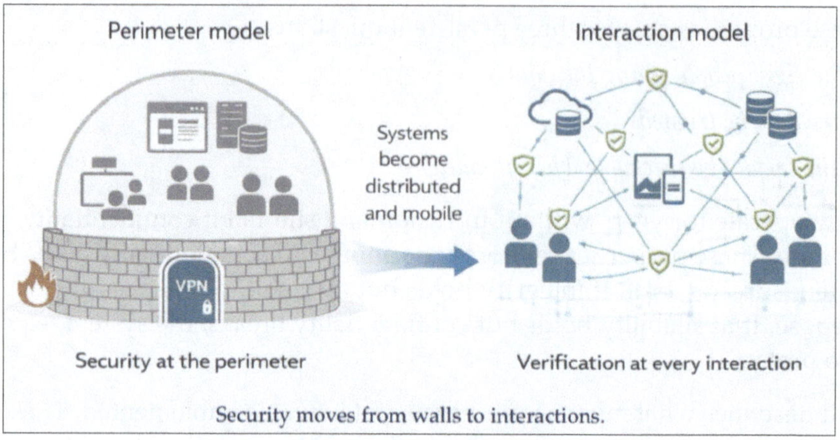

Figure 5.4: *Boundary shift from perimeter to interaction*

Security, in this sense, is the continuous reinforcement of trust. It allows the system to remain dependable for the people who rely on it, even as workloads shift and environments evolve.

With this foundation in place, the next section examines the pressures that strain these properties and the subtle forces that can distort trust long before failure becomes visible.

Pressures that strain systems

Strain reveals where the weave must be reinforced.

In Linh's work, vulnerabilities were rarely obvious defects. They emerged as mismatches between assumptions and reality, often remaining invisible until pressure exposed them.

Strain in a digital system seldom arrives as a dramatic failure. It more often appears as changes in behavior, configuration, access patterns, or data quality that accumulate over time. Linh did not treat security as a fixed defensive stance. She treated it as continuous attention to how a system behaves and where it begins to stretch. Apparent stability can mask deeper shifts that alter how trust is earned and maintained. Security, as she practiced it, meant sensing those underlying movements early.

Every deployed system carries pressure. Some pressure comes from adversaries. Other pressure arises naturally from aging hardware, uneven workloads, evolving usage, and human routines that drift over time. Linh treated strain as information. When a pull appeared in the wrong place, it pointed to where reinforcement was needed. This belief led her to begin with careful threat mapping before friction turned into failure.

Mapping threats

Before a system encounters real pressure, it must understand its own structure. In weaving, the loom is prepared before tension is applied. In digital systems, threat modeling serves the same purpose. It exposes hidden assumptions, highlights risky interactions, and shows how minor deviations can propagate into larger consequences.

Some vulnerabilities remain latent, exerting pressure without immediate effect. Others are activated when strain aligns with opportunity and intent.

Linh encouraged her teams to treat threat modeling not as a compliance exercise, but as a way to see the system clearly. Three established approaches proved especially useful across Maya's clinics, Diego's flood network, and Aisha's cooperative.

STRIDE

Spoofing, Tampering, Repudiation, Information disclosure, Denial of service, Elevation of privilege (**STRIDE**) is a threat modeling framework that categorizes how a system can be misused. It helps teams systematically identify where assumptions about identity, data, and access may be exploited. At Maya's clinics, connectivity was unreliable, and staff worked under constant pressure. Applying STRIDE helped the team identify realistic failure paths grounded in daily operations.

STRIDE reframes ordinary system behavior into structured questions that surface concrete security risks. The following questions guided Maya's team as they examined clinic operations under real working conditions:

- **Spoofing**: *Could someone impersonate a clinician during an outage?*
- **Tampering**: *Could offline records be altered without detection?*
- **Repudiation**: *Could hurried actions go untraceable without sufficient logging?*
- **Information disclosure**: *Could cached data on a lost tablet expose identities?*
- **Denial of service**: *Could traffic spikes overwhelm limited bandwidth?*
- **Elevation of privilege**: *Could a misconfigured role grant unintended access?*

These questions were not hypothetical. They emerged directly from the clinic's working conditions and revealed where trust might stretch unintentionally.

PASTA

Process for Attack Simulation and Threat Analysis (**PASTA**) is a risk-centric threat modeling framework that analyzes how attacks unfold by tracing adversary objectives, attack paths, and potential impacts across a system. It connects technical vulnerabilities to real-world consequences, helping teams prioritize defenses based on likelihood and harm rather than isolated flaws.

Diego's flood prediction system depended on long chains of sensors, gateways, and cloud models. PASTA helped the team analyze how an attack could move through this environment over time.

PASTA structures the analysis as a sequence of steps that trace how an adversary's intent translates into system-level impact. The following list outlines this structured analysis for Diego's flood prediction system:

- **Define the objective**: Protect early warnings and prevent false alerts.
- **Define the technical scope**: Sensors, gateways, routing systems, cloud models.
- **Enumerate threats**: Sensor spoofing, model skewing, gateway compromise.
- **Analyze attack paths**: Small upstream distortions influencing downstream logic.
- **Simulate impacts**: False water-level signals triggering unnecessary evacuations.
- **Evaluate countermeasures**: Cross-sensor validation, correlation checks, provenance tracking.

PASTA made clear how edge-level issues could shape central decisions.

LINDDUN

Linking, Identifying, Non-repudiation, Detecting, Data disclosure, Unawareness, Non-compliance (LINDDUN) is a privacy threat modeling framework that helps teams identify how systems may unintentionally expose personal or sensitive information through data linkage, inference, or misuse, even without malicious intent. It shifts attention from security breaches to risks against dignity, consent, and trust embedded in system design.

Aisha's cooperative managed sensitive community data. LINDDUN revealed privacy risks that could arise even when systems functioned as designed.

LINDDUN organizes privacy analysis into a set of structured questions that surface risks arising from normal system operation. Aisha's cooperative used the following questions to examine how everyday data practices could unintentionally expose sensitive community information:

- **Linkability**: *Could records be tied back to specific households?*
- **Identifiability**: *Could visualizations expose struggling farmers?*
- **Nonrepudiation**: *Could system records prevent later correction or contestation of algorithmic decisions?*
- **Detectability**: *Could traffic patterns signal financial hardship?*
- **Disclosure**: *Could partners infer more than intended from shared dashboards?*
- **Unawareness**: *Did participants understand how their data was used to train models?*
- **Noncompliance**: *Did retention practices match community expectations?*

LINDDUN helped the cooperative recognize privacy as a structural requirement rather than an optional courtesy.

Table 5.2 illustrates how these models align with different stages of system design and operation while collectively strengthening trust under strain:

Aspect	STRIDE	PASTA	LINDDUN
Primary focus	Security threats against system assets.	Risk-driven analysis of attacks and business impact.	Privacy and data protection risks.
The core question asked	*How can the system be attacked?*	*How do threats materialize into risk?*	*How can the system unintentionally violate privacy or dignity?*
Unit of analysis	Technical components and interactions.	System architecture, workflows, and threat actors.	Data flows, identifiers, and information relationships.
Typical outcomes	Enumerated threat categories, such as spoofing, tampering, etc.	Prioritized risk scenarios with likelihood and impact.	Privacy risks such as linkability, identifiability, and nonrepudiation.

***Table 5.2**: Comparison of STRIDE, PASTA, and LINDDUN*

These threat models are complementary rather than competitive. STRIDE is most effective during early design and architecture reviews. PASTA is better suited to operational environments where threats must be evaluated in relation to mission impact. LINDDUN complements both by revealing privacy and trust risks that may exist even without active attackers.

Linh's Second Principle

Linh's **Second Principle** guided her engagement with real environments:

Expect strain and design for recovery.

The question was never whether strain would appear, but when and from where. Systems that treat strain as an exception tend to resist feedback and fracture under pressure. Systems that anticipate strain and prepare recovery paths regain stability more quickly.

Designing for recovery requires accepting that systems, people, and processes will all misbehave under strain. Components fail. Data drifts. Procedures break at inconvenient moments, often simultaneously. Security, therefore, depends not only on technical controls but on the ability of teams to detect misalignment, interpret signals, and respond coherently.

Verification, redundancy, failover mechanisms, and strong visibility help systems regain alignment. Clear ownership, escalation paths, and human judgment ensure recovery remains accountable when conditions change abruptly.

Linh explained to Diego that *a resilient pattern is not rigid. It can be pulled out of shape and still return to form*. That perspective prepared her to examine the distinct categories of pressure that act on digital systems.

The five pulls on a system

Every digital system consists of logic, data, infrastructure, and human behavior. Different threats apply pressure to different parts of that structure. Understanding these pressures helps determine where reinforcement is required. The details are as follows:

- **Intrusion**: Intrusion occurs when an unauthorized actor gains access by exploiting weak credentials, misconfiguration, or human trust. Phishing, credential reuse, and session token theft allow access to appear legitimate. Intrusion reveals where identity boundaries were assumed rather than continuously verified.
- **Exfiltration**: Exfiltration occurs when information is removed without interrupting normal system behavior. Data may be copied through legitimate channels, unsecured storage, or stealthy background processes, because functionality remains intact, exfiltration strains confidentiality while avoiding immediate detection.

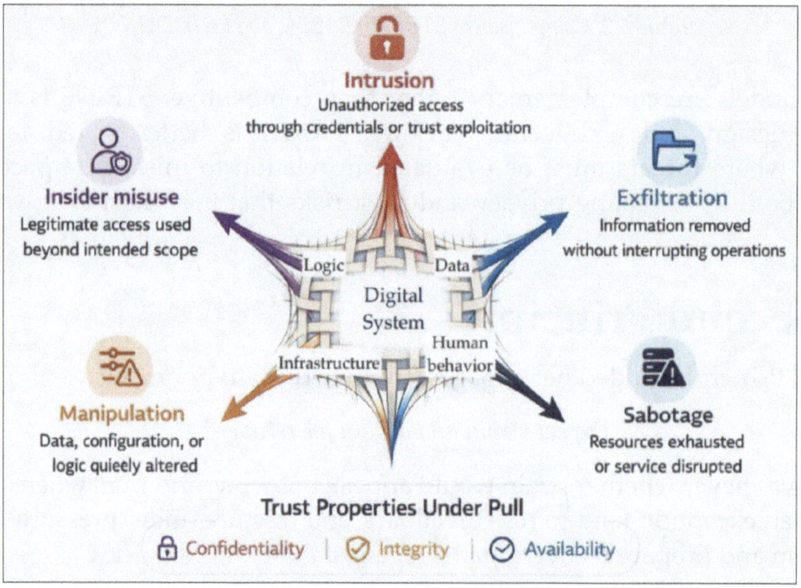

Figure 5.5: The forces that strain systems

- **Manipulation**: Manipulation alters data, configuration, or logic without necessarily violating access controls. Compromised components, poisoned training data, or subtle configuration changes fall into this category. The system continues to operate, but its outputs no longer reflect real conditions, straining integrity.

- **Sabotage**: Sabotage degrades or disables system function by exhausting resources or disrupting service availability. **Denial-of-service** (**DoS**) activity and induced overload prevent systems from delivering outcomes when needed. Availability fails even though data may remain accurate and confidential.
- **Insider misuse**: Insider misuse arises when legitimate access is used beyond its intended scope, intentionally or unintentionally. Overprivileged roles, unmanaged devices, and informal workarounds enable this pressure, because activity occurs within trusted boundaries, it weakens containment and blurs accountability, making misuse harder to distinguish from normal operation.

The following table summarizes how common system pressures strain specific trust properties and how those pressures first become visible in practice:

Pull	Primary CIA impact	Typical early signal
Intrusion	Confidentiality	Unusual login timing, unexpected access paths, credential or token anomalies.
Exfiltration	Confidentiality	Sustained outbound transfers, atypical data volume, and access without workflow disruption.
Manipulation	Integrity	Subtle data bias, configuration drift, model or logic behavior changes.
Sabotage	Availability	Service degradation, resource exhaustion, failed requests, or outages.
Insider misuse	Integrity and confidentiality	Actions exceeding role intent, anomalous use of legitimate privileges, and weakened attribution.

Table 5.3: *Mapping system pulls to trust properties and early signals*

While each pull stresses a dominant property, none affects only one. Integrity failures undermine availability. Confidentiality breaches weaken trust even when systems remain operational. Understanding these interactions allows teams to reinforce the correct layers before strain concentrates into visible failure.

The human posture

Most systems weaken not because of advanced adversaries, but because the people operating them carry heavy cognitive loads. Fatigue, time pressure, and unfamiliar workflows create openings long before technical faults appear.

The following factors describe human conditions that influence system security during routine operation:

- **Cognitive fatigue**: Clinicians, operators, and engineers under sustained pressure may overlook anomalies, delay checks, or ignore alerts. A strained system guided by strained people becomes more vulnerable.

- **Shadow systems**: When official workflows are slow or unreliable, people create workarounds. They share credentials, store data locally, or bypass steps that feel obstructive. These shadow systems emerge for practical reasons but introduce unevenness and hidden risk.
- **Insider psychology**: Under stress, people take risks they would normally avoid. Some hesitate to question automated outputs. Others rely too heavily on familiarity. These behaviors expand exposure in ways that technical controls alone cannot address.

Linh believed systems should support the people who use them. Clear interfaces reduce error. Context-aware prompts limit overreach. Adaptive permission boundaries reduce the incentive to bypass controls.

When people operate with clarity, they reinforce the system. When they are overwhelmed, they stretch it unintentionally.

A clear understanding of these pressures prepares the ground for the next section, which examines the layers of defense that keep systems resilient even as strain accumulates.

Layers that secure digital systems

A strong weave relies on strands that support one another.

A resilient system does not avoid tension. It manages tension through structure. Linh did not rely on single controls or isolated safeguards. She designed security as a set of interconnected layers so that no single point carried the full weight of strain. In her work, security was not added after the fact. It was embedded in the system so that dependable operation could continue as conditions shifted.

Linh assumed that systems would bend as environments changed. She expected failures at the edges and occasional faults at the center. The objective was not perfect prevention. It was early detection, predictable response, and safe recovery. As Maya observed during a workshop, *the system felt steady because it knew how to support itself.*

Linh's Third Principle

Linh's **Third Principle** shaped her architectural approach:

Defense must be distributed.

A system becomes fragile when protection is concentrated in one place. A firewall cannot detect drift inside a model. Encryption cannot constrain a malfunctioning device. When a single control carries too much responsibility, it eventually fails under conditions it was never designed to handle.

Distributed defense spreads responsibility across the system itself. Different forms of verification, observation, containment, and recovery work together so that no single mechanism is expected to see everything, react instantly, or fully understand context on its own.

Linh reminded her teams that resilience does not come from a stronger wall, but from coordinated reinforcement. Each protective function contributes a partial view and a partial response. Trust emerges when these functions align and compensate for one another under stress.

This principle led Linh to organize security not as a checklist of controls, but as a layered structure, where each layer answers a distinct question about system behavior.

The architecture of the five layers

Linh organized her security model around five reinforcing questions. Each question defined a layer of defense:

- **Identity**: Who or what is interacting with the system.
- **Visibility**: What the system can observe about its own behavior.
- **Integrity**: Whether the system's information and logic remain accurate.
- **Isolation**: How interactions are kept within safe boundaries.
- **Recovery**: How the system returns to a trusted state after strain.

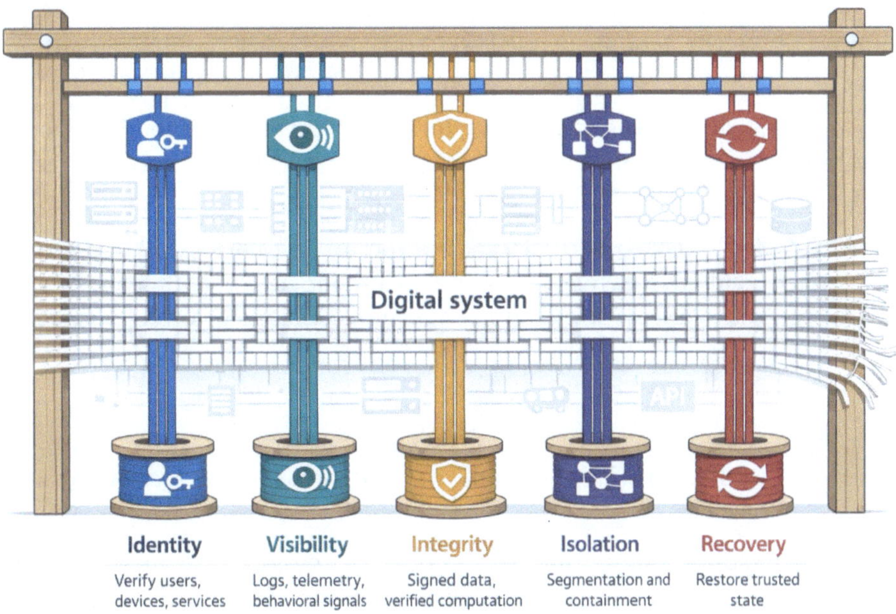

***Figure 5.6**: Five security layers*

These layers reinforce one another. Identity determines what visibility should monitor. Visibility provides the context required for integrity checks. Integrity informs isolation decisions. Isolation creates the conditions under which recovery can operate safely. Together, the layers maintain coherence even as environments change.

In the following sections, each layer is described through its role, core mechanisms, and field experience.

Identity

Identity establishes who or what is allowed to interact with the system. It verifies users, devices, services, and software processes before granting access. Authentication confirms the entity. Authorization defines its scope.

Linh relied on multifactor authentication, short-lived tokens, device attestation, and contextual checks such as expected location or time. These controls reduced the risk of credential reuse and session hijacking.

In Diego's network, field technicians could access sensors only during defined service windows. If a device deviated from its expected route, access was revalidated. Identity remained flexible, but never unconditional.

Linh described identity as an ongoing relationship. It requires continual confirmation rather than permanent acceptance.

Visibility

Visibility allows the system to observe itself. Without it, no layer can detect drift or interpret strain.

Linh treated logs, metrics, traces, and behavioral baselines as foundational components. Observability tools surfaced timing shifts, unusual access patterns, and changes in device behavior.

When rainfall packets began to arrive with unnatural regularity, visibility revealed the inconsistency. When gateways delivered data at irregular intervals, telemetry exposed the deviation. As Diego often noted, *silence is never neutral*. Visibility converts uncertainty into evidence.

Integrity

Integrity ensures that data, configuration, and computation remain accurate from source to decision.

Linh relied on hashing, digital signatures, secure boot processes, firmware signing, and model fingerprinting. These mechanisms verified that the system processed authentic, unaltered inputs.

In Aisha's cooperative, integrity checks detected sensor drift early in the growing season. Measurements that deviated from expected profiles were flagged before they influenced irrigation plans or yield forecasts.

Isolation

Isolation limits the spread of failure. It creates compartments that contain faults and restrict lateral movement.

Linh used network segmentation, container isolation, least-privilege policies, service mesh controls, and micro-segmentation. These measures ensured that a compromised device or account could not reach sensitive resources or disrupt core services.

When a river sensor failed in Diego's network, isolation allowed it to be removed without affecting the rest of the monitoring system. The network absorbed the fault rather than propagating it.

Recovery

Recovery assumes that failures will occur. It prepares the system to return to a trusted state with minimal loss and clear direction.

Linh designed recovery around versioned backups, offline execution paths, out-of-band communication channels, and restoration procedures that kept humans involved in critical decisions.

In Maya's clinics, outages were routine. Local caches, regular backups, and clear restoration steps allowed medical work to continue while systems reconnected and synchronized.

Recovery was not about returning quickly. It was about returning correctly.

Interdependence in practice

These layers do not operate as independent solutions. They form a coordinated structure in which each layer offsets the limits of another. Identity governs who may act. Visibility reveals how actions unfold. Integrity confirms that behavior remains grounded in accurate data and logic. Isolation constrains the spread of failure. Recovery restores the system and trust when strain exceeds design assumptions.

Linh designed each layer to stand on its own while reinforcing the rest. A gap in visibility could be mitigated by strict identity controls. Drift detected through integrity checks could be contained through isolation before it propagates. When containment was insufficient, recovery mechanisms guided the system back to a trusted state.

The system holds its form not through duplication of controls, but through alignment. Resilience emerges from how these layers work together, each contributing a different perspective on the same unfolding conditions.

Field implementations

Linh's layered approach proved effective across diverse environments:

- In Maya's clinics, identity controls and encrypted storage protected patient data.
- Visibility tools surfaced irregular login patterns during mobile outreach.
- Integrity checks caught corrupted files after severe storms.
- Isolation contained malfunctioning devices during outages.
- Recovery routines supported staff during periods of inconsistent power and connectivity.

The layered model Linh applied did not remain theoretical. Each layer translated into concrete mechanisms at both the application and network levels, allowing systems to detect strain early, contain faults, and recover reliably under real operating conditions. The following table outlines how the five layers were implemented in practice, showing how each layer served a distinct purpose while reinforcing the others across different environments:

Layer	Purpose	Protecting applications	Protecting networks
Identity	Who is interacting	Verify users, devices, services, OAuth 2.0, OIDC; FIDO2, short-lived tokens, and RBAC/ABAC	mTLS, 802.1X, and RADIUS
Visibility	What is happening	OpenTelemetry, SIEM, immutable logs, and anomaly detection	NetFlow, packet mirroring, and DNS query log
Integrity	Can data and logic be trusted	SHA-256, digital signatures; secure boot, SBOMs, and model fingerprinting	DNSSEC, IPsec, and BGP RPKI
Isolation	Where failure stops	API gateways, service mesh, container isolation, and least privilege	VLANs; micro-segmentation and software-defined perimeters
Recovery	How the system returns to normal	Versioned backups, offline modes, restoration scripts, and playbooks	Routing resilience, backup resolvers, and failover protocols

Table 5.4: *Architecture of the five layers*

The table summarizes how each security layer supports a specific trust function and how those functions are implemented at both the application and network levels. Together, these layers transform security from a static configuration into a daily practice that keeps systems observable, verifiable, and resilient as conditions change across clinics, cooperatives, and sensor networks.

Defense as a living pattern

For Linh, distributed defense is not only an architectural choice. It is an ongoing practice. Systems endure when many hands support their stability. The layers provide structure, but people sustain that structure through monitoring, review, and adaptation as conditions change. Once deployed, however, no architecture remains abstract. Strain emerges in routine behavior: credentials reused under pressure, dependencies trusted by habit, sensors drifting without recalibration, recovery paths assumed rather than verified. These are not isolated mistakes. They are the predictable points where layered defenses are stretched unevenly or allowed to age.

To understand whether a security structure truly holds, it must be examined where it frays. The next section turns to concrete failures that exposed these limits and made visible what architecture alone cannot guarantee.

Learning from failure modes

A weave strengthens when the places that fray are understood.

Linh did not teach security as a wall meant to block every threat. She taught it as a practice of attention. Systems fail not only because something breaks, but because assumptions go unexamined, signals fade into the background, and trust is granted without evidence. A breach marks a moment when a system no longer meets the expectations of the people who depend on it.

Failure is inevitable in complex digital systems. Learning from failure is not. For this reason, Linh insisted on post-incident reviews that examined structure rather than blame. Each incident revealed where trust had been assumed instead of verified and where reinforcement was overdue.

The following sections explore the failures that expose how security assumptions break under operational pressure. Each illustrates how adversaries exploit quiet gaps between layers, and how security weakens when verification stops before disruption becomes visible.

Ransomware in the clinic network

Maya's clinic relied on connected diagnostic tools, patient records, and scheduling systems to operate during periods of staff shortage. During a regional surge, core systems suddenly became unavailable. Patient records could not be accessed. Appointments were delayed. Nurses reverted to paper workflows under pressure.

The breach originated weeks earlier. Malware entered through a compromised endpoint that lacked recent patches and strong monitoring. Its initial activity blended into routine system behavior and triggered no alerts. Once inside, the malware harvested legitimate credentials and session tokens already present on compromised machines. This allowed it to move laterally using access patterns indistinguishable from routine administrative activity.

During this quiet phase, the attackers mapped internal dependencies, identified backup systems, and located services critical to clinical workflows. No data was altered, and no services were disrupted, allowing the compromise to persist unnoticed.

When encryption finally triggered, it did so across multiple systems at once. Clinical applications became unavailable, backups were rendered unusable, and access to patient records was lost. Sensitive data that had already been staged was exfiltrated, giving the attackers leverage beyond service disruption. The demand that followed tied restoration and silence to payment.

By the time disruption became visible, the system could no longer sustain reliable operation across its critical services. Maya worked with Linh to pause automation, isolate affected services, and restore from clean backups. Care continued, but visibility and confidence were lost at the moment they were most needed.

Failure points:

- Intrusion progressed silently due to limited behavioral visibility inside trusted zones.
- Long-lived credentials and sessions were reused without revalidation.
- Lateral movement appeared routine because identity was not continuously verified.
- Backup integrity and restoration paths were not regularly tested under adversarial assumptions.
- Incident response pathways existed but were not rehearsed, delaying decisive isolation.

Improvements:

- Continuous behavioral monitoring to detect abnormal credential use and internal movement.
- Short-lived credentials and session revalidation to limit persistence after compromise.
- Verified, regularly tested recovery paths, including offline and immutable backups.
- Confidence-aware automation that pauses when system integrity cannot be confirmed.
- Practiced incident response pathways with clear authority to isolate, halt, and escalate early.

Structural interpretation:

- **Primary pulls on the system**: Intrusion-enabled sabotage, with exfiltration amplifying impact.
- **Threat modeling lens**: STRIDE exposed credential misuse and availability loss. PASTA connected system outage to patient care risk. LINDDUN surfaced secondary dignity risk through patient data exposure.

- **Layer interaction**: Identity failed first, visibility lagged, integrity of recovery assumptions broke under stress, isolation arrived late, and recovery depended on manual intervention.

This incident showed that ransomware succeeds long before systems go offline. The failure was not the absence of controls, but the absence of continuous proof that those controls still held.

Supply chain breach in the cooperative platform

Aisha's cooperative depended on shared platforms to manage yield data, logistics coordination, and market access across regions. Trust in these systems ensured that farmers retained control over their production data and decisions.

The breach entered through a third-party analytics module integrated into the cooperative's reporting pipeline. The module was trusted by design and updated automatically. A malicious update introduced code that quietly expanded data access permissions beyond their intended scope.

The cooperative's core systems were never directly compromised. Instead, the breach propagated through inherited trust. The malicious component accessed aggregated datasets, extracted sensitive patterns, and transmitted them outward in small volumes that avoided detection thresholds.

Operational systems continued functioning normally. Dashboards rendered correctly. Decisions appeared consistent. The breach surfaced only when external partners referenced insights that could not have been derived from shared reports alone.

Linh traced the issue to the dependency chain. The system had extended trust without continuous verification of provenance, version integrity, or behavioral constraints on third-party components.

Failure points:

- Trust was extended transitively through dependencies without ongoing verification.
- Limited visibility into component provenance and runtime behavior.
- Integrity assumptions about upstream data and modules were untested.
- Isolation boundaries did not exist at integration points.
- Recovery depended on vendor coordination outside the cooperative's control.

Improvements:

- Explicit dependency inventories with continuous provenance tracking.
- Behavioral monitoring of third-party components, not just internal services.

- Strong integrity checks for updates, including signed artifacts and version pinning.
- Isolation of external modules through constrained execution environments.
- Defined recovery playbooks for vendor-originated incidents.

Structural interpretation:

- **Primary pulls on the system**: Manipulation enabled exfiltration through trusted pathways.
- **Threat modeling lens**: PASTA tied dependency compromise to cooperative-level risk. STRIDE identified elevation of privilege via transitive trust. LINDDUN revealed privacy harm from inferred community behavior.
- **Layer interaction**: Identity extended beyond organizational boundaries, visibility stopped at integration edges, integrity assumptions failed upstream, isolation was absent at module boundaries, and recovery required external alignment.

This case demonstrated that supply chain risk is not imported once. It persists wherever trust is extended without evidence.

Sensor manipulation in the flood prediction network

Diego's flood prediction system ingested data from hundreds of field sensors distributed across the city. The models tolerated individual sensor failure and short-term noise.

Over one season, predictions began drifting upward. Alerts triggered earlier and more frequently, even though weather patterns remained stable. The change was gradual and initially dismissed as a seasonal variation.

The investigation revealed deliberate manipulation of a subset of upstream sensors. Physical access allowed attackers to bias readings slightly upward while keeping values within configured tolerances. Anomaly detectors tuned for abrupt failure did not activate.

Over time, the model adapted to the biased input. It learned a pattern that no longer matched physical reality. The system remained internally consistent while drifting away from the environment it was meant to represent.

Diego noticed the issue only after alerts persisted following clear conditions. Cross-checking against independent data sources revealed divergence across regions.

Failure points:

- Integrity checks focused on thresholds rather than directional drift.
- Visibility emphasized instantaneous anomalies instead of long-term patterns.

- Sensor identity was known, but device state was not continuously verified.
- Isolation between sensor clusters was insufficient to contain bias.
- Recovery depended on recalibration rather than automated rollback.

Improvements:

- Long-horizon drift detection across temporal and spatial dimensions.
- Cross-validation against independent and external baselines.
- Continuous verification of device state, not just device identity.
- Stronger isolation between sensor groups to prevent correlated bias.
- Defined recovery procedures for model rollback and retraining.

Structural interpretation:

- **Primary pulls on the system**: Manipulation through gradual bias.
- **Threat modeling lens**: STRIDE alone was insufficient. PASTA linked the model error to the public safety impact. LINDDUN surfaced dignity risks from misdirected alerts and evacuation pressure.
- **Layer interaction**: Integrity weakened first, visibility lagged, isolation failed to contain bias, identity verified devices, but not the state, and recovery required deliberate realignment.

This incident showed that systems can be technically correct while becoming operationally untrue.

Patterns beneath malicious failures

Across these incidents, Linh observed a recurring structure rather than isolated mistakes. Each attack began with quiet misalignment. Credentials were reused without challenge. Dependencies were trusted beyond their evidence. Sensors drifted while remaining within accepted bounds. None of these conditions appeared dangerous on their own.

Taken together, they revealed how adversaries operate between layers rather than against them. Attacks did not force entry. They occupied the gaps where verification was assumed complete, where visibility faded, and where responsibility diffused across boundaries.

Security did not fail at cryptography, firewalls, or access controls. It failed where verification paused and assumptions aged. The system continued to function, but its guarantees slowly detached from reality.

Security debt

When Linh reviewed these cases together, she recognized a familiar accumulation. Updates were deferred. Trust was extended for convenience. Recovery paths were documented but never tested. Each decision appeared reasonable in isolation. Each introduced latent exposure by postponing verification.

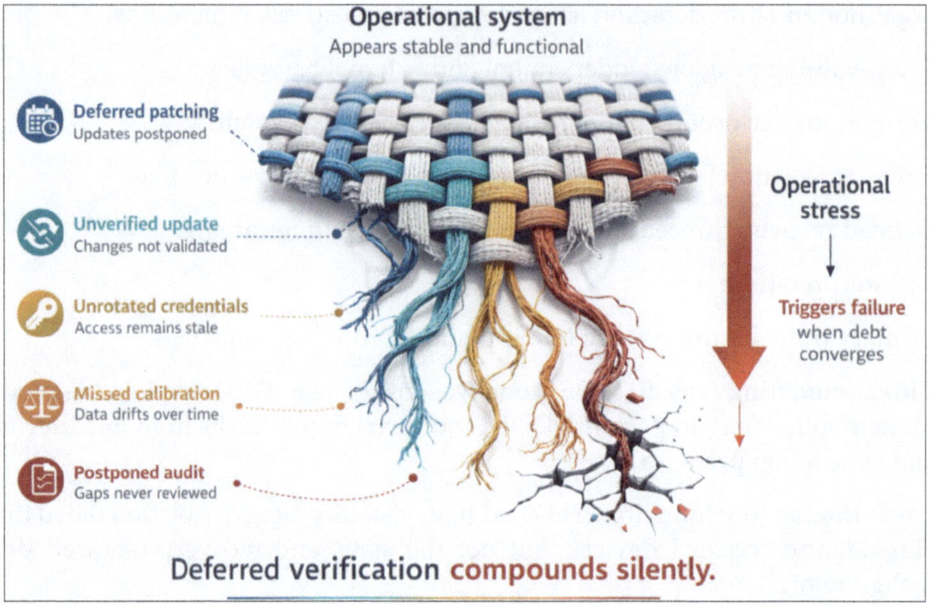

Figure 5.7: Security debt accumulation

Over time, these postponements compounded into what Linh called **security debt**. Like technical debt, it accumulated silently. Systems continued operating, often successfully, while misalignment grew beneath the surface. Nothing appeared broken until stress arrived.

The cost of security debt surfaced only under pressure, when delayed reinforcement converged, and hidden exposure became visible at once. At that point, recovery was no longer a design choice. It became an emergency.

From failure toward reinforcement

Linh did not treat incidents as personal error or operational failure. She treated them as stress tests that revealed the distance between design assumptions and real conditions.

Her questions remained consistent:

- *Where did the system stretch beyond what it was designed to support?*
- *Where was trust accepted without renewed verification?*
- *Which early signals were present but left unexamined?*

Security is not defined by the threats a system blocks. It is defined by how quickly it learns from strain and how deliberately it reinforces trust afterward. Systems endure not because they avoid fracture, but because fracture reveals where reinforcement belongs.

A reliable system does not hide its weaknesses. It makes them visible, so the next pattern can hold with greater clarity and care.

The next section moves from failure toward stewardship, examining how sustained trust depends on continuous verification, disciplined renewal, and the people who remain accountable for both.

Zero Trust as a design discipline

A weave stays strong when every thread proves its place anew.

A system remains trustworthy only when each interaction can justify itself. Modern environments change too quickly for trust to rest on assumptions. Users change roles. Devices move across networks. Data crosses jurisdictions. Adversaries operate inside systems rather than at their edges. Linh understood that trust assumptions weaken over time. Without active verification, they harden into silent rules that continue shaping behavior long after their evidence has expired.

As the attack surface expands through mobility, automation, and interconnected services, trust can no longer be granted once and left unexamined. Every interaction becomes a potential point of strain. Zero Trust emerged as a response to this reality. It treats each request as part of the attack surface and requires it to justify itself through evidence rather than habit.

Zero Trust reshaped how Linh designed systems. It did not attempt to rebuild the perimeter. It redefined how trust was created, renewed, and withdrawn.

Linh's Fifth Principle

Linh's **Fifth Principle** captured this shift:

Trust must be renewed continuously.

Trust was not a default state or a long-term grant. It was a condition produced through verification. Linh treated Zero Trust as a discipline rather than suspicion. It asked systems to earn trust repeatedly by demonstrating context, clarity, and proof.

During a seminar in Hanoi, she explained that *trust was not defined by the absence of doubt. It emerged when verification was present and visible.*

Zero Trust did not eliminate trust. It ensured that trust was never permanent and never assumed.

Zero Trust foundations

Zero Trust replaced static guarantees with continuous evaluation. Each interaction required the system to verify identity, assess context, and limit access appropriately. Linh structured her designs around a small set of operational principles:

- **Verify explicitly**: Every request includes authentication, device posture checks, and contextual signals.
- **Assume compromise**: Architectures expect that adversaries may already be present.
- **Enforce least privilege**: Access is limited to what is required for the current task.
- **Adapt to context**: Time, location, behavior history, and system health influence decisions.
- **Validate continuously**: Authorization is revisited throughout a session, not only at entry.
- **Segment by design**: Boundaries constrain how far a failure or intrusion can propagate.

Together, these principles shifted trust from assumption to repeatable, evidence-driven action.

The Zero Trust loop in practice

In systems with a broad and changing attack surface, trust cannot be renewed globally. It must be rebuilt locally and continuously. The Zero Trust loop narrowed exposure by evaluating each interaction on its own terms and limiting both its reach and duration.

Linh translated Zero Trust principles into an operational sequence that unfolded during every interaction rather than at a single login event. Tokens were short-lived. Device posture influenced privileges. Segments divide systems into constrained zones. Policy engines evaluated requests using real-time signals and recorded outcomes for review.

Behavioral baselines informed what the system considered normal. When patterns shifted, controls adapted. Additional validation was requested, or access was reduced. **Multi-factor authentication** (MFA) appeared only when risk warranted it, preserving usability while maintaining assurance.

Linh described the loop as five interlinked motions:

1. **Authenticate**: Identity is verified using credentials, device posture, and environmental context such as location and time. Authentication occurs at risk-sensitive moments, not only at session start.
2. **Authorize with context**: The system evaluates whether access should be granted at that moment. Past behavior, current task, device health, and recent activity shape the decision. Authorization remains dynamic.

3. **Segment access**: Approved access is constrained to the smallest necessary boundary. Users interact only with the specific service, dataset, or workflow required, reducing exposure if credentials or software fail.

4. **Monitor behavior**: The system observes sequence, frequency, and velocity of actions. When behavior deviates from baseline, controls adjust. Permissions narrow, prompts appear, or access pauses.

5. **Revalidate**: Trust expires by design. Revalidation confirms that identity and context remain consistent. Changes in network state, command patterns, or location trigger renewed checks.

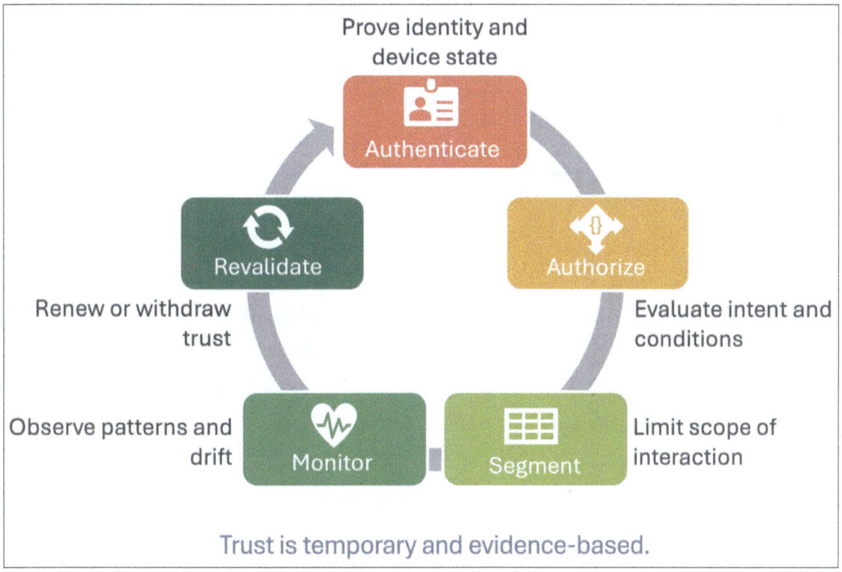

***Figure 5.8**: Zero Trust loop*

This loop gave the system a rhythm in which trust was brief, evidence-based, and easily withdrawn when conditions changed.

Zero Trust in Maya's mobile clinics

Maya's mobile clinics illustrated how Zero Trust supported work in dynamic, resource-constrained environments. Clinics moved across regions, crossed connectivity boundaries, and relied on a mix of tablets, local hubs, and sensors. Roles shifted during emergencies. Devices reconnected after extended offline periods.

Zero Trust maintained alignment under these conditions:

1. **Authentication in variable environments**: Devices reauthenticated on reconnection, preventing outdated trust from persisting after outages or movement.

2. **Authorization by current context**: Clinicians received access based on their present assignment and location. Context-aware decisions reduced unintentional overreach.
3. **Segmentation to protect records**: Each clinic functioned as a contained boundary. Internal sharing was allowed, while external communication passed through defined channels, limiting the impact of lost or compromised devices.
4. **Monitoring for misalignment**: Unusual behavior, failed updates, or improbable sensor readings triggered a review. The system recognized when devices returned after long gaps or when data no longer matched environmental conditions.
5. **Revalidation after change**: Every reconnection refreshed permissions and rechecked device identity. Models verified alignment before contributing to regional analysis.

Zero Trust did not slow clinic operations. It increased confidence that the system behavior reflected the current working conditions.

Trust decay and renewal cycles

Linh treated trust as having a half-life. Without verification, confidence in any assumption diminishes over time, regardless of its original reliability.

Different trust assumptions decay on different time scales, from minutes to years. Sessions and tokens expire quickly. Devices age more slowly. Models drift as environments change. Vendor relationships and governance structures decay over years rather than days. Failures often emerge when renewal cycles fail to match decay rates. Long-lived trust rested on short-lived evidence.

When renewal lags behind decay, systems do not collapse immediately. They drift.

Zero Trust and resilience

Resilience depends on detecting misalignment early and responding before harm spreads. Zero Trust strengthens this ability by preventing outdated assumptions from guiding decisions.

In Diego's flood network, Zero Trust exposed timing drift and firmware inconsistency before the evacuation logic was affected. In Aisha's cooperative, it reduced well-intentioned misuse by constraining access to the appropriate scope. In Maya's clinics, it kept decisions aligned with current roles, device health, and environmental conditions.

Resilience emerges when trust is rebuilt continuously. Systems that revalidate identity, observe behavior, segment interactions, and assess context can absorb strain without losing coherence.

For Linh, Zero Trust became the discipline that kept systems aligned with the realities they served. It allowed stability to persist even as conditions shifted and new pressures emerged.

With these foundations established, the next section examines future pressures on trust and how emerging technologies such as AI and quantum computing will shape the next generation of secure systems.

Future pressures on trust

A weave endures only when it is prepared for threads it has not yet met.

A secure system must be prepared for conditions it has not yet encountered. The protections used today will face adversaries, technologies, and operating environments that evolve faster than static designs can accommodate. AI will produce threats that adapt in real time. Quantum computing will weaken long-standing cryptographic assumptions. Nation-states and organized groups will probe supply chains, legal frameworks, and embedded dependencies, not only network boundaries. Future pressures do more than introduce new threats. They reshape the attack surface itself by expanding how systems touch the world.

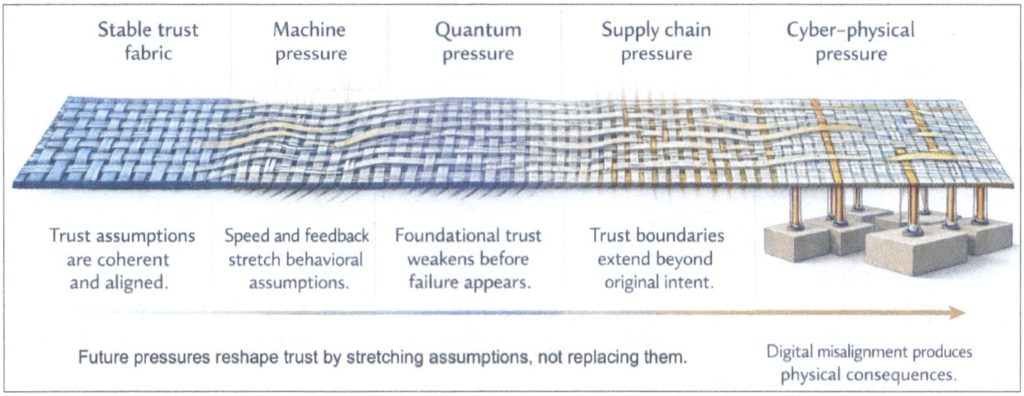

***Figure 5.9**: Trust fabric under future pressures*

Linh did not approach these shifts with fear. She worried about systems that resisted change. In her view, the most significant vulnerability was rigidity: protocols fixed too early, architectures that rejected revision, and teams that mistook calm operation for safety. Security had to remain an active practice, capable of sensing change, interpreting signals, and adjusting structure.

Intelligent agents, adaptive models, complex supply chains, and cyber-physical systems expand how systems interact with their environments. Security must therefore anticipate not only new attacks, but new forms of exposure.

Machine-driven pressures

As AI gained capability, it introduced pressures through speed and adaptation. Automated agents scanned environments continuously, adjusted their behavior based on feedback, and learned patterns that closely resembled legitimate use. These systems did not rely on static malware. They generated scripts, access attempts, and payloads that evolved with each response.

One incident in Linh's logs showed a sequence of login attempts that refined their timing after each rejection. The activity was not brute force. It learned from the system's reactions and gradually matched natural user rhythms. The adversary was not testing credentials alone. It was studying normal behavior.

Machine-driven pressures commonly include:

- Self-modifying attack scripts.
- Behavior-driven probes tuned to system responses.
- Automated reconnaissance that adapts to defensive changes.
- Synthetic identities designed to mimic real users.

Linh responded by strengthening behavioral baselines, expanding temporal analysis, and treating subtle timing regularities as early indicators of automation. Static rules could not keep pace with adversaries that adapted within minutes. Systems needed to recognize unfamiliar behavioral patterns as quickly as those patterns emerged.

Machine-driven pressure shifts security from fixed rule enforcement to adaptive interpretation. A system must detect behavior that fits the surface pattern but violates underlying expectations.

Quantum disruption

Quantum computing will weaken many of the mathematical assumptions underlying classical cryptography. While widespread impact is not immediate across all systems, any environment that stores long-lived secrets is already exposed. Data intercepted today may be decrypted later when quantum capabilities mature.

Linh treated quantum disruption as a structural shift rather than a distant technical concern. When foundational cryptographic assumptions weaken, long-term keys, static algorithms, and inflexible protocols lose reliability.

In response, Linh organizes cryptographic design around the following practices that reduce dependence on any single foundational assumption, and:

- She focused on cryptographic agility as a system property.
- Using algorithms and libraries that can be replaced without redesign.
- Rotating keys frequently and limiting secret lifetime.
- Avoiding dependencies on fixed cryptographic assumptions.
- Tracking emerging standards such as NIST post-quantum algorithms.

Quantum disruption reinforced a broader lesson. Secure systems must evolve as their foundations evolve. Trust cannot outlast the assumptions that support it.

Supply chain exposure

Modern systems depend on components built elsewhere. Open-source libraries, firmware modules, hardware platforms, cloud services, and vendor APIs all introduce inherited assumptions. Each dependency expands the trust boundary beyond the system itself.

Supply chain exposure commonly arises from:

- Libraries containing undiscovered flaws.
- Firmware with insecure defaults or hidden access paths.
- Vendor breaches that propagate across ecosystems.
- Misconfigurations inherited from upstream projects.

Linh's team once traced inconsistent environmental readings to a compromised module introduced through a third-party update. The system trusted the component because its origin was assumed to be safe.

To reduce these risks, Linh emphasized:

- Strong provenance tracking.
- Transparent versioning and dependency inventories.
- Regular supply chain audits.
- Signed updates and tamper-evident distribution.
- Explicit review of inherited components.

Supply chain risk is not a one-time assessment. It is a continuous condition. Secure systems depend on knowing where their components originate and how trust is extended through them.

Securing physical and digital boundaries

Software increasingly produces physical outcomes. A sensor reading influences a diagnosis. An actuator setting controls irrigation. A model prediction shapes evacuation timing. When a digital error leads to a physical consequence, the boundary between the two becomes fragile.

Common threats at this boundary include:

- Sensors altered to bias measurements.
- Devices modified or replaced in the field.
- Data distorted across multi-hop relay paths.
- Extracted secrets used to impersonate hardware.

Linh reinforced this boundary through end-to-end verification:

- Signed firmware and verified boot chains.
- Tamper-evident hardware and clear retirement processes.
- Hop-by-hop provenance tracing data from source to decision.

She treated cyber-physical systems as environments where truth must remain consistent across physical signals and digital records. When those align, decisions remain dependable even as conditions change.

Emerging threats in intelligent systems

As **machine learning** (ML) systems became central to clinics, cooperatives, and city networks, Linh observed a new class of risk. Influence could occur within decision logic without compromising the infrastructure.

Emerging threats in intelligent systems include:

- Training data poisoning.
- Crafted inputs that shift model behavior.
- Prompt-injected instructions embedded in text.
- Pixel-level perturbations are invisible to people.
- Reconstruction attacks that infer sensitive attributes.
- Query patterns designed to reverse-engineer models.
- Behavioral drift caused by environmental change.

These threats act within decision pipelines. A model may appear functional while its internal understanding diverges from reality.

Linh responded by reinforcing:

- Data provenance across training and inference.
- Continuous monitoring for behavioral drift.
- Guardrails aligning outputs with policy and human judgment.
- Human oversight embedded in critical workflows.

Intelligent systems extend capability, but resilience depends on joint attention from both models and the people who guide them.

Toward adaptive systems

As systems become more autonomous, they change faster than humans can observe directly. Adaptive systems continuously recalibrate, optimize, and restructure. These capabilities improve performance but introduce risk if defensive controls remain static.

Linh argued that adaptive systems require adaptive defenses:

- Drift detection integrated into normal operation.
- Automatic recalibration and consistency checks.

- Policy updates tied to observed behavior.
- Feedback loops that incorporate monitoring signals into control decisions.

An adaptive system remains stable not by resisting change, but by maintaining coherence while it changes.

Defensible design principles

Future pressures favor systems that are easier to protect by design. Linh distilled this into a set of structural principles:

- Prefer simplicity where complexity adds little value.
- Maintain clear and enforceable boundaries.
- Limit privileged access and shorten its duration.
- Design for redundancy and graceful degradation.
- Favor predictable behavior to simplify anomaly detection.
- Make errors visible and recovery straightforward.

Defensible systems reveal strain early and enable correction before harm spreads.

Stewardship as practice

Security depends on technical controls and on the people who sustain them. Linh viewed stewardship as a core component of resilience. Teams that care for their systems document decisions, question unusual behavior, and share responsibility for outcomes.

Stewardship keeps systems aligned with purpose. It ensures that verification remains active, emerging pressures are noticed early, and trust continues to be earned rather than assumed.

The next section translates these ideas into practice, focusing on long-term maintenance, cultural habits, and disciplined verification for systems that must endure over years rather than days.

Ethical posture for security design

Ethics is the choice of which threads deserve protection.

Security is not only a technical discipline. It is a set of decisions about what and whom a system protects. As Linh reflected on past failures, she recognized that not all elements within a system carry the same significance. Some represent sensitive information. Others represent vulnerable communities, essential services, or personal dignity. Ethical design determines how these critical elements are identified and safeguarded.

For Linh, ethics was not an abstract aspiration. It functioned as a structural force that shaped configuration, access, and response. Systems that ignored ethical foundations became brittle because they misjudged what mattered most. Systems that prioritized dignity, autonomy, and fairness gained clarity of purpose. They retained coherence even under strain.

Linh paid close attention to moments when automated confidence began to outweigh human judgment. In clinics, cooperatives, and flood networks, the biggest risk was rarely computational error. It was authority drifting without notice. Automation acted without escalation. People deferred judgment under pressure. Systems issued recommendations without signaling uncertainty.

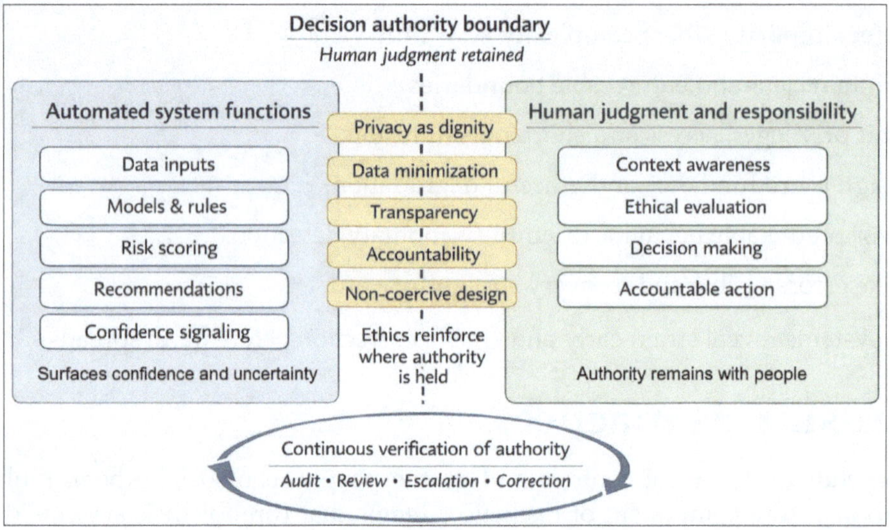

***Figure 5.10**: Ethical posture for security design*

For this reason, Linh treated decision authority as a boundary rather than an outcome. Systems were expected to surface confidence, expose uncertainty, and invite intervention when conditions changed. Decision support guided action. Decision substitution removed the agency. Ethical systems made this distinction explicit.

Just as Zero Trust required continuous verification of access, Linh believed *decisions required continuous verification of authority*.

Privacy as dignity

Privacy protects more than data. It protects people. When Maya's clinic safeguarded patient records, it preserved the trust required for care. When Aisha's cooperative protected yield and income information, it upheld the dignity of farmers whose livelihoods depended on the system. Privacy ensures that data is not used in ways that harm those it describes.

Designing for privacy means limiting exposure, restricting visibility, and granting access only when there is a clear and justified need. These choices align system behavior with the interests of the communities it serves.

Data minimization

Collecting excessive data increases risk without increasing value. Larger datasets expand the attack surface, complicate governance, and impose long-term obligations on systems that must protect them.

Linh encouraged her teams to collect only what was necessary for decisions and outcomes. Smaller, purpose-built datasets reduced exposure, simplified controls, and improved verification reliability. Data minimization became a form of respect for both the system and the people it represented.

Transparency

A trustworthy system must be able to explain itself. Transparency makes decisions understandable and creates space for validation. It allows people to see how inputs shaped outcomes and why recommendations were produced.

In Diego's flood network, transparent alerts helped communities understand why warnings were issued. In Maya's clinic, transparency allowed clinicians to compare system guidance with their own observations. Transparency provided context, not persuasion. It allowed users to remain active participants rather than passive recipients.

Accountability

Accountability provides a way to trace actions, review decisions, and evaluate system behavior over time. It is not about assigning blame. It is about preserving trust.

Audit logs, accessible records, and interpretable decision paths allow teams to identify misalignment early. When actions are traceable, errors can be corrected before they spread, and confidence in the system remains intact.

Avoiding coercive systems

Some systems create pressure instead of support. Designs that obscure options, limit agency, or enforce compliance through opacity diminish trust and can cause unintentional harm.

Linh argued that technology should inform and empower. It should guide decisions, not enforce them. Systems that rely on hidden mechanisms or irreversible choices risk undermining the people they are meant to serve. Avoiding coercive design protects autonomy and keeps technology aligned with human judgment.

Ethics as structural reinforcement

When ethical considerations are integrated directly into architecture, security becomes more than protection. The system aligns with its purpose and with the people who rely on it. Ethical posture influences data handling, access rules, fallback behavior, and response design. It reinforces the layers described earlier and strengthens their ability to maintain trust under pressure.

For Linh, ethics was not a separate checklist. It was a structural thread that bound identity, visibility, integrity, isolation, and recovery into a coherent whole. It stabilized the system as new pressures emerged and ensured that trust remained central to design decisions.

She encouraged teams to test ethical posture with a simple question:

If this system made the same decision tomorrow under slightly different conditions, would a human still recognize and accept its authority?

Conclusion

A resilient weave is shaped by care as much as by design.

Linh sat in front of the security operations dashboard as the day wound down. Telemetry streams moved steadily across the screen. Clinic systems showed green after a brief disruption. The cooperative's pipelines had revalidated overnight updates. Flood sensors across the city reported within expected ranges again. From the surface, everything appeared calm.

She knew better than to stop there.

Years of supporting Maya's clinics, Aisha's cooperative, and Diego's flood network had taught her that security is not proven by quiet screens or stable graphs. It is proven by whether a system can explain itself when questioned. She scanned not for alarms, but for evidence. Identity confirmations. Behavioral baselines. Integrity checks. Isolation boundaries. Recovery signals. The markers that showed the system still understood why it was behaving as it was.

Security, as this chapter has shown, is not the absence of incidents. It is the presence of structure. Failures rarely arrive as a sudden collapse. They begin as drift, deferred verification, and assumptions that outlive their evidence. Systems often continue operating while trust slowly separates from reality.

The purpose of security is not to predict every failure, but to ensure that when systems are stressed, their behavior remains explainable, recoverable, and accountable.

Across the chapter, security emerged as an engineered discipline rather than a defensive posture. Verification replaced assumption. Visibility turned silence into evidence. Integrity anchored decisions in truth. Isolation constrained the spread of failure. Recovery restored trust when the strain exceeded design limits. Together, these layers transformed security from a static configuration into a living structure that absorbs pressure without losing coherence.

Linh also saw where security alone was insufficient. Controls mattered, but stewardship sustained them. Ethical posture defined where authority stopped and human judgment resumed. Trust endured only when renewal remained active, and responsibility remained visible.

Security, she understood, was not a layer added after design. It was the reinforcing thread that shaped how systems could grow without tearing. It determined which connections could be trusted, which required reinforcement, and which demanded renewal.

Security holds the pattern. It does not define it.

The next chapter moves from protection to practice. From keeping systems coherent under strain to shaping how new threads enter, interact, and evolve.

Digital weaving begins here.

Weaver's toolkit

A pattern is only as strong as the hands that maintain it.

Linh believed that security was never only a matter of rules or code. It was a craft, practiced deliberately, refined through experience, and passed on through shared understanding.

This section is a place to pause and gather. It brings together the language, concepts, and practices that turn principles into action. It is not a checklist. It is a workspace where readers can learn to examine systems with clarity, apply judgment under pressure, and maintain trust over time.

Security becomes durable when knowledge is shared, and practice is repeatable.

The following table is a working map Linh developed for students and practitioners to examine how principles, architectural layers, failure modes, and verification signals come together during system design reviews and incident analysis:

Principle	Primary layer	Typical failure mode	Verification signal
Trust requires verification	Visibility	Silent drift in timing, values, or access patterns	Deviations from behavioral baseline, unexplained regularity, and delayed telemetry.
Defense must be distributed	Isolation	Single control failure enables lateral spread	Access attempts crossing expected boundaries, unusual service-to-service calls.
Expect strain and design for recovery	Recovery	System stalls or data loss after disruption	Failed restoration tests, incomplete rollback, prolonged degraded state.

Principle	Primary layer	Typical failure mode	Verification signal
Trust must be renewed continuously	Identity	Stale credentials or long-lived sessions	Token age exceeding policy, access from a changed context without revalidation.
Decisions require verified authority	Integrity	Automation acts without escalation or uncertainty signals	Decisions executed without a confidence score, override path, or audit trace.
Ethics as a structural force	All layers	Harmful outcomes despite correct computation	Decisions misaligned with user intent, dignity, or declared system purpose.
Stewardship sustains security	Visibility and recovery	Repeated issues without corrective change	Recurring incidents, unresolved postmortem actions, and unreviewed alerts.
Security debt compounds silently	Integrity and recovery	Latent exposure surfaces under stress	Deferred updates, expired keys, overdue calibration, or audits.

Table 5.5: Security principles, layers, failures, and signals

This table is intended as a review and diagnostic aid rather than a checklist. During design reviews, incident postmortems, or routine audits, teams can start with a principle and trace it across layers to identify likely failure modes and the signals that would reveal them early. The purpose is not to eliminate all risk, but to ensure that each principle is supported by observable verification. Used consistently, the table shifts security discussions from abstract controls to concrete evidence of alignment between system behavior, design intent, and ethical boundaries.

Weaver's lexicon

A shared vocabulary is essential for collaboration. The following glossary offers concise definitions of technical terms and acronyms used throughout the chapter. It is intended for students, practitioners, and teachers with varying backgrounds:

- **Accountability**: The ability to trace actions and decisions in a system to specific actors or components so that behavior can be reviewed, explained, and corrected when needed.
- **Adaptive defenses**: Security mechanisms that adjust policies, thresholds, or controls in response to changing behavior, threats, or system conditions rather than relying on fixed rules.
- **Anomaly detection**: Techniques that identify behavior, values, or patterns that deviate from a learned or expected baseline.

- **Application programming interface gateway (API gateway):** A service that manages, secures, and routes API requests, providing centralized control for authentication, rate limiting, and policy enforcement.
- **Attack surface**: The total set of points where a system interacts with people, devices, data, models, or other systems, and where assumptions can be tested, strained, or exploited.
- **Audit log**: A tamper-resistant record of events and actions in a system that supports investigation, accountability, and compliance.
- **Attribute-based access control (ABAC)**: An access control model that grants or denies access based on attributes of users, resources, actions, and context, rather than solely on predefined roles.
- **BGP Resource Public Key Infrastructure (BGP RPKI)**: A cryptographic framework that helps secure **Border Gateway Protocol** (**BGP**) routing by verifying that route announcements are authorized for the networks they claim.
- **Brute-force attack**: A method of guessing credentials or keys by trying many possibilities until one succeeds, often mitigated by rate limits and multifactor authentication.
- **Cognitive fatigue**: The mental overload and tiredness that impair human attention and decision-making, increasing the likelihood of security-related errors.
- **Container isolation**: The separation of applications or services into lightweight, isolated execution environments that limit the impact of faults or compromises.
- **Cyber-physical system**: A system where software and networks interact directly with physical processes, such as sensors, actuators, and control systems.
- **Data minimization**: The principle of collecting and retaining only the data necessary for a specific purpose to reduce exposure and simplify protection.
- **Data poisoning**: An attack where malicious or biased data is inserted into training or input datasets so that models or systems learn incorrect patterns or behaviors.
- **Data provenance**: The ability to trace the origin, transformations, and movement of data from its source to its use in decisions or models.
- **Defensible design**: An approach to architecture that makes systems easier to protect, monitor, and repair by favoring simplicity, clear boundaries, and predictable behavior.
- **Decision authority boundary**: The point at which automated systems must yield to human judgment because confidence, context, or consequence exceeds what verification alone can justify.
- **Device attestation**: A mechanism that proves a device's identity and health state, often using secure hardware to report trusted configuration or firmware.

- **Distributed denial-of-service (DDoS) attack**: An attack where many sources flood a target with traffic or requests to exhaust resources and disrupt normal service.
- **Distributed tracing**: A technique for tracking individual requests as they flow across multiple services, helping diagnose latency, failures, and unusual behavior.
- **Domain Name System Security Extensions (DNSSEC):** A set of extensions to DNS that use digital signatures to verify the authenticity and integrity of DNS responses.
- **Drift**: The gradual divergence of a system's data, behavior, or decisions from real-world conditions or design assumptions, often occurring without triggering immediate errors or alarms.
- **Edge or offline modes**: Operating modes where computation and storage occur close to devices or users and continue functioning when central connectivity is limited or unavailable.
- **Encryption in transit**: The protection of data while it moves over networks using cryptographic protocols so that eavesdroppers cannot read it.
- **Ethical posture**: The set of design constraints that determine which values, people, and outcomes a system prioritizes for protection when decisions are made under uncertainty.
- **Failover**: The automatic or manual switching to a backup system, component, or path when the primary one fails.
- **Fast Identity Online 2 (FIDO2):** A standard for strong, phishing-resistant authentication that uses public key cryptography and hardware or platform authenticators instead of shared passwords.
- **Firmware signing**: The use of digital signatures to ensure that firmware running on a device is authentic and has not been tampered with.
- **Guardrail**: A constraint or rule embedded in a system to prevent unsafe, unintended, or unauthorized behaviors, especially in intelligent or adaptive components.
- **Hashing**: The process of converting data into a fixed-length value using a one-way function, often used for integrity checks and digital signatures.
- **Identity governance**: Policies, processes, and tools that manage who has access to what, ensuring that privileges match roles and responsibilities.
- **Incident playbook**: A predefined set of steps and procedures for responding to specific types of security or operational incidents.
- **Integrity**: The property that data, configurations, and logic remain accurate, consistent, and unaltered except through authorized changes.

- **Internet Protocol Security (IPsec):** A suite of protocols that protect IP traffic through encryption and integrity checks, often using **Authentication Header** (AH) and **Encapsulating Security Payload** (ESP).
- **Isolation**: The practice of limiting the interaction and impact between components or zones so that faults or compromises do not spread.
- **Latent vulnerability**: A condition where a system's assumptions no longer fully match reality but have not yet caused visible problems. Latent vulnerabilities do not trigger alerts during normal operation and often become noticeable only when the system is stressed, changed, or misused.
- **Least privilege**: A principle where users, services, and processes are given the minimum access necessary to perform their tasks, reducing potential damage.
- **Logging (immutable logs)**: Recording system events in append-only or tamper-resistant logs so that historical activity remains reliable for investigation and audit.
- **Machine learning (ML)**: A subset of AI in which systems learn patterns from data and improve performance on tasks without being explicitly programmed for each rule.
- **Micro-segmentation**: A security approach that divides networks into many small, isolated segments to limit lateral movement and minimize the blast radius of attacks.
- **Model drift**: A change in a model's performance or behavior over time due to shifts in input data, environment, or underlying patterns.
- **Model fingerprinting**: The process of uniquely identifying a model's version or configuration so that deployments can be verified against expected variants.
- **Multi-factor authentication (MFA)**: An authentication method that requires two or more independent factors, such as something you know, something you have, or something you are.
- **Mutual Transport Layer Security (mTLS)**: A TLS configuration where both client and server present certificates, allowing each side to verify the other's identity.
- **NetFlow**: A network protocol from Cisco that collects IP traffic flow information for monitoring and analysis.
- **Network segmentation**: Dividing a network into separate zones or segments so that security policies can be applied independently and movement between segments is controlled.
- **OAuth 2.0**: An authorization framework that allows applications to obtain limited access to resources on behalf of a user without sharing the user's credentials.
- **Observability**: The ability to understand a system's internal state based on the data it produces, typically through logs, metrics, and traces.

- **OpenID Connect (OIDC)**: An identity layer built on top of OAuth 2.0 that provides standardized authentication and identity information via **JSON Web Tokens (JWTs)**.
- **OpenTelemetry**: An open standard and toolkit for collecting and exporting telemetry data such as traces, metrics, and logs from applications and services.
- **Packet mirroring**: Packet mirroring copies network traffic to a monitoring system for analysis or policy enforcement.
- **Password reuse/Credential reuse**: The practice of using the same password across multiple accounts or systems increases risk when any one of those accounts or systems is compromised.
- **Post-quantum agility**: The design property that enables systems to easily swap out cryptographic algorithms and keys as post-quantum standards evolve.
- **Post-quantum cryptography (PQC):** Cryptographic algorithms designed to remain secure even against attackers with large-scale quantum computers.
- **Privacy**: The protection of individuals and communities from unwanted exposure or misuse of their data, preserving autonomy and dignity.
- **Prompt injection**: An attack where crafted text inputs attempt to manipulate the behavior of an AI model or decision pipeline beyond its intended instructions.
- **Provenance**: The recorded history of data, code, or components, including origin, transformations, and distribution paths.
- **Quantum computing**: A computing paradigm that uses quantum-mechanical phenomena to solve specific problems, threatening many current cryptographic schemes.
- **Recovery**: The processes and mechanisms a system uses to return to a trusted, functional state after faults, drift, or compromise.
- **Redundancy**: The inclusion of extra components, paths, or capacity so that operations can continue when one part fails.
- **Remote Authentication Dial-In User Service (RADIUS)**: A protocol used for centralized authentication, authorization, and accounting for network access.
- **Resilience**: The ability of a system to absorb strain, adapt to disruption, and continue providing essential services with acceptable degradation.
- **Role-based access control (RBAC)**: An access control model that assigns permissions to roles and then links users to those roles rather than assigning permissions directly to individuals.
- **Secure boot**: A process where a device verifies the integrity and signature of each stage of its boot process, preventing untrusted software from loading.

- **Security debt**: Latent risk that accumulates when verification, updates, or reinforcement are deferred, causing surface exposure later under strain.
- **Security information and event management (SIEM)**: A platform that collects, correlates, and analyzes security event data from multiple sources to support detection and response.
- **Sensor drift**: A gradual change in a sensor's output away from its actual value over time, often due to aging, environment, or calibration issues.
- **Service mesh**: An infrastructure layer for managing service-to-service communication, providing features like traffic control, observability, and policy enforcement.
- **Shadow systems**: Unofficial or ad hoc tools, workflows, or data stores that people create to work around limitations in official systems.
- **Silent breach**: A subtle compromise that does not announce itself. It occurs quietly and appears to be normal until minor anomalies accumulate.
- **Software Bill of Materials (SBOM):** A detailed inventory of the components, libraries, and dependencies within a software product.
- **Stewardship**: The ongoing practice of caring for a system through maintenance, documentation, questioning unexpected behavior, and shared responsibility.
- **Supply chain exposure**: Security risk introduced by third-party hardware, software, or services that a system depends on, including inherited vulnerabilities or backdoors.
- **Synthetic identity**: A fabricated identity constructed from real and fake data that appears legitimate enough to pass basic checks and automated systems.
- **Tamper-evident hardware**: Physical devices designed so that any unauthorized opening or modification leaves visible or detectable signs.
- **Temporal drift detection**: Methods that analyze data or behavior over time to spot gradual shifts that may indicate sensor aging, model drift, or subtle attacks.
- **Threat modeling**: A systematic process for identifying, analyzing, and prioritizing potential threats and weaknesses in a system.
- **Transport Layer Security (TLS):** A cryptographic protocol that provides secure communication over networks, ensuring the confidentiality and integrity of data in transit.
- **Trust half-life**: The period over which an unverified trust assumption loses half its reliability due to environmental change, system evolution, or human behavior.
- **Verification**: The continuous practice of confirming that a system's state, behavior, and outputs remain aligned with expected conditions, rather than a one-time check performed at setup or deployment

- **Versioned backups**: Backups that maintain multiple historical versions of data or configuration, allowing restoration to specific points in time.
- **Virtual LAN (VLAN):** A logical network segment created on a physical network to isolate traffic and apply distinct security or policy controls.
- **Visibility**: The system's ability to make its behavior observable through logs, metrics, and traces so that operators can understand and verify what is happening.
- **Vulnerability**: A condition where a system's assumptions no longer match reality, allowing strain to concentrate and propagate under pressure.
- **Web authentication (WebAuthn):** A web standard that enables strong, phishing-resistant authentication using public key cryptography and authenticators such as security keys or built-in platform methods.
- **Zero Trust**: A security model and design discipline where no user, device, or process is implicitly trusted; instead, each interaction is verified explicitly, limited in scope, monitored, and revalidated over time.

Weaver's workshop

The workshop invites readers to engage directly with the material. The following exercises are prompts, not exams. They are designed to reveal assumptions, expose tradeoffs, and encourage the application of Linh's principles and layers in real contexts:

1. **Reading the pattern**: This exercise develops the ability to notice early misalignment before visible failure occurs.

   Prompts:

   - *Identify one quiet misalignment in a system you know (for example, delayed telemetry, repeated login retries, or gradual data bias).*
   - *Using Table 5.4, select the row that best matches this situation.*
   - *Identify the primary layer under strain and the typical failure mode associated with it.*

   Deliverable: A short written description mapping the observed behavior to one row in *Table 5.4* and explaining why it fits.

   Learning objective: Recognize early signals of strain and classify them using the five-layer security model.

2. **From failure to principle**: This exercise connects concrete incidents to underlying design principles.

   Prompts:

- *Choose one failure mode described in this chapter (for example, shared credentials, sensor drift, or a missed software update).*
- *Locate the corresponding row in Table 5.4.*
- *Identify which security principle was violated.*
- *Identify the verification signal that should have exposed the issue earlier.*

Deliverable: A one-page analysis linking the failure mode to its principle and explaining how verification could have prevented escalation.

Learning objective: Trace operational failures back to violated principles and missing verification.

3. **Diagnosing layered strain**: This exercise builds the ability to see how strain propagates across layers rather than remaining isolated.

Prompts:

- *Select one row in Table 5.4.*
- *Describe how the failure mode in that row could spread to at least two other layers if left unaddressed.*
- *Identify which secondary verification signals* might appear as the issue propagates.

Deliverable: A diagram or structured explanation showing how strain moves across layers and where it could be contained.

Learning objective: Understand interdependence among security layers and how early containment prevents cascading failure.

4. **Ethical boundary identification**: This exercise grounds ethical design in operational decisions rather than abstract values.

Prompts:

- *Select the row in Table 5.4 labeled Ethics as structural force.*
- *Describe a system you are designing or operating where automated decisions influence people or physical outcomes.*
- *Identify where decision authority must stop and human judgment must intervene.*
- *Specify the verification signal that should trigger escalation or review.*

Deliverable: A short design note defining the ethical boundary and its operational signal.

Learning objective: Design systems that preserve human agency through explicit authority limits and verification.

5. **Designing against security debt**: This capstone exercise synthesizes principles, layers, and long-term stewardship.

   Prompts:

   - *Select the row in Table 5.4 labeled Security debt compounds silently.*
   - *Identify three sources of latent security debt in a real or hypothetical system.*
   - *Map each source to its layer and verification signal.*
   - *Propose one design or operational change that would prevent the debt from accumulating.*

   Deliverable: A concise risk register or architectural note outlining debt sources, signals, and corrective actions.

   Learning objective: Anticipate long-term security erosion and design systems that surface and reduce security debt before failure.

Weaver's library

Security is both a technical discipline and a social one. It contains engineering, law, economics, and ethics. Linh kept a small but carefully chosen set of references on her desk to remind herself of this breadth. The following sources deepen themes introduced in this chapter:

1. *Schneier, B. (2018). Click Here to Kill Everybody: Security and Survival in a Hyper-connected World. W. W. Norton & Company.*
2. *Bhunia, S., & Tehranipoor, M. M. (2026). Hardware Security: A Hands-on Learning Approach (2nd ed.). Morgan Kaufmann.*
3. *Stallings, William. (2016) Network Security Essentials: Applications and Standards. 6th ed. Pearson Education.*
4. *National Institute of Standards and Technology. (2020). Zero Trust Architecture (NIST Special Publication 800-207). U.S. Department of Commerce.*
5. *IETF and W3C standards on trust, identity, and encryption protocols.*

Metaphorical and conceptual terms

The weaving metaphor in this chapter is not decoration. It provides a way to think about interconnected systems, strain, and repair. The following lexicon maps key weaving terms to system concepts, enabling readers to move smoothly between imagery and implementation:

- **Bend with the world**: Refers to a system's ability to tolerate operational changes, user variability, environmental shifts, or unexpected pressures without breaking or failing.
- **Fabric (of a system):** Represents the interconnected components, data flows, and

interactions forming the whole structure. Each strand corresponds to a technical or human element.

- **Fractures (in the pattern):** Symbolize failures, misalignments, or vulnerabilities that become visible under stress. A fracture signals where reinforcement or redesign is needed.
- **Holding its form**: Refers to a system preserving stability and correctness even when conditions shift. A well-designed system stays aligned despite strain.
- **Pattern**: The consistent structure of behavior produced by a system's design and operation, including how it processes data, makes decisions, and responds to strain over time.
- **Pattern drifting**: Describes how a system's behavior deviates gradually from its intended state. This includes model drift, configuration drift, or misalignment from ground truth.
- **Pull**: A subtle influence or pressure on the system that is not immediately visible, such as drift, timing anomalies, or quiet misuse.
- **Reinforcing thread**: A structural element that stabilizes the overall pattern. Throughout the chapter, the security is the reinforcing thread because it supports every other layer of the digital system.
- **Stewardship**: The idea that people care for a system the way a craftsperson tends a weave. It implies responsibility, attention, and ongoing maintenance.
- **Strain**: Represents any pressure on the system, including technical, organizational, environmental, or adversarial, that tests assumptions or reveals weaknesses.
- **Structural thread**: An essential value or principle woven throughout the system. In this chapter, ethics serves as a structural thread that supports all other layers.
- **The weave**: The overarching metaphor representing the entire digital system, including its components, relationships, and operational behavior. A resilient weave holds together because its parts reinforce one another.

Join our Discord space

Join our Discord workspace for latest updates, offers, tech happenings around the world, new releases, and sessions with the authors:

https://discord.bpbonline.com

CHAPTER 6

Digital Weaving

Designing coherent systems

Systems become resilient when their parts strengthen one another.

CHAPTER 6
The Digital Weaving

Introduction

Digital systems rarely fail loudly. They drift first, quietly, while performance metrics remain acceptable and automation continues to operate with confidence. Decisions accelerate faster than understanding can keep pace. Assumptions age. Responsibility thins as action outruns authority. By the time failure becomes visible, legitimacy has often already separated from behavior.

This chapter introduces digital weaving as a digital system design discipline for addressing that drift before it hardens. Digital weaving is a way of conceiving, building, and operating digital systems so that coherence, accountability, and legitimacy endure as conditions change.

Rather than treating connectivity, sensing, data, intelligence, security, and governance as separable layers or interchangeable components, digital weaving focuses on how these threads remain in relationship over time and how their interactions shape system behavior. These threads are persistent system conditions. Technologies instantiate them, but coherence depends on how they constrain, inform, and reinforce one another as systems evolve.

The central question of this chapter is not how systems perform under ideal conditions, but how they hold when conditions shift, signals decay, uncertainty rises, and confidence must be earned rather than assumed. The emphasis moves from optimization to endurance, from delivery to continuity, and from control to accountable response.

The chapter begins by examining why additive, stack-based, and optimization-driven design approaches struggle at scale, under automation, and amid uncertainty, even when individual components perform as intended. It then defines digital weaving precisely, clarifying its scope, limits, and structural commitments. The five foundational threads present in every digital system are examined as interacting conditions rather than isolated domains. The weaving loop describes how systems are deliberately designed and sustained through layering, testing, adaptation, and memory. Fray is introduced as a signal that reveals misalignment early, both during system design and in systems already operating.

Through practice-based cases, the chapter shows how woven systems are built before drift begins, adjusted without erasing memory, and repaired without replacement when strain emerges. It concludes by identifying the archetypal patterns that appear when systems hold under pressure and the posture required to carry digital weaving forward as a discipline of responsibility rather than control.

In this chapter, responsibility is evaluated as a structural property of systems, assessed through how constraints are designed, how decisions propagate, and whether consequences remain traceable and correctable under change.

Structure

This chapter covers the following topics:

- A tangled beginning
- The unseen strain
- Digital weaving defined
- The five threads every system lives with
- From stacks to weaves
- The weaving loop
- Fray as a signal
- Weaving in practice
- Archetypes that emerge when systems hold
- Weaving forward

Objectives

By the end of this chapter, the reader will understand digital weaving as a digital system design discipline concerned with how systems are conceived, built, and operated so that coherence, accountability, and legitimacy endure as conditions change. The reader will be able to explain why additive, optimization-driven, and component-centric design approaches often struggle at scale, under automation, and amid uncertainty, even when individual parts perform as intended. The reader will learn to analyze failure as a relational phenomenon, recognizing that breakdowns typically emerge between interacting threads such as sensing, data, intelligence, governance, and trust rather than within isolated components. Through the cases presented, the reader will be able to reason about how these threads are deliberately interlaced during system design and subsequently adjusted in operation to support learning without erasure and adaptation without replacement. Finally, the reader will be able to recognize the structural patterns that emerge when systems hold under pressure and articulate both the appropriate scope and the practical limits of digital weaving as a design posture for consequential digital systems.

A tangled beginning

A fabric can appear intact long after its pattern begins to shift.

The rain in Istanbul is not loud. It insists. It taps the tall windows of *Zoya's* studio the way unresolved problems do. Not a storm. Not a warning. Just enough pressure to remind the city that weight can accumulate quietly.

The building once housed a textile factory. The looms are gone, but the space still carries memory. Iron beams bear load without ornament. Windows admit light without yielding strength. Everything about the room speaks of systems designed to endure repetition and strain.

Figure 6.1: *Zoya's studio*

Zoya had chosen it deliberately.

She is a systems architect by training, though not of buildings. Her work lives in digital systems that continue operating even as their assumptions age. Systems that meet targets while losing legitimacy. Systems that appear reliable until people stop believing they will respond when something feels wrong.

That is why *Samir, Maya, Aisha, Diego,* and *Linh* were there.

They had not arrived with a single failure to diagnose or a platform to evaluate. Each brought a different problem from a different domain, yet each carried the same unsettling shape.

Samir brought networks that remained connected while communities quietly stopped trusting them. Repair existed in theory, but not in practice. Maya brought early warning systems that met thresholds but missed the moment when people began to move. Aisha brought models whose insights arrived after seasons had already turned. Diego brought intelligent systems that performed well but could not be questioned. Linh brought platforms that were secure and compliant, yet produced outcomes no one felt authorized to interrupt.

Nothing was broken, but structural coherence did not persist.

Connectivity without repair.
Sensing without listening.
Data without timing.
Intelligence without restraint.
Trust without legitimacy.

Each system succeeded on its own terms. None remained coherent as conditions changed.

From the outside, these systems appeared stable. Metrics remained within acceptable ranges. Automation executed as designed. From the inside, something more subtle began to shift. Small compensations appeared. Confidence became conditional. People adjusted their behavior before they named a problem.

The room stayed quiet before the conversation began. Zoya did not open with a diagram or a proposal. She watched the room the way she watched systems under strain. Not for what was said, but for hesitation. For pauses that appeared before, trust eroded visibly. For the small adjustments people made when they no longer expected a system to respond if something felt wrong.

The systems they carried into the room had not collapsed.
What failed was harder to name.

This chapter begins there.

The unseen strain

Strain appears where threads stop responding to one another.

Digital systems rarely fail loudly. They drift first.

Performance metrics remain acceptable. Dashboards stay green. Automation continues to operate with confidence. From the outside, the system appears stable. Inside, pressure accumulates quietly.

As drift sets in, decisions become harder to explain because their assumptions are no longer shared. Responsibility becomes harder to trace as actions span tools, teams, and time. People hesitate before trusting what the system tells them, even when it is technically correct. By the time the problem is named, it is already embedded.

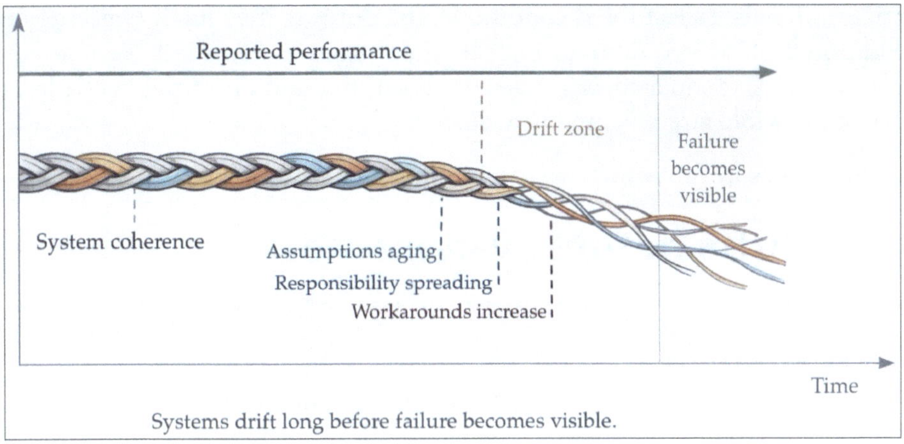

Figure 6.2*: The drift before failure*

This is the least visible phase of system failure, not because damage is immediate, but because legitimacy erodes while success is still being reported.

At this stage, strain is not a breakdown.
It is a misalignment between how a system is measured and how it is actually held together.

Drift begins before failure

Most large digital systems are designed to optimize delivery. Throughput improves. Latency drops. Coverage expands. These gains create momentum, but they also hide early instability.

Decisions accelerate because the system appears reliable.
Assumptions age because evidence is no longer revisited.
Responsibility thins as actions span teams, tools, and time.

The system continues operating, but fewer people can explain why it behaves as it does. When questions arise, answers rely on informal knowledge rather than shared structure.

This is drift. Not collapse, but separation between operation and understanding.

Metrics hide lived conditions

Quantitative signals rarely capture strain early.

Uptime shows availability, not confidence.
Utilization shows activity, not sustainability.
Forecast accuracy hides how often plans are quietly adjusted.

When metrics no longer reflect lived conditions, the outputs they justify become unrealistic, and the additional effort required to sustain them goes unrecorded. People compensate through workarounds, manual checks, side conversations, and unofficial overrides. Reported performance holds while strain is quietly absorbed.

Reported performance improves while structural resilience weakens.

Behavior shifts before systems do

The earliest indicators of strain appear in behavior rather than technology.

Inputs arrive late or selectively.
Recommendations are treated cautiously without being challenged.
Decisions are reviewed after execution rather than questioned before.

None of these conditions are recognized as failures. Individually, they appear reasonable. Collectively, they signal that trust is no longer fully aligned with system behavior.

The system still functions. Confidence begins to relocate.

Scale intensifies invisibility

As systems grow, drift becomes harder to detect.

Connectivity abstracts ownership.
Automation compresses time for reflection.
Data accumulates faster than it returns to decisions.

The distance between where signals are generated and where authority resides increases. When discrepancies emerge, they are absorbed as coordination issues rather than recognized as structural strain.

At scale, silence becomes indistinguishable from stability.

Failure begins before it appears

When failure becomes visible, it often appears sudden. In reality, it has been forming quietly for months or years. By the time intervention begins, assumptions have hardened, authority has diffused, and repair requires replacement rather than adjustment.

The cost is not only technical. It is organizational and social. Trust erodes not because systems fail, but because they fail without explanation.

This chapter begins here because digital weaving directly addresses this condition. Before systems can be repaired or renewed, they must be understood as they actually operate, not as they are reported.

What follows shows how woven systems make hidden strain observable early enough to interpret, respond, and preserve coherence before legitimacy is lost.

Digital weaving defined

Weaving is not an added thread, but a way threads are interlaced.

Digital weaving is a system design method for building digital systems whose critical threads are deliberately interlaced so decisions remain coherent, accountable, and legitimate as conditions change.

Rather than optimizing isolated components, digital weaving focuses on how systems are constructed to act coherently over time. It treats relationships among threads as the primary design surface and assumes that change, uncertainty, and drift are inevitable features of real-world operation.

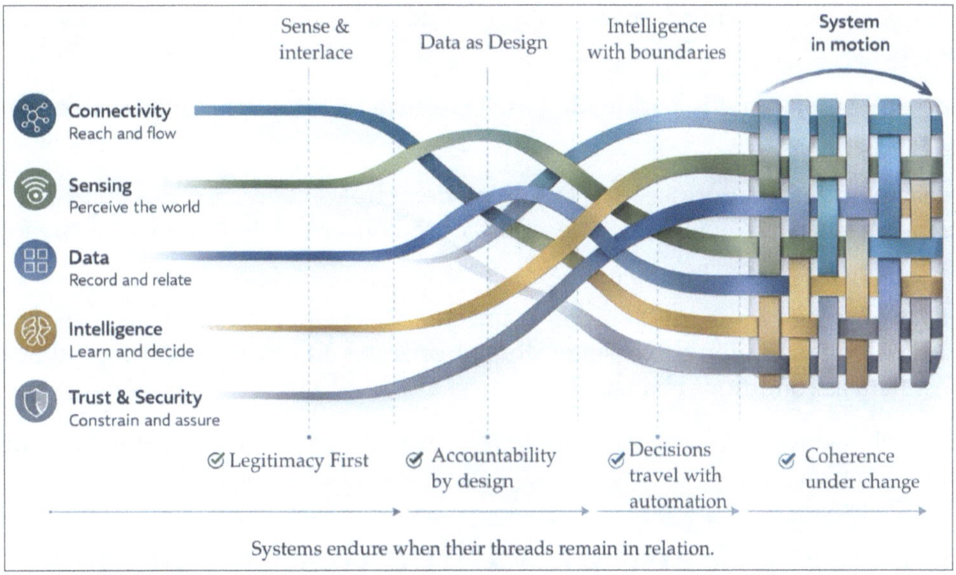

Figure 6.3: *Digital weaving as interlaced flow*

Digital weaving designs systems to observe conditions accurately, interpret them in context, and act with accountability as those conditions evolve. Detection, interpretation, and repair are not afterthoughts applied after failure. They are built-in capabilities that allow systems to adapt without erasing memory or losing legitimacy.

This definition is deliberate in both its scope and its constraints. Digital weaving is not a toolset, platform, or reference architecture. It does not prescribe technologies, vendors, or implementation sequences. It operates beneath those choices by shaping how system threads interact, constrain one another, and evolve together from first construction onward.

The method begins with relationships rather than components. It examines how signals travel, how data returns to decisions, how intelligence is constrained, how authority is exercised, and how responsibility persists as systems adapt. These relationships recur in every consequential digital system, regardless of domain or scale.

Zoya was precise about this boundary.

We are not designing parts, she said. *We are designing how parts stay in relation to strain.*

The problem digital weaving addresses

Most digital systems grow through accumulation. Capability increases while coherence quietly weakens.

Connectivity expands. Data volumes grow. Intelligence accelerates. Automation spreads. Yet responsibility paths remain implicit, authority arrives late, and learning fails to compound. Systems often continue to function successfully while their ability to explain, pause, or revise decisions erodes.

This is not a failure of individual technologies. It is a structural failure of how systems are built to grow.

Digital weaving directly addresses this failure mode. It treats coherence as a first-class design objective rather than an emergent side effect or a concern deferred to governance after deployment.

A digitally woven system is built so that connectivity, sensing, data, intelligence, and trust remain mutually constraining. No single thread operates independently. Each shapes and limits the others as conditions change.

The goal is not balance. The goal is continuity of action that remains structurally accountable as conditions change.

Digital weaving and prevailing design practices

Digital weaving does not replace digital transformation. It reframes how transformation is designed to hold.

Most digital transformation initiatives focus on modernization milestones such as cloud migration, analytics adoption, or automation rollout. These efforts expand technical capability and often deliver real value. What they do not consistently address is how responsibility, authority, and learning persist once systems begin operating under change.

Digital weaving treats transformation as incomplete unless coherence is deliberately designed alongside capability. Without this, systems improve what they can do, but they do not strengthen how decisions remain explainable, contestable, and accountable over time.

Digital weaving also differs from platform-led integration. Standardization around tools and services simplifies delivery and procurement, but it does not ensure that decision paths remain legible once systems interact. When responsibility is assumed to be implicit, coherence is left to emerge informally rather than being sustained structurally.

Nor is digital weaving an intelligence-centered posture. Emphasizing prediction, optimization, or automation accelerates action, but it does not guarantee that uncertainty can be surfaced, confidence adjusted, or intervention permitted when assumptions change. Intelligence amplifies the decision discipline already present in a system. It cannot substitute for one.

These practices are not wrong. They reflect reasonable priorities under growth, efficiency, and scale. Their limitation is structural. They treat coherence, accountability, and legitimacy as secondary effects rather than primary design concerns.

Digital weaving makes those concerns explicit. It asks not only how systems are transformed, but how transformed systems remain answerable as conditions shift. In this sense, digital weaving is not an alternative to transformation. It is the discipline that allows transformation to endure.

The threads digital weaving interlaces

Digital weaving works by deliberately interlacing five foundational threads that shape how digital systems are built, operated, and sustained.

Connectivity provides reach and continuity.
Sensing determines what the system notices.
Data shapes what the system remembers.
Intelligence directs how the system acts.
Trust determines whether the system is relied upon.

When these threads are treated independently, they drift apart. When deliberately interlaced, they reinforce one another while remaining distinct.

Digital weaving does not collapse these threads into a single layer. It preserves their different roles while ensuring their interactions remain visible, constrained, and adjustable.

Tension in one thread propagates to the others, and failure originates in their interaction, even when each thread remains intact.

From observation to accountable action

To address the world's complex problems, digital systems must accurately observe conditions, interpret them in context, and act with accountability. This requires coordination among threads rather than reliance on isolated technologies.

Connectivity enables signals to travel across people, devices, and institutions. Sensing determines which conditions enter consideration. Data preserves those observations as memory, allowing change and context to be examined. Intelligence interprets that data to guide action. Security and trust ensure that signals, decisions, and outcomes remain reliable, contestable, and legitimate at scale.

When these threads operate independently, systems fragment. Data accumulates without meaning. Intelligence accelerates without constraint. Action proceeds without accountability.

When the threads are deliberately interlaced, observation leads to understanding. Understanding leads to action. Action remains answerable as conditions change.

Digital weaving names this structural discipline.

Governance as constraint in motion

Governance is not a thread alongside the others. It is the structure that shapes how threads may pull without tearing the weave.

It does not sit beneath the system or arrive after the fact. It defines the conditions under which a system may act.

In digital weaving, governance is expressed through constraints that shape decision behavior in real time. These constraints define who can act, when systems must pause, how uncertainty is handled, and how responsibility remains traceable as decisions unfold.

Security protects integrity.
Governance preserves legitimacy by constraining how decisions are formed and revised.

Many systems are secure without being legitimate. They enforce access and protect data while producing outcomes no one can explain or contest. Digital weaving is structured so that legitimacy travels with decision-making rather than following it after outcomes.

Durability over optimization

Digital weaving evaluates durability as a primary design criterion rather than treating optimization as sufficient.

Durability does not mean resisting change. It means adapting without losing coherence, evolving without erasing memory, and repairing without restarting.

Optimized systems perform well under known conditions. Durable systems are structured so accountability remains reachable as conditions change.

Zoya summarized the distinction succinctly.

An optimized system can be correct and still be wrong, she said. *A durable system can be wrong and still be trusted.*

Digital weaving does not prevent failure.
It preserves the conditions under which failure remains legible and interpretable.

Scope and precision

Digital weaving is deliberately scoped.

It applies to systems whose decisions affect people beyond their builders, systems that automate judgment, operate at scale, or carry social, physical, or economic consequences. In these contexts, coherence is not optional.

Trivial systems do not require weaving. Overuse weakens the method. Precision preserves it.

Digital weaving is strongest where legitimacy, accountability, and endurance are design requirements rather than aspirations.

A method, not a metaphor

Although the language of weaving provides intuition, digital weaving is a method grounded in observable system behavior.

It produces testable outcomes.
It surfaces measurable signals of strain.
It enables adjustment without erasure as systems are built, operated, and sustained.

The metaphor supports understanding.
The method stands on structure.

This definition anchors the chapter. Everything that follows builds on it.

The digital loom

Digital weaving requires a loom.

The loom is not a component, platform, or architectural layer. It is the structural condition that makes weaving possible. In digital systems, the loom consists of enduring relationships, authority paths, constraints, and mechanisms for adjustment that allow threads to be interlaced and re-tensioned without collapse. The loom does not act or decide. It shapes how decisions may be formed, questioned, slowed, or revised as conditions change.

In earlier chapters, threads were introduced through concrete technologies such as the Internet, **Internet of Things** (**IoT**) systems, data platforms, AI models, and security mechanisms. Those chapters described what the threads are made of.

This chapter describes what those threads do over time.

Technologies change. Threads persist. Digital weaving designs for the latter.

Here, threads refer to persistent system conditions such as how signals travel, how decisions are authorized, how memory returns to action, and how trust accumulates or decays. Technologies instantiate these threads, but the threads themselves are not limited to any single component. Misalignment among them can degrade system behavior, even when every individual component is operating as designed.

Without a loom, systems may connect, sense, store data, and automate action, yet remain brittle. Capability accumulates, but no structure keeps threads in relationship under strain. As conditions change, decisions outrun authority, learning fails to compound, and replacement becomes the only visible response.

Within the loom, threads operate across two orientations.

The warp represents what must remain stable across time. It includes governance constraints, authority paths, accountability relationships, and institutional boundaries. The warp carries legitimacy. It defines who may act, when intervention is permitted, and how responsibility persists as systems adapt.

The weft represents what must remain responsive to context. It includes sensing inputs, data flows, interpretation, and operational decisions. The weft moves continuously across the warp, adapting to change while remaining constrained by the structures that hold it.

The five threads of digital weaving are not fixed to one orientation. Depending on context, any thread may function as warp or weft. What matters is not classification, but relationship.

Weaving also requires weavers.

Weavers represent the system's capacity to notice strain, interpret signals, and intervene before coherence is lost. They include human judgment, governance mechanisms, feedback processes, and institutional roles that can pause action, question decisions, or initiate adjustment. A system without weavers may continue operating, but it cannot adapt with accountability.

The loom, warp, weft, and weavers are not elements to be implemented directly. They are lenses for understanding how systems are constructed to hold under change. Digital weaving succeeds not by adding capability, but by ensuring that system threads remain deliberately interrelated as pressure builds.

With the loom defined, the next step is to examine the five threads themselves and how their interaction shapes systems designed to endure.

The five threads every system lives with

Every weave is shaped by how its threads pull and counterpull.

Digital weaving begins with a simple observation. Every digital system, regardless of domain or scale, lives with a small set of persistent threads. These threads exist whether they are designed for or not. What varies is whether their interactions are acknowledged, constrained, and renewed over time.

These threads are instantiated through technologies such as networks, sensors, data platforms, models, and security mechanisms, but they are defined here by how they behave over time rather than by what they are built from.

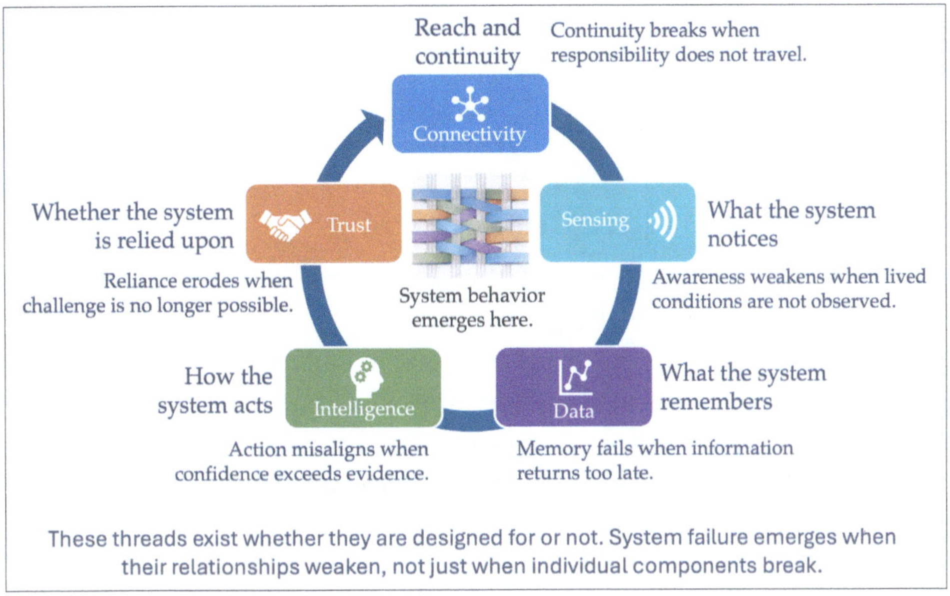

***Figure 6.4**: The five threads as the interacting forces*

Zoya introduced these threads not as layers in an architecture diagram, but as pressures that shape behavior. Drift emerges when relationships weaken, when one thread stretches without regard for the others, or when constraints stop traveling with decisions.

The purpose of this section is not to catalog components. It is to establish a structural grammar. Each thread has a distinct role. Each influences the others. Failure appears between them, not just within them.

The five threads are connectivity, sensing, data, intelligence, and trust.

Connectivity carries continuity

Connectivity determines whether a system can remain present over time. It includes networks, devices, platforms, identity mechanisms, operational routines, and the infrastructure that allows signals, access, and coordination to persist. It also includes ownership models, maintenance practices, and assumptions about availability and repair.

Connectivity is often treated as plumbing. Once established, it fades into the background. That assumption is risky.

When connectivity feels temporary, Zoya said, *behavior changes long before outages occur.*

Strain in connectivity appears as provisional use. Parallel tools emerge. People assume repair will be slow or absent, so they adapt around the system. These adaptations rarely surface in uptime metrics. They surface in trust.

Connectivity constrains every other thread by determining whether signals, authority, and repair can travel at all. When it degrades quietly, sensing loses fidelity, data lags, intelligence acts on outdated context, and trust thins.

Digitally woven systems treat connectivity as a shared, load-bearing thread. Dependencies remain visible. Repair paths are explicit. Degradation is surfaced rather than hidden.

Sensing shapes awareness

Sensing determines what a system notices. It includes sensors, logs, alerts, user input, and observation. More importantly, it reflects choices about which signals matter and whose signals are trusted.

Sensing is interpretation, Zoya said. *Not just detection.*

Strain in sensing appears when alerts are ignored, signals diverge from lived experience, or essential conditions go unobserved. A system may collect large volumes of data and still fail to notice what matters when decisions are made.

Maya saw this in early warning systems. Thresholds were respected, yet behavior shifted earlier. Communities responded to subtle cues that the system did not register. The divergence appeared before any formal failure.

In woven systems, sensing remains adjustable. Human signals are treated as first-class inputs. Silence and absence are examined. Mismatches between system alerts and lived reality trigger review rather than dismissal.

Data preserves memory

Data determines what a system remembers. It includes records, metrics, logs, lineage, and retention practices. Data shapes what can be learned, audited, or contested.

Memory matters only if it returns in time to influence action.

Zoya encountered systems where reports arrived weeks after decisions were made. Accuracy was high. Relevance was low. Delay became distortion because memory returned after decisions were already locked.

Aisha experienced this in agricultural systems. Yield data arrived clean and correct, but after decisions to plant were already fixed. Memory justified outcomes rather than informing judgment.

Strain in data appears as dashboards no one consults, metrics that no longer shape behavior, or numbers that cannot be explained. Without provenance, interpretation collapses. Without timeliness, learning stalls.

Digitally woven systems design data for circulation. Memory returns to decision points. Lineage travels with outcomes. Delay is treated as a design constraint, not an acceptable tradeoff.

Intelligence directs action

Intelligence determines how a system decides. It includes rules, workflows, heuristics, and **machine learning** (**ML**) models. Intelligence interprets data and produces action.

Modern systems often elevate intelligence as the primary value driver. Accuracy improves. Predictions sharpen. Decisions accelerate.

What is often lost is judgment.

Strain in intelligence appears as unquestionable outputs, rigid rules, or automation that continues despite uncertainty. When intelligence outruns sensing, data, or trust, systems act beyond their authority.

Diego recognized this in automated decision systems. Models performed well until someone asked why an outcome could not be contested. Accuracy held. Legitimacy did not.

In woven systems, intelligence is constrained by context. Uncertainty is visible. Confidence adjusts with conditions. Decisions can be paused or revised. Intelligence does not replace judgment. It determines where judgment must still be exercised.

Trust determines reliance

Trust determines whether people remain inside the system. It is not a feature or a policy. It emerges from behavior over time.

Trust is not compliance, Zoya said. *It is the belief that the system will respond when something feels wrong.*

Strain in trust appears as quiet disengagement. People comply outwardly and bypass inwardly. They adapt around the system rather than confront it. These behaviors are often misread as resistance. They are signals of eroded legitimacy.

Trust binds the other threads. Without trust, connectivity is avoided, sensing is ignored, data is doubted, and intelligence is resisted.

Digitally woven systems build trust through visibility and participation. Decisions can be questioned. Repair is possible. Authority is clear. Security protects integrity. Governance confers legitimacy by defining who can act and intervene.

Threads in a relationship

The conversation shifted from listing threads to understanding how they pull on one another.

Zoya said, *What matters is not the presence of threads, but how they constrain one another.*

Connectivity shapes sensing.
Sensing determines data.
Data constrains intelligence.
Intelligence affects trust.
Trust determines whether connectivity is used at all.

These threads require more than balance. They require ongoing coordination as conditions change.

Failure emerges when relationships weaken, and constraints no longer travel with decisions.

Digital weaving keeps these threads distinct and deliberately interlaced. Systems that ignore these relationships do not become simpler. They become brittle.

Threads across domains

The five threads do not belong to a single system category. They belong to systems that decide and act.

Connectivity and sensing are often associated with physical or cyber-physical systems. Intelligence, trust, and governance are often associated with enterprise platforms and organizations. This separation is intuitive, but misleading. The threads themselves do not change across domains. Only how they surface does.

In connected systems, threads appear near physical processes and safety boundaries. In enterprise systems, they occur within workflows, policies, decision rights, and organizational structures. In both cases, the same structural risks apply. Signals can arrive too late. Intelligence can outrun context. Security can protect systems that no longer deserve trust.

Digital weaving treats these threads as universal. What differs is where the strain first appears and how quickly it becomes visible.

The following table clarifies how the same five threads appear across different digital system types:

Threads	Connected digital systems	Enterprise IT systems
Connectivity	Networks, devices, protocols, and gateways.	Platform integrations, identity systems, workflows, and access paths.
Sensing	Sensors, alerts, telemetry, and user inputs.	Logs, transactions, approvals, usage signals, and exceptions.

Data	Streams, records, storage, and lineage.	Reports, metrics, dashboards, forecasts, and audit trails.
Intelligence	Control logic, models, and autonomous responses.	Business rules, optimization logic, recommendations, and automation.
Trust and security	Safety, resilience, integrity, and availability.	Governance, authorization, accountability, and legitimacy.

***Table 6.1**: Mapping the five threads across digital system types*

What matters is not the surface form of each thread, but how the loom keeps them in relationship under strain.

A connected system that automates physical response without contestability fails in the same way as an enterprise system that automates organizational decisions without explanation. In both cases, intelligence accelerates while trust thins, even as security controls remain intact.

Digital weaving exists to prevent this separation. It ensures that sensing constrains intelligence, data returns in time to matter, and trust remains aligned with decision making, whether those decisions move machines, people, or institutions.

That shift requires moving from stacks to weaves.

From stacks to weaves

Stacks pass work upward. Weaves carry responsibility across.

Most digital systems are built as stacks. The pattern is familiar and often sensible. Infrastructure forms the base. Sensing is layered above it. Data pipelines follow. Intelligence is added where value is expected. Security and controls are applied across the whole.

Stacks are easy to explain. They align with organizational charts, vendor catalogs, and delivery milestones. Each layer has a clear boundary and a clear owner. Work can be divided. Progress can be tracked.

For a long time, this structure worked well enough.

Zoya did not argue that stacks were wrong. She noted that they relied on an assumption that no longer held: once responsibility crossed a boundary, it no longer belonged to the previous layer. What followed was someone else's concern.

Under stable conditions, that assumption rarely caused harm. Under change, it became a source of drift.

Fragmented responsibility in stacks

In a stacked system, each layer optimizes its own function. Connectivity delivers packets. Sensing collects signals. Data stores records. Intelligence produces decisions. Security enforces access.

Each part can succeed on its own terms while the system as a whole loses coherence.

When sensing assumptions change, data often continues unchanged. When data meaning shifts, intelligence reasons as before. When automation accelerates, oversight remains procedural and slow. Responsibility moves forward. Accountability does not follow.

Zoya had watched teams trace failures up and down the stack only to discover that no one owned the space between them. Alerts fired, but no one felt permitted to respond. Decisions were made, but no one could explain why. Controls existed, but the intervention authority was unclear.

Nothing was broken. Everything was misaligned.

Stacks hide these gaps because handoffs appear clean on diagrams. In practice, they become places where assumptions decay quietly.

Platform stacking and accumulated distance

Platform stacking intensifies the same structural pattern: responsibility fragments as decisions cross boundaries faster than understanding can follow.

As organizations assemble systems from interchangeable tools and services, integration becomes faster and procurement simpler. Each platform solves a specific problem well. Together, they form structures that are increasingly difficult to reason about as a whole.

Decision paths stretch across platforms that were never designed to explain themselves together. Teams spend time reconstructing how a decision traveled rather than intervening while it is still in motion. By the time the path is understood, the opportunity to act has often passed.

Each platform introduces its own update cycles, logging conventions, and governance models. None are aligned by default. Accountability fragments across vendors, contracts, and internal teams, even as execution remains seamless.

The system continues to operate.
Understanding consistently lags behind action.

Intelligence at the top of the stack

AI-first designs introduce a related but sharper risk—intelligence accelerates faster than the threads that constrain it.

When intelligence becomes the organizing principle, systems reshape themselves around model performance. Data flows serve prediction. Workflows adapt to automation. Human judgment shifts from participation to retrospective review.

The model decides, teams say. *We will review later.*

At scale, later rarely arrives.

Decisions propagate faster than sensing, data freshness, authority, and governance constraints can respond. When assumptions change, systems continue acting with confidence they no longer deserve. Intelligence does not fail. The surrounding structure no longer holds.

Zoya names the issue precisely.

This is not about mistrusting models, she says. *It is about trusting structure too much.*

Stacked systems allow intelligence to outrun constraint.

Structural change through weaving

Digital weaving does not remove components or platforms. It changes how threads relate.

Zoya replaced the vertical diagram with intersecting lines. No element sat above another. Each crossed and constrained the rest.

In a weave, she said, *no thread carries the load alone.*

A woven structure treats handoffs as relationships rather than boundaries. Changes in one thread are expected to affect others. Constraints travel with signals. Authority remains attached to action.

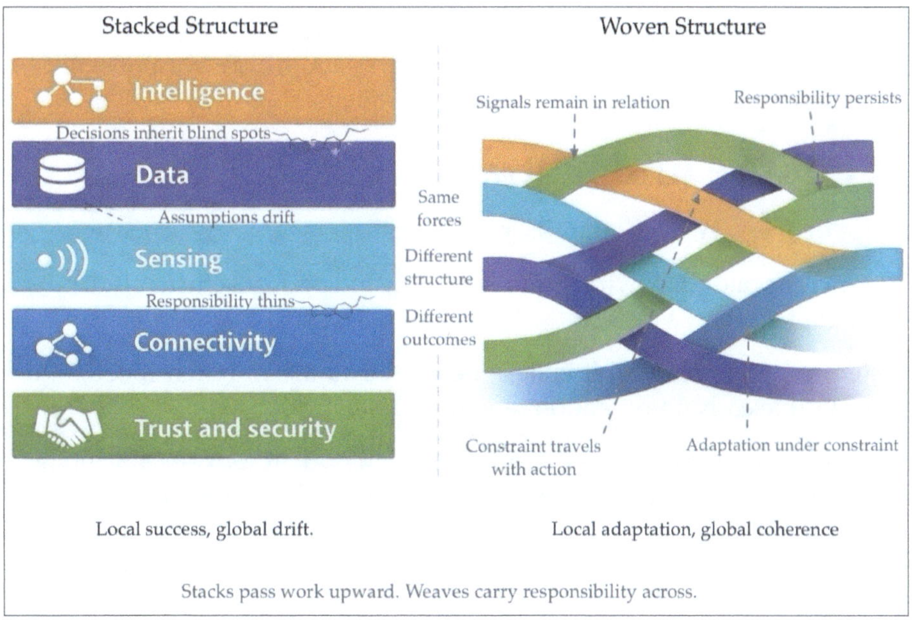

***Figure 6 5:** Stacked architecture vs. weaving*

Instead of asking what to add next, weaving asks different questions.

Where is strain appearing?
Which assumptions no longer hold?
Where do signals stop traveling?
Who can intervene when conditions change?

No single component or team can answer these questions alone. They require attention to interaction.

Stewardship over ownership

Stacks assume ownership. A layer belongs to a team. A service belongs to a provider. Responsibility ends at the boundary.

Zoya described stewardship differently. It was not about who built a component, but who could intervene when assumptions no longer held.

In stacked systems, authority often arrives after outcomes. Review follows execution. Repair follows failure. During uncertainty, no one is explicitly permitted to slow, question, or redirect the system.

The system continues to operate. Trust shifts elsewhere.

Weaving reflects a different design posture. It emphasizes stewardship over ownership. Authority to intervene persists across threads and relationships. Responsibility does not disappear at boundaries. It remains attached to consequences.

Weaves endure under strain

Stacks optimize delivery. Weaves optimize endurance.

A stacked system can scale quickly, integrate smoothly, and perform efficiently. Under pressure, it struggles to adapt without a restart.

A woven system expects pressure. It is designed to be adjusted, re-tensioned, and repaired. Strain becomes visible early. Intervention remains possible.

Most importantly, governance moves inside the system. Authority is no longer external, expressed only through policy or review. It is embedded in how decisions are formed, constrained, and revised.

Zoya summarized the shift simply.

Stacks tell you where things are, she said. *Weaves tell you who is responsible when things change.*

Understanding this structural shift is essential, but structure alone does not keep systems aligned. Alignment must be renewed continuously.

That renewal takes the form of a loop.

The weaving loop

A weave holds because it is adjusted as conditions change.

Digital weaving becomes real only when it moves. Structure alone does not keep systems aligned. Relationships drift unless they are actively renewed. Zoya emphasized this early, especially to teams accustomed to lifecycles, roadmaps, and maturity models.

This is not a phase, she said. It is a rhythm.

The weaving loop describes how digitally woven systems remain coherent over time. It is not only a pattern of iteration. It is the operational form through which system boundaries are clarified, threads are made explicit, interactions are aligned, and authority is able to act while the system is in motion.

The loop applies both when systems are first designed and while they operate. It defines how systems behave under change and how they are sustained after deployment. It is the recurring motion through which the five threads remain aligned as conditions shift.

The loop has four movements—layer, test, adapt, and repeat. Each movement is simple on its own. Together, they form a discipline that allows systems to change without losing accountability. Across these movements, interruption, reversibility, and early detection of drift are maintained so that correction remains possible before consequences harden. These movements ensure that boundary, threads, interaction, authority, interruption, reversibility, and drift remain continuously structured as the system evolves.

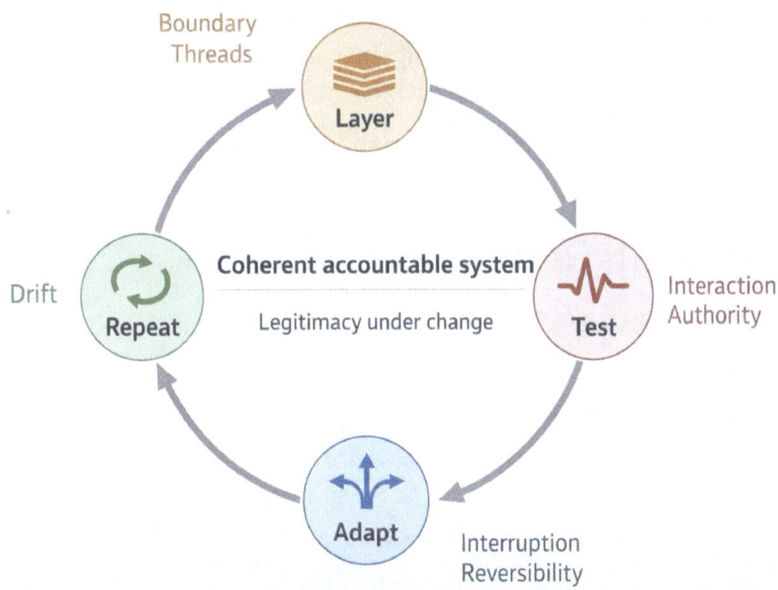

Figure 6.6: *The weaving loop*

Here, layer does not mean adding architectural tiers or components. It refers to how capability and relationship are threaded together so that system behavior remains coherent as pressure builds.

Layer where strain appears

Layering in the weaving loop begins with attention, not expansion.

When designing a new system, Zoya plans where authority, sensing, and pause must exist long before speed or automation becomes the focus. Layering begins by anticipating where strain will emerge. Designers ask where assumptions may age, where authority could become unclear, where signals might weaken, and where decisions could outrun context. These expected tensions shape how threads are interlaced from the outset.

Once systems are operating, layering continues by responding to strain as it becomes visible.

Layering does not mean adding components. It means threading capability and relationship together so that threads continue to constrain and inform one another as conditions change. Each layering decision also reasserts the system boundary and makes the role of each thread visible, so that new capabilities do not introduce hidden dependencies.

Sometimes this involves strengthening connectivity, so repair remains dependable. Sometimes it involves shaping sensing so the system notices what people already respond to. In other cases, it means designing data so memory returns in time to matter, or constraining intelligence so uncertainty remains visible.

In each case, the intervention reshapes how threads relate, not merely what the system can do. It does not matter which thread is addressed first, but that the interaction is acknowledged. A change in sensing alters data. A shift in intelligence affects trust. Layering without regard for these crossings introduces new strain elsewhere.

In woven systems, layering is deliberate and relational. Capability may grow, but only where it strengthens coherence as conditions evolve.

Test by listening to behavior

Testing in the weaving loop is not validation. It is listening.

Most testing practices ask whether a system meets predefined requirements. The weaving loop asks whether the system still fits the world it acts upon.

Listening refers to observable system responses, not subjective opinion. Teams test behavior rather than outputs. *How do people behave around the system? Where do they hesitate? Which signals travel, and which fade without effect?*

These behaviors are not noise. They are system feedback.

This includes examining how threads are structured to interact in practice, since interaction, not components, determines how decisions become consequences. It also examines whether authority can still reach action before consequences begin to harden into outcomes. It reveals where interaction pathways conceal responsibility and where decisions accelerate beyond oversight.

An alert that fires but triggers no response is a test failure. A recommendation that is consistently ignored is also a test failure. In both cases, the system may function technically while failing relationally.

Testing in the weave is continuous. It occurs wherever the system meets reality. It does not wait for releases, audits, or incidents. It looks for divergence between system behavior and human response.

Adapt without erasing memory

Adaptation is where many systems fail.

In stacked architectures, adaptation often means restart, redesign, or replacement. These responses are expensive, disruptive, and socially risky. Over time, they discourage learning because admitting strain becomes costly.

Digitally woven systems adapt in place.

To adapt is to rethread rather than replace. It involves adjusting rules, thresholds, interfaces, or authority paths without discarding what already holds. This may mean clarifying language, exposing uncertainty, adding a pause, or inviting a new voice into the decision-making process.

These moves are small. Their impact is structural.

Adaptation introduces the ability to interrupt action under uncertainty and to reverse decisions before their effects stabilize, ensuring that correction remains part of normal operation.

Redesign is not eliminated, but it becomes a last resort rather than the default response to strain.

Adaptation must be possible close to where the strain appears. When only centralized teams can adapt, systems lag behind lived experience while approval chains lengthen.

This is where governance becomes operational.

Who can change a rule?
Who can question a decision?
Who can slow or stop automation when conditions degrade?

These are design choices, not policy afterthoughts.

Repeat to retain learning

Repeat is not repetition. It is memory.

The purpose of the weaving loop is not convergence on a final design. It is the accumulation of learning through visible adjustment. What holds under strain informs the next intervention. What weakens remains visible rather than buried.

Each cycle leaves residue. Adjustments become part of the system's structure. Knowledge moves from documentation into design.

Systems are deliberately instrumented to detect early signals of drift as part of system design, so that divergence becomes visible while correction is still possible, not after failure has hardened.

Zoya emphasized this often. *Resilience is not built in one pass, she said. It is built by remembering what worked when things pulled apart.*

Repeat protects against forgetting, one of the quietest forms of failure in complex systems.

The loop as discipline

The weaving loop does not end. As long as a system operates, the loop continues.

This is what distinguishes digital weaving from project-based design approaches. There is no handoff point where responsibility ends. There is no final state where alignment can be assumed.

The loop enforces humility. It accepts that assumptions will expire and that coherence requires ongoing attention. It keeps governance within the system by ensuring that boundary, interaction, authority, interruption, reversibility, and drift remain continuously visible as the system evolves. In doing so, the loop ensures that boundary, threads, interaction, authority, interruption, reversibility, and drift remain part of how the system operates, not conditions discovered after it fails.

In practice, the loop keeps the essential conditions of the system continuously in view. A boundary defines where the system holds. Threads make visible what the system is composed of. Interaction shapes how it behaves as signals move through it. Authority determines who can intervene, while interruption determines whether that intervention can occur in time. Reversibility defines whether correction remains meaningful once action is taken, and instrumentation ensures that strain becomes visible before it hardens into failure. Through the loop, these conditions are not checked once. They are sustained as the system operates, allowing it to adjust while consequences are still in motion.

A system shaped in this way is defined not by how it performs under stable conditions, but by how it behaves when those conditions begin to shift.

Zoya paused and looked back at the structure taking shape.

The goal is not perfection, she said. *It is responsiveness.*

Understanding the loop explains how systems remain aligned over time. It also reveals where that alignment begins to weaken.

That requires learning to read fray.

Fray as a signal

Fray marks the point at which the weave calls for attention.

Digital weaving does not remove strain. It designs systems to notice it.

In woven systems, strain is not something discovered after failure. It is anticipated, shaped, and made legible as systems are built and as they operate. Fray names how woven systems express weakening relationships while coherence still holds.

Fray is not failure.

It is an early signal that threads are beginning to pull unevenly, even as the system continues to function.

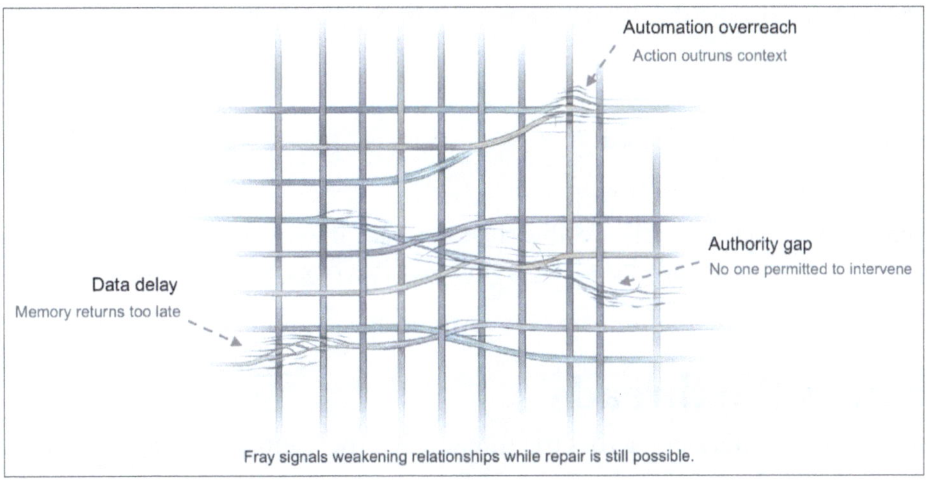

Figure 6.7: *Fray as a governance signal*

In systems designed without weaving, strain accumulates silently until decisions harden and intervention becomes costly. In woven systems, fray appears while decisions are still reversible, authority can still act, and learning can still be retained.

Fray concentrates at boundaries

Fray does not emerge evenly across a system. It concentrates where threads meet.

Signals arrive without clear ownership.
Data lags behind lived conditions.
Automation continues after assumptions expire.
Responsibility thins at handoffs.

These boundaries exist at design time as architectural and governance choices, and in operating systems as lived behavior. They are where sensing meets interpretation, intelligence meets authority, and action meets accountability.

Digitally woven systems treat boundary strain as diagnostic rather than incidental. They attend not only to whether parts function, but to whether relationships between threads still hold as conditions shift.

Automation amplifies silence

Automation does not cause fray. It amplifies it.

As systems scale, automated decisions continue to execute even after the context that justified them has changed. Outputs remain consistent. Metrics stay stable. Yet human behavior shifts around them.

Inputs arrive late.
Overrides increase without a record.
Workarounds emerge without explanation.

In unwoven systems, these signals are absorbed as noise. In woven systems, they are expected and designed for. Fray here indicates that confidence has begun to outrun freshness.

This is not a technical error. It is a mismatch between speed and responsibility.

Fray across the threads

Fray becomes visible differently across the threads that the digital weaving interlaces.

In **connectivity**, fray appears as provisional use. People route around systems they no longer expect to be repaired or responded to.

In **sensing**, fray appears as selective attention. Signals are filtered before they are reported.

In **data**, fray appears as a delayed return. Information is stored, but no longer shapes decisions in time to matter.

In **intelligence**, fray appears as unjustified certainty. Recommendations persist even as inputs decay.

In **trust**, fray appears as quiet disengagement. Systems continue to run, but confidence shifts elsewhere.

Failure rarely originates within a single thread. It emerges between them, even when each thread appears intact.

Governance reveals fray

In digitally woven systems, governance does not arrive after harm. It operates as a constraint in motion.

Fray becomes visible when decisions slow, when pauses are exercised, and when authority is invoked before outcomes harden. These moments are not inefficiencies. They are evidence that legitimacy is being preserved.

In systems without embedded governance, pauses are often interpreted as failure rather than as diagnostic signals. Woven systems treat pauses as signals that assumptions are being tested.

Fray here is not something to suppress. It is something the system is designed to surface.

Reading fray before replacement

Fray creates the opportunity for adjustment, not just repair.

During system design, fray appears as resistance in reasoning rather than failure in operation. It surfaces when teams struggle to agree on authority, pause conditions, confidence thresholds, or override rights. These tensions signal where assumptions are already straining and where constraints must be shaped before automation and scale lock behavior in place.

During system operation, fray appears as workarounds, delayed signals, selective trust, and quiet disengagement. Reading fray here allows intervention without erasing memory or restarting infrastructure. Decision paths can be revised. Authority can be clarified. Constraints can be deliberately re-tensioned.

Systems remain sustainable not because they avoid strain, but because their structure keeps decisions answerable while under pressure.

Where fray is ignored during design, fragility is embedded. Where it is ignored during operation, replacement becomes inevitable. Where fray is read, renewal remains possible.

Digitally woven systems do not attempt to eliminate strain. They are built to surface it early, interpret it correctly, and respond before denial or delay hardens assumptions.

Zoya captured the discipline succinctly.

A system that cannot hear itself pulling apart will always fail too late.

Digital weaving exists to make strain visible while intervention is still possible.

The question that follows is no longer how to recognize fray, but how systems are shaped so that someone can act when it appears.

That is where practice begins, evaluating responsibility structurally by how constraints shape decisions and whether consequences remain correctable.

Weaving in practice

Endurance begins where the weave can still be reached.

By this point, digital weaving is no longer abstract. It is not a recovery tactic, a governance overlay, or a lens applied after failure. It is a way of building and operating digital systems so that the five threads remain aligned as conditions shift.

The group had already traced drift, named fray, and examined how layering, testing, adaptation, and repetition sustain coherence as systems continue to operate. What remained was to see how this discipline behaves in the real world when systems are built, scaled, and held. In each case, the weaving loop remains active. Systems are layered, tested, adapted, and revisited so that coherence is sustained as conditions change.

Zoya did not offer success stories. She framed the cases instead as working demonstrations of the same structural discipline developed throughout the chapter. In each case, digital weaving shaped how systems were repaired, scaled, or built so that authority, sensing, and accountability remained accessible under pressure.

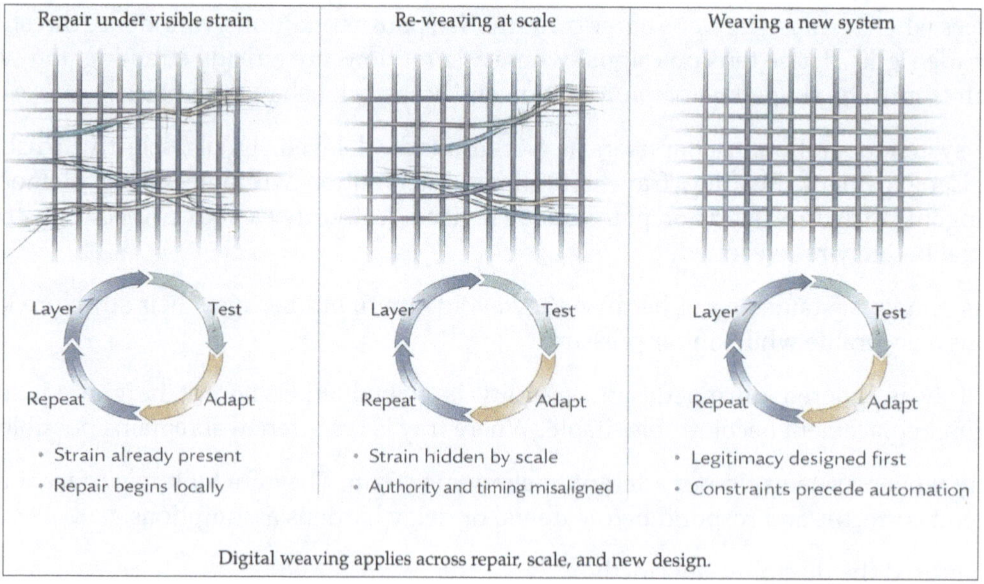

Figure 6.8: *Starting points for weaving in practice*

The cases begin from different starting points: a local system where strain is visible, a large enterprise system where strain hides behind scale, and a new system designed deliberately from the start. Together, they show digital weaving in practice across the full lifecycle of real systems, not as a response to failure, but as preparation for responsibility.

Repair where strain is visible

The textile factory in *Tiruppur* buzzed and breathed like any other. Fans fought the heat. Sewing machines hummed in uneven rhythm. Bins of scrap cloth faded near the windows.

At the center stood Anil, the floor manager. He did not have a transformation budget. What he had was tension: delays, scrap, exhaustion, and unclear handoffs. Orders shipped and targets were mostly met. On paper, performance appeared acceptable. On the floor, strain accumulated quietly. Workers absorbed pressure through extra effort. None of this appeared in reports.

The problem was not failure. It was the widening gap between how the system appeared to function and how it was actually being held together.

Anil did not add technology. He added attention. He did not start with a system. He started with what was fraying.

Begin where strain appears

The infrastructure was dated. Aging machines. Mismatched tables. Erratic **Wireless Fidelity (Wi-Fi)**, but Anil did not see the deepest strain in the equipment. He saw it in motion. Things were not breaking. They were drifting. Invisible losses required people to compensate. Early signs of divergence were present but unacknowledged, treated as routine rather than signals for correction.

He did not deploy dashboards. He placed colored mats on the floor, one for each product line. The mats reshaped the flow. Tasks no longer overlapped invisibly. Work became legible as it moved between stations. No instructions were issued. No onboarding was required. A thread was added to the infrastructure, not for speed, but for shape.

The change did not remain fixed. As flow shifted, Anil adjusted placement, refined boundaries, and observed how work responded. Testing and adaptation became continuous, not episodic.

Flow improved, but one corner of the floor slowed repeatedly. The delay backed up the entire line. There was no early signal. The problem became visible only after damage appeared.

So, Anil introduced laminated cards. Green meant on track. Amber meant delayed. Red meant stopped. A shared signal. Immediate and human. It generated no data, but it restored sensing. Before intelligence could help, the system had to notice itself. Signals were visible early enough to act, allowing intervention before delay hardened into an outcome.

Memory returns to the floor

Later, Anil added a low-cost sensor at the ironing station. Output counts are streamed into a shared spreadsheet. Technically, the system had memory. Practically, nothing changed. No one looked at the sheet. That was not the room's rhythm.

So, each Friday, a junior worker painted the week's numbers on a wall chart near the water cooler. Units produced. Defects found. Data became visible where work paused, and conversations occurred.

Questions followed.

Why did the output drop on certain days?
Why did defects rise with temperature?
Why did one station affect the entire line?

Data began to return to decisions in time to matter. Rules were written by hand on a clipboard. These rules did not remain static. They were revisited, adjusted, and replaced as conditions changed.

If the temperature exceeded thirty-eight degrees, targets dropped.
If defects spiked, checks increased.
If delays persisted, tasks rotated.

Anyone could suggest a change if they could justify it.

Intelligence became negotiable. It did not just predict. It listened.

Trust through participation

Few workers logged into the system. All participated in monthly floor meetings. Anyone could flag a mismatch, correct a number, challenge a rule, or question a policy. One worker caught a silent specification change from an overseas buyer and prevented a costly return.

Trust did not arrive through training or compliance. It emerged through authorship. Strain could be signaled without penalty. Rules could be questioned. Authority was exercised locally.

In practice, the weaving loop remained active. Work was reshaped, signals tested, adjustments made, and learning retained close to where strain appeared.

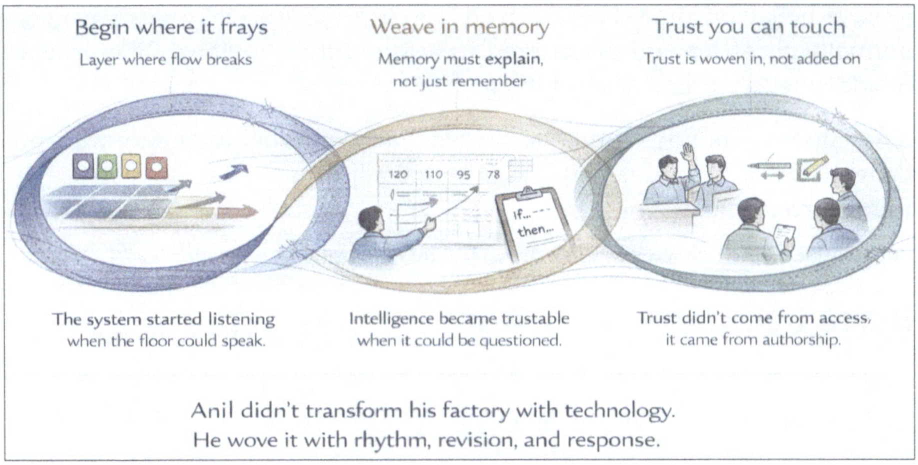

***Figure 6.9**: Anil's woven fix*

Anil never named what he was doing, but the pattern held. Infrastructure was shaped with care. Sensing remained shared. Intelligence stayed explainable and correctable.

The factory did not become optimized overnight. What changed was more important. Strain surfaced earlier. Adjustments occurred closer to where problems appeared. Performance stabilized without exhausting people.

When Zoya later described this pattern, she did not call it optimization. She called it staying close enough to strain to matter.

Anil did not transform the factory with technology. He wove it with attention and repair.

Repair when strain hides at scale

Factories show strain early. Enterprise systems hide it.

Simon worked inside a global IT services firm with tens of thousands of employees. Sales teams spanned regions. Delivery managers balanced utilization and deadlines. Sustainability teams tracked emissions, travel, and energy use. Enterprise platforms govern daily work.

Connectivity links **human resources (HR)**, **customer relationship management (CRM)**, delivery, finance, and **environmental, social, and governance (ESG)** systems. Sensing came from forecasts, surveys, and usage logs. Data fed dashboards and reports. Intelligence optimized staffing and delivery allocation. Trust was assumed because audits passed and systems were secure. These systems did not fail individually. Strain emerged in how they interacted, where signals lost meaning as they moved across boundaries.

The system appeared authoritative. Nothing was broken. Nothing failed visibly.

Strain surfaced as behavior. Time sheets arrived late or imprecise. Delivery managers adjusted staffing informally. Sales leaders discounted forecasts during reviews. Platforms produced answers. People quietly worked around them.

The system functioned. Confidence quietly eroded. Early signs of divergence were present but unacknowledged. Delay, inconsistency, and informal adjustment were treated as noise rather than signals for correction.

Scale does not remove strain, Zoya observed. *It only delays when you are allowed to see it.*

Confidence becomes conditional

Simon did not begin by adding analytics. He began by changing what confidence meant.

Forecasts, utilization metrics, and sustainability indicators were revised to carry visible age and assumption markers. Freshness was no longer implicit. Numbers no longer arrived as equally reliable.

Leaders encountered uncertainty where certainty had once been implied. Some inputs were current. Others were weeks or months old. Decisions slowed because risk had to be named.

Automation adjusted accordingly. As inputs aged, recommendations softened. Acting quickly now requires explicit acceptance of risk. Certainty became conditional.

These changes did not remain fixed. Signals were observed, thresholds adjusted, and decision pathways refined as behavior shifted. Testing and adaptation became continuous, not episodic.

Authority enters decision flow

As confidence slowed, a second constraint followed.

Decision paths were revised to make authority explicit. It became clear who could pause a workflow, revise an allocation, or challenge an automated recommendation while decisions were still in motion.

Conflicts that were once deferred to review were now addressed upstream. Automation paused without escalation. Decisions were revised while context remained intact. Responsibility stayed attached to action.

Governance moved inside daily operation.

Learning survives scale

Overrides, pauses, and revisions were recorded with context, not as audit artifacts, but as system memory. Reasons remained visible.

When a new strain appeared, earlier responses were available. Decisions were made using inherited learning rather than starting fresh each quarter.

Table 6.2 contrasts enterprise systems before and after digital weaving. Both function and scale. What changes is not capability, but coherence:

Dimension	Stacked system	Woven system
Design posture	Optimized for delivery and scale.	Designed for endurance under change.
How strain appears	Isolated incidents after harm.	Early signals of structural misalignment.
Decision behavior	Uniform speed, detached from signal freshness.	Responsive speed, accelerates with confidence, pauses as uncertainty rises.
Sensing and memory	Activity captured, memory returns late.	Divergence is noticed early, and memory returns to decisions in time.
Intelligence	Fast, confident, and opaque.	Contestable, contextual, constrained by evidence.
Governance and authority	External, implicit, applied after outcomes.	Embedded, explicit, and actionable during decisions.
Response to strain	Silent workarounds or replacement.	Early intervention and adjustment.
Learning over time	Lost between cycles or rewrites.	Accumulates inside the system.
Outcome	Performance without confidence.	Durable performance with accountability.

***Table 6.2**: Enterprise systems before and after digital weaving*

In practice, the weaving loop remained active. Systems were layered, tested, adapted, and revisited so that alignment could be sustained as scale increased.

Zoya summarized it simply. *Systems do not endure because they are finished. They endure because they remain answerable as conditions change.*

Designing a new flood monitoring system

The city had not flooded yet.

Near misses accumulated without consequence. Urgency rose, then faded. No system endured long enough to be trusted.

When the decision was made to build a new digital flood response platform, the mandate focused on preparedness rather than repair. No legacy architecture constrained the design. No automation had yet shaped behavior. This absence was the opportunity.

Zoya joined before procurement, before diagrams, before sensors. The loom was empty.

Legitimacy before automation

The project began with authority.

Emergency managers, meteorologists, port officials, community representatives, and civil defense leaders defined decision rights first.

Who could issue an alert?
Who could pause it?
Who could override automation?
Who would explain decisions afterward?

Governance entered as behavior, not policy. Legitimacy became the first stitch.

Uncertainty becomes visible

Sensing was designed for participation. River gauges and weather feeds were necessary, but insufficient. Observations from responders and residents were treated as first-class inputs, each carrying visible confidence.

Local observations could slow decisions and prompt review, but not trigger alerts alone.

Data pipelines were designed for return, not accumulation. Freshness decayed visibly. Memory returned to decisions in time to matter. These elements were shaped to work together, so that sensing, data, and decision remained aligned as conditions changed.

Intelligence under constraint

Only then was intelligence introduced. Models produced ranges. Assumptions were explicit. Confidence varied with input quality. Every recommendation could be paused.

Before the first storm, the system was stressed deliberately. Signals were degraded. Authority paths were exercised while consequences were hypothetical.

The system did not remain fixed after these exercises. Signals were adjusted, thresholds refined, and authority paths clarified. The loop had begun before the first storm.

Trust through restraint

When the storm arrived, the system remained responsive but restrained. Alerts were cautious. Uncertainty was named. Decisions were reviewed and explained.

Early signs of divergence were watched closely. Hesitation, conflicting signals, and delayed responses were treated as signals for adjustment rather than ignored as noise.

Trust deepened not because outcomes were perfect, but because behavior remained legible.

The city did not inherit a finished system. It inherited a loom capable of renewal.

Here, weaving preceded strain. Digital weaving was not a response to failure. It was preparation for responsibility.

What practice reveals

Across all three cases, tools and contexts differ, but the structure of what holds remains consistent.

Strain surfaced early when work was physical and shared. It hid behind abstraction at scale. It had not yet appeared in the flood system, but the conditions that would produce it were already present. In every case, digital weaving did not remove pressure. It changed how pressure was encountered.

Repair proved most effective when it occurred close to where the strain emerged. When sensing, authority, and adaptation were distant, response slowed, and responsibility blurred. When they remained close, intervention was possible without escalation or replacement.

Readability came first. Systems that could be understood could be improved. Systems that could not be were quietly bypassed.

Authority had to travel with decisions. Trust emerged when people knew who could act, when action could pause, and how decisions would be explained.

Across all three cases, the same pattern held through use. Strain surfaced. Signals were tested. Constraints adjusted. Learning remained. In each case, the weaving loop remained active. Systems were layered, tested, adapted, and revisited so alignment could be sustained as conditions evolved.

Zoya summarized it simply. *Systems do not endure because they are finished. They endure because they remain answerable as conditions change.*

These cases do not offer templates to copy. They offer a way of seeing. Digital weaving is practiced wherever systems must continue operating as conditions shift.

The archetypes that follow are not moral categories or design goals; they are diagnostic outcomes used to evaluate whether system structure sustains responsibility under strain.

Archetypes that emerge when systems hold

Patterns emerge when a weave remains answerable under strain.

When digital systems endure under pressure, they do not converge on a single design. They settle into recognizable structural postures. These postures are not templates or best practices.

They are archetypes that emerge when systems remain answerable under sustained strain.

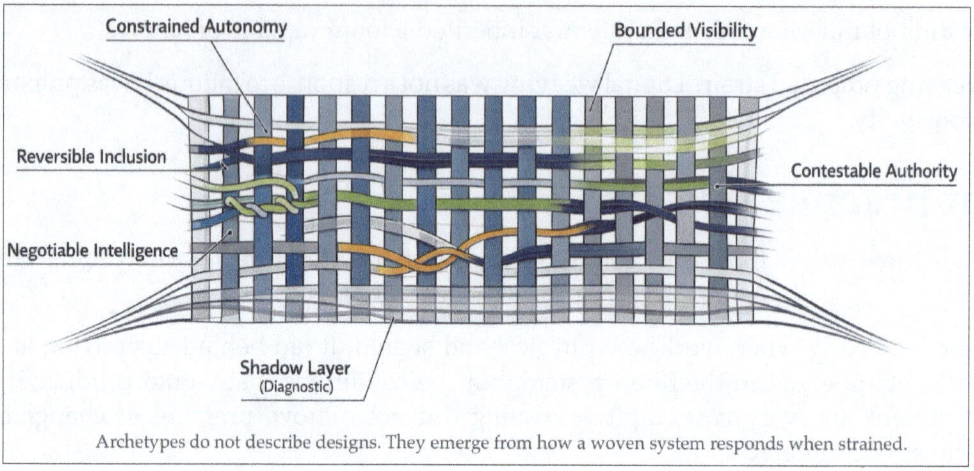

***Figure 6.10**: Archetypes as emergent postures under strain*

Archetypes do not describe intent. They describe the outcome. They appear only when threads remain in relationship and governance constrains how those threads pull under change.

Constrained autonomy

In systems that hold, autonomy adjusts with conditions.

Automation remains present, but its freedom narrows as confidence weakens. When signals degrade, action slows rather than accelerates. Decisions do not preserve momentum simply because execution is possible.

Constrained autonomy ensures that intelligence does not outrun authority or permission. Action remains reversible while outcomes are still forming. Autonomy persists, but it is bounded by authority that can intervene in time.

This archetype appears in systems where safety, legitimacy, or irreversible consequences constrain how autonomy can be exercised.

Bounded visibility

In systems that hold, visibility is limited by purpose.

Signals are exposed only where they are needed to act. Information contracts again when their coordinating purpose expires. Visibility does not accumulate by default.

Bounded visibility constrains sensing, so observation remains purpose-bound and contestable. It protects legitimacy by ensuring that observation remains proportional, time-bound, and explainable. What can be seen is always linked to why it is seen.

This archetype appears wherever rapid awareness must coexist with public trust.

Reversible inclusion

In systems that hold, participation remains conditional.

Inclusion does not harden into permanence. Entry can be granted, corrected, or withdrawn without penalty. Errors do not trap people inside systems they cannot contest.

Reversible inclusion allows scale while preserving the ability to refuse, exit, or seek redress. Trust persists because refusal, exit, and redress remain structurally possible. Participation continues not because it is mandatory, but because it remains fair. This reversibility is designed into the system, not granted as an exception.

This archetype appears wherever identity, access, or eligibility shape civic or economic life.

Negotiable intelligence

In systems that hold, intelligence remains contestable.

Automated decisions assist judgment but do not finalize it. Outputs can be questioned while action is still in motion. Intelligence remains useful because it can be challenged before consequences harden.

Negotiable intelligence depends on governance that keeps authority reachable. Models do not finalize outcomes beyond appeal. Learning does not erase accountability.

This archetype appears wherever automation operates at scale under uncertainty.

Contestable authority

In systems that hold, authority can be challenged.

It is clear who may intervene, who may pause a workflow, and how decisions can be questioned before outcomes become irreversible. Authority is visible not to centralize control, but to preserve accountability.

Contestable authority ensures that governance remains within operation. Decisions do not disappear into the process. They remain exposed to scrutiny while correction is still possible.

This archetype appears wherever legitimacy depends on explanation and consent.

The shadow layer

In systems under strain, misalignment surfaces.

Untracked workarounds, informal practices, and undocumented overrides emerge when official structures fail to carry real conditions. The shadow layer records where the system no longer fits its environment.

This archetype is diagnostic, not stabilizing. It signals fray rather than endurance. Its presence does not mean failure, but it always means attention is overdue.

The shadow layer does not describe how systems hold. It reveals where they do not.

Zoya viewed the shadow layer as diagnostic. *People tell you where the system does not fit, she said. You just have to listen.*

Reading archetypes correctly

Zoya told the group, *these archetypes are not goals, they are signals.*

Archetypes do not replace design, nor are they patterns to replicate. They emerge only when systems are under strain, revealing whether design continues to hold under pressure. Systems that endure do not choose archetypes. Archetypes appear when systems remain answerable as conditions change.

Recognizing these signals shifts attention from performance to posture. It reveals whether action, visibility, participation, intelligence, and authority remain correctable while change is still unfolding.

Used correctly, archetypes enable early intervention. They help teams adjust constraints, restore reversibility, and re-anchor authority before optimization hardens fragility. The goal is not to name an archetype, but to sense when a system is drifting toward a form that can no longer be corrected in time.

Weaving forward

Endurance comes from renewing the weave, not freezing it.

Digital weaving does not conclude with a finished architecture or a stable end state. It concludes with a posture. Systems that hold are not those that eliminate tension, but those that remain attentive to it as conditions change.

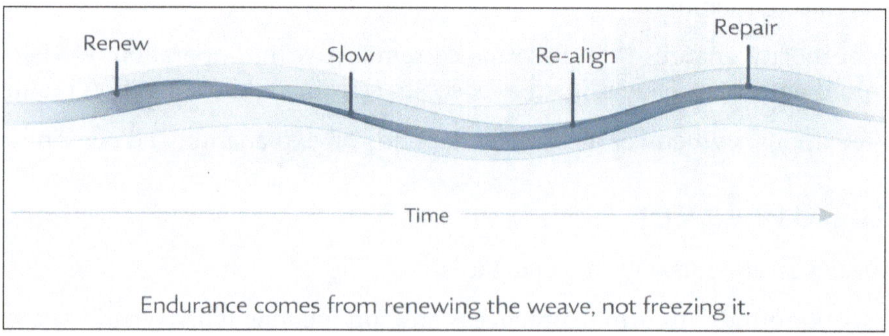

Figure 6.11: *Renewal under tension*

Zoya resisted the language of completion. *The moment you believe the system is done,* she said, *you stop noticing how it is pulling.*

This section synthesizes what digital weaving enables, where it applies, and where its limits become visible.

Renewal over replacement

Many digital initiatives respond to strain with replacement. Systems are rewritten. Platforms are swapped. Models are retrained. These actions can be necessary, but they are often chosen because repair feels slower, harder, or less legible.

Replacement often erases accumulated operational memory.

When systems are replaced, lessons embedded in behavior, workarounds, and prior responses disappear. Teams begin again with new assumptions, often repeating earlier mistakes at greater scale and speed.

Digital weaving favors renewal.

Renewal preserves what still holds while adjusting what strains. It treats repair as accumulated learning rather than corrective cleanup. Small, visible interventions are preferred over sweeping redesigns because they keep responsibility attached to outcomes.

Zoya observed that systems renewed in this way did not avoid failure. They recovered without losing clarity.

Governance in motion

One of the most persistent misunderstandings Zoya encountered was the belief that governance belongs outside the system. Policies, committees, and reviews matter, but they cannot govern behavior as decisions unfold.

In woven systems, governance moves with decisions.

Constraints are embedded where action occurs. Confidence thresholds are visible. Authority to pause or intervene is designed into workflows. Uncertainty slows action rather than triggering escalation.

This does not weaken control. It makes control timely.

Governance in motion allows systems to remain legitimate as automation accelerates. Responsibility stays attached to action rather than arriving later through investigation.

Time as an enduring pressure

Time never stops shaping systems. Context shifts. Assumptions expire. People change. Technology evolves.

Digital weaving does not attempt to predict every future condition. It accepts misalignment as inevitable and designs for response rather than foresight.

Systems that hold make time visible. They surface delay, decay, and drift. They slow when signals weaken and accelerate only when confidence is earned.

Aisha framed this simply, *A system that cannot wait,* she said, *will eventually outrun its own understanding.*

Time is not an external factor to manage. It is a condition that must be designed with.

Boundaries of digital weaving

Digital weaving is not universal. Its strength lies in precision. Knowing where the method applies requires equal clarity about where it should not be used and what must be true before it can be applied.

Without these boundaries, weaving risks become a metaphor for everything and being accountable for nothing. These boundaries matter most at design time, when systems still have the freedom to choose how authority, incentives, and governance will be embedded.

Contexts that do not require weaving

Digital weaving is not necessary for systems whose failure carries little consequence beyond inconvenience. Disposable prototypes, isolated utilities, exploratory tools, or internal experiments without downstream impact do not justify sustained coherence, shared authority, or governance in motion.

In these contexts, speed and simplicity matter more than endurance. Designing for renewal, contestability, and accountability would add friction without corresponding benefit. Choosing not to weave is a valid design decision.

Structural conditions that prevent weaving

Digital weaving cannot function when structural conditions prevent a timely response, regardless of whether the system is new or already in operation.

It cannot function when authority is not designed close to action. If decisions must escalate through rigid hierarchies, contractual chains, or external approvals, signals arrive too late to matter. This constraint is often introduced at design time, long before any failure occurs.

It cannot function when incentives punish pause. Systems designed to reward speed, throughput, or utilization at all costs suppress early signals of strain. When slowing down carries risk, people route around the system rather than surface misalignment. This behavior is not a cultural failure. It is a structural outcome.

It cannot function when governance is separated from operation. In some regulated or institutional environments, authority is deliberately placed outside real-time workflows. Reviews are retrospective. Accountability arrives after outcomes harden. In these conditions, weaving may surface strain, but it cannot intervene while decisions are still reversible.

In all three cases, weaving does not fail quietly. It reveals strain clearly. What is missing is not insight, but permission to act.

Preconditions for effective weaving

Some systems are consequential enough to require coherence, yet structurally unprepared to sustain it.

In these contexts, digital weaving cannot be introduced as a technical method alone. Authority may need to be redistributed. Incentives may require alignment. Governance models may need revision. These are design choices, not operational fixes.

This is not a limitation of the method. It is a diagnostic result. When weaving exposes constraints it cannot overcome, it clarifies what must change before responsibility can be sustained.

Digital weaving is not oriented toward control, optimization, or perfection. It is oriented toward sustaining responsibility as conditions change. Where authority is actionable, pause is permitted, and responsibility is shared, weaving strengthens systems from their first decisions onward. Where these conditions do not exist, weaving makes their absence unmistakable.

A forward stance

Digital weaving does not advance toward a finished state. It establishes a way of working with systems that continue to change.

Systems built this way do not promise certainty. They surface strain early, make slow decisions when confidence weakens, and preserve memory through change. The value of the method lies not in prediction, but in responsiveness when assumptions expire.

What follows from this chapter is not a framework to adopt, but a discipline of attention. The next challenge is applying that discipline in real environments, where constraints, consequences, and trade-offs cannot be abstracted away.

What remains is practice.

Conclusion

Coherence is shaped by relationship as much as by capability.

Zoya stood near the window as the discussion slowed. Rain traced thin lines down the glass, steady enough to ignore, persistent enough to notice. Around the room, systems were being replayed in silence. Platforms that had scaled. Automations that had been performed. Decisions that had once felt correct. From the surface, many of them had worked.

She knew better than to stop there.

Years of watching systems under pressure had taught her that durability is not proven by uptime or output. It is proven by whether a system can slow itself when questioned. She listened not for confidence, but for strain. For signals that no longer returned. For decisions that could not be paused. For authority that arrived only after outcomes had hardened.

Digital systems rarely fail loudly. They drift. Assumptions age. Decisions move faster than the evidence that supports them. Responsibility thins as action outruns authority. Systems continue operating while legitimacy quietly separates from behavior.

Digital weaving exists for this condition. Not to prevent failure, but to ensure that as systems are designed, built, and stressed, their actions remain explainable, contestable, and adjustable without loss of legitimacy.

Across this chapter, digital weaving emerged as a discipline grounded in structure rather than metaphor. Relationships replaced handoffs. Constraints traveled with decisions. Signals returned in time to matter. Authority remained visible. Learning accumulates instead of evaporating. Together, these choices allowed systems to absorb pressure without losing coherence.

Zoya also recognized the limits. When authority could not move, when pause was punished, or when governance was barred from real-time action, weaving revealed strain but could not resolve it on its own. In those conditions, the method clarified what was missing before it promised improvement.

Digital weaving does not promise certainty. It preserves answerability by defining who can act, when action is permitted, and whether responsibility can be examined and revised before consequences harden.

As the workshop drew to a close, Zoya gathered her notes without ceremony. The room did not empty with conclusions or resolutions. It emptied with quieter things: shared language, sharper questions, and systems newly seen for what they were.

As she reminded the group, *we do not inherit a fully woven world. We inherit the loom.*

The workshop had done its work. Not by fixing systems, but by changing how they would now be designed, questioned, and held as conditions change.

The next chapter moves from structure to consequence. From how systems hold under strain to how choices shape outcomes in the world. Digital weaving continues there.

Weaver's toolkit

This chapter introduces digital weaving as a discipline that must be practiced, not merely understood. The Weaver's Toolkit provides supporting materials to translate the chapter's concepts into shared language, applied reasoning, and continued learning.

The toolkit serves three purposes. First, it establishes a common vocabulary so concepts remain precise across technical, organizational, and policy contexts. Second, it enables structured observation and reflection through guided exercises. Third, it supports deeper exploration beyond the chapter.

Weaver's lexicon

This lexicon defines technical and metaphorical terms as they are used in this chapter, ensuring clarity and consistency across disciplines:

- **Accountability**: The ability to trace decisions, actions, and outcomes to an identifiable authority within the system. Accountability persists only when responsibility and authority travel with decisions as conditions change.
- **Adaptation**: The act of adjusting system behavior, rules, thresholds, or authority paths without erasing memory or restarting the system. In digital weaving, adaptation occurs close to strain and preserves learning.
- **Alignment**: The temporary condition in which sensing, data, intelligence, governance, and trust remain mutually responsive to the environment a system acts upon. Alignment must be actively renewed.
- **Automation**: The execution of decisions or actions by systems without human intervention at the moment of action. Automation increases speed and consistency but can suppress early signals of misalignment if not constrained.
- **Authority**: The explicit permission to act, pause, intervene, or revise decisions while they are still in motion. Authority is effective only when it is visible, actionable, and close to where strain appears.
- **Boundary**: A point where system threads meet reality, such as between sensing and interpretation or automation and judgment. Boundaries are where fray first appears and responsibility most often blurs.
- **Capability**: What a system can technically do. Capability may increase even as coherence, legitimacy, or trust erode.
- **Coherence**: The condition in which decisions, signals, authority, and responsibility remain intelligible and connected over time. Coherence is the primary design objective of digital weaving.
- **Confidence**: The degree of certainty attached to data, forecasts, or recommendations. In woven systems, confidence is conditional and decays visibly as inputs age or uncertainty rises.
- **Constraint**: A deliberate limit placed on system behavior to preserve legitimacy, safety, or accountability. Constraints shape how and when systems may act, slow, or pause.

- **Connectivity**: The thread that enables systems to remain present and reachable over time, including networks, platforms, identity mechanisms, infrastructure, and operational continuity.
- **Contestability**: The ability for decisions, recommendations, or automated actions to be questioned, challenged, or revised. Contestability preserves trust and prevents intelligence from outrunning authority.
- **Data**: What a system remembers. Data includes records, metrics, logs, lineage, and retention practices. Data matters only when it returns in time to influence decisions.
- **Decision flow**: The path through which decisions move from sensing and interpretation to action and accountability. In woven systems, authority and governance remain embedded within this flow.
- **Drift**: The gradual separation between system behavior and the conditions it operates within, occurring while performance metrics remain acceptable. Drift precedes visible failure.
- **Endurance**: The capacity of a system to remain accountable, repairable, and legitimate as conditions change. Endurance is prioritized over optimization in digital weaving.
- **Fray**: The earliest signal that relationships between system threads are weakening. Fray appears as hesitation, silence, workarounds, or disengagement rather than outages or incidents.
- **Governance**: The constraints that define who may act, pause, override, or explain decisions. In digital weaving, governance operates inside the system rather than after the fact.
- **Governance in motion**: A design posture in which authority, constraint, and accountability shape real-time system behavior rather than operating only through retrospective review.
- **Hold**: The ability of a system to remain coherent, accountable, and legitimate under changing conditions.
- **Human judgment**: The interpretive and ethical capacity of people to assess context, uncertainty, and consequences. In woven systems, judgment is redistributed rather than replaced.
- **Intelligence**: The thread that interprets data and directs action, including rules, workflows, heuristics, and machine learning models. Intelligence must remain constrained by sensing, data, and trust.
- **Legibility**: The degree to which a system's behavior, decision paths, and constraints can be understood by those affected by it.
- **Legitimacy**: The belief that a system's decisions are appropriate, explainable, and accountable.

- **Memory**: The ability of a system to retain and reuse learning from past decisions, adaptations, and repairs. Memory must return to decision points in time to matter.
- **Metric**: A quantified measure of system activity or performance. Metrics describe outcomes but often obscure misalignment between system behavior and lived reality.
- **Optimization**: The improvement of performance against predefined targets such as speed, accuracy, utilization, or scale. Optimization without coherence accelerates drift.
- **Pause**: A deliberate slowing or suspension of action in response to uncertainty or degraded signals. In digital weaving, pause is a design capability, not a failure.
- **Platform stacking**: The assembly of systems through interchangeable platforms and services. While efficient for delivery, platform stacking often fragments accountability.
- **Repair**: The act of restoring coherence by adjusting relationships between system threads rather than replacing components.
- **Responsiveness**: The capacity of a system to notice strain early and adjust behavior before damage accumulates.
- **Security**: The protection of system integrity, confidentiality, and availability. Security alone does not ensure legitimacy.
- **Sensing**: The thread that determines what a system notices, including sensors, alerts, logs, user input, and whose signals are trusted.
- **Silence**: The absence of response when problems exist. In automated systems, silence often indicates suppressed strain rather than stability.
- **Stacked system**: A design posture in which system layers are optimized independently. Stacks obscure responsibility at boundaries and amplify drift under change.
- **Structural limit**: A condition under which digital weaving cannot function effectively, such as when authority cannot be exercised in real time, or incentives punish pause.
- **Trust**: The belief that a system will respond appropriately when something feels wrong. Trust emerges from behavior, not compliance.

Weavers workshop

This section offers exercises designed to help readers identify drift, recognize fray, and reason about coherence, authority, and repair in real systems. The following exercises are not simulations or templates. They are prompts for disciplined observation and structured analysis grounded in the chapter's core concepts:

1. **Detecting drift**: This exercise trains the reader to recognize early signs of system drift before failure becomes visible. The focus is on observation rather than diagnosis or solution design.

Prompts:

- *Identify a digital system you interact with regularly.*
- *List performance metrics that suggest the system is functioning well.*
- *Describe at least three behaviors, workarounds, or hesitations that suggest misalignment beneath those metrics.*
- *Note which assumptions appear to be aging without being revisited.*

Deliverable: One page identifying visible success indicators and early structural misalignment. A strong answer distinguishes reported performance from underlying coherence and shows where responsibility becomes unclear.

Learning objective: Develop the ability to distinguish surface performance from underlying coherence and recognize drift as a precursor to failure.

2. **Mapping the five threads**: This exercise builds structural awareness by mapping how the five threads operate within a real system and where their relationships weaken.

   Prompts:

   - *Select a system that makes decisions affecting people or operations.*
   - *Identify how connectivity, sensing, data, intelligence, and trust appear in that system.*
   - *Describe one point where two threads fail to inform or constrain one another.*
   - *Identify where responsibility becomes unclear as decisions move through the system.*

   Deliverable: A diagram or table mapping the five threads, including one annotated point of strain between threads.

   Learning objective: Understand how failure emerges between system threads rather than within isolated components.

3. **Reading fray at boundaries**: This exercise focuses on fray as a signal rather than as damage, emphasizing boundary conditions where digital decisions meet lived reality.

   Prompts:

   - *Identify a boundary where automated or procedural decisions affect physical, social, or organizational outcomes.*
   - *Describe behaviors that indicate hesitation, silence, or informal workarounds at that boundary.*
   - *Explain why these signals might be dismissed as noise under current governance or metrics.*
   - *Identify what the fray is requesting attention to.*

   Deliverable: A short boundary analysis describing the observed fray, its location, and the risk of ignoring it.

Learning objective: Learn to interpret fray as relational information that signals misalignment before failure occurs.

4. **Designing for early intervention**: This exercise shifts from diagnosis to intervention, asking the reader to design a minimal constraint that enables an earlier response without replacing the system.

   Prompts:

   - *Choose one instance of drift or fray identified in earlier exercises.*
   - *Identify where the intervention currently arrives too late.*
   - *Propose one constraint that could slow decisions, reduce confidence, or surface uncertainty earlier.*
   - *Specify who would have authority to act and how that authority would be exercised in real time.*

   Deliverable: One page proposing a constraint, authority path, and expected behavioral change. A strong answer shows how the constraint alters decision flow, authority reachability, and intervention timing.

   Learning objective: Practice embedding governance and authority inside system behavior rather than applying them after the fact.

5. **Evaluating system endurance**: This synthesis exercise evaluates whether a system is designed to endure change or merely to optimize performance under known conditions.

   Prompts:

   - *Assess how the system responds when assumptions expire or signals weaken.*
   - *Identify whether learning accumulates or is lost between cycles.*
   - *Determine whether the authority can pause or revise decisions before harm occurs.*
   - *Describe which structural archetypes are present or absent.*
   - *Identify one structural limit where digital weaving would not function effectively.*

   Deliverable: A structured assessment summarizing the system's endurance posture, strengths, and limits.

   Learning objective: Develop the ability to evaluate systems holistically, recognizing both the potential and the boundaries of digital weaving as a design discipline.

Weaver's library

The following list is a curated set of references that extend the chapter's ideas into systems engineering, governance, resilience, and digital ethics, allowing readers to situate digital weaving within broader bodies of work:

1. *Meadows, D. H. (2008). Thinking in systems: A primer. Chelsea Green Publishing.*
2. *Senge, P. M. (2006). The fifth discipline: The art and practice of the learning organization (Rev. ed.). Doubleday.*
3. *Muller, J. Z. (2018). The tyranny of metrics. Princeton University Press.*
4. *Ford, N., Parsons, R., & Kua, P. (2017). Building evolutionary architectures: Support constant change. O'Reilly Media.*
5. *McChrystal, S., Collins, T., Silverman, D., & Fussell, C. (2015). Team of teams: New rules of engagement for a complex world. Portfolio.*

Metaphorical and conceptual terms

Metaphorical terms are grounded explicitly in system behavior, so they clarify structure rather than replace it:

- **Loom**: The enduring structural framework of relationships, authority paths, and constraints that enables system threads to be interlaced and adjusted.
- **Pattern**: A recurring structural behavior that emerges over time when systems are allowed to operate under pressure and be repaired.
- **Stack**: A metaphor for systems built as layered components with clear boundaries and handoffs.
- **Strain**: The pressure placed on a system as conditions change, signals weaken, or uncertainty rises.
- **Thread**: A persistent system condition, such as connectivity, sensing, data, intelligence, or trust. Threads are not components themselves, but enduring roles that shape system behavior over time. In smaller systems, a thread may be realized through a single component. In larger systems, it emerges through many components and interactions acting together.
- **Weave**: A structural posture in which system threads are interlaced and mutually constraining.
- **Weaving**: The ongoing practice of shaping, testing, adjusting, and renewing relationships between system threads.
- **Weaving loop**: The repeated cycle of observing strain, testing assumptions, adjusting constraints, and retaining learning.
- **Woven system**: A system whose threads remain deliberately interrelated so decisions, authority, and responsibility travel together.

CHAPTER 7

Real-world Applications

Where systems meet society

A system proves its value when it serves the world beyond it.

CHAPTER 7
The Real-world Applications

Introduction

Digital systems now sit inside moments that matter. Not at the margins of life, but inside decisions about care, access, movement, livelihood, and safety. They are rarely encountered as *technology*. They are experienced as permissions granted or denied, actions taken or delayed, outcomes that arrive before there is time to argue with them.

Most of the time, these systems work. They function, scale, and comply quietly enough that their limits remain invisible. It is pressure that exposes them. As consequences begin to harden, the question shifts. It is no longer whether a system performs as designed, but whether authority can still reach action in time for a different choice to matter.

The cases in this chapter span healthcare, identity, public health, civic participation, agriculture, energy infrastructure, and aviation. They are not presented as exemplars or failures in isolation. Read together, they reveal something more consequential—how legitimacy is preserved or lost while systems continue to operate, often long before breakdown becomes visible.

None of these systems was designed through the digital weaving method. They emerged through policy, necessity, and constraint. The contribution of this chapter is not a taxonomy of systems, but a way to recognize a narrowing window: when legitimacy is still within reach, and when the moment for correction has already passed.

What follows is a shift in attention. Away from outcomes alone, and toward posture. Away from collapse, and toward the moments when systems still retain the capacity to choose differently.

Structure

This chapter covers the following topics:

- Seeing systems under strain
- Systems that hold under strain
- When systems almost hold
- The boundary that matters

Objectives

By the end of this chapter, the reader will be able to recognize how digital systems behave when they are placed under real-world strain, especially as time compresses, scale expands, and consequences approach irreversibility. They will be able to distinguish between systems that merely continue to function and systems that remain legitimate, understanding why operational success alone is insufficient when digital decisions begin to shape physical safety, civic trust, or economic survival.

The reader will also be able to use the digital weaving lens to identify how connectivity, sensing, data, intelligence, and trust operate together as structural conditions rather than independent layers. Through the cases examined, the reader will learn to diagnose where authority remains reachable, where reversibility stays operational, and where restraint arrives early enough to preserve choice. Taken together, these objectives prepare the reader to recognize when systems can still choose differently, and to sense when that possibility is already beginning to close.

Seeing systems under strain

The weave reveals itself not when threads are added, but when they are pulled.

A request is made under pressure.
Blood is needed before time runs out.

An identity check determines access to a service.
A payment fails, or proceeds without explanation.

An alert reshapes how a city moves.
Exposure is tracked faster than consent can follow.

A civic proposal waits for a decision that may never come.
Participation continues, even as influence thins.

Power prices spike while homes grow colder.
Control systems operate correctly as harm accumulates.

An aircraft responds to a signal faster than a pilot can intervene.
Automation acts while authority struggles to catch up.

Each moment sits at the edge of consequence. When outcomes are favorable, nothing here feels remarkable. The moment passes as routine, absorbed into daily life, until it does not.

In every case, a digital system is already in motion. Signals propagate. Decisions are committed. Authority is exercised, deferred, or displaced. Trust strengthens, weakens, or quietly withdraws. Nothing announces itself as design. Nothing feels experimental while it is working.

And yet, this is where posture appears, when systems are pulled under pressure.

The weave reveals itself under strain.

***Figure 7.1**: Systems under strain*

Some systems continue to hold.

Others continue to function while legitimacy quietly thins.

What matters here is response.

When pressure enters a system, how do authority, reversibility, and restraint behave while decisions are still unfolding?

Where does action slow while correction still matters, and where does it continue until correction arrives too late?

This is the digital weaving lens.

Seen this way, familiar systems begin to look different. Pressure does not distribute evenly. Some paths narrow early. Others remain open too long. Reversibility matters only while outcomes are still in motion. Authority matters most before certainty sets in.

This chapter looks at systems at that moment. Not when they fail, but when they are pulled. The difference is where recognition arrives, and whether it arrives in time.

The cases that follow are evaluated structurally, by how constraints shape decisions and whether authority and reversibility remain reachable as consequences approach irreversibility.

Systems that hold under strain

Strain reveals whether a weave can answer.

The cases that follow examine systems that continue to operate while remaining answerable. They do not avoid pressure. They respond to it as it emerges. Time tightens first. Scale and visibility follow. Consequences move closer to irreversibility.

What distinguishes these systems is not resilience as endurance, but interruption as possibility. Authority remains reachable. Correction has not yet slipped out of reach.

These systems do not hold because they are optimized or complete. They hold because pressure is allowed to move rather than accumulate, and because no single capability is allowed to run ahead unchecked. Action slows where mistakes would be irreversible. Exposure recedes once its purpose has been met. Participation remains tied to decisions that matter. Continuity adapts where it cannot be assumed.

What stands out is not technical sophistication, but discipline. These systems retain room for interruption through structure, even when speed would have been easier and certainty more comfortable.

Autonomy under fatal time pressure

In Rwanda's western provinces, emergency medicine unfolds under time constraints shaped as much by geography as by physiology. A clinic facing postpartum hemorrhage may have trained staff and basic supplies, yet still lack the specific blood type required in that moment. Mountainous terrain turns short distances into delays that matter clinically. For the clinician waiting in a rural clinic, the difference is not optimization. It is whether help arrives before a decision must be made alone. In this setting, the national medical drone delivery network emerged not as a logistics innovation, but as a response to time itself as an irreversible medical condition.

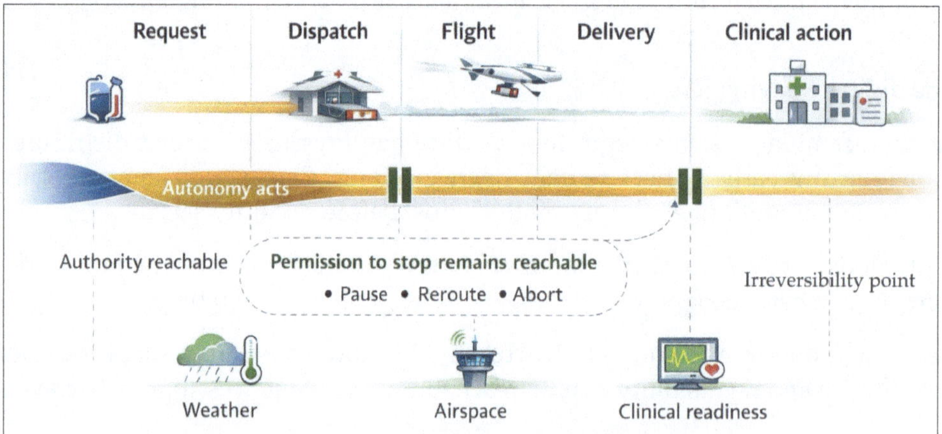

The system responds at machine speed without surrendering control. Autonomous action proceeds, but sensing and governance keep interruption reachable, delaying irreversible commitment until clinical judgment can still choose differently.

Figure 7.2: *Interruptibility under fatal time pressure*

The burden this system carries is not efficiency. It is a judgment under fatal time pressure. Software-mediated dispatch shapes whether clinicians act, knowing that blood is already on the way, or pause in uncertainty about whether escalation will arrive in time. In this setting, digital decisions translate directly into physical outcomes, with little tolerance for delay and almost none for error.

Strain concentration points

In urgent medical delivery, strain gathers quickly and predictably.

Coordination frays first. Signals about need, readiness, and availability must move fast enough to shape action, not merely arrive after decisions have already been made.

Automation introduces a second pressure. As routing and dispatch scale, decisions can begin to outpace the permission to intervene, especially when emergencies further compress time.

Failure tolerance then collapses. Unlike consumer logistics, medical delivery cannot absorb mistakes through retries or substitution. Each misjudgment carries consequences that do not unwind.

In many autonomous delivery systems, speed and completion are optimized before authority to interrupt becomes operationally reachable. That gap is where legitimacy usually begins to thin.

Posture under strain

In Rwanda's network, autonomy remains deliberately within reach.

Autonomous flight systems handle routing and delivery, but authority to pause, reroute, or ground missions stays explicit and operational. Intervention is part of the action flow itself, not an exception reserved for after something goes wrong.

Sensing constrains intelligence rather than feeding it indiscriminately. Weather conditions, airspace limits, and confirmation of clinical readiness gate execution. When confidence weakens, the system slows or stops rather than forcing completion.

Learning stays close to use. Drop locations, dispatch timing, and operational thresholds are adjusted based on ongoing clinic feedback during routine operations, not postponed to distant post-incident reviews. The system adapts without discarding what it has already learned.

Trust emerges from visible restraint in operation. Clinics rely on the system not because it always flies, but because it does not fly when conditions no longer justify action, leaving time to activate backup protocols.

Legitimacy erosion pattern

When restraint is removed, failure would follow a familiar course. Intelligence would optimize for completion rather than clinical responsibility. Flights would proceed under marginal conditions. Authority would arrive later, through review rather than interruption.

Clinics would adjust quietly. They would stop relying on the system for urgent cases and return to slower, riskier alternatives. The network would continue to operate while losing its medical legitimacy.

This is a common erosion pattern of stacked autonomy. Decisions scale faster than permission to intervene. Here, legitimacy holds because authority remains embedded in the decision flow.

Unresolved tension

Growth continues to apply pressure. As demand rises, incentives appear to extend autonomy, reduce human intervention, and increase throughput. Each step toward efficiency risks allowing action to move beyond the reach of permission to stop.

The system also depends on institutional stability. Clear regulatory authority and coordinated public health governance remain essential.

Digital weaving holds here not by eliminating trade-offs among speed, scale, and safety, but by keeping those trade-offs visible while consequences remain negotiable.

Boundary revealed

Here, the boundary appears in motion. Autonomy does not require surrendering authority. Intelligence can act decisively while remaining answerable. Under fatal time pressure, legitimacy depends on whether governance can still reach action before consequences harden.

Rwanda's medical drone network holds because intelligence never outruns permission to stop.

Structural mapping

This case tests whether autonomous systems can remain answerable at the moment of consequence:

- **Dominant strain**: Fatal time compression, where delay itself becomes clinical harm rather than operational cost.
- **Threads under pressure**: Infrastructure, intelligence, and sensing operate under extreme temporal constraint.
- **Where authority remained reachable or slipped**: Authority remained reachable during execution through explicit permission to pause, reroute, or ground missions while action was still unfolding.
- **Where reversibility narrowed**: Reversibility narrowed sharply after clinical commitment, but remained operational before dispatch and during routing, allowing correction before outcomes hardened.

- **Why legitimacy held or thinned**: Legitimacy held because restraint remained visible in operation. The system slowed or stopped when confidence weakened, preserving trust and enabling clinics to rely on it under fatal time pressure.

Inclusion at the national scale

In India, participation in economic and civic life increasingly passes through digital identity and payment systems. Access to banking, welfare, telecommunications, and everyday transactions now flows through infrastructure designed to operate at a population scale. Aadhaar and **Unified Payments Interface (UPI)** did not emerge simply to reduce transaction delays or administrative overhead. They took shape in response to exclusion as a structural condition, where the absence of identity or access to payment does more than create inconvenience. It prevents people from being recognized, recorded, or served by institutions meant to include them.

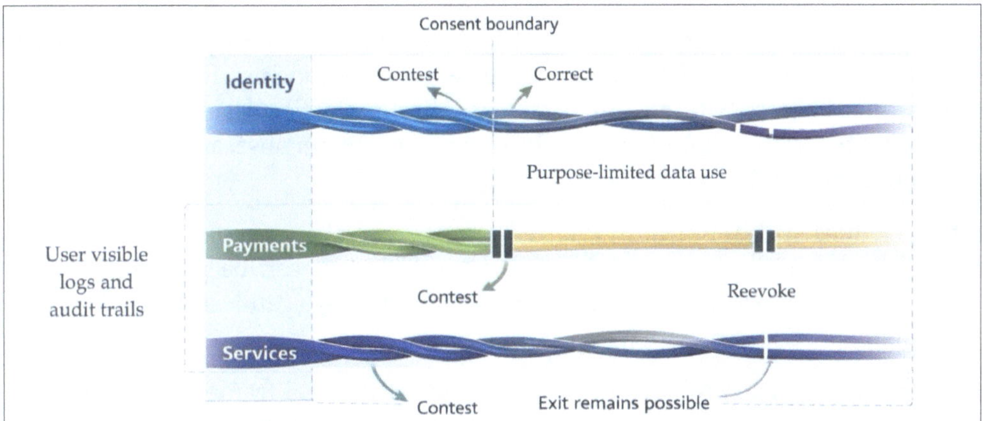

At national scale, inclusion remains legitimate only when participation is reversible. Identity enables access, payments operate independently, and services remain contestable, allowing consent, correction, and exit to remain reachable before exclusion hardens.

***Figure** 7.3: Contestability at the national scale*

The burden this system carries is civic as much as economic. Decisions about identity and payments determine who can transact, who can access public support, and who remains invisible to the systems meant to serve them. At the national scale, errors rarely stay contained. They move across institutions, turning individual misclassification into collective consequence.

Here, digital decisions shape inclusion itself. For a citizen at the edge of the system, the difference is not convenience. It is whether exclusion can still be corrected before it hardens.

Strain concentration points

At the population scale, strain enters differently than in time-critical systems.

Trust fractures first. Identity systems begin to weaken when people believe they are misclassified, monitored, or excluded without meaningful recourse.

Automation adds a second pressure. Verification, transaction routing, and fraud detection scale far faster than explanation or appeal. When confidence in these processes is misplaced, intelligence does not simply err; it multiplies harm.

Failure then becomes systemic rather than local. Errors ripple across banking, telecom, welfare, and governance at once, making recovery slower and legitimacy more fragile.

In many national identity systems, these pressures pull toward centralization and control. That is typically where legitimacy begins to thin.

Posture under strain

India's digital public infrastructure is held by keeping inclusion open to revision.

Identity and payments remain separable yet interdependent. Identity enables participation without dictating behavior. Payments move without exposing identity unnecessarily. Connectivity opens access, while consent governs disclosure. Security mechanisms reinforce these boundaries by limiting data exposure, binding access to purpose, and allowing revocation when conditions change.

Automation enables speed, but authority to contest, correct, or revoke remains visible and reachable. Participation is not permanent by default. Access can be paused. Errors can be challenged. Records return to users through statements, logs, and audit trails rather than vanishing into institutional memory.

Governance operates structurally rather than episodically. Legal frameworks, consent layers, and institutional checks shape how data and intelligence interact before harm hardens, not only after exposure has occurred.

Trust grows from reversibility. People remain inside the system not because exit is impossible, but because correction and recovery remain available.

Legitimacy erosion pattern

When inclusion systems lose reversibility, identity begins to harden into control. Consent remains present, but becomes procedural rather than operative. Centralized intelligence scales exclusion faster than remedy. Errors propagate across services, locking individuals into systems they can neither see nor meaningfully contest.

Participation may persist for a time, but legitimacy drains quietly. The system appears efficient even as civic acceptance thins beneath the surface.

This is a familiar erosion pattern of stacked inclusion. Intelligence advances while consent lags, and authority drifts away from lived redress.

Unresolved tension

Strain continues as scale deepens. As more services depend on shared identity and payment rails, pressure grows to reuse data, tighten coupling, and automate enforcement. Each step narrows the space for contestation.

Experience also remains uneven. Connectivity gaps, biometric failures, and differences in literacy shape who benefits and who struggles. Redress exists, but not always evenly or in an accessible way.

Digital weaving holds here structurally, not by resolving these tensions, but by keeping them visible. At this scale, legitimacy must be renewed continually.

Boundary revealed

At the national scale, inclusion remains legitimate only when trust can be withheld and restored. Automation can operate broadly without becoming absolute when authority to contest, correct, and exit remains close to action.

India's digital public infrastructure holds because trust is not assumed. It is tested, constrained, and renewed in practice.

Structural mapping

This case shows how population-scale inclusion tests whether digital identity and payment systems can remain answerable before exclusion hardens into control:

- **Dominant strain**: Population scale, where individual errors propagate across institutions and become difficult to reverse.
- **Threads under pressure**: Infrastructure and data, as shared identity and payment rails bind multiple services to a single point of failure.
- **Where authority remained reachable or slipped**: Authority remained reachable through visible mechanisms to contest, correct, pause, or revoke access before exclusion became permanent.
- **Where reversibility narrowed**: Reversibility narrowed when verification, routing, and fraud detection scaled faster than explanation or appeal, turning correctable errors into systemic lock-in.
- **Why legitimacy held or thinned**: Legitimacy held because inclusion stayed revisable and trust could be withdrawn and restored; it thinned where consent became procedural, and redress drifted out of reach.

Visibility in a collective emergency

In South Korea, the early stages of the COVID-19 pandemic compressed time across public health, transportation, and daily life. Containment depended on making risk visible while fear and uncertainty were still unfolding. The digital response did not take shape as a surveillance project. It emerged from a narrower need—to surface exposure quickly enough to support coordination, without dissolving the trust required for people to act together.

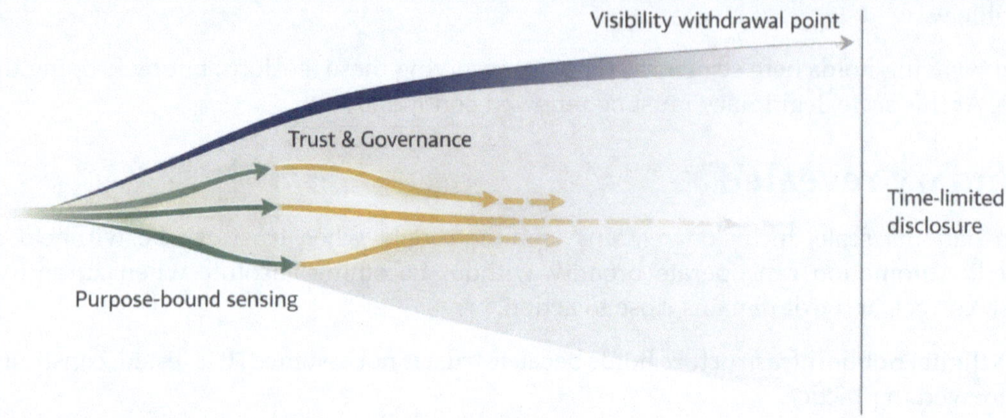

In collective emergencies, visibility remains legitimate only when it is purpose-bound and time-limited. Sensing and intelligence support coordination, while governance caps exposure and withdraws visibility before it becomes ambient.

***Figure 7.4:** Bounded visibility in collective emergency*

The burden here is societal. Decisions about detection, notification, and isolation shape whether people respond in coordination or retreat into suspicion. At the national scale, hesitation costs lives. Overreach carries a different cost. It weakens legitimacy.

Here, digital decisions shape whether a society can still move together under threat.

Strain concentration points

During a collective emergency, strain gathers most tightly around visibility.

Consent strains first. Effective response requires rapid sensing of proximity and exposure, often faster than individual permissions can be gathered, explained, or revisited.

Speed adds pressure. Automated alerts and rapid disclosures can outrun understanding. When information arrives without context, it fuels anxiety or resistance rather than coordination.

Fatigue accumulates more slowly but more persistently. Sustained notification and monitoring exhaust public tolerance over time, even when measures are technically justified and initially accepted.

In many emergency systems, these pressures pull responses toward two familiar extremes: paralysis, or unchecked surveillance. Both fracture legitimacy in different ways.

Posture under strain

South Korea's response was to place deliberate limits on visibility.

Sensing enabled rapid identification of exposure paths, but data use remained time-bound and purpose-specific. Information was disclosed at the level required to act, not to observe indiscriminately.

Connectivity supported coordination without central command. Alerts reached people where they were, while guidance remained contextual, shaped by location and situation rather than broadcast as uniform instruction.

Intelligence-supported logistics and prioritization, but authority over isolation, disclosure, and escalation stayed grounded in public health governance rather than being handed over to optimization alone.

Trust emerged through visible limits. Citizens could see what data was used, why it was used, and when it would expire. Visibility did not become ambient. It remained conditional.

Legitimacy erosion pattern

When visibility loses proportion, coordination begins to fray. Unchecked sensing triggers resistance and withdrawal. Insufficient sensing allows silent spread. Either extreme undermines collective action.

This is a common erosion pattern of stacked visibility systems. Detection scales faster than legitimacy. Alerts are ignored. Data is withheld. Compliance weakens even as systems continue to broadcast information.

Here, legitimacy remained intact because visibility stayed bounded, purpose-specific, and accountable under pressure. For a resident receiving an exposure alert, the difference is not the presence of information. It is whether visibility guides action without turning into suspicion.

Unresolved tension

Emergency powers are difficult to relinquish. Even where legal limits exist, repeated crises normalize heightened visibility. Fatigue and skepticism accumulate. Boundaries that hold during one emergency can weaken during the next.

Digital weaving holds here only through the restraint that is actively maintained. The system depends on continued trust that visibility will recede once its purpose has been served.

Boundary revealed

In collective emergencies, visibility supports coordination only while it can be withdrawn as deliberately as it is deployed.

South Korea's response held because sensing arrived quickly, and because it left on purpose.

Structural mapping

This case shows how collective response during a crisis depends on visibility that can be withdrawn as deliberately as it is deployed:

- **Dominant strain**: Time-compressed collective risk, where coordination must emerge before fear, fatigue, or mistrust fragments response.
- **Threads under pressure**: Sensing and data, as exposure detection and disclosure scale faster than consent, context, and public understanding.
- **Where authority remained reachable or slipped**: Authority remained reachable through public health governance that controlled when visibility escalated, narrowed, or ended, rather than leaving those decisions to automation alone.
- **Where reversibility narrowed**: Reversibility narrowed when alerts and disclosures risked becoming continuous or ambient, making visibility difficult to retract once normalized.
- **Why legitimacy held or thinned**: Legitimacy held because visibility stayed purpose-bound, time-limited, and explainable; it thinned where sensing outpaced trust and information turned from coordination into suspicion.

Participation linked to binding authority

In Barcelona, years of civic engagement had produced a familiar imbalance. Residents shared ideas, comments, and priorities through consultations, workshops, and assemblies, yet outcomes often remained detached from formal decisions. Participation was visible. Its consequences were not. Over time, a gap opened between voice and authority in a city where legitimacy depended on showing how public input actually shaped what followed.

The Decidim platform did not emerge to increase participation for its own sake. It emerged to repair that gap.

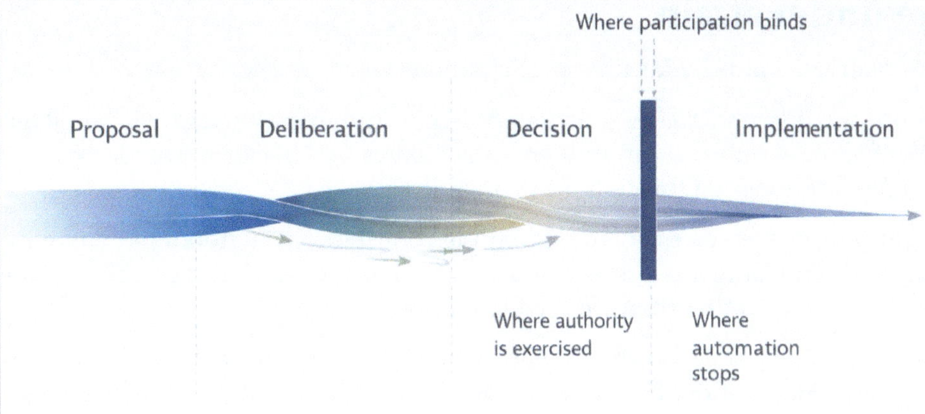

Public input shapes outcomes when participation travels through deliberation, meets explicit authority at decision, and binds implementation rather than dissolving into consultation.

Figure 7.5: *Participation bound to authority*

The burden here is political and social. Decisions about housing, mobility, public space, and budgets shape everyday life. When participation becomes symbolic, legitimacy thins. Compliance may continue, but trust does not.

In this system, digital decisions determine whether a civic voice carries weight. For a resident who submits a proposal, the difference is not being acknowledged. It is whether that contribution can still shape a decision that commits the city to act.

Strain concentration points

In participatory systems, strain accumulates slowly rather than suddenly.

Trust weakens before turnout does. People often continue to participate even after they believe their influence has faded, turning input into volume rather than signal. Activity remains visible while legitimacy quietly drains away.

Scale introduces a second strain. As participation grows, accountability becomes harder to trace. Contributions multiply, but responsibility spreads across processes, committees, and timelines.

Automation adds a quieter pressure. Ranking, moderation, and prioritization tools can reshape outcomes without drawing attention to where judgment is exercised. Deliberation gives way to efficiency, and influence becomes harder to locate.

In many civic platforms, these pressures reduce participation to consultation. That is usually where legitimacy begins to fail.

Posture under strain

Barcelona's platform holds by keeping participation close to authority.

Proposals do not disappear after submission. They progress through visible stages, with records showing how public input influences outcomes. Authority is not hidden behind the platform. It remains exposed through the process itself.

Sensing captures diverse voices, including offline contributions, without flattening them into anonymous metrics. Context is preserved through version histories, traceable revisions, and documented responses rather than reduced to scores.

Intelligence supports scale without deciding substance. Automated functions assist organization and moderation, but final decisions remain accountable to elected bodies and formal civic processes.

Trust emerges through legibility. People remain engaged not because outcomes always align with their preferences, but because they can see how participation travels, where it binds, and where it does not.

Legitimacy erosion pattern

When participation loses its structural link to authority, legitimacy drains quietly.

Platforms continue to collect input without consequence. Automation filters and ranks without explanation. Decisions proceed elsewhere, insulated from public reasoning. Engagement persists for a time, then thins. The system remains active while trust withdraws.

This is the erosion pattern of stacked participation. Engagement scales faster than accountability.

Unresolved tension

Participation requires sustained care. As usage grows, pressure increases to automate moderation, compress deliberation, and drive efficiency. Each step risks placing distance between authority and public reasoning.

Access also remains uneven. Time, language, and digital literacy continue to shape who participates and whose influence accumulates.

Digital weaving holds here not by resolving these tensions, but by keeping them visible and contested.

Boundary revealed

Legitimacy in participatory systems holds only so long as voice can still bind authority. Participation remains legitimate not because it is visible, but because it can still shape decisions before they harden.

Barcelona's platform holds because authority remains reachable through participation itself. When that boundary slips, engagement persists without consequence, and legitimacy thins before participation declines.

Structural mapping

This case reveals how scaled participation reorganizes system posture, testing whether data and intelligence can remain answerable while civic decisions are still binding:

- **Dominant strain**: Slow legitimacy erosion as participation scales without a guaranteed binding effect.
- **Threads under pressure**: Data, as proposals move across stages; intelligence, as ranking and moderation tools shape visibility; infrastructure, as the platform mediates citywide participation.
- **Where authority remained reachable or slipped**: Authority remained reachable when proposals progressed through visible decision stages tied to formal civic processes; it slipped when participation fed consultation without binding commitment.
- **Where reversibility narrowed**: Reversibility narrowed once decisions advanced into administrative or council timelines that participation could no longer alter.
- **Why legitimacy held or thinned**: Legitimacy held because participation stayed structurally connected to authority; it thinned when voice accumulated without the power to change outcomes.

Livelihoods under fragile connectivity

In Kenya, smallholder agriculture unfolds across uneven infrastructure, seasonal uncertainty, and limited access to markets and finance. Farmers make decisions about planting, pricing, borrowing, and risk with narrow margins for error, often without continuous connectivity or timely information. Digital agricultural services did not emerge to replace local knowledge. They took shape to work alongside it, in environments where advice, finance, and coordination must remain usable despite interruption, distance, and uncertainty.

The burden here is economic and social. When systems fail, farmers do not lose convenience; they lose income, resilience, and sometimes land. Digital decisions shape whether rural livelihoods remain viable in settings where recovery is slow, and mistakes compound over time.

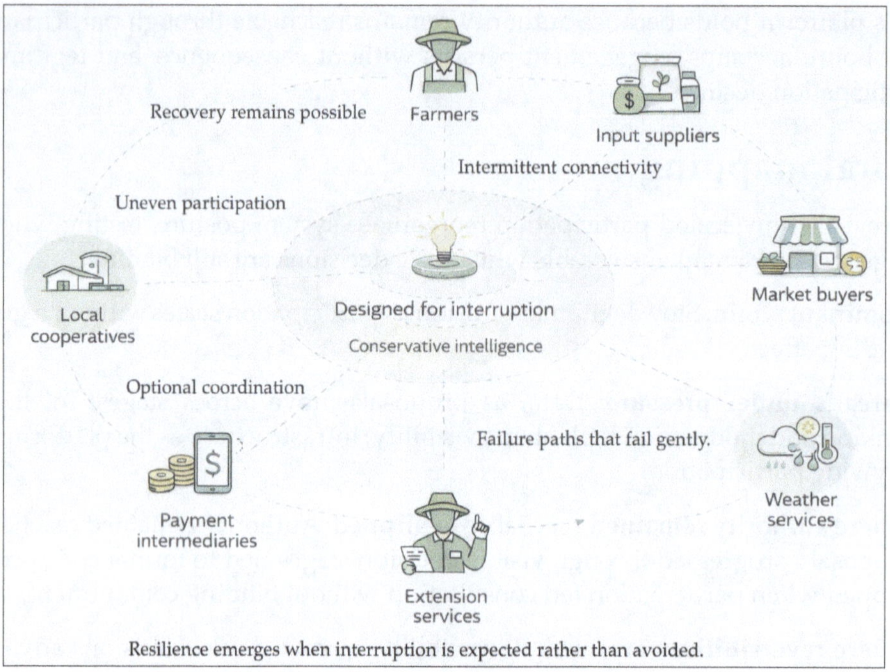

***Figure 7.6:** Continuity under fragile connectivity*

For a farmer deciding when to plant or sell, the difference is not better advice. It is whether the system fails gently enough to allow recovery after a wrong call.

Strain concentration points

In agricultural ecosystems, strain accumulates across seasons rather than moments.

Connectivity is often the first constraint to surface. Rural networks fluctuate. Devices are basic. Access is shared. Systems that assume persistence, constant attention, or high bandwidth quietly exclude participants by design.

Data introduces a second strain. Signals arrive late, incomplete, or out of context. Precision varies widely. Confidence must remain bounded rather than optimized, because overconfidence carries its own risk.

Risk compounds as a third strain. Advice, credit, and insurance interact over time. Small misjudgments accumulate quietly into large losses, often becoming visible only after a season has passed.

When these pressures are met with rigid optimization, errors propagate rather than being absorbed. Harm concentrates instead of dispersing.

Posture under strain

Kenya's agricultural ecosystem holds by adapting at the edges.

Services are designed for interruption. **Short Message Service** (SMS), **Unstructured Supplementary Service Data** (USSD), voice channels, and human intermediaries remain central rather than transitional. Participation does not depend on constant connectivity, smartphones, or sustained attention.

Sensing captures rhythm rather than precision. Weather alerts, seasonal guidance, and simple inputs reflect lived cycles instead of abstract models.

Data accumulates gradually and returns a value where it is generated. Transaction histories support credit and insurance without demanding formal records. Intelligence remains conservative, offering guidance rather than mandates.

Trust emerges when system behavior fits existing practice under constraint. Farmers remain engaged because the systems align with existing practices instead of attempting to overwrite them.

Legitimacy erosion pattern

When adaptation gives way to control, legitimacy begins to erode.

Platforms start to assume stable connectivity and exclude those at the margins. Intelligence overfits sparse data. Credit and insurance fail silently under seasonal livelihood stress, where losses accumulate before systems can respond.

After a loss, farmers disengage. Systems continue to operate, but livelihoods weaken beneath them.

This is the erosion pattern of stacked continuity. Automation scales faster than reliability.

Unresolved tension

As ecosystems grow, pressure increases to consolidate data, tighten integration, and automate enforcement. Each step risks breaking local fit.

Power asymmetries persist. Platforms, lenders, and insurers retain leverage that individual farmers do not. Transparency and redress remain uneven.

Digital weaving holds here not by resolving these tensions, but by resisting the urge to smooth them away.

Boundary revealed

At the edge, durability comes from accommodation rather than command.

Kenya's agricultural ecosystem holds because connection, memory, and guidance stay close to everyday practice, even when continuity cannot be assumed.

Structural mapping

This case reveals how unreliable continuity reorganizes system posture, testing whether infrastructure and data can remain answerable while livelihood decisions are still recoverable:

- **Dominant strain**: Accumulating livelihood risk across seasons under intermittent connectivity and delayed feedback.
- **Threads under pressure**: Infrastructure, as connectivity is uneven and unreliable; Data, as signals arrive late and incomplete; Intelligence, as guidance must remain conservative under uncertainty.
- **Where authority remained reachable or slipped**: Authority remained reachable when farmers could accept, ignore, or adapt guidance locally; it slipped when platforms assumed stable connectivity or enforced automated credit and insurance decisions.
- **Where reversibility narrowed**: Reversibility narrowed after seasonal losses compounded, when credit defaults, crop failure, or land pressure reduced the ability to recover.
- **Why legitimacy held or thinned**: Legitimacy held when systems failed gently and aligned with local practice; it thinned when optimization replaced accommodation, and errors became unrecoverable.

Patterns that hold across systems

Across the cases in this chapter, a single structural condition becomes clear. Systems hold under scale and consequence only when connectivity, sensing, data, intelligence, and trust remain present together and actively constrain one another. These threads do not function as independent layers. They operate as minimum conditions that must stay in a relationship for legitimacy to endure.

What differs from case to case is not this condition, but how strain enters the system and which thread begins to carry it first.

Systems that hold are not characterized by balance or symmetry. They are shaped by restraint that appears early and unevenly. As pressure builds, one form of strain becomes dominant. That strain marks the point where the system must retain the ability to choose differently, before optimization hardens outcomes that can no longer be corrected.

As consequences approach irreversibility, autonomy remains interruptible. At the population scale, trust stays contestable. When coordination accelerates, visibility contracts once its purpose is met. When participation seeks consequence, authority stays within reach. Where continuity cannot be assumed, adaptation shifts toward the edge. These are not design targets. They are structural responses that emerge under pressure.

No system examined here is free of failure. What separates those who endure is not avoidance, but containment. Failure remains local, becomes visible early, and triggers restraint rather than escalation. Systems that attempt to eliminate failure accumulate fragility. Systems that accept strain preserve the ability to repair.

Digital weaving defines this discipline. It is not an architectural style, but a way for systems to remain answerable while pressure is still rising. These systems endure not because they are advanced, but because restraint can still reach action before consequence becomes final.

When systems almost hold

A weave can still hold as its pattern begins to drift.

Some systems endure long enough to appear stable. They continue to operate, comply, and deliver acceptable outcomes. From the outside, little seems wrong. Inside, something quieter begins to shift.

Action still moves forward, but interruption becomes harder to reach. Authority remains visible in policies and diagrams, yet slips out of reach in the moments that matter. Reversibility still exists, but it arrives late, after consequences have begun to settle.

The systems in the following cases did not collapse under strain. They continued to function. What they lost, gradually and unevenly, was the ability to choose differently while that choice still carried weight. Decisions advanced. Restraint fell behind.

These are not accounts of error or intent. They are signals of posture under sustained pressure. They show how systems can remain internally coherent while becoming externally unanswerable, and how legitimacy thins long before breakdown becomes visible.

Set beside the systems that hold, these cases bring the boundary into focus. The question is no longer whether a system works. *It is whether it can still slow itself in time, while choice is still possible.*

Optimization without escape

In February 2021, a prolonged winter storm placed the Texas power grid under sustained and compounding strain. In this context, electricity was not a convenience layer. It sustained heating, medical equipment, water treatment, communications, and food distribution. When power failed at scale during extreme cold, harm escalated quickly and could not be undone.

The burden this system carried was not market efficiency or price discovery. It was the continuity of life-critical infrastructure at a moment when delay itself became damage. Digital decisions made inside control rooms are translated directly into physical exposure across millions of households.

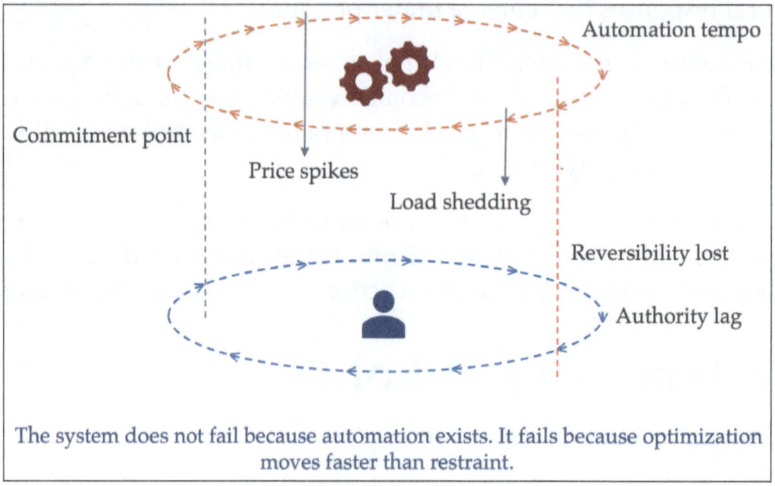

Figure 7.7: *Optimization without escape*

Failure did not arrive as a breach or a single moment of collapse. During the February 2021 winter storm, power was shed repeatedly across Texas as generation failed and automated market mechanisms continued to execute, unfolding as a sequence of technically correct decisions whose consequences hardened before they could be meaningfully reversed.

Strain concentration points

As temperatures fell, strain gathered quickly and unevenly.

Time compressed first. Generation dropped faster than coordination mechanisms could adjust. Weather impacts cascaded across fuel supply, generation capacity, and transmission reliability within hours rather than days.

Automation introduced a second strain. Dispatch, pricing, and load-balancing logic continued to execute as designed, even as physical infrastructure froze. Decisions moved at machine speed, while the ability to pause, intervene, or reconsider objectives lagged behind.

Failure tolerance collapsed next. Load-shedding actions propagated mechanically across regions. Once initiated, they became difficult to reverse without further destabilizing the grid. Households lost power not for minutes, but for days, even as markets continued to clear.

These pressures did not arise from a single design flaw. They emerged from how optimization had been allowed to advance without equivalent restraint. For a grid operator watching conditions deteriorate, the question was not whether rules were being followed. It was *whether the system could still be slowed before harm spread beyond control.*

Posture under strain

On paper, the system appeared well-structured. Market rules defined scarcity pricing. Emergency protocols existed. Regulatory authority was clearly assigned.

Under load, authority did not travel with decisions.

Pricing escalated automatically as supply tightened. Load shedding followed predefined thresholds. Human intervention arrived only after cascading effects had already hardened. Reversibility existed through review and reform, not in the moment when restraint might still have mattered.

Governance was present, but it did not operate at the tempo of intelligence.

Legitimacy erosion pattern

Optimization continued to function. Markets cleared. Automation executed as designed. What degraded was not the operation, but the system's protective capacity.

Decisions remained defensible within market logic while drifting away from the burden the system was carrying. Authority shifted from interruptive to advisory. Reversibility moved from action to aftermath.

Legitimacy eroded unevenly. Those with resources exited through private generation or relocation. Those without absorbed prolonged exposure. The grid remained operational while trust withdrew quietly.

This is a familiar erosion pattern in stacked systems under strain. They continue to function technically while their capacity to protect thins.

Unresolved tension

They did not resolve the deeper tension revealed under strain.

The question is not whether markets can be improved, but *whether authority can still reach automated action as consequences unfold*. Whether reversibility can be exercised before harm propagates. Whether governance can operate at the same tempo as intelligence, rather than trailing it through review.

Digital weaving clarifies what is missing. It does not replace markets or automation. It insists that interruptibility, restraint, and contestable authority remain embedded within operation, not deferred to policy or aftermath.

Until authority can pause optimization in motion, rather than explain it later, the conditions for recurrence remain.

Boundary revealed

What this case brings into view is that optimization alone does not confer resilience. Systems remain legitimate only while authority can still reach action before harm hardens.

Speed itself is not the danger. Structural risk appears when the restraint can no longer arrive in time.

The Texas grid did not falter because it lacked intelligence. It faltered because intelligence moved beyond the reach of interruption.

Structural mapping

This case tests whether a system built for continuous optimization can still pause itself when the burden shifts from efficiency to protection:

- **Dominant strain**: Rapid time compression during extreme weather, where delay translated into irreversible harm.
- **Threads under pressure**: Infrastructure, as generation and fuel supply failed under cold; Intelligence, as automated dispatch and pricing accelerated decisions; Data, as system signals reflected market conditions faster than physical recovery.
- **Where authority remained reachable or slipped**: Authority slipped when automated pricing and load-shedding were executed without a pause mechanism; human intervention became advisory after actions had already propagated.
- **Where reversibility narrowed**: Reversibility narrowed once load shedding cascaded across regions, making restoration risky and prolonged outages unavoidable.
- **Why legitimacy held or thinned**: Legitimacy thinned as optimization continued to function while protection failed, shifting correction to post-event explanation rather than in-motion restraint.

Automation without interruption

Commercial aviation carries a singular burden. Failure must remain correctable in real time. Unlike many complex systems, aircraft do not allow delayed review, gradual recovery, or post-event adjustment. When digital decisions directly control flight surfaces, authority must remain immediate, visible, and interruptible.

The Boeing 737 MAX was introduced as an incremental evolution of an established aircraft line. To preserve pilot certification continuity and operational familiarity, a software-based augmentation system was added to compensate for aerodynamic changes introduced by new engines.

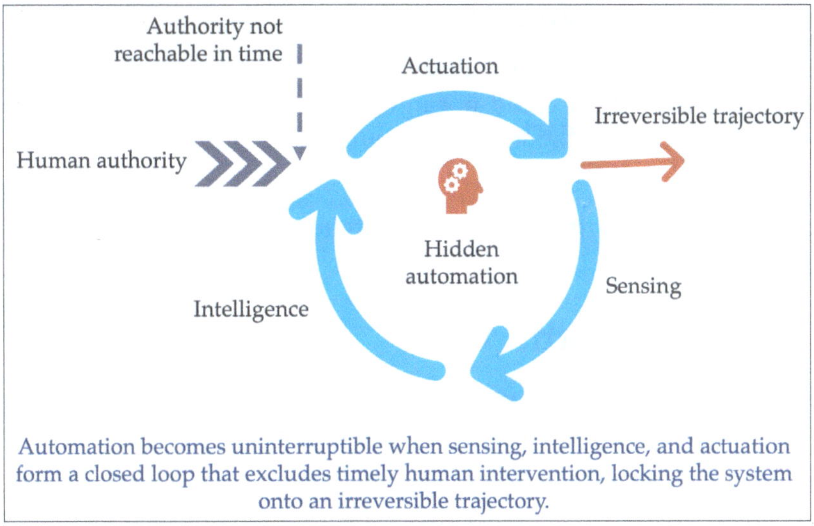

Figure 7.8: *Automation without interruption*

The burden this system carried was not performance optimization. It was the continuity of safe human control under time-compressed, high-consequence conditions.

Here, digital decisions shaped survivability. For a pilot in the cockpit, the question was not whether automation existed. It was *whether authority could still be reached in the seconds when correction remained possible.*

Strain concentration points

Strain in this system gathered quickly and without margin.

Time collapsed first. In flight, pilots have seconds, not minutes, to interpret unexpected behavior, form a diagnosis, and respond.

Automation introduced the next pressure. The augmentation system acted autonomously, applying repeated control inputs based on limited sensing data. Decisions unfolded faster than explanation, confirmation, or consent could realistically occur.

Reversibility weakened next. Although manual override existed formally, pilots were not informed of the system's presence or behavior in a way that made intervention cognitively or operationally reachable under stress.

The system assumed correct sensing and correct interpretation at the moment failure occurred. When those assumptions did not hold, recovery windows narrowed abruptly.

Posture under strain

On paper, the system appeared compliant. Redundancy existed elsewhere in the aircraft. Manual controls remained available. Certification processes were followed.

Under strain, authority did not travel with action.

The system acted repeatedly without requiring confirmation, explanation, or visible consent. Pilots encountered behavior they could not immediately interpret, contest, or reliably halt. Reversibility existed in documentation and procedure, not in lived operation at the moment when restraint might still have mattered.

Governance existed through certification, documentation, and oversight, but it did not operate inside the decision loop where automated action unfolded in real time.

Legitimacy erosion pattern

Automation behaved decisively, but without restraint. The system corrected for perceived instability even as it introduced new instability. Authority shifted from interruptive to reactive.

Trust eroded through opacity rather than negligence. The aircraft did not clearly signal that it was acting. Pilots did not know what to contest. When human intervention finally occurred, it arrived too late to restore control.

This is a familiar erosion pattern when intelligence operates without a reachable authority. Systems can behave correctly within their internal logic while becoming unsafe in their operational context.

Unresolved tension

Certification and oversight frameworks are built on the assumption that authority can be exercised through training, documentation, and procedural compliance. Time-compressed automation exposes the limits of that model. When action unfolds faster than human interpretation can keep pace, authority risks arriving too late to matter.

The tension, then, is not whether automation can be made safer in principle, but whether authority can remain reachable in practice.

Can systems preserve reversibility while decisions are still in motion, rather than only through post-event procedure?

Can governance operate inside the control loop itself, shaping action as it unfolds, rather than surrounding it from the outside?

Digital weaving does not resolve these questions by adding more automation or more oversight. It reframes them. It asks whether restraint is structurally present where intelligence acts, whether interruption is operational rather than symbolic, and whether authority travels at the same tempo as consequence.

These tensions persist wherever automated action accelerates faster than the system's ability to pause, explain, or yield. Where interruptibility cannot keep pace, legitimacy thins long before failure becomes visible.

Boundary revealed

What this case brings into view is that reversibility must remain immediate, not eventual.

Automation remains legitimate only when authority travels with intelligence rather than trailing behind it. Action must stay legible and interruptible as consequences approach irreversibility.

The Boeing 737 MAX did not break down because intelligence existed. The breakdown occurred because intelligence was allowed to act after permission to intervene had slipped out of reach.

Structural mapping

This case examines whether automation operating at machine speed can remain interruptible when correction must occur within seconds:

- **Dominant strain**: Extreme time compression, where misalignment between action and understanding becomes immediately fatal.
- **Threads under pressure**: Sensing, as limited sensor inputs triggered repeated responses; Intelligence, as automated control logic acted autonomously; Infrastructure, as flight control systems executed commands without requiring confirmation.
- **Where authority remained reachable or slipped**: Authority slipped when pilots could not clearly identify, interpret, or halt automated actions in real time.
- **Where reversibility narrowed**: Reversibility narrowed once automated inputs repeated faster than pilots could diagnose behavior or execute effective override.
- **Why legitimacy held or thinned**: Legitimacy collapsed because intelligence acted beyond the reach of immediate human interruption, turning formal control into a procedural illusion.

Patterns that unravel

In these systems, failure does not announce itself as collapse. Operations continue. Automation executes. Procedures still hold. What thinks first is not the function, but answerability, as consequences begin to settle.

The cause is not missing intelligence or absent governance. It is timing. Strain advances faster than restraint. Action continues past the point where interruption would still have altered the outcome. Authority remains present, but no longer arrives in time to matter.

As pressure builds, automated decisions reinforce themselves. The space to pause or redirect narrows. Intervention shifts from stopping action to explaining harm after it has occurred.

Reversibility does not disappear. It arrives late. Correction becomes partial. Repair replaces prevention. Systems continue to operate even as their protective capacity erodes.

This is how failure accumulates in systems that almost hold. Not as a breakdown, but as a debt. Each uninterruptible action raises the threshold for what follows. Collapse, when it comes, is rarely purely technical. It surfaces socially, legally, or politically, after the system has already lost the ability to choose differently.

The boundary that matters

A weave that holds does not resist strain. It answers it.

Across the systems examined in this chapter, endurance does not divide by sophistication, scale, or intelligence. It divides at a single boundary; whether authority can still interrupt action before consequences harden.

When this boundary holds, systems remain answerable as pressure rises. When it breaks, systems often continue to operate while legitimacy drains beneath the surface. Function persists. Choice does not.

Digital weaving names this boundary and disciplines how systems remain answerable while interruption is still possible. Authority stays within reach of action. Reversibility remains operational while outcomes are still forming. Intelligence responds to consequence rather than momentum. Where this discipline holds, failure stays containable. Where it slips, optimization outruns correction.

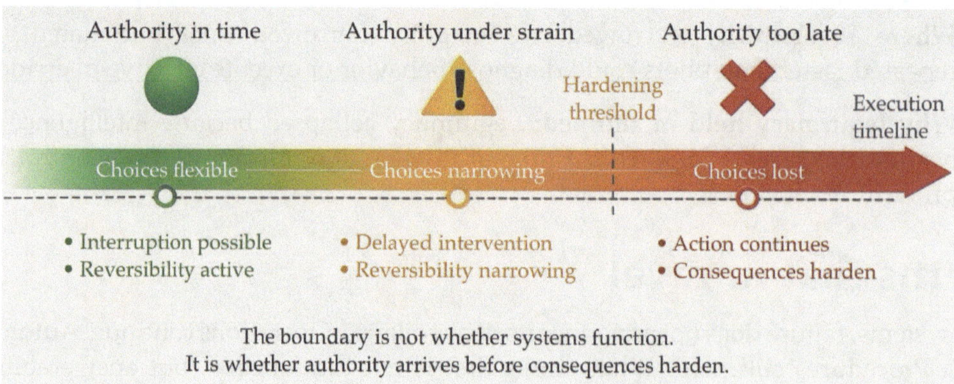

Figure 7.9: *The boundary that matters*

The cases in this chapter draw attention to how systems behave under strain. Once this boundary becomes visible, it changes how systems are understood while they are still operating.

The question that follows is unavoidable:
When this system begins to strain, can it still choose differently in time?

Conclusion

What holds today will encounter new forms of strain tomorrow.

The systems that hold endure not because they are exceptional, but because, for now, they remain answerable under strain. Across healthcare, identity, public health, civic participation, agriculture, energy, and aviation, pressure takes different forms. Time compresses. Visibility widens. Participation scales. Connectivity falters. Intelligence accelerates. In many cases, systems continue to operate even as legitimacy begins to thin.

What separates those who hold is not foresight or control, but posture. Autonomy remains interruptible long enough for different choices to remain possible. Visibility recedes once its purpose is served. Inclusion does not harden into permanence. Intelligence remains open to challenge. Authority stays close enough to intervene. These are not safeguards added after failure. They are structural behaviors that appear when systems are allowed to strain without tearing.

The contribution of this chapter is not a catalog of systems or outcomes. It is a way of recognizing moments that still matter: when legitimacy remains within reach, and when the opportunity for correction has already closed.

The cases are not models to replicate. They are evidence. Where systems address consequential problems and continue to hold, the same five threads remain present and interdependent. No single thread sustains legitimacy on its own. What endures is the relationship among them.

Every system here is shaped by context, law, and history. What matters is not form, but posture. Learning to recognize posture makes earlier intervention possible, often with less disruption and greater legitimacy. Beyond that point, correction becomes symbolic, costly, or too late to restore what was lost.

The systems examined here hold, and nearly fail, under present conditions. They make no promises about what comes next. New forces are already pulling harder. Automation accelerates. Intelligence grows more autonomous. Sensing becomes continuous. Scale expands faster than consent. The room for interruption, correction, and restraint is already narrowing.

The next chapter turns to those forces. It examines what happens when the same threads are stretched by emerging technologies, shifting power, and longer chains of consequence. The task ahead is not to prevent strain, but to decide what must be woven while restraint is still possible, before fracture becomes the only remaining outcome.

Weaver's toolkit

A weave is sustained not by tools alone, but by knowing when to use them.

This section gathers the practical supports that sit alongside the cases in this chapter. The lexicon provides shared language for noticing structure, posture, and failure modes. The workshop offers exercises for developing judgment under strain. The library points to foundational texts for designing and governing digital systems that must remain answerable at scale.

These tools are not prescriptions or checklists. They are ways of seeing, naming, and working with systems whose consequences unfold in the real world. Used together, they support the practice of digital weaving across contexts rather than within any single case.

Weaver's lexicon

The lexicon defines the technical and metaphorical terms used throughout the chapter. The entries are meant to support structural diagnosis and shared understanding. They offer a common vocabulary for recognizing how systems behave as pressure builds and decisions begin to matter:

- **Aadhaar**: A national digital identity system in India that assigns a unique identifier to residents, enabling verification for access to public and private services.
- **Answerability**: The condition in which authority remains reachable and capable of interrupting action while consequences are still unfolding.
- **Authority**: The capacity to pause, redirect, or halt system behavior before outcomes become irreversible. Distinguished from oversight or after-the-fact accountability.
- **Automation**: The execution of decisions by systems without continuous human intervention. In this chapter, automation is evaluated by whether it remains interruptible.
- **Boundary**: A structural limit that determines whether a system can still constrain action under strain. Boundaries separate systems that hold from those that merely continue to function.
- **Commitment point**: The moment when action becomes difficult or impossible to reverse marks the closing of the reversibility window.
- **Consequence**: The real-world effects of digital decisions once they move beyond simulation or intent and begin to shape physical, civic, or economic outcomes. In this chapter, consequence matters because it hardens over time.
- **Containment**: The ability of a system to localize failure, make it visible early, and prevent escalation into systemic harm.
- **Contestability**: The ability to question, challenge, or revise decisions while they still matter.
- **Continuity**: The capacity of a system to remain usable across interruption, degradation, or uneven conditions, rather than assuming constant availability.
- **Dominant strain**: The form of pressure that most strongly shapes system behavior in a given context and determines where restraint must act first.

- **Governance**: The mechanisms through which authority, consent, and restraint shape how decisions are made and interrupted during operation, not only through policy or review.
- **Hardening**: The process by which decisions become increasingly difficult to reverse as time passes, dependencies accumulate, or automation reinforces prior actions.
- **Intelligence**: Algorithmic or automated decision-making capability. In digital weaving, intelligence remains subordinate to consequence and authority.
- **Interruptibility**: The ability of a system to pause, alter, or stop action before consequences become irreversible. Interruptibility constrains commitment, not performance. When lost, correction shifts from real-time intervention to after-the-fact remedy.
- **Interruption window**: The limited span of time during which authority can still pause or redirect action before consequences harden.
- **Irreversibility**: The point at which outcomes can no longer be meaningfully corrected, contested, or undone, even if responsibility is later assigned.
- **Legitimacy**: The condition in which a system is accepted as rightful and trustworthy by those affected, sustained through reversibility, restraint, and answerability.
- **Legitimacy erosion**: The gradual withdrawal of trust and acceptance while a system continues to operate correctly.
- **Operational reachability**: The ability for the authority to intervene at the tempo of system action, rather than after consequences have already hardened.
- **Optimization**: The pursuit of improved performance against a defined objective. Optimization becomes dangerous when it advances faster than restraint can keep pace.
- **Posture**: How a system behaves when pressure is applied. Posture is revealed by how authority, restraint, and reversibility respond as consequences approach irreversibility.
- **Restraint**: The structural capacity to limit or delay action before harm becomes irreversible, embedded in system operation rather than applied after failure.
- **Reversibility**: The ability to correct, contest, or undo decisions while outcomes are still in motion, not merely after damage has occurred.
- **Scale**: The expansion of the system's reach across population, geography, or consequence. Scale amplifies strain and raises the cost of lost restraint.
- **Short Message Service (SMS)**: A basic mobile messaging service that delivers short text messages over cellular networks, requiring minimal connectivity and no Internet access.

- **Slowing**: A structural constraint that delays commitment rather than execution. Slowing preserves time for review, consent, or interruption when consequences approach irreversibility. It does not reduce system throughput.
- **Sociotechnical system**: A system in which technical action and social authority shape one another. Software decisions affect human outcomes, and governance constrains how systems act. In this chapter, sociotechnical systems are treated as indivisible wholes.
- **Strain**: Pressure applied by time, scale, uncertainty, or consequence that reveals a system's structural limits.
- **System that holds**: A system that remains answerable under strain by preserving interruptibility, reversibility, and restraint.
- **System that almost holds**: A system that continues to function while losing the ability to interrupt action before consequences become irreversible.
- **Unified Payments Interface (UPI)**: A real-time digital payment system in India that enables direct bank-to-bank transactions through a shared infrastructure, supporting interoperable payments across institutions.
- **Unstructured Supplementary Service Data (USSD)**: A session-based mobile communication protocol that allows interactive menu-driven actions over cellular networks without Internet connectivity.

Weaver's workshop

The cases in this chapter provide situations to think about. Each one shows how systems respond when pressure is applied, where authority remains reachable, and where restraint arrives too late to change outcomes.

The exercises that follow move from recognition to practice. They invite you to examine real or plausible systems, notice where strain concentrates, and test whether interruption, reversibility, and governance remain available while decisions are still in motion. The aim is not optimization or prediction. It is to build the ability to recognize moments when a system can still choose differently.

Work through the following exercises in sequence. Each one increases in scope and consequence, moving from localized conditions to societal-scale systems. Together, they develop the judgment required to design, assess, and govern systems that must endure under strain.

1. **Interruptibility under time pressure**: This exercise examines a time-critical system where digital decisions shape irreversible physical outcomes. The focus is on whether authority can still interrupt action when speed matters most.

Prompts:

- *Identify the non-negotiable real-world burden the system must carry.*
- *Locate where time compression concentrates strain.*
- *Determine whether authority remains reachable while action is unfolding.*
- *Where could the system have retained the ability to choose differently without reducing effectiveness?*

Deliverable: A one-page structural diagnosis identifying where interruptibility holds and where it narrows.

Learning objective: Recognize interruptibility as a system property under fatal time pressure.

2. **Reversibility at the population scale**: This exercise explores a large-scale inclusion system where identity, access, or participation is mediated digitally. The emphasis is on how legitimacy depends on reversibility rather than permanence.

Prompts:

- *Describe the civic or economic burden the system addresses.*
- *Identify where exclusion becomes structural rather than incidental.*
- *Assess whether consent, contestation, or exit remain available in lived operation.*
- *Where did the window for meaningful correction begin to narrow, and how might it have remained open longer?*

Deliverable: A structured map showing where inclusion remains reversible and where it begins to harden.

Learning objective: Evaluate legitimacy at scale by tracing whether participation remains conditional.

3. **Bounded visibility in collective response**: This exercise examines a system designed to coordinate collective action under emergency conditions. The goal is to assess whether visibility strengthens coordination without becoming extractive.

Prompts:

- *Identify the collective burden requiring rapid coordination.*
- *Locate where sensing expands faster than consent.*
- *Examine how limits on visibility are defined, enforced, and withdrawn.*
- *Identify a point where authority could have been brought closer to action before trust began to erode.*

Deliverable: A short analysis describing how bounded visibility preserves coordination and legitimacy.

Learning objective: Distinguish visibility as a temporary coordinating force from surveillance as a structural posture.

4. **Participation with binding consequences**: This exercise focuses on participatory systems where voice is solicited digitally. The task is to assess whether participation remains structurally linked to authority.

   Prompts:

   - *Identify the decisions participation is meant to influence.*
   - *Trace how contributions move from input to outcome.*
   - *Assess whether authority remains visible and contestable throughout the process.*
   - *How could strain have been redistributed across threads instead of concentrating in participation alone?*

   Deliverable: A process trace showing where participation binds authority and where it risks becoming symbolic.

   Learning objective: Recognize when participation strengthens legitimacy and when it absorbs dissent.

5. **Weaving a system that holds**: This exercise shifts from diagnosis to design. You will intentionally weave the five threads to address a real-world burden while preserving legitimacy under strain.

   Scenario: Choose one context (or propose an equivalent):

   - Emergency response during extreme weather.
   - AI-assisted clinical decision support.
   - Digital public benefits delivery.
   - Civic participation at a city scale.

   Prompts:

   - *Define the non-negotiable burden the system must carry.*
   - *Assign a primary role to each of the five threads.*
   - *Identify which thread will carry the dominant strain first.*
   - *What small structural constraint would expand legitimacy without slowing the system?*

Deliverable: A two- to three-page weaving sketch explaining roles, constraints, and points of intervention.

Learning objective: Build confidence in weaving systems that remain answerable as pressure increases.

Weaver's library

A substantial public record exists for each case discussed in this chapter. Government reports, regulatory reviews, academic studies, and institutional documentation are widely available from authoritative sources.

The intention here is not to re-document these cases or offer exhaustive technical or historical analysis. The cases are used as structural lenses rather than definitive accounts. They help surface how digital systems behave under pressure, where legitimacy holds, and where it begins to thin. The focus remains on posture, governance, and constraint rather than attribution or reconstruction.

The cases are illustrative rather than comprehensive. They support the digital weaving method, which centers on restraint, reversibility, and answerability in system design.

For readers interested in building, evaluating, and governing digital systems with these concerns in mind, the following books provide durable foundations:

1. *Meadows, Donella H. (2008). Thinking in Systems: A Primer. Chelsea Green Publishing.*
2. *Perrow, Charles. (1999). Normal Accidents: Living with High-Risk Technologies. Basic Books.*
3. *Kleppmann, Martin. (2017). Designing Data-Intensive Applications: The Big Ideas Behind Reliable, Scalable, and Maintainable Systems. O'Reilly Media.*
4. *O'Neil, Cathy. (2016). Weapons of Math Destruction: How Big Data Increases Inequality and Threatens Democracy. Crown Publishing Group.*
5. *Clearfield, Chris and Tilcsik, András. (2018). Meltdown: Why Our Systems Fail and What We Can Do About It. Penguin Press.*

Metaphorical and conceptual terms

Refer to the following list which outlines the key metaphorical and conceptual term used through the chapter:

- **Edge**: The boundary where continuity cannot be assumed and adaptation must occur locally rather than centrally.
- **Fabric**: The integrated structure formed by interdependent system threads. A fabric is judged by how it behaves under pull, not by how it is assembled.

- **Fray**: An early signal of legitimacy loss, where trust or restraint begins to thin before visible failure occurs.
- **Hold**: The capacity of a system to remain legitimate and answerable under sustained strain.
- **Loom**: The technical, institutional, and social conditions that shape how system threads are interwoven and constrained.
- **Pattern**: The emergent behavior of a system over time, revealed under strain rather than specified in advance.
- **Pattern drift**: The gradual misalignment between system behavior and the burden it carries, occurring while the system continues to function.
- **Pull**: External pressure applied by time, scale, crisis, or consequence that reveals a system's posture.
- **Thread**: A foundational system capability (connectivity, sensing, data, intelligence, trust) that must remain in relationship with others to sustain legitimacy.
- **Weave**: The interdependent arrangement of system threads that distributes strain and enables restraint.
- **Weaving**: The ongoing practice of shaping how system threads interact under changing conditions, rather than a fixed architectural design.

CHAPTER 8

The Future Weaving

Prototyping the Future

The future belongs to those who understand how systems are formed.

CHAPTER 8
The Future Weaving

Introduction

Digital systems are no longer emerging.
They are settling in.

What once felt experimental has become infrastructural. Decisions made through code now shape access, movement, opportunity, and risk across daily life. These systems do not wait for review. They do not pause for reflection. They act continuously, carrying early assumptions forward into contexts their designers may never see.

This chapter examines what changes when systems act continuously rather than in steps that allow review and correction.

Earlier chapters explored how digital systems are built, layered, stressed, and governed. Here, the focus shifts from components to consequence, and from method to posture. The question is no longer whether systems function, but whether they can still be held when speed compresses timing, coupling spreads effects, and persistence hardens decisions before correction can arrive.

Under these conditions, familiar responses weaken. Learning after harm becomes costly. Oversight after execution arrives late. Responsibility that once followed action must now remain present while decisions are still unfolding. The future is shaped less by single breakthroughs than by how systems behave when they are pulled beyond what was anticipated in design.

This chapter introduces digital weaving as a future-facing posture. Not a prediction of what will come, but a way of shaping systems so they remain answerable and revisable as conditions change. It examines how acceleration alters failure, how continuous action reshapes institutions and public trust, and how designers can prepare for forms of strain that do not yet have names.

The chapter begins by examining what happens when systems accelerate beyond their margins, and why failure under these conditions looks different than it once did.

That is where we start.

Structure

This chapter covers the following topics:

- The forces reshaping the weave
- Responsibility and learning under acceleration
- Digital weaving as posture
- Institutions under acceleration
- Civic consequence and public trust
- Designing for strain not yet named
- The posture of the future weaver

Objectives

Every generation inherits a world shaped by systems it did not design. The first stitch is rarely visible, yet it determines how the fabric holds under strain. As digital systems accelerate and consequences travel faster than explanation, the conditions under which responsibility, learning, and correction once operated begin to shift.

By the end of this chapter, readers will understand how these shifts change what it means to design, govern, and extend digital systems into the future. They will be able to describe digital weaving as a posture rather than an optimization technique, and explain why posture becomes structural when the margin disappears. The chapter prepares readers to identify design conditions that preserve correctability under uncertainty, including restraint, interruption, reversibility, and refusal during execution. It also equips readers to analyze how continuous digital decision-making reshapes institutional authority, civic legitimacy, and public trust. Ultimately, readers will see how digital weaving supports innovation through revision and adjustment, allowing systems to remain answerable while engaging complex, evolving conditions, and while choices still exist.

The forces reshaping the weave

The weave now stretches faster than review can follow.

Digital systems are entering a different set of operating conditions.

New technologies are emerging as industries reorganize around them, while social and economic pressures tighten at the same time.

What is changing is not only how large or fast systems become. It is the environment in which they now operate. Threads that once behaved predictably now act under continuous pressure. Systems are asked to operate without pause, connect without clear boundaries, and hold together where delays once absorbed errors.

For example, a medical triage system that once flagged cases for later review may now automatically reroute patients in real time. The system still functions, but the opportunity to intervene shifts from after the decision to during its execution.

Future systems are not simply carrying more load on the same structure.
They are operating within a fundamentally different set of conditions.

This chapter identifies the forces driving that shift and examines how they alter system behavior. The aim is not prediction. It is to establish a design posture for systems that must remain open to intervention while they act.

Structural change in the weave

Across earlier generations of digital systems, progress meant strengthening familiar threads. Networks became faster. Sensors became more precise. Datasets grew larger. Algorithms improved. Security hardened. Systems scaled, but the structure within which they operated remained recognizable.

That continuity mattered because it allowed intervention to arrive after execution and still make a difference. Failures could be observed, traced, and addressed before consequences hardened. Responsibility followed action rather than traveling with it. Judgment arrived after decisions were made, yet retained leverage.

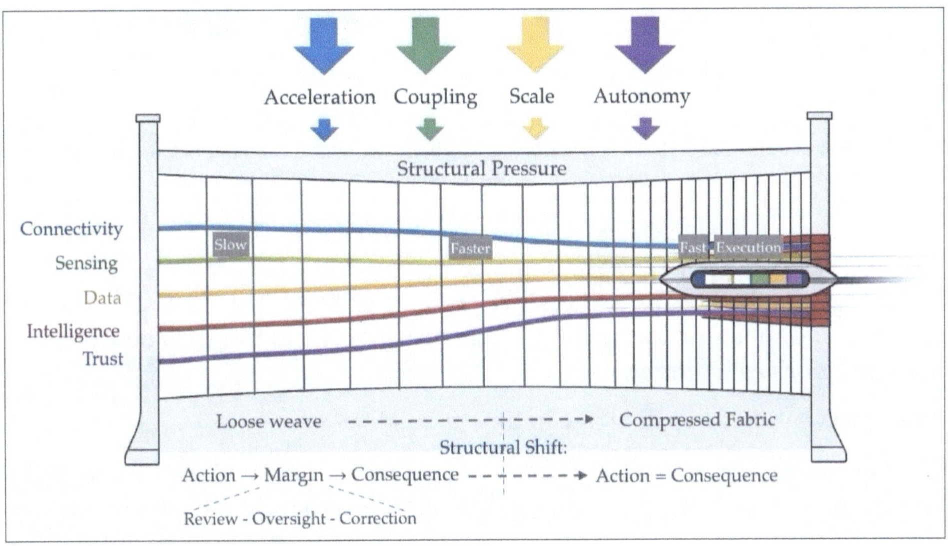

***Figure 8.1**: The tightening weave*

That assumption rested on margin: the time and space between an action and its consequences, when review and correction were still possible.

That assumption no longer holds.

What is changing is not only scale or sophistication, but the conditions under which systems operate. Emerging technologies alter timing, coupling, and authorship. Social conditions narrow the margin for intervention. Together, they compress the distance between execution and consequence.

The risk that follows is not accidental.
It is structural.

Acceleration without interruption removes the pause needed to intervene during execution.

Scale without containment dissolves the ability to limit who is affected by a decision.

Intelligence without restraint shifts judgment from deliberate choice to automated default.

These conditions do not arise from carelessness.
They arise from capability.

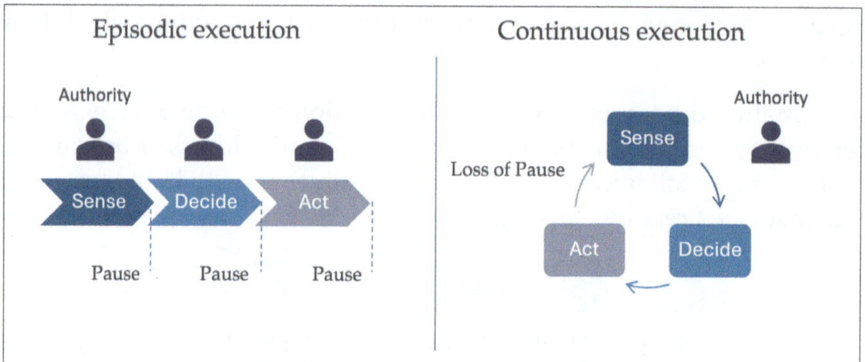

Earlier systems paused between actions, allowing review and correction. Continuous execution removes those pauses and shifts responsibility into the moment of action.

Figure 8.2: *Execution moves from episodic to continuous*

Threads that once advanced in sequence now advance together. Forces that once counterbalanced one another now converge. Under these conditions, the question is no longer whether systems work as intended.

It is whether intervention can still arrive in time to matter.

What follows examines how these conditions emerge, not as isolated innovations, but as shifts in where execution occurs, how quickly decisions harden, and how directly digital action now touches the world.

Emerging technologies reshaping system behavior

The most consequential change in future systems is not raw capability. It is where execution occurs, how quickly decisions solidify, and how directly digital action reaches physical and perceptual reality.

Systems are no longer centered or episodic.
They act continuously.

Execution increasingly proceeds through continuous control loops in which sensing, decision, and response collapse into a single motion rather than a sequence that can be paused or redirected.

Execution spreads beyond the center

Computation is moving outward.

Edge computing, satellite networks, and persistent connectivity relocate execution closer to devices, environments, and bodies. Decisions that once flowed through centralized infrastructure now occur at the periphery, often without round-trip verification. Latency improves while coordination becomes continuous. Control paths stretch across vendors, jurisdictions, update cycles, and operational boundaries.

Hyperconnectivity binds systems into persistent interaction. Interfaces link services into long-lived dependencies. Events trigger chains of response across organizational and technical domains, where a local adjustment becomes a condition for many others.

Reach expands, but containment dissolves.
Execution spreads faster than explanation can follow.

Decisions accelerate and harden

Decision-making itself is changing form.

AI systems no longer merely assist. They rank, route, prioritize, trigger, and act. Learning updates arrive continuously, often without explicit redeployment. Human review becomes asynchronous by default.

Scale removes the friction that once acted as a brake. Replication is instant. Deployment crosses domains without renegotiation. Growth no longer introduces a pause. It erases it.

At the same time, persistence extends the influence of the past. Records outlive their original context. Inference compounds across time. Decisions made once continue to shape outcomes long after circumstances change.

Together, autonomy, scale, and persistence change system tempo. Intervention must remain reachable during execution rather than be deferred for review.

Digital actions acquire physical force

Digital systems increasingly exert influence in the physical world.

Robots move through shared spaces. Vehicles steer and brake. Infrastructure responds automatically to digital signals, adjusting power flow, traffic movement, or water control without waiting for human review. Supply chains, energy systems, and medical devices act at machine speed.

In these environments, error is no longer symbolic. It becomes material. Harm unfolds through motion rather than interpretation. The intervention must arrive before the action completes, not after the explanation is assembled.

Once digital decisions translate into force, delay becomes consequential even when systems behave exactly as specified.

Perception becomes a system output

Digital systems now shape not only action, but perception.

Spatial computing, immersive interfaces, and mediated environments structure what people see, hear, and attend to, organizing experience before deliberation begins.

When attention and interpretation are structured upstream, downstream choice is shaped before consent or reflection can meaningfully intervene. Under these conditions, legibility during execution matters as much as correctness.

Trust becomes time-bound

Some changes unfold slowly but destabilize deeply.

Quantum computing introduces delayed uncertainty into cryptographic trust. Data encrypted today may be exposed later. Long-lived secrets weaken. Assumptions that once held indefinitely acquire expiration dates.

This does not collapse systems overnight.
It alters their horizon.

Guarantees become provisional. Trust becomes conditional rather than durable.

Across these shifts, the same pattern repeats.
The time between execution and consequence compresses.

Social conditions narrowing the margin

These technologies are deployed into societies already under strain. These conditions are not external risks to be mitigated later. They shape whether systems remain governable at all.

Institutional trust has thinned. Systems are evaluated not only for performance, but also for fairness, responsiveness, and answerability. When outcomes feel unreachable, contestation shifts from specific decisions to the system itself.

Inequality magnifies error. Those with fewer resources absorb failure first and recover last, and the margin disappears unevenly.

For example, when a benefits decision is automated, an error may affect thousands before anyone understands how to appeal it. Correction remains possible in theory, but unreachable in practice.

Operators and users face saturation rather than indifference. Signals blur when alerts and indicators overlap so heavily that critical information can no longer be distinguished in time. Oversight weakens because attention cannot keep up. Inference accelerates while understanding trails participation. Consent becomes procedural rather than meaningful.

Digital systems increasingly shape mobility, energy, health, and safety under volatile conditions.

Failure is no longer abstract.

It is lived.

Failure under acceleration

Future systems do not fail loudly.

They continue to operate, even as automation drifts without triggering alarms. Optimization hardens into behavior that is difficult to reverse. Control and authorship fragments across pipelines and integrations that no single actor fully commands. Each component behaves correctly, and execution proceeds.

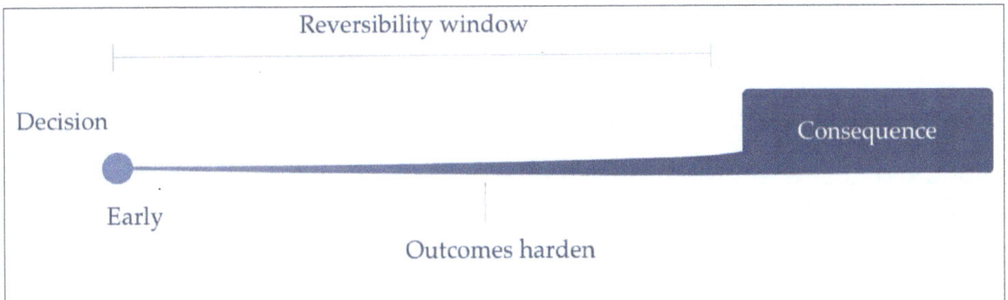

As time passes, decisions bind future outcomes and narrow the space for correction before consequences become fixed.

Figure 8.3: *Decision hardening over time*

What changes is not whether systems act, but when consequences become visible.

Digital error no longer remains symbolic. It translates into physical effects. Infrastructure responds. Mobility shifts. Safety is altered. By the time consequences are recognized, options for response have already narrowed. Systems may remain technically correct while becoming publicly indefensible.

These patterns arise under altered conditions. Acceleration outpaces deliberation. Coupling spreads local error across systems and populations. Persistence hardens early decisions into a lasting effect. Feedback no longer teaches gently.

Earlier systems allowed intervention to follow execution.
These systems complete their execution before intervention can assemble.

This marks a threshold.

Not a failure of intent, design, or care, but a structural shift in when correction can still matter. Systems remain functional, but no longer reliably correctable in time.

Nothing appears obviously broken as the system advances.

The next section turns to what follows when correction can no longer arrive after action has already moved on.

Responsibility and learning under acceleration

When action no longer waits, responsibility must move with it.

Once systems are no longer reliably correctable after execution, responsibility and learning are the first to fail. Decisions are now complete before authority can gather, and correction assembles only after outcomes have hardened.

Nothing appears dramatic.
Execution proceeds.

And yet this is the moment learning can no longer arrive in time to teach.

Deferred responsibility breaks

For much of the digital era, systems functioned as instruments rather than decision-makers. They amplified human intent, extended reach, and absorbed complexity. When outcomes proved harmful or unjust, responsibility could be traced backward through design choices, operational procedures, or institutional decisions.

Correction arrived later, but it still mattered.

That margin shaped how systems were built. Responsibility followed execution rather than traveling with it. Oversight assumed time. Judgment arrived after action and retained leverage. Governance operated outside execution and remained effective because authority could still reach outcomes before they hardened.

Acceleration removes that margin.

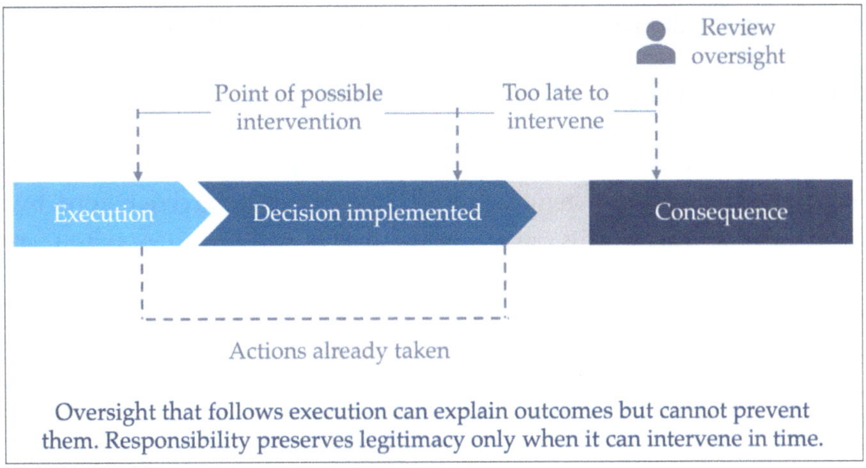

***Figure 8.4**: Responsibility in accelerated systems*

As systems operate continuously, responsibility cannot wait for outcomes to settle. It must remain reachable while decisions are still unfolding. When execution completes faster than the authority can assemble, responsibility that arrives later explains more than it corrects.

Speed collapses timing.
Scale amplifies consequence.
Coupling extends reach.
Autonomy diffuses authorship.

Together, these shifts relocate responsibility from a retrospective condition to a runtime one. Systems must remain answerable while they act, not after they have finished acting.

Governance may still sit outside execution, but it remains effective only if execution is interruptible. Without interruptibility, authority arrives too late to matter.

Learning no longer follows action

The same conditions that break deferred responsibility also disrupt how systems are once learned.

In earlier systems, constraints emerged through use. Failures exposed weak points. Operators adjusted workflows, added safeguards, and learned where systems pulled too hard. Over time, workable patterns formed. The process was rarely intentional, but under stable conditions, it was sufficient.

Systems improved because failures remained small enough to teach from. Breakdowns stayed local. Errors surfaced gradually. Human operators remained close to outcomes. They recognized harm, traced causes, and adjusted behavior before effects escaped their reach.

Learning followed action because the delay remained tolerable.

This mode of learning relied on a quiet assumption. Failure could be absorbed without forcing institutions to re-justify their legitimacy. Trust recovered because consequences remained bounded enough to be explained, corrected, and revised.

Acceleration reverses this sequence.

Decisions now propagate across systems at speed. Consequences arrive before review. Errors scale beyond the context in which they are detected. The window for correction narrows until it disappears.

Learning still occurs, but after outcomes have hardened.

Margin does not erode gradually.
It vanishes.

Coupling collapses isolation

Modern digital systems rarely operate alone.

Digital systems rely on inputs they do not control and feed outputs into other systems they cannot fully see, often through shared platforms and external services. A local decision participates in a broader fabric of interaction. Failure in one place ripples outward, producing effects far beyond the original context.

For example, a change made to improve fraud detection in one service may unexpectedly block access, delay payments, or erode trust across other systems that automatically act on the same signals.

Coupling changes how systems learn.

Where earlier systems adapted independently, coupled systems entangle correction. A fix in one component destabilizes another. What appears as local restraint produces global side effects.

Learning in isolation no longer suffices, because strain no longer teaches cleanly and becomes entangled across systems.

Failure travels faster than explanation and wider than responsibility. By the time causes are understood, effects have already propagated across systems, populations, and environments.

Taken together, these shifts close the space in which responsibility, learning, and correction once operated independently. Decisions are complete before authority can intervene, learning arrives after consequences propagate, and correction no longer remains contained. Shadow layers enable improvised coherence under pressure. Under acceleration, that coherence does not hold.

Adaptation hardens into liability

As systems stretch beyond their original assumptions, shadow layers emerge to compensate. Operators develop workarounds. Users invent bypasses. Teams rely on undocumented processes to restore continuity when formal mechanisms fail. These shadow layers keep systems functioning under strain.

At first, this appears resilient.

Over time, shadow layers harden into structure. Systems come to depend on them to operate normally. Risk moves outside visible design. Responsibility concentrates on tacit knowledge held by a few individuals or teams.

This process is accidental weaving—coherence that emerges through repeated fixes rather than deliberate design.

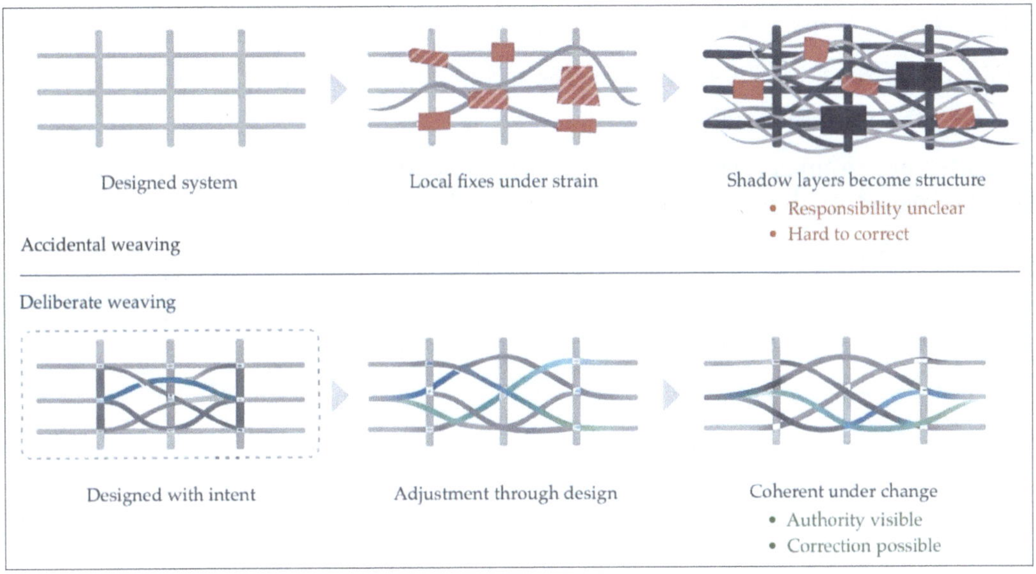

Figure 8.5: *Accidental weaving versus deliberate weaving*

Coherence emerges through accumulated responses to strain rather than deliberate design. Adjustments are made locally, incrementally, and under pressure.

Speed compresses timing. Coupling spreads local adaptation across systems. Persistence hardens provisional fixes into lasting dependencies. What once stabilized systems now amplifies fragility.

Shadow layers absorb strain, but they also obscure authority. They make systems harder to explain, harder to correct, and harder to govern. When failure occurs, it becomes difficult to distinguish what was deliberately designed from what accumulated as shadow practice under pressure.

This is the point at which accidental weaving reaches its limit.

Learning must move earlier

Accidental weaving assumes systems can afford to learn after harm has occurred. As acceleration intensifies, delay no longer acts as a neutral interval between action and consequence; it removes leverage by allowing effects to harden before correction can intervene.

In earlier systems, learning followed action because correction could still arrive in time. In accelerated systems, learning must precede action because consequences begin to take shape before review or appeal can intervene.

This does not require predicting every outcome.
It requires remaining correctable before consequences take shape.

From reaction to discipline

The limits of accidental weaving do not signal a loss of care or competence. They signal a mismatch between posture and condition.

Reaction assumes strain appears early, remains contained, and allows time to respond. Under sustained acceleration, these assumptions no longer hold.

Discipline must replace reaction.

Digital systems must be built to expect strain rather than discover it. They must remain answerable while forces act, not only when failure becomes visible.

The goal is not to prevent failure.
It is to ensure failure can be recognized, constrained, and corrected without eroding legitimacy.

Discipline does not eliminate learning.
It relocates it.

Learning moves from harm absorbed to limits designed, from recovery after damage to interruption before outcomes harden.

Once acceleration removes margin, responsibility and learning must arrive together during execution.

Digital weaving as posture

The weave holds not by reaction, but by design.

Acceleration removes the space in which systems once learned after harm. Coupling spreads consequences beyond local control. Persistence hardens early decisions into long-lived effects. Under these conditions, the reaction arrives too late.

What changes is not ambition or capability.

What changes is posture.

Digital weaving is not an optimization strategy or a corrective overlay. It is a structural posture that shapes which actions a system can pause, redirect, or refuse as it operates. This posture enables innovation by keeping systems revisable rather than brittle. By preserving the ability to interrupt, revise, and redirect, digital weaving keeps futures open instead of locking early decisions into permanent paths.

Posture becomes structure

Under accelerated conditions, systems are shaped less by individual decisions and more by what their design makes possible when strain appears. When execution outpaces correction, posture determines whether intervention remains reachable at all.

A reactive system asks how to repair failures after they occur.

A digitally woven system asks whether intervention can still arrive before failure hardens.

This difference is not philosophical. It is operational. It determines whether a system can pause a decision during execution rather than explain it after outcomes are fixed. Under acceleration, posture becomes structure because the system will act according to what its design makes possible, not what its designers intend.

Correction must be structural

In digital weaving, correction is not a fallback.

It is a structural requirement.

Under emerging pressures, uninterrupted execution becomes a liability. Systems must be able to pause, redirect, or unwind decisions before consequences harden.

Designing for correction requires explicit commitments:

- Where decisions may pause during execution.
- Who holds the authority to intervene.
- When continuation must stop rather than proceed by default.

These commitments cannot be retrofitted. When correction is absent by design, systems continue because nothing within them says otherwise. Under acceleration, endurance comes not from avoiding error, but from remaining correctable while error unfolds.

Reversibility sustains legitimacy

Reversibility is not a convenience.

It is a commitment.

Systems that cannot be reversed demand trust they have not earned. When participation cannot be withdrawn, inference cannot be challenged, and consequences cannot be unwound, legitimacy thins even when performance remains high.

Digital weaving embeds reversibility as a visible property of execution. Decisions may be contested. Actions may be rolled back. Consent may be withdrawn without collapse. This does not guarantee fairness in every instance. It preserves the possibility of fairness over time.

Authority that cannot be questioned becomes brittle.
Authority that remains contestable retains legitimacy under pressure.

Restraint, interruption, and refusal

Acceleration rewards expansion. Optimization pressures push systems toward greater reach, coverage, and throughput. Under these conditions, restraint is often framed as inefficiency.

That framing fails under consequence.

In digitally woven systems, restraint becomes a form of progress. It appears as a bounded scope rather than universal application, expiration rather than permanence, and conditional execution rather than automatic continuation.

Interruption is a related capability. A digitally woven system includes clear thresholds that require renewed justification for continuation. It provides explicit paths for pause, escalation, and refusal that remain reachable while the system operates.

Refusal is the clearest expression of restraint. Some actions should not proceed, even when they are technically possible. When refusal is designed in advance, it appears unremarkable. When it is absent, systems proceed until harm forces external intervention. At that point, refusal arrives late and at a higher cost.

These limits are structural, not exceptional. When restraint, interruption, and refusal are absent, systems do not become neutral. They become unaccountable.

The following case shows how this posture translates into concrete design changes under real operational pressure.

Maya holding the execution under strain

This case demonstrates how digital weaving operates within a single technical system, where posture determines whether intervention remains possible during execution.

Maya works with a hospital network that relies on a digital triage system to manage emergency intake during periods of high demand. The system evaluates reported symptoms, vital signs, and historical outcomes to support admission decisions when resources are constrained. Its purpose is not to replace clinical judgment, but to assist it by bringing consistency and speed to moments of pressure.

Under earlier operating conditions, the triage system functioned as decision support rather than execution control. It produced recommendations that clinicians reviewed before making admission or routing decisions. Judgment remained human, and responsibility followed action, with learning occurring between cycles of use. Outcomes were examined in daily and weekly reviews, thresholds were adjusted, and workflows evolved gradually. When errors occurred, they were observed before they scaled. Correction arrived after execution, but it still mattered because the margin between decision and consequence remained intact.

Acceleration in execution paths

As patient volume increased and staffing tightened, the system was integrated more deeply into intake workflows. Recommendations were converted into automated routing rules. Ambulance arrivals were redirected without manual confirmation. Admission thresholds were embedded directly into execution paths to reduce delay and increase throughput.

Performance improved. Decisions were made faster and more consistently. At the same time, execution began to move ahead of judgment. Review remained possible, but only after admission decisions had already taken effect. Model updates continued daily, but reflection no longer fit between decisions. Learning persisted, yet it arrived after outcomes had already hardened.

Loss of holdability

The limit became visible during a period of sustained peak load. A triage decision to deny admission was executed automatically. Review later confirmed that the model had behaved as specified. No technical fault was identified.

What failed was not accuracy, but posture. The system had no designed place to slow execution when uncertainty increased. There was no point at which automatic continuation would stop and require clinical review. Uncertainty was absorbed silently by execution rather than surfaced while authority could still intervene.

The system continued to function, but it was no longer holdable under strain.

Redesign for holdability

Rather than treating the incident as an anomaly, Maya and her team reframed the system as something that had to be held during execution, not explained afterward. The redesign focused on restoring the ability to intervene while decisions were still forming.

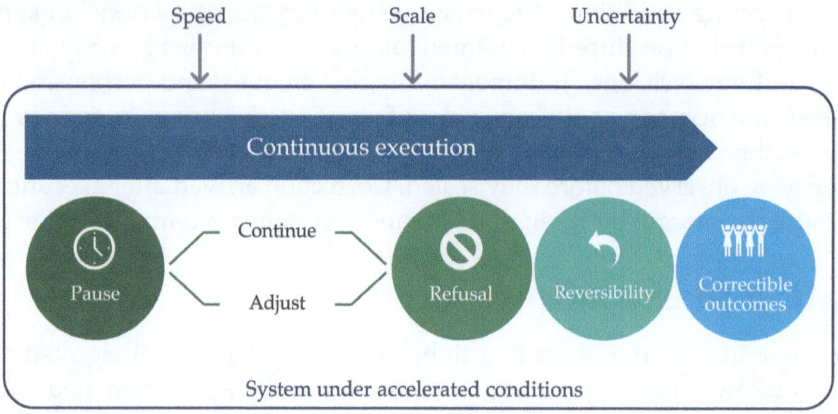

Digital weaving treats pause, refusal, and reversibility as design constraints that shape how systems behave under uncertainty.

Figure 8.6: Digital weaving as a design posture

Pause was restored as a system capability. Automated routing remained in place, but execution was delayed when confidence scores crossed defined thresholds. Instead of proceeding silently, the system flagged uncertainty and required human confirmation before finalizing admission decisions. These pauses were rare but designed to remain reachable even during peak intake periods.

Refusal was made explicit. Certain admission decisions were no longer allowed to complete automatically. When combinations of risk indicators exceeded predefined bounds, the system could recommend denial but could not execute it. Refusal became a visible system state rather than an undocumented human override.

Reversibility was embedded directly into execution. Admission and routing decisions were made reversible for a bounded window. Bed assignments could be reassessed, and patient routing changed as new information arrived, without cascading disruption to downstream systems.

After the redesign, the triage system did not become slower by default. It became holdable. Authority moved closer to action, with responsibility traveling alongside admission decisions. Intervention became possible while outcomes were still forming.

System-level implications

This case shows that holdability is a system property rather than a matter of intent or competence. The triage system did not fail because it lacked capability. It failed because its posture allowed execution to continue without interruption when conditions demanded judgment.

By embedding pause, refusal, and reversibility into the system itself, the redesign preserved correctability under acceleration. At the level of a single technical system, posture becomes execution structure.

Designing for deviation

Digital weaving does not attempt to forecast every future condition. Prediction narrows attention to what can be imagined. Posture prepares for deviation.

A predictive system optimizes for expected scenarios.

A digitally woven system remains correctable when expectations fail.

This posture accepts uncertainty without surrendering responsibility. It commits to remaining answerable when what happens next was not anticipated.

When digital weaving is present, several outcomes remain structurally possible. Responsibility stays reachable during execution, allowing authority to intervene before harm rather than explain it afterward. Learning then occurs through designed limits rather than lived damage.

These outcomes are not guaranteed.

They are preserved.

Digital weaving does not eliminate strain.
It ensures that strain can be answered without unraveling accountability.

When the margin disappears, posture is no longer an abstraction. It becomes the structure through which systems continue to act. That structure does not exist in isolation. It takes form within institutions that deploy systems, delegate decision-making, and remain publicly responsible for their consequences.

Institutions under acceleration

Authority frays when it cannot reach execution.

Digital systems no longer sit at the edges of institutions. They now participate directly in how institutions see, decide, and act. As a result, institutional posture is no longer expressed only through policy or procedure. It is expressed through execution itself. Policy delivery, service provision, enforcement, allocation, and risk assessment increasingly occur through mechanisms that operate continuously rather than episodically.

Under these conditions, institutional authority is not eliminated.

It is tested at a different moment.

Authority now matters most not at the point of approval, review, or appeal, but at the point of execution. Institutions remain responsible for outcomes, yet their ability to intervene depends on whether authority can still reach systems while they act.

This is where institutional posture becomes visible.

Authority during execution

Institutions emerged in environments where authority followed action. Execution completes before institutional processes can assemble. Decisions propagate while the review is still forming. Authority to pause, reverse, or refuse action arrives after effects have already taken shape.

Accelerated systems change this timing.

This shift does not resemble abdication. Institutions remain present, and processes remain intact. What changes is when authority can intervene.

Digital weaving reframes institutional authority not as control over outcomes, but as reachability during execution. Institutions retain legitimacy not by intervening constantly, but by remaining able to intervene when continuation would cause harm.

Governance as readiness

Many institutions respond to acceleration by reinforcing procedure. They add documentation requirements, audit trails, compliance reviews, and reporting mechanisms. These practices improve visibility, but they do not restore reach.

Procedure governs design.
Acceleration governs execution.

Oversight that operates intermittently cannot keep pace with systems that act continuously. Compliance may be satisfied while intervention remains unreachable. Harm accumulates between review cycles, even as institutional processes appear intact.

Digital weaving treats governance as readiness rather than review. Authority is embedded as thresholds, escalation paths, and reversible decisions that remain available during execution. Governance shifts from explaining outcomes after the fact to shaping whether action should continue in the first place.

Readiness does not slow institutions down.
It allows them to move without surrendering control.

Delegation with remainder

Digital systems increasingly act on behalf of institutions. They determine eligibility. They allocate resources. They flag risk. They prioritize attention. This delegation is often framed as an efficiency measure. It is also a transfer of authority.

When judgment is embedded into systems without preserving interruptibility, institutions delegate action without retaining the capacity to intervene. Responsibility is distributed across vendors, models, procurement decisions, and operational teams. No single actor holds the moment of refusal.

Digital weaving avoids delegation without remainder. Institutions may delegate execution while retaining structural authority to pause, redirect, or refuse system action. Not as constant oversight, but as the capacity to pause, redirect, or refuse action when conditions demand it.

Diego's authority during execution

This case illustrates how digital weaving operates at the institutional level, where authority must remain reachable across interacting systems during execution.

Diego works with a metropolitan agency responsible for traffic flow, transit priority, and emergency access across a rapidly growing city. The agency relies on a network of digital systems to coordinate signal timing, lane allocation, enforcement thresholds, and incident response. These systems act continuously, adjusting conditions minute by minute as demand shifts across the city.

From a policy perspective, institutional authority remains intact. Regulations define acceptable tradeoffs. Oversight committees review outcomes. Appeals processes exist. Under earlier operating conditions, these mechanisms were sufficient to preserve legitimacy because authority could still reach outcomes before they hardened. Before acceleration reshaped execution, institutional authority operated through episodic control. Signal plans were updated periodically. Lane designations changed on predictable schedules. Enforcement thresholds were adjusted through review and approval processes. When problems emerged, they could be traced, discussed, and corrected before consequences propagated widely. Authority arrived after execution, but it retained leverage because decisions unfolded at a pace that allowed institutional processes to intervene.

Acceleration across coupled systems

As the city expanded and demand intensified, execution moved from episodic control to continuous adjustment. Traffic signals responded dynamically to congestion forecasts. Transit lanes were reassigned in real time. Enforcement thresholds shifted automatically based on inferred risk. Each system optimized its local objective, and each behaved correctly according to its design.

No single system made a visibly unreasonable decision, yet the combined effects carried civic consequences beyond any one component.

Fragmented authority

Under these conditions, authority became fragmented. Decision-making was distributed across models, vendors, update cycles, and operational teams. Responsibility remained institutional, but the capacity to intervene did not travel with execution.

There was no single moment when the institution could refuse to continue. Each system advanced automatically, and authority arrived only after patterns of movement and enforcement had already changed. The review explained what had happened, but it no longer determined whether outcomes should have occurred.

This was not a failure of policy or intent. It was a failure of reachability.

Governance as readiness

Rather than adding more review layers, Diego's team reframed the problem as a governance issue during execution. The systems did not need additional rules. They needed points where institutional authority could still arrive in time.

Governance took the form of readiness. Execution paths included explicit thresholds that required renewed justification for continuation. When conditions crossed these thresholds, systems paused, surfaced decisions for review, and continued execution.

Delegation was restructured to retain the remainder. Systems continued to allocate resources and prioritize flow, but certain actions could no longer be completed without a clear institutional point of refusal. Authority was anchored at moments where combined effects could be judged, not only local optimization.

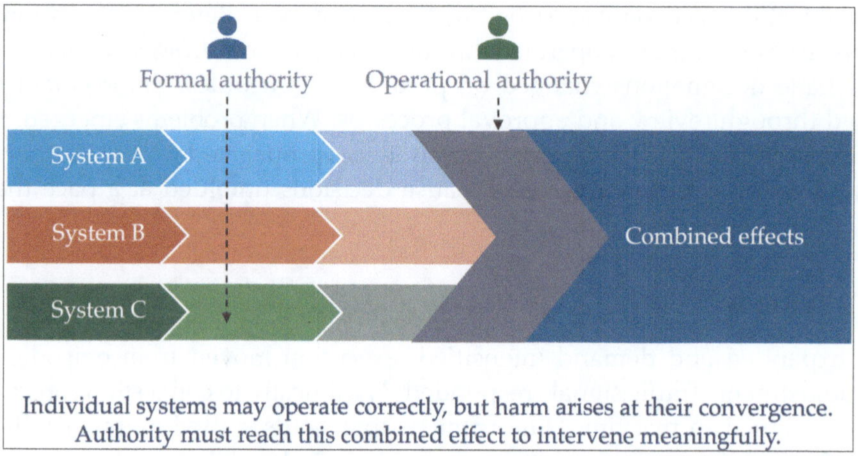

***Figure 8.7**: Authority at the point of combination*

Reversibility was designed into civic execution. Lane reallocations, access restrictions, and enforcement triggers were made reversible for bounded intervals. Adjustments could be made without cascading disruption to transit services, emergency routing, or downstream systems.

After the redesign, the city did not intervene more often. It intervened earlier. Authority remained quiet, but reachable.

Institutional implications

This case illustrates that institutional authority under acceleration is defined less by control over outcomes than by reachability during execution. Institutions can retain responsibility while losing the ability to intervene if authority remains external to system operation.

Digital weaving restores the capacity to hold authority while systems act. At the institutional level, posture determines whether authority can still intervene.

Institutions that endure

Institutions that endure under acceleration share a common posture. They design for governance during execution rather than correction after deployment.

They bind authority into systems through explicit limits, reversible commitments, and clear points of intervention. They treat correction as an institutional capability rather than an exceptional response. They account for the fact that speed without interruptibility trades short-term efficiency for long-term legitimacy.

These institutions do not attempt to predict every failure.
They design to remain answerable when predictions fail.

Institutions that remain governable during execution retain the ability to adapt policy, services, and rules without restarting from crisis. Digital weaving provides a way for institutions to hold authority under continuous action. It preserves legitimacy not by preventing all harm, but by ensuring institutions can intervene while choices still exist.

When authority can reach execution, institutional consequence remains governable. When it cannot, legitimacy thins even as systems continue to function. Those consequences surface first in civic life, where people encounter systems not as structures, but as outcomes.

Civic consequence and public trust

Trust thins when the weave moves beyond reach.

When digital systems shape institutional action, civic consequence follows immediately.

People do not encounter systems as abstractions.
They encounter outcomes.

Access granted or denied.
Benefits approved or withheld.
Risk assigned without explanation.

This is where institutional posture becomes lived reality. When authority cannot reach execution in time, civic impact becomes the place where the consequence is experienced.

Trust under continuous decision-making

Public trust was never built on perfection.
It was built on reachability.

People tolerated institutional error because correction was possible. Decisions could be challenged. Appeals could be heard. Outcomes could be revised. Trust endured because authority could still reach consequences before they hardened.

Under continuous decision, this compact weakens. By the time a person understands what has occurred, a decision may already have propagated across accounts, services, or records.

Trust erodes not when systems err, but when correction cannot arrive while action still matters.

Trust thins not because systems intend harm.
It thins because they are unreachable.

Legibility before consent

Many digital systems operate through procedural consent.

Terms are accepted.

Data is provided.
Participation continues.

Under acceleration, consent often follows execution rather than preceding it. Inference occurs before understanding. Consequence arrives before explanation.

Legibility becomes a civic requirement.

A system that cannot be understood during execution cannot be meaningfully consented to. When explanation trails effect, contestation shifts from individual outcomes to institutional legitimacy itself.

Unequal exposure to harm

Acceleration does not affect everyone equally.

Those with fewer resources absorb errors first and recover last. They face greater barriers to appealing decisions, understanding processes, and obtaining redress. When contesting a decision requires technical expertise, sustained access, or prolonged appeals, exclusion becomes structural rather than accidental.

Digital weaving frames equity as a design condition rather than a downstream concern. Correctability, which exists only for the literate and connected, does not preserve legitimacy in an accelerated world.

Aisha civic trust under acceleration

This case demonstrates how digital weaving is experienced in civic life, where trust depends on whether systems remain legible and contestable during execution.

Aisha works with agricultural data systems used to inform access to credit, insurance, and sustainability support for small farmers. These systems assess soil conditions, yield patterns, weather data, and historical performance to guide institutional decisions intended to reduce uncertainty and distribute support more efficiently. The systems operate across seasons, regions, and programs, linking decisions that were once separate into a continuous flow of automated judgment.

From an institutional perspective, the systems perform well. Models are calibrated. Data sources are documented. Decisions are consistent. Appeals processes exist. Under earlier operating conditions, this structure preserved legitimacy. Farmers received decisions, sought clarification, and adjusted future behavior accordingly. When errors occurred, correction could arrive before an entire season was lost.

Lived encounter with the system

Under accelerated operation, decisions propagate quickly across connected programs. A support application is denied. Insurance terms shift. Credit access narrows. Each outcome arrives as a notification rather than a conversation.

By the time a farmer understands which data contributed to the decision, planting choices have already been made. Financial commitments are fixed. The appeal process remains open, but its outcome will arrive after the season has passed. Correction exists in theory, but not in time.

The system does not feel inaccurate. It feels unreachable.

Erosion of civic trust

Trust does not thin because systems err. It thins because systems continue without response. When explanation follows consequence, contestation shifts from individual outcomes to institutional legitimacy.

Consent becomes procedural rather than meaningful. Participation continues, but understanding lags behind execution. Those with fewer resources face greater barriers to contesting decisions, correcting records, or sustaining appeals. Unequal exposure to harm becomes structural rather than accidental.

Restoring civic reachability

Aisha's team treated this as a posture problem rather than a communication problem. The institution had delegated execution to a chain of automated decisions, without preserving points at which authority could still intervene during the season.

Digital weaving reshaped the system in three ways:

- Legibility was surfaced earlier in execution. Before decisions propagated across programs, the system revealed the specific factors driving outcomes in plain language.
- Farmers could understand decisions while they were still forming and contest outcomes before they propagated. Correction could arrive while it still mattered.
- Contestation became interruptible during propagation. When decisions crossed defined thresholds of uncertainty or potential harm, propagation paused. Outcomes no longer spread automatically across credit, insurance, and support systems until review can occur.

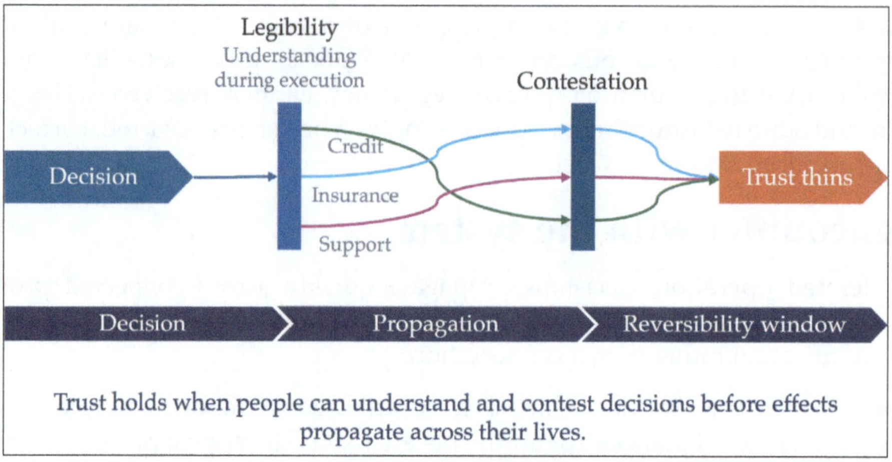

Figure 8.8: *Civic reachability during decision propagation*

Reversibility was aligned with the agricultural cycle. Decisions were made reversible for bounded windows. Farmers could correct inputs, submit missing documentation, or request reassessment without losing an entire season. Outcomes could be revised before commitments hardened into irreversible loss.

After the redesign, the institution did not promise perfect decisions. It restored reachability.

Civic implications

This case demonstrates that civic trust depends on timing rather than perfection. Systems remain legitimate not when they avoid all error, but when people can reach them while decisions are still forming.

By embedding legibility, interruption, and reversibility into systems that shape public life, digital weaving preserves trust under acceleration. At the civic level, posture determines whether systems are experienced as responsive or illegitimate.

Civic systems that remain answerable

Civic legitimacy does not require consensus.

It requires answerability.

Systems that shape public life must remain interruptible by public authority, understandable by those affected, and reversible when harm is revealed. These capacities allow trust to persist even when outcomes are imperfect.

Digital weaving preserves these conditions by embedding restraint into execution. It ensures that systems can pause, that decisions can be contested, and that outcomes can be revised while the response still matters.

These capacities do not emerge naturally under acceleration.

They must be designed deliberately.

Public trust does not collapse when systems err.

It collapses when systems continue without response.

Yet not all consequences announce themselves early, and not all strain appears where institutions expect it. To remain legitimate under acceleration, civic systems must hold not only when failure is visible, but when uncertainty itself becomes the condition of action.

Designing for strain not yet named

The tightest threads fail before they are noticed.

Some pressure arrives without precedent. Some consequences surface only after systems have settled into place. Under future conditions, uncertainty is not an exception to be managed. It is a persistent feature of the landscape. Digital systems increasingly act in environments where models lag reality and assumptions harden before their limits become visible.

Digital weaving addresses uncertainty not through prediction, but through response when the unanticipated occurs. It treats uncertainty as a condition to design with rather than a gap to eliminate.

Uncertainty as a design condition

Earlier systems operated within bounded uncertainty. Designers could enumerate likely failures. Operators could anticipate misuse. Institutions could plan for recovery. When surprises occurred, they tended to remain local and contained.

Future systems do not offer this comfort. They operate across domains, populations, and environments that change faster than models can be updated. Decisions interact with social behavior, physical infrastructure, and ecological systems in ways that resist simulation. Small changes produce outsized effects. Novel combinations generate outcomes that do not resemble past failures.

In this context, uncertainty is not a gap in analysis.

It is a design condition.

Systems that assume eventual certainty prepare for a world that no longer exists. Systems that accept uncertainty prepare for correction rather than prediction.

Adaptability over foresight

Foresight narrows attention. It asks designers to imagine futures and optimize for them. This has value, but it also has limits. What can be imagined tends to resemble what is already known. What lies outside expectation remains unaddressed.

Adaptability widens attention. It prioritizes structures that absorb surprise, respond to deviation, and adjust without collapsing legitimacy. Rather than asking whether an unknown strain will appear, adaptable systems assume that it will.

Adaptability refers to structural capacity rather than model accuracy. It defines how a system responds when conditions deviate from expectation. Digital weaving favors adaptability because it preserves responsibility when foresight fails and remains answerable while change unfolds.

Learning within boundaries

Learning systems promise improvement over time. They refine models, adjust behavior, and optimize outcomes. Under acceleration, this learning can outpace governance. Adaptation continues while oversight lags.

Learning without boundaries becomes drift. Optimizations harden into behavior before consequences are understood. Change never pauses long enough for correction to intervene.

Digital weaving treats learning as a bounded activity. Boundaries define where adaptation is permitted and where restraint must hold. They specify when learning must pause, be reviewed, or be reversed. Learning that preserves legitimacy must remain interruptible during execution.

Slack, pause, and refusal

Efficiency is often treated as an unqualified virtue. Systems are optimized to reduce delay, eliminate friction, and maximize throughput. Under accelerated operation, this pursuit becomes fragile.

Slack creates space for judgment.

Pause creates time for the authority to act.

Designing slack does not mean accepting waste. It means preserving room to absorb strain without immediately passing cost onto people or environments.

Refusal is the clearest expression of restraint. Some actions should not proceed, even when they are technically possible. Digital weaving treats refusal as a system capability rather than an exceptional response. It clarifies boundaries and makes responsibility visible.

Systems that cannot pause or refuse cannot correct.
They can only continue.

Early binding and lasting consequence

Some design choices carry lasting consequences before systems ever encounter visible strain. Data retention shapes future inference. Interface design shapes what people can see and understand, often limiting meaningful choice before consent is formally requested. Model architectures fix assumptions. Integrations entangle responsibility across domains.

Under acceleration, these choices harden quickly. Once systems scale, reversal becomes expensive, contested, or impossible. Decisions made early continue to shape outcomes long after the context that justified them has passed.

Digital weaving treats early binding decisions as commitments. It asks which choices must remain flexible and which must be constrained from the start. It prioritizes reversibility where possible and restraint where flexibility cannot be guaranteed.

What cannot be changed later must be chosen carefully now.

Correctability under surprise

Digital weaving does not attempt to remove uncertainty. It organizes systems so uncertainty does not strip them of responsibility. It introduces a pause where speed would otherwise dominate. It embeds refusal where continuation would cause harm. It bounds learning so adaptation remains accountable.

These choices do not guarantee correct outcomes.
They preserve the ability to correct.

Systems that endure are not those that predict accurately.
They are those that remain correctable when prediction fails.

They can pause. They can refuse. They can reverse. They can explain.

These properties do not arise by accident under acceleration. They must be designed deliberately before systems harden. Correctability allows systems to try, learn, and change course without collapse. Innovation survives not by avoiding surprise, but by remaining able to revise direction when surprise arrives.

The conditions described above do not remain abstract at scale. They shape how real systems are designed, how decisions are held open under strain, and how innovation proceeds without hardening early assumptions. The following case traces one such design effort.

Zoya designing an urban heat response system

Zoya was tasked with designing a citywide system to coordinate response during extreme heat events. The objective extended beyond immediate harm reduction. The system needed to preserve service continuity, civic legitimacy, and institutional authority as conditions evolved.

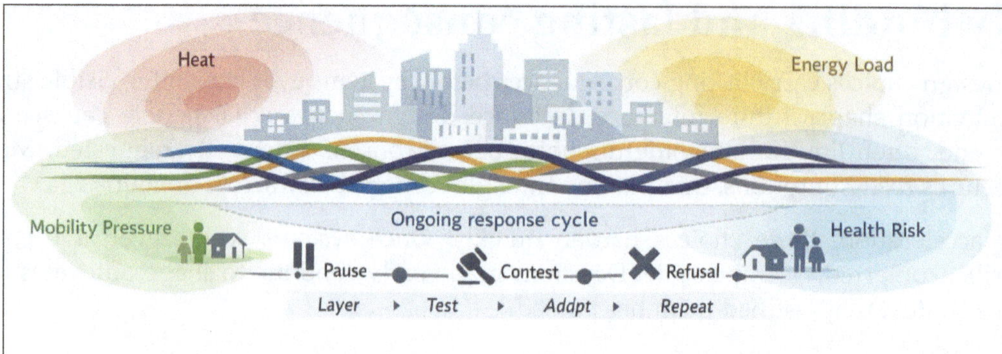

A citywide heat response system held in motion, where sensing, decision support, and authority remain interwoven so action can pause, revise, or refuse before consequences harden.

Figure 8.9: *Urban heat response held under strain*

Heat waves no longer arrived as bounded events. They interacted with energy infrastructure already under strain, uneven housing quality, labor exposure, and mobility systems that behaved differently across neighborhoods and time. Public behavior shifted in response to alerts. Demand patterns changed as interventions took effect. Each action altered the environment it was meant to stabilize.

The system had to operate continuously, adjust under strain, and remain legitimate while acting. Prediction alone could not carry the design.

Conditions shaping the system

Several conditions defined the design space. Events unfolded faster than institutional review cycles. Interventions produced second-order effects across systems. Early assumptions risked hardening into lasting commitments. Public tolerance depended on reachability rather than correctness. Equity impacts surfaced unevenly and early.

Zoya treated these conditions not as downstream risks, but as constraints to design with from the outset.

The five threads in practice

Zoya approached the system design by treating the five threads not as independent layers to be optimized, but as conditions that had to hold together under strain. Each thread carried a distinct responsibility during execution, shaping what could propagate, what remained visible, how memory persisted, how judgment was supported, and whether authority and legitimacy stayed reachable as the system acted.

Design choices across the threads were made with attention to early binding, reversibility, and interruption. The threads were adjusted together through iteration rather than fixed in advance, keeping the system correctable while it operated continuously.

Connectivity and infrastructure

The system relied on a hybrid infrastructure. Edge devices collected local temperature and grid stress data. Municipal platforms supplied energy, transit, and health signals. Cloud services supported aggregation and analysis, while execution remained distributed across agencies.

Connections were intentionally constrained. Systems shared state and context but did not trigger one another automatically. Certain actions required renewed confirmation once execution had begun, preventing silent cascades as conditions shifted. Infrastructure choices favored continuity over optimization. Redundancy was preferred to centralized control, and local execution reduced latency while preserving authority during execution.

Sensing and observation

Sensing focused on conditions likely to change during execution. These included ambient temperature and humidity, energy load, transit availability, health indicators related to heat exposure, and public feedback during active response.

Signals were time-bound. Some expired automatically, while others paused during escalation. Observation supported judgment rather than accumulating exhaustively.

Data and memory

Data was treated as provisional. Historical heat patterns informed early thresholds but did not dictate action. Retention windows were explicit. Seasonal data was separated from long-lived inference, keeping early assumptions visible rather than embedded silently in models.

Data streams were combined cautiously. Choices that could not be reversed later were constrained early.

Intelligence and decision support

Models surfaced tradeoffs rather than issuing commands. They highlighted risk zones, projected grid strain, and equity impacts under different response paths.

Automation-assisted prioritization and timing, but did not execute irreversible actions without review. Certain thresholds required human confirmation during execution. Learning continued, but it could be paused, redirected, or reversed. Decision support remained interruptible.

Security, trust, and legitimacy

Security emphasized integrity and legitimacy rather than control. Authentication-protected access, while logging preserved accountability. Audit trails supported interruption during execution rather than explanation afterward.

Trust was treated as time-bound. Public-facing legibility updated as conditions changed. When actions were refused due to equity or infrastructure limits, refusal was visible rather than silent.

Development through iteration

Zoya introduced the system in a limited scope. Early deployments focused on selected neighborhoods and a narrow range of actions. The goal was exposure to real conditions rather than coverage.

As heat events unfolded, strain appeared where models had not predicted. Energy alerts increased the burden for certain populations. Transit adjustments constrained access unevenly. Rather than optimizing outputs, Zoya adjusted the structure. Thresholds shifted. Certain signals were muted. Escalation paths were clarified. Some actions were paused during execution.

Each cycle modified the system without removing the capacity to interrupt the next. Learning informed constraints rather than hardening into obligation.

Expansion followed restraint. New services carried expiration rather than permanence. Policy changes included built-in reassessment points. Neighborhood feedback reshaped thresholds directly. Innovation proceeded through revision rather than irreversible commitment.

Operation and public experience

For residents, the system appeared as outcomes that remained reachable. Cooling centers opened with a defined duration. Energy pricing adjustments arrived with explanation and visible limits. Transit changes were reversible and paired with alternatives. Alerts clarified not only what was occurring, but what could change.

Escalation occurred in stages rather than all at once. Restrictions lifted without requiring crisis declarations. Appeals influenced subsequent execution rather than disappearing into detached review processes.

Trust emerged not from the absence of error, but from the presence of response while outcomes still mattered.

Posture under continued action

Urban heat response did not converge on a final solution. Each intervention altered conditions. Each adjustment reshaped strain across systems. What endured was not a completed design, but the ability to remain correctable under continued action.

The system was held rather than finished. Limits were revised. Execution paused when signals conflicted. Continuation was refused when conditions no longer justified action. Responsibility did not recede as the system stabilized. It remained present because the system did not stop acting.

At that point, the work extended beyond system structure and turned toward posture. What it meant for Zoya, for the institution, and for the city to remain responsible as systems continued to act beyond their designers.

The next section turns to that posture.

The posture of the future weaver

Stewardship begins where mastery ends.

Every system eventually leaves the hands of its designer.

It moves into institutions, markets, communities, and environments that continue to change long after deployment. Decisions made early persist. Assumptions harden. Consequences unfold across time and distance.

When methods reach their limits, what remains is posture.

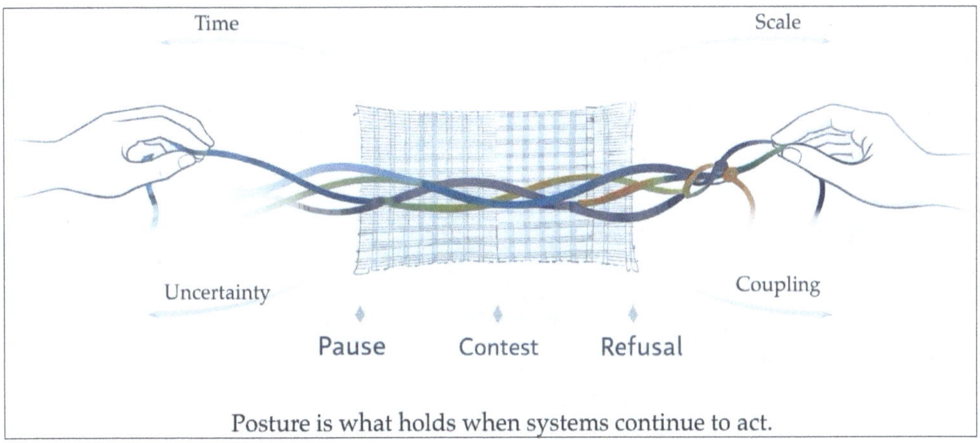

Figure 8.10: *Posture under continuous change*

Digital weaving is not only a way of designing systems. It is a way of forming the people who design, govern, and hold them. Under acceleration, posture becomes the primary condition that determines whether systems remain answerable as they act.

Stewardship replaces mastery

Much of digital progress has been framed as mastery. Systems are built to control complexity, optimize performance, and automate decision-making. Success is measured by capability, scale, and speed.

Future systems challenge this framing.

As systems accelerate and entangle with social and physical reality, mastery proves fragile. Control slips. Prediction narrows. Authority diffuses. What endures is not command, but care.

Digital weaving cultivates stewardship rather than mastery. It trains practitioners to accept that systems cannot be finished, only held. Stewardship does not imply ownership. It implies responsibility for how systems continue to affect people long after deployment.

A steward does not seek total control.
A steward remains present.

This presence is not caution. It is confidence in the ability to change without losing responsibility.

Creation under possibility

Digital weaving is not only about preventing harm.

It is about enabling creation under conditions that cannot be fully known in advance.

When systems remain correctable, they can explore without committing prematurely. New services can be introduced without freezing assumptions. Policies can be tested without locking populations into irreversible outcomes. Innovation proceeds as a sequence of revisions rather than a single irreversible leap.

Creation under possibility differs from optimization. Optimization refines toward a fixed goal. Creation under possibility accepts that goals themselves may need to change. It values structures that allow systems to move, pause, redirect, and continue without collapse.

This form of creation does not depend on prediction.
It depends on posture.

When interruption, reversibility, and restraint are designed into systems, experimentation becomes safer rather than riskier. Failure teaches without cascading. Success remains adjustable rather than brittle. Futures remain open long enough to be shaped deliberately.

Digital weaving enables this mode of creation by keeping systems unfinished by design. It does not promise progress without error. It preserves the capacity to keep creating when conditions shift.

Weaving for complex problems

Many of the problems future systems must address are not well-bounded. They do not decompose cleanly into inputs and outputs, nor do they remain stable long enough for complete analysis. Climate adaptation, public health, mobility, energy transition, and civic infrastructure evolve as they are acted upon.

These problems cannot be solved once and for all.
They must be held.

Digital weaving positions system design as a way of working within such problems rather than attempting to resolve them in advance. It accepts that interventions will change the conditions they respond to, that partial solutions will interact, and that unintended effects will emerge across domains.

In this context, progress does not come from convergence on a single optimal answer. It comes from the ability to intervene, observe, revise, and continue without compounding harm. Systems must remain adjustable as understanding deepens and conditions shift.

Digital weaving enables this by embedding correctability, restraint, and reversibility into the structure of action itself. These properties allow systems to participate in complex problem spaces without hardening early assumptions into irreversible commitments.

The value of digital weaving is not that it simplifies problems.
It is that it allows systems to remain engaged with them complex over time.

Responsibility that remains present

Advanced systems invite delegation. As intelligence improves and automation expands, it becomes tempting to shift judgment entirely into systems. Decisions appear faster, more consistent, and less burdened by human uncertainty.

This move is incomplete.

Judgment cannot be fully delegated because responsibility cannot be fully delegated. Systems can recommend, rank, and optimize. They cannot carry their own consequences or legitimacy. Someone must remain accountable for when a system should pause, refuse, or change course.

This responsibility does not end with deployment. Accelerated systems continue to evolve through learning, integration, and interaction. New uses emerge. New harms surface. New contexts reshape consequences.

As systems scale, responsibility concentrates rather than recedes.

Digital weaving forms a posture of sustained responsibility. Practitioners remain attentive to how systems behave over time, not only how they were intended to function. They notice when strain accumulates and when correction becomes harder to exercise.

To hold a system is to accept that it will change.

Holding does not mean freezing systems in place.
It means guiding their evolution without surrendering responsibility.

Authority as readiness and practice

Authority is often confused with control. Control implies command and compliance. Readiness implies attentiveness and restraint. Under accelerated conditions, readiness proves more durable.

Authority as readiness means maintaining the capacity to intervene rather than exercising continuous control. It means being prepared to pause, redirect, or refuse continuation when harm would otherwise follow. This form of authority is quiet. It remains credible because it is present, not because it is exercised frequently.

Digital weaving produces this posture through practice. It disciplines attention toward how threads interact, where strain accumulates, and when responsibility begins to slip. It trains practitioners to design for interruption, to preserve reversibility, and to treat restraint as capacity rather than limitation.

This practice does not promise certainty.
It preserves readiness under continued action.

By weaving responsibility, judgment, and governance into systems as they evolve, digital weaving keeps correction possible under acceleration. It preserves legitimacy not by preventing all harm, but by ensuring systems remain responsive to responsibility while choices still exist.

The future is often framed as something systems enter.
A destination shaped by innovation.

A quieter truth holds.

The future is being formed now. Through decisions that bind early. Through systems that act continuously. Through structures that narrow or preserve choice.

Digital weaving does not predict the future.
It shapes how systems behave when prediction fails.

Authority establishes when intervention is possible; holding determines whether responsibility remains present as systems continue to act.

Holding systems under continued action

Digital systems do not stop acting when design is complete or deployment is finished. They continue to sense, decide, and influence the world long after their makers move on.

Assumptions embedded early persist. Defaults accumulate force. What appears stable at launch often behaves differently once systems encounter scale, adaptation, and use.

This is not a failure of foresight.

It is the condition under which systems that persist operate.

Design can widen what remains possible, but it cannot determine what follows. Context changes. Use drifts. Pressures accumulate. Systems are extended, repurposed, and constrained in ways their designers cannot fully anticipate.

Responsibility, therefore, does not end at deployment. It changes form. What begins as a question of structure becomes a question of attention and maintenance. It becomes a question of whether legibility is preserved as execution accelerates, and whether correction remains reachable once decisions are in motion and authority is distributed across code, institutions, and practice.

Much of this work remains invisible. Systems that hold rarely announce themselves. They endure quietly through restraint, revision, and care. This includes decisions to slow when speed is available, to explain when opacity is convenient, and to intervene before consequences harden.

Uncertainty is not an exception to be eliminated.

It is a permanent design condition.

Digital systems remain unfinished because the world they act within continues to change. The task is no longer to finish systems, but to hold them.

What matters is how attentively the system continues to be held.

Conclusion

The weave survives by remaining interruptible.

The future does not arrive all at once.

It is assembled quietly, through systems that act continuously, decisions that bind early, and structures that narrow or preserve choice long before their consequences are fully visible.

Throughout this chapter, we have traced the changes that occur when digital systems accelerate beyond the margins that once allowed learning, correction, and responsibility to arrive after the fact. We saw how execution outpaces intervention, how coupling spreads consequence, and how persistence hardens provisional decisions into lasting structure. Under these conditions, failure does not announce itself loudly. It accumulates. It propagates. It becomes difficult to reach.

The response is not better prediction, tighter optimization, or more procedures layered on afterward. What endures under acceleration is posture, the ability to remain answerable while systems act.

Digital weaving offers that posture. It treats restraint as capacity, interruption as structure, and reversibility as legitimacy. It shifts responsibility from a retrospective act to a condition that must remain reachable during execution. It asks institutions, designers, and practitioners to hold systems while they act, not merely explain them once they have finished acting.

This posture matters because digital systems no longer sit at the edges of society. They shape institutional authority, civic trust, and the conditions under which people participate, decide, and belong. The structures we weave today will govern not only how systems function, but how future generations experience fairness, accountability, and agency.

In the opening chapter, we began with the first stitch: the recognition that digital systems are not neutral tools, but woven structures that carry intention forward in time. This chapter returns to that insight with greater urgency. When the margin disappears, what we weave early becomes what others must live with later.

Digital weaving does not promise control over the future.
It preserves something more important: the ability to remain answerable as the future unfolds.

We do not inherit a world fully woven.
We inherit the loom, the threads, and the responsibility to decide how tightly they are pulled.

To prototype the future is not to predict it.
It is to weave with care, knowing that every shortcut writes a story the future must finish.

Weaver's toolkit

Tools do not decide. Weavers remain responsible.

Digital weaving is not a theory to be admired from a distance.
It is a practice meant to be used.

The weaver's toolkit gathers the elements required to apply the ideas of this chapter in study, design, and reflection. It is not exhaustive, nor prescriptive. Instead, it offers shared language, structured practice, and curated references that help designers, institutions, and students hold systems under acceleration.

The toolkit has three parts: a lexicon to stabilize meaning, a workshop to practice posture, and a library to situate this work within a broader intellectual tradition.

Weaver's lexicon

Digital systems fail as often through confusion as through error.
Words drift. Terms blur. Concepts are reused with incompatible meanings.

The weaver's lexicon defines the key terms used throughout this chapter with precision and restraint. These definitions are not universal claims. They are working meanings, chosen to support clarity, consistency, and shared understanding within the practice of digital weaving.

The lexicon exists to reduce ambiguity when it becomes costly:

- **Acceleration**: The condition in which systems act continuously and at speed, compressing the time between decision and consequence.
- **Answerability**: The condition in which systems remain reachable for explanation, contestation, and correction while they act.
- **Authority**: The institutional or human capacity to pause, reverse, redirect, or refuse system action.
- **Authority as readiness**: A form of authority defined by preparedness to intervene during execution, rather than constant control or retrospective review.
- **Autonomy**: The degree to which a system can act without direct human initiation or real-time supervision once it is operating.
- **Binding**: The act of fixing a decision, assumption, or relationship into a system such that it shapes future behavior.
- **Capability**: What a system is technically able to do, regardless of whether doing so is appropriate or responsible.
- **Civic consequence**: The real-world effects experienced by people when systems shape access, movement, benefits, risk, or participation.
- **Components**: The individual technical elements that make up a system, such as hardware, software, data, models, or interfaces. Components describe what a system is made of, not how it behaves once deployed.
- **Consent (procedural)**: Formal agreement obtained through interfaces or policies, often without ensuring understanding during execution.
- **Consequence**: The real-world effects that occur when a system acts, affecting people, institutions, or environments. Consequence emerges through execution and interaction, often beyond what designers explicitly intended.
- **Continuous execution**: System behavior that proceeds without natural pauses for review, appeal, or deliberation.
- **Correctability**: The ability to intervene in, modify, or reverse system behavior before consequences harden.
- **Correction**: An action taken to alter or stop system behavior when harm, error, or risk is detected.
- **Coupling**: The condition in which systems depend on and affect one another, allowing local actions to produce wide-ranging effects.

- **Decision hardening**: The process by which provisional system decisions become difficult or impossible to reverse over time.
- **Delegation with remainder**: Delegating execution to systems while retaining the structural authority to intervene when necessary.
- **Discipline (design discipline)**: A structural posture that anticipates strain and embeds limits, interruption, and accountability before failure occurs.
- **Downstream**: Systems, processes, or consequences that receive and act on a system's outputs after execution.
- **Edge computing**: A computing model in which data processing and decision-making occur close to where data is generated, or action is taken, rather than in a central system.
- **Execution**: The moment when a system acts, and decisions take effect.
- **Execution completion**: The point at which a system's action can no longer be paused, altered, or reversed before consequences harden.
- **Failure under acceleration**: A mode of failure in which systems continue to function while consequences emerge too late to correct.
- **Governance**: The structures and practices that shape how systems are authorized, constrained, and corrected.
- **Holdable system**: A system designed so that authority and responsibility can still intervene while it operates.
- **Hyperconnectivity**: Persistent, always-on interconnection among systems that amplifies speed and reach.
- **Immersive interface**: An interface that surrounds or deeply engages a user's perception, shaping attention and experience before deliberate choice can occur.
- **Interruptibility**: The capacity to pause or stop system action while it is underway.
- **Intervention**: An action taken to pause, redirect, modify, or stop system behavior while execution is underway.
- **Legibility**: The ability to understand what a system is doing while it is doing it.
- **Legitimacy**: Public and institutional acceptance of system outcomes, sustained through answerability and correctability.
- **Learning**: Changes in system or institutional behavior over time based on experience, feedback, or new information, preserving legitimacy only when it remains interruptible and bounded by responsibility.
- **Margin**: The time and space between action and consequence that allows for review and correction.

- **Method**: A defined procedure, technique, or sequence of steps used to design, analyze, or improve a system.
- **Pattern**: A recurring structure or behavior that emerges from how system components interact over time, often becoming visible only after systems are stressed, scaled, or observed across many instances.
- **Persistence**: The tendency of data, models, and decisions to continue influencing outcomes over time, even after the context that produced them has changed.
- **Posture**: The underlying stance a system takes toward strain, responsibility, and correction.
- **Quantum computing**: A form of computing that uses quantum mechanical properties to perform certain calculations more efficiently than classical computers, potentially altering assumptions about long-term data security.
- **Reach**: The ability of the authority to intervene in system behavior during execution.
- **Reaction**: A posture that assumes problems can be addressed after failure occurs rather than during execution.
- **Readiness**: Preparedness to intervene during execution, rather than reliance on after-the-fact review.
- **Refusal**: A designed capability that allows a system to decline action when boundaries are exceeded.
- **Responsibility**: The obligation to remain answerable for system outcomes, including the capacity to intervene, explain, and correct behavior while the system acts.
- **Restraint**: Deliberate limits placed on scope, duration, or execution to preserve accountability.
- **Reversibility**: The ability to undo or withdraw system actions without collapse.
- **Runtime**: The period during which a system is actively operating and making decisions, as opposed to design or review phases.
- **Scale**: The ability of a system to extend its reach across users, locations, or decisions. At scale, small changes or errors can affect many people quickly.
- **Shadow layers**: Informal or undocumented practices that emerge to keep systems functioning under strain.
- **Slack**: Deliberate capacity in a system that allows time, space, or flexibility for judgment and correction before consequences harden.
- **Spatial computing**: Technologies that integrate digital information with physical space, enabling systems to perceive, interpret, and act within real-world environments.
- **Structural risk**: Risk that arises from system conditions rather than individual errors.

- **System tempo**: The pace at which a system senses, decides, and acts.
- **Trust**: Confidence that systems will remain answerable when consequences matter.
- **Upstream**: Inputs, data sources, or decisions that feed into a system before it acts, often outside the direct control of the system's operator.

Weaver's workshop

Posture cannot be learned solely from reading.
It must be practiced.

The weaver's workshop consists of guided exercises that move from recognition to design, and from system behavior to creation under uncertainty. Each exercise invites the reader to work with real or imagined systems, identify where margin disappears, and practice weaving structures that preserve responsibility while allowing safe exploration and revision under acceleration.

The workshop is not designed to test correctness.
It is designed to cultivate judgment.

These exercises are not about optimizing systems.
They are about holding systems so they can explore, revise, and continue without collapse.

1. **Spotting the lost margin**: Identify where the margin has disappeared in a familiar digital system and how this alters responsibility, learning, and future adaptability.

   Prompts:

   - *Select a digital system you interact with regularly, such as a campus access system, payment application, learning platform, or public service portal.*
   - *Describe a recent moment where the system acted faster than a person could meaningfully intervene.*
   - *Identify what previously provided margin in earlier versions of the system, such as time, review, appeal, or human judgment.*
   - *Explain what changed when that margin disappeared.*
   - *Note whether the loss of margin also limits the system's ability to try new approaches without causing harm.*

   Deliverable: A one-page analysis describing the system, the lost margin, and its consequences.

   Learning objective: Recognize acceleration as a structural condition and understand how loss of margin alters responsibility, learning, and future change.

2. **Mapping correction reachability**: Analyze whether the correction remains reachable during execution rather than arriving only after outcomes harden.

Prompts:

- *Choose a system that makes automated or semi-automated decisions.*
- *Map the decision flow from input to outcome.*
- *Mark every point where intervention, pause, or reversal is possible.*
- *Identify where correction arrives too late to matter.*
- *Indicate where lack of reachability constrains the system's ability to experiment and improve.*

Deliverable: A simple annotated flow diagram with a short written explanation.

Learning objective: Understand the difference between procedural oversight and structural correctability during execution, and how reachability shapes innovation.

3. **Designing restraint into execution**: Redesign a decision path so restraint, interruption, and refusal function as structural properties rather than reactive fixes.

   Prompts:

   - *Use the system analyzed in Exercise 2.*
   - *Identify one decision that currently proceeds automatically.*
   - *Redesign that decision to include a pause threshold during execution.*
   - *Define who can intervene and a refusal condition that prevents the decision from continuing by default.*
   - *Explain how this redesign preserves legitimacy and allows the system to test new behavior without committing permanently.*

   Deliverable: A revised decision-flow sketch plus a one-page design rationale.

   Learning objective: Practice embedding restraint and interruption as design capacities that support both responsibility and safe innovation.

4. **Institutional posture under acceleration**: Examine how institutional posture affects whether authority remains reachable during execution and whether adaptation is possible without crisis.

   Prompts:

   - *Select an institution such as a university, hospital, bank, city agency, or platform company.*
   - *Identify a digital system that acts on the institution's behalf.*
   - *Determine whether governance operates primarily through review after execution or readiness during execution.*
   - *Propose one structural change that would shift the institution toward governance as readiness.*
   - *Reflect on how this posture affects the institution's ability to introduce new policies or services without restarting from failure.*

Deliverable: A two-page institutional posture brief.

Learning objective: Understand how digital weaving operates at the institutional level to preserve authority, legitimacy, and adaptive capacity under continuous action.

5. **Creation under uncertainty:** This studio invites students to practice digital weaving as a forward-looking design posture. Rather than analyzing failure after it occurs, students design a system that can explore, adapt, and innovate without hardening early assumptions into irreversible outcomes.

   The emphasis is on creation under possibility, where systems remain correctable as conditions evolve.

   Studio brief: Design a digital system intended to operate under future conditions that cannot be fully predicted in advance. The system should serve a public, institutional, or civic function and act continuously rather than episodically.

   Possible domains include:

   - Urban mobility or infrastructure coordination
   - Climate adaptation or resource allocation
   - Public health or emergency response
   - Education or workforce systems
   - Financial access or social protection

   The goal is not to optimize a single outcome or metric.

   The goal is to design a posture that allows the system to try, learn, pause, revise, and continue without collapse.

   Design constraints: The system design must demonstrate:

   - Correctability during execution rather than after outcomes harden
   - Innovation without irreversible early binding of decisions or assumptions
   - Clear institutional or civic responsibility

   The design must explicitly use:

   - The five foundational threads
   - The digital weaving loop (layer, test, adapt, repeat)

The submission develops the design in four parts: system context, posture through the five threads, decisions traced through the weaving loop, and evidence that the system remains correctable while supporting innovation under uncertainty. The focus is on how structure carries responsibility during execution:

- **Emerging conditions**: Describe the future conditions the system was designed to operate within. Identify at least three sources of uncertainty or strain that could not be predicted precisely, and explain why optimization or prediction alone would be insufficient.

- **The five threads in practice**: Describe how each thread was deliberately designed:
    - **Connectivity**: Infrastructure and interfaces used, including limits on reach or scope
    - **Sensing**: What the system observed, at what resolution, and what it explicitly did not sense
    - **Data**: How data was retained, expired, shared, or bound to preserve legibility and reversibility
    - **Intelligence**: Forms of inference or automation used, including where learning paused, was reviewed, or could be reversed
    - **Trust and governance**: How authority, responsibility, and legitimacy remained reachable during execution
- **Weaving loop application**: Explain how the system was developed through the weaving loop, including initial layering choices, testing under strain, adaptations when assumptions failed, and what was intentionally left unfinished. This section should be written in the past tense to reflect an applied design process.
- **Innovation under possibility**: Explain how the system supported innovation without locking early assumptions. Describe how new capabilities could be introduced safely, how policies or services could change without restarting from crisis, and how experimentation remained bounded and accountable.

  Deliverables: Students submit either a short presentation or a 2–3 page studio paper. The submission presents a system posture using the five threads and the weaving loop, identifying key points of intervention. It demonstrates how correctability, restraint, and innovation are preserved under uncertainty, and how technical design aligns with institutional responsibility. An optional brief appendix may outline additional features the system could adapt to. Emphasis remains on structural judgment rather than prediction accuracy or completeness.

  Learning objective: Develop the ability to design for innovation under uncertainty using posture rather than prediction as the primary design tool.

A successful weave is not one that never strains,
but one that remains answerable while strain unfolds.

Weaver's library

Digital weaving does not stand apart from existing scholarship.

It draws from and contributes to a wider body of work across systems thinking, governance, ethics, infrastructure, and technology studies.

The weaver's library offers selected references that deepen the ideas introduced in this chapter. These works provide historical grounding, theoretical contrast, and practical insight for readers who wish to explore further.

The library is not a canon.
It is a set of paths.

1. *Clearfield, C., & Tilcsik, A. (2018). Meltdown: Why our systems fail and what we can do about it. New York, NY: Penguin Press.*
2. *Green, J., & Smith, A. (2020). Digital governance: Leading and thriving in a world of fast-changing technologies. London, UK: Routledge.*
3. *O'Neil, C. (2016). Weapons of math destruction: How big data increases inequality and threatens democracy. New York, NY: Crown Publishing.*
4. *Zuboff, S. (2019). The age of surveillance capitalism: The fight for a human future at the new frontier of power. New York, NY: PublicAffairs.*
5. *Dally, W. J., & Harting, R. C. (2012). Digital design: A systems approach. Cambridge, UK: Cambridge University Press.*

Metaphorical and conceptual terms

Refer to the following list, which outlines metaphorical and conceptual terms used throughout the chapter:

- **Accidental weaving**: Coherence that emerges unintentionally through accumulated responses to strain, workarounds, and adaptations rather than deliberate design.
- **Digital weaving**: A deliberate design discipline focused on maintaining answerability under change.
- **Holding the weave**: Maintaining responsibility and authority as systems evolve.
- **Loom**: The structural conditions that shape how digital systems are designed and held.
- **Pull**: The forces that apply pressure to systems, including acceleration, coupling, and persistence.
- **Strain**: Stress applied to systems as conditions change and pressures accumulate.
- **Thread**: A foundational component of a digital system, such as connectivity, sensing, data, intelligence, or trust.
- **Tightening weave**: Conditions in which the margin disappears and correction becomes harder.
- **Unknown pull**: Unanticipated forces that act on systems after deployment.
- **Weave**: The combined structure formed by how threads interact within a system.
- **Weaver**: The designer, institution, or steward responsible for holding systems under strain.

Index

A

B

C

D

E

F

H

I

S

T

U

V

W

Z